The History of
SCOTTISH LITERATURE

Volume 1

THE HISTORY OF SCOTTISH LITERATURE
general editor Cairns Craig

Volume 1   Origins to 1660 *editor R D S Jack*
Volume 2   1660 to 1800 *editor Andrew Hook*
Volume 3   Nineteenth Century *editor Douglas Gifford*
Volume 4   Twentieth Century *editor Cairns Craig*

DICTIONARIES from AUP

THE SCOTTISH NATIONAL DICTIONARY
(18th century to the present day)
in ten volumes

THE COMPACT SCOTTISH NATIONAL DICTIONARY
in two volumes

A DICTIONARY OF THE OLDER SCOTTISH TONGUE
From the twelfth century to the end of the seventeenth
Volumes 1 to 6 (and continuing)

THE CONCISE SCOTS DICTIONARY
editor-in-chief Mairi Robinson

GAELIC DICTIONARY
Malcolm MacLennan

The History of
SCOTTISH LITERATURE

Volume 1

Origins to 1660
(Mediæval and Renaissance)

edited by R D S Jack

general editor Cairns Craig

ABERDEEN UNIVERSITY PRESS

820·9941
H 15

First published 1988
Aberdeen University Press
A member of the Pergamon Group

© The Contributors 1988

The publisher acknowledges subsidy from the Scottish Arts Council towards the publication of this volume.

British Library Cataloguing in Publication Data

The History of Scottish literature.
  Vol. 1: Mediæval and Renaissance
  1. English literature—Scottish authors
  —History and criticism 2. Scottish
  literature—History and criticism
  I. Jack, R D S
  820.9'9411   PR8511

  ISBN 0-08-035054-2

Printed in Great Britain
The University Press
Aberdeen

Contents

List of Contributors

ALEX AGUTTER has been a lecturer in the Department of English Language, University of Edinburgh since 1978. Her publications and research cover many aspects of historical and modern Scots language.

PRISCILLA BAWCUTT, now an independent scholar, was formerly lecturer in English at the Universities of London and Durham and a Fellow of the Institute for Advanced Studies at Edinburgh. She has edited and is the author of various books and articles on Scottish and Mediæval English literature.

SARAH CARPENTER is a graduate of Oxford and a lecturer in English at Edinburgh University. She has an interest in practical theatre and perform-ance, and has published articles and reviews on mediæval drama. She is currently working on a book on 'Masks in the Mediæval Theatre'.

RONALD D S JACK is Professor of Scottish and Mediæval Literature at the University of Edinburgh. His publications include *Scottish Prose 1550–1700*, *The Italian Influence on Scottish Literature*, *A Choice of Scottish Verse 1560–1660*, *Alexander Montgomerie* and *Scottish Literature's Debt to Italy*.

WILLIAM GILLIES is Professor of Celtic at the University of Edinburgh. His Gaelic interests include both early and contemporary literature. For the Mediæval period his research has centred mainly on the Book of the Dean of Lismore, from which he has published a number of poetical texts, and on the Red and Black Books of Clanranald, of which he is currently preparing an edition for the Scottish Gaelic Texts Society.

HAMISH HENDERSON, poet, essayist, song-writer, was born in Blairgowrie in 1919. His publications include *Ballads of World War II* and *Elegies for the Dead in Cyrenaica* (Somerset Maugham Award 1949). He was the first translator into English of Gramsci's prison letters, and of several modern Italian poets. A founder member of the School of Scottish Studies, Edinburgh University, he also lays claim to being the discoverer of Jeannie Robertson.

GREGORY KRATZMANN is a Senior Lecturer in English at La Trobe University, Melbourne. A graduate of Edinburgh University, his main research interests are in fifteenth- and sixteenth-century Scots and English poetry and prose. He is the author of *Anglo-Scottish Literary Relations*, 1430–1550, editor of *Colkelbie Sow* and *The Talis of the Fyve Bestes*, and the joint-editor of a collection of essays of Mediæval English religious and ethical literature. He is currently working on English fictional prose printed in the Netherlands.

R J LYALL is Titular Professor in Scottish Literature at the University of Glasgow, where he has taught since 1975, having previously lectured in English at Massey University in New Zealand. He is currently preparing a new edition of Lindsay's *Satyre of the Thrie Estaits*, and working on the manuscript culture of late mediæval Scotland.

MATTHEW P MCDIARMID, a graduate of Glasgow and Balliol College, Oxford, was Senior Lecturer at Belfast University and Reader at Aberdeen University. He was one of the founders of the series of international conferences on Mediæval and Renaissance Scots literature, and has contributed literary and historical studies to books and periodicals published in Britain and Europe. For the Scottish Text Society he has edited *The Poems of Robert Fergusson*, Hary's *Wallace*, and been co-editor of *Barbour's Bruce*.

ALASDAIR A MACDONALD read English at Edinburgh University, where he also presented his doctorial thesis—a study of the religious lyric verse of Mediæval Scotland. He has taught at the Universities of Leeds and Ghana, and been a Fellow of the Institute for Advanced Studies in the Humanities at Edinburgh. In 1980 he moved to the Kathalieke Universiteit of Nijmegen, and since 1986 he has been Professor of English at the Rijksuniversiteit, Groningen.

JAMES G MACQUEEN, a graduate of Magdalen College, Oxford, has been on the staff of the Department of Classics and Archaeology at Bristol University since 1959 where he is now Reader in Classics and Ancient Middle Eastern Studies. His publications range from *Neolithic Anatolia* to *Scottish Latin Poetry of the 18th Century*.

JOHN MACQUEEN, a graduate of Glasgow and Cambridge, has held posts in Washington University, St Louis, Missouri and in Edinburgh University. He has published many books and articles, including *Robert Henryson* and *Numerology*. He is currently engaged on an edition of *Scotichronicon*, Books I to V.

WINIFRED W MACQUEEN, a graduate of Glasgow and Cambridge, has held posts in Glasgow and Edinburgh Universities, in Washington University, St Louis, Missouri and in various Edinburgh Schools. She has published an edition of *Miracula Nynie Episcopi*, and has collaborated on an anthology of Middle Scots Verse, and is currently engaged on an edition of *Scotichronicon*, Books I to V.

DAVID REID was educated at the Universities of St Andrews and British Columbia. He has taught at the Universities of Salonica, New Hampshire and British Columbia, and is currently a lecturer at the University of Stirling.

FELICITY RIDDY taught in the English Department at Stirling University for twenty years before taking up a Readership in English at the University of York in 1988. She is co-editor, with Priscilla Bawcutt, of *Longer Scottish*

Poems, 1375–1650 and a selection of the poetry of Henryson and Dunbar. She has also co-edited, with Michael Alexander, *Macmillan's English Literary Anthologies: Mediæval* and is the author of *Sir Thomas Malory*.

MICHAEL SPILLER, a graduate of Edinburgh and Oxford, is a lecturer in English Literature and Cultural History at the University of Aberdeen. He has published work on the history of science, Renaissance poetry and prose, Scottish literature and critical theory.

Abbreviations

BL:	British Library
CUL:	Cambridge University Library
DNB:	*Dictionary of National Biography*
EETS:	Early English Text Society
ELH:	*English Literary History*
FMLS:	*Forum for Modern Language Studies*
GGB:	*Gude and Godlie Ballatis*
K:	Kinsley edition of Dunbar
NLS:	National Library of Scotland
PMLA:	Publications of the Modern Language Association of America
SGTS:	Scottish Gaelic Texts Society
SHR:	*Scottish Historical Review*
SHS:	Scottish History Society
SLJ:	*Scottish Literary Journal*
SS:	Scottish Studies
SSL:	*Studies in Scottish Literature*
STS:	Scottish Text Society
TGSI:	Transactions of the Gaelic Society of Inverness

Introduction

R D S JACK

The twin tasks I have set myself in this Introduction are to discuss the ways in which I believe this history helps us to see Scottish Literature in a more accurate light and what directions it points for further research. Before I tackle these issues, however, it is necessary to indicate two features which distinguish this volume from those which follow it, features which pose particular problems and impose particular contraints upon the contributors.

The first of these concerns the time span. The earliest poems mentioned are Latin hymns dating from the second half of the sixth century and the earliest prose writer is Adomnan, ninth abbot of Iona, who flourished in the mid and later seventh century. As the remit of this volume ends in 1660, this implies that one volume covers about a thousand years of literature and the latter three, just over three hundred years between them. Of course, the amount of literature preserved in the later periods exceeds ours, but historically we move from the very founding of the kingdom of Scotland to the Restoration of Charles II. This vast historical time span is particularly important, not only because of the very different political and social pressures of the different centuries but because there is a danger of forgetting chronological differentials the further back in time we go. Would those, for example, who label Henryson a Scottish Chaucerian, do so with so easy a mind if they remembered that he lived as long after the English poet as T S Eliot after Wordsworth?

Secondly, there is the evidence with which we are working. Although, throughout, we base our conclusions on the best available texts, the date, provenance and reliability of the witnesses vary greatly, as Priscilla Bawcutt and Felicity Riddy correctly highlight in their 'Note on the Texts' for *Longer Scottish Poems* Volume I.[1] The first major vernacular Scots poem, *The Bruce*, for example, was written in the late fourteenth century but survives in two manuscripts dated 1487 and 1489. The best witnesses for Henryson's *Morall Fabillis*, with the exception of the Asloan copy of 'The Two Mice', are dated almost a century after the poet's death. The major vernacular anthology of the sixteenth century, the Bannatyne Manuscript, has an editor who sometimes alters religious poems to bring them into conformity with the theological views of the Reformed church. And as Scottish texts come to be printed in England anglicised forms are introduced by the intermediaries in the printing houses, making conclusions about language singularly difficult to maintain. Such niceties may not greatly concern all readers of this book. Yet it is as well to be aware of them at the outset.

1

'But to our tale.' Most obviously an attempt has been made not only to assess written vernacular prose and verse but also the oral tradition and the very important contributions made by writers in Gaelic and Latin. Hamish Henderson in 'The Ballad and Popular Tradition to 1660' links the Scottish ballad to European analogues but also to the work of storytellers from Turkey, Iran and India. In a more 'parochial' context he addresses himself to the question of why folklorists and singers generally agree that of all the ballads of the British Isles, the Scots contribution is the finest. Professor Gillies traces the very different social and educational forces which produced the verse of the Gaelic bards and in particular the major contribution made by the MacMhuirich family, reminding us that geographical proximity can go along with a quite distinct poetic tradition.

If I lay most emphasis, in this context, on the Latin contribution, it is for two major reasons. First of all, while modern critics have dealt well and at length with both the ballad and with Celtic writings, there has been very little attempt to link Scottish vernacular literature with Latin and that despite the fact that the origins of Scottish literature are Latin; Latin was also for most of our period the preferred medium for literary composition and the universal language of the Universities. Secondly, the Latin and Scots traditions very often (and not surprisingly) go hand in hand. To study the work of late sixteenth and early seventeenth century vernacular writers such as Alexander and Drummond without being aware of the contemporary Latin verse contained in the *Delitiae Poetarum Scotorum* is resolutely to study a tradition with one eye determinedly shut.

To provide an example of what I mean, I turn to the tradition of regal panegyric. Prior to the Union of the Crowns panegyrics in both Scots and Latin conform to the major characterics of classical panegyric. They are usually part of a ceremony or at least presuppose an audience. They establish the monarch as a personification of virtue and the writer, often for clear political reasons, adopts the voices of counsellor and prophet. Dunbar's *The Thrissill and the Rois* for example clearly meets all these criteria. It is written for an occasion, the marriage of James (the thistle) to Margaret Tudor (the rose). The virtues of both are ingeniously presented not only through the central idea of Dame Nature calling representative animals, birds and plants but by heraldic symbolism. The poet in prophetic mode looks forward to a future drawing together two opposed nations but also takes the opportunity to warn the King against continuing his philandering ways. The same traditionalism and conventionality can be found later in Montgomerie's *The Navigatioun*, which celebrates James VI.

But all the methods employed in *The Thrissill and the Rois* or *The Navigatioun* are also used by the Latin writer Patrick Adamson in 'Genethliacum Serenissimi Scotiae, Angliae et Hiberniae Principis Jacobi VI'. The extravagant optimism of the piece begins with the title. James is referred to as the ruler of Scotland, England and Ireland. His personal virtues are somewhat hopefully deduced from the character of his parents, greathearted ('magnanimus') Darnley and Mary of the generous heart ('generoso pectore') and chaste morals ('casti mores')! It is, however, James's own destined greatness which forms the major concern of the poem. He is seen as the Sun bringing light to a darkened land and ushering in the golden age of Saturn. The unification of Britain this time takes the form of a vision in which the River Tweed as boundary obeys a divine command. On the west it returns to its source and on the east rejoins the sea. It then addresses its Nymphs who, presumably, have suddenly found themselves out of their element:

> Non has Superi regnator Olympi
> Perpetuas dederat sedes, nec littora nobis
> Haec semper pulsanda: alio sub sole penates
> Quaerendi.

(The ruler of celestial Olympus had not given this seat in perpetuity, nor must we always beat against these shores. Beneath another sun we must seek a dwelling).

The last mark of division thus eloquently disappears.

Adamson is addressing a clearly defined audience, he highlights the virtues of James, he prophesies his future greatness and he warns him against hubris. Both Latin and Scots writers are following the same conventions. Recently, however, Robert Cummings has brilliantly analysed the ways in which the Union of the Crowns at once destroyed the natural audience for Scottish panegyric, and the mood of optimism both with regard to James's political virtues and Scotland's future role.[2] As a result when Drummond composes his seventeenth century vernacular panegyric *Forth Feasting*, he subtly reinterprets the panegyrical mode. The loss of a Scottish court results in a personal rather than a public focus. Praise of James, though still strong, mingles with a line of complaint addressed to an absentee monarch. The striking thing from our point of view is that Latin panegyrists made very much the same alterations. Thomas Craig, who in 1566 had welcomed James's birth with a powerful traditional panegyric, addresses the absentee king in another poem 'Dulcis amor populi'. This, while it remains true to all the central criteria of the panegyric, entirely changes the spirit and the focus of the mode. The King is still praised as sole light of the fatherland ('Patriae lux unica'); the poem still celebrates an occasion (though now a private one); and he still draws on evidence from the past and divination of the future to see James's virtue reaffirmed by his predecessor and carried on by his children. But the context and the content is now domestic. For a Scot returning to his homeland the greater political plans are irrelevant so he proffers personal love rather than political counsel. The image of the Sun is continued but to bless James's wife and family rather than herald a united land.

And if the positive side of panegyric becomes in this way more personal, domestic concerns replacing political; love becoming not so much the King's supreme virtue as the supreme appeal of the poet himself, so the negative side of warning becomes a direct complaint on behalf of Scotland. She, for Craig as for Drummond, becomes a neglected lover. The unifying image of the Sun is cleverly employed to bring home this message:

> Iam repeto patrii tristia tecta soli.
> Triste solum sine Sole, suo sine Principe cernam.

(Now I seek again the sad roofs of my native country. I will look upon a country that is sad without its Sun and without its own Prince).

Craig ends his poem by relinquishing his barren songs ('steriles Musas et carmina'). Their purpose, once enjoyed in the presence of the King, has disappeared now that they are separated. James must live on, as the double call of 'Vive, vale!' proclaims but that optimistic cry is seriously undercut by our knowledge that it goes along with Craig's own poetic death.

Both Drummond and Craig work their way towards a re-definition of regal panegyric, capable of coping with the changed political situation as it affects Scotland. But this is only a slight example of the sort of comparative criticism which becomes possible once the wealth of Latin literature within the period is seriously studied. I, therefore, make no apology for devoting some space within a general Introduction to these particular analyses for they pinpoint perhaps the greatest single critical failure within our period. I equally hope that the attention paid to the Latin tradition within this volume will encourage students to redress it.

The aim of the remaining chapters—those concerned with vernacular prose and verse—is a simple one. They aim to chart with as much precision as possible and in as comprehensive a manner as possible the development of Scottish literature through historical events as cataclysmic as the Wars of Independence, the Reformation and the Union of the Crowns. A number of quite important editorial decisions, however, further shape the particular approach adopted. First it was decided to open with a Chapter devoted entirely to language in its relationship to the literature of the Mediaeval and Renaissance periods. Apart from in itself acknowledging the crucial importance of a proper understanding of linguistic change in discussing the work of our authors, this decision was made with two further aims in mind. Most basically, a clear account of the distinctive features of Middle Scots is essential for those readers not directly acquainted with it. And, at a greater level of sophistication, it was thought valuable to have a professional linguist's views on the crucial problem of the gradual erosion of the Middle Scots Standard by the Southern English Standard from the late sixteenth century onwards.

The second decision in this area was to achieve maximum coverage by using chapters which were chronologically defined (e.g. Chapters 8, 9, 11 and 12); chapters which focused on literary movements and forms (e.g. Chapters 2 and 3) and chapters dealing solely or primarily with the work of the acknowledged 'greats' (e.g. Chapters 4 and 5). This triple approach seems to me to have worked well, although I am conscious that a few poems of more than passing interest (such as *The Three Priests of Peebles* and *The Freiris of Berwick*) receive less attention than is their due. It implies, of course, that occasionally the same texts will be approached from different viewpoints. In such cases I tried to ensure that new insights were being offered and that there was no needless repetition. No attempt was made to reconcile value judgements passed by different critics on the same work.

Finally, this *History* is being written at a time when genuine critical interest in all of vernacular Scottish Literature, and not just the work of a chosen few, has been at last awakened. Consequent on this, the defensive stage of critical patriotism with its tendency to overpraise in order to counterbalance long seasons of neglect should have passed. It is, therefore, hoped that the book, while transmitting the enthusiasm of the specialists concerned, will serve as an accurate critical assessment of the literature of the period.

This leads me directly to the most difficult portion of this Introduction. It is not my intention in any major fashion to anticipate the findings of the various chapters and where possible I have chosen to back up general con- clusions with examples other than those found in the body of the text, rather than steal the thunder of the contributors, who would rightly resent such highhandedness. There is one area, however, in which this approach does not work for, with great frequency, writers have called into question some of the rather simplistic conclusions until now confidently held as truths. Dr Carpenter, for example, shows how the Reformers, generally held to condemn drama in all its forms, actually used dramatic performances to further their case. Professor Lyall subtly reassesses the notion that as a prosewriter Knox was an out and out angliciser. And a number of authors from different viewpoints challenge the belief that the Union of the Crowns was the sole influence, drawing writers away from Middle Scots to English. The full arguments I shall not anticipate hoping to stave off interference through brevity. It is, however, surely inevitable that as research becomes more soph- isticated, so simple answers give way to rather more complex ones and apparently obvious conclusions fall in the face of more detailed knowledge.

Throughout our period Scotland is of course a separate nation, but its literary tradition while different from England's is not totally separate and the various types of interrelationship form an important part of this volume's concern. Sometimes, for example, a notable English movement simply takes longer to arrive in Scotland. This is the case with alliterative poetry and with the sonnet form. Usually too, the delay goes along with distinctively Scottish features. For the sonnet, the popularity of the interlacing rhyme scheme, the reluctance to compose long love sequences and the broader thematic range all mark out a specifically Scottish re-interpretation of English conventions.

This phenomenon comprehends source preferences. The political closeness for much of the period between France and Scotland resulted in Scots writers turning more regularly for inspiration to France than to other countries (often including England). Notably, when Petrarchism was at its height in England Scottish lyric writers generally preferred to base their imitative works on the writers of the Pléiade. Only after the Union, when Petrarchism was on the decline in England, did Drummond and others turn to Italian sources with enthusiasm.

The reasons for the popularity of Petrarchism among Scottish courtier poets at this time are fairly obvious. Petrarch's work had long been known in Scotland but these poets had not been associated with the glut of Petrarchan

imitation during Elizabeth's reign and so did not share the general English
satiety with the Italian's work. Those who came to London came to a foreign
court, aware of their foreignness; aware particularly that English was a
language not wholly natural to them but anxious to cultivate this new poetic
diction and align themselves with English poetic practice. What more natural
than that they should imitate the mode until that time most widely practised?
In addition, as Leonard Forster has highlighted,[3] Petrarchism offered 'something supremely imitable' for those trying to create a new poetic diction.
Petrarch's own association with the quest for purity in language, the clearly
defined conceits and rhetorical devices of the Petrarchan mode, had drawn
the creation of new poetic dictions and the influence of Petrarch together
before and, not surprisingly, did so again.

Once more, however, major differences between Scottish and English practice emerge. Alexander and Drummond prefer to imitate closely the later
Petrarchists rather than the master themselves. When they do use Petrarch
as a model, their imitation is much freer. More importantly, while English
lyricists had shown more interest in the physical side to Petrarchan love, the
Scottish lyricists come much closer to the original in valuing the spiritual
lessons of love for a Laura. This bias had been anticipated by William Fowler
whose *Tarantula of Love* ends by admitting that the lady had led him
unknowingly towards a true understanding of the love of God. Likewise, for
Drummond as for Petrarch, the visions after his beloved's death teach even
more valuable lessons than those taught in life. Once more we are concerned
not only with a gap in time but with important modifications of the English
tradition.

For the most part Scottish and English literatures work with the same
poetic forms, bringing them to the forefront of popularity perhaps at
different times, perhaps with different biases but the overall tradition within
which they are working is essentially the same. There are exceptions to this
generalisation, however. The flyting tradition was one which was enthusiastically developed in Scotland but not in England. Yet, major differences
between the two countries from a literary viewpoint are usually due to unique
religious or political movements or outstanding political figures drawing
literature into their service. The Calvinistic Reformation in Scotland with its
distrust of certain types of imagery and its heavy reliance on Biblical material
inevitably produced a very different sort of poetry and prose than did the more
pragmatic religious revolution under Henry VIII. The proclaimed intention of
James VI to be a Maecenas to his chosen poetic group at the Edinburgh court
along with the set rules and warnings he mapped out for them equally
guaranteed that verse written under his auspices would be distinguishable
from English verse composed at the same time.

These differences are fully treated in the text by Professor MacDonald, by
David Reid and by myself. As an additional example, I turn to the reign of
Mary Queen of Scots.[4] Here the combined notoriety of the Queen and the
rules for writing 'Reformed' verse resulted in a distinct tradition, devoted to
discrediting the Queen and all she stood for. Extreme protestants such as
Robert Sempill employed the vogue for broadsheets to criticise the Queen

for her behaviour throughout her reign. I shall concentrate on this group, looking first at its treatment of other characters in the drama before focusing specifically on Mary.

Within this tradition there is always stern opposition to Rizzio:

> And brocht in ane to reule with raggit clais:
> Thocht he wes blak and Moriane of hew,   [swarthy, Moorish]
> In credit sone and gorgius clais he grew:
> Thocht he wes forraine, and borne in Piemont.

This is coupled with an almost incredible idealizing of Darnley, whose murder is presented in the most pathetic light possible:

> Ane King at evin, with Sceptur, Sword, & Crown,
> At morne bot ane deformit lumpe of clay.

His achievements, when viewed posthumously, assume a heroic dimension quite at odds with established fact:

> In deidis he soulde have bene lyke Deiphoebus,
> Had feinyeit Fortoun favourit him to ring,   [reign]
> Or Theseus, or gentill Julius,
> In gentill featis ferand for ane King.

Bothwell is 'ane monstuire full of fylthyness', worse than Sardanapalus, Nero or Heliogabalus, who is more than once accused of having employed his knowledge of the black arts to bewitch the Queen. The action of the confederate Lords in deposing a ruling Scottish monarch is resolutely defended:

> Behalding than the actis execrabill
> That in this countrie hes committit bene,
> The schame, the lack, the bruit abhominabill,   [rumours]
> That saikles men with sorow did sustene,   [innocent]
> Ane privat hart it mycht prik up with tene,   [anger]
> To seik redres and mend that cairfull caice;
> Far mair the nobillis of the Royall raice,

while the joint hope for the future is firmly placed on the shoulders of the regent Moray and the infant James.

The bitterness and spite vented against Mary herself and conveyed mainly by comparisons with classical and Biblical villainesses may most economically be exemplified by analysing in detail one of *The Sempill Ballatis*, 'Declaring the Nobill and Gude Inclination of our King'. In this work the poet meets a youth, lamenting the death of Darnley and questions him on the subject. The boy, while drawing a grossly inflated portrait of the dead King, likens Mary to Delilah, being the betrayer of a brave and godfearing husband; to Jezebel in her viciousness and in having drawn her husband into a false religion; to Clytemnestra and Semiramis as husband murderer and voluptuary. He urges the Lords to sweep to vengeance like Joshua but also fervently hopes that his Queen may die in horrible agony like Creusa and Dido. He wishes on her head all the curses which Ovid crowded into his venomous invective Ibis (though actually having managed quite well on his own!); goes through a series of imaginary encounters in which the Queen plays hare to his hound, mouse to his cat, bairn to his boar or rabbit to his ferret before finally plunging her deep in Hell:

> My spirit hir spirit sall douke in Phlegethon,
> Into that painfull fylthie flude of hell;
> And thame in Styx and Lethee baith anone,
> And Cerbereus, that cruell hund sa fell   [hound]
> Sall gar hir cry, with mony yout and yell,   [cry]
> O wallaway that ever sho was borne!   [alas]
> Or with tresoun be ony maner mell   [mingle]
> Quhilk from all blis sould cause hir be forlorne.

The poet then thanks the child for having delighted him with this 'sweit figureit speiche' and they part to spread the tale of the Queen's viciousness throughout the world in song and verse.

It is difficult for modern readers to adapt to such outspoken, dogmatic bitterness, especially when placed in the mouth of a youth and given a supposedly religious context. Yet this poem follows the approved techniques of protestant vituperative verse in the period. Similar invectives, employing similar literary devices could be analysed in 'The Testament and Tragedie of umquhile King Henrie Stewart', 'Ane Exhortatioun to the Lordis', 'Ane Declaratioun of the Lordis Just Quarrel' and the 'Diallog betwix Honour, Gude Fame, and the Author heirof in a Trance'. Such an investigation would not, however, add much to the vision presented in 'Declaring the Nobill and Gude Inclination of our King'. For this group, with Sempill at its head, Mary was and remained the 'whore of Babylon' and 'double Daliday'.

There was a less powerful group of poets countering vituperation with Marian panegyric. But *The Sempill Ballatis* show how the combination of a particular religious movement with firm views on the limits of poetic expression coupled with a Queen who did not, like Elizabeth or James, know how to manipulate literature into her service, can produce verse not precisely paralleled anywhere in the English tradition.

Inevitably comparisons with English literature will reveal the smaller, Scottish movement more often omitting than complementing. This is especially the case towards the end of our period. The late sixteenth and early seventeenth century in England produced drama of the highest quality, the poetry of Spenser and Milton as well as a rich and varied prose tradition. In the equivalent period Scotland saw only the turgid Senecan dramas of Alexander and the lightweight *Philotus*. Its finest poet was the 'literary chameleon' Drummond and its most talented prosewriter the idiosyncratic Thomas Urquhart. It would, in short, have been nice to end the volume on a high point but this is not the case.

Contributory reasons can be adduced to account for this state of affairs. Perhaps one should first ask, however, whether it is reasonable to expect a relatively small country such as Scotland to vye with its much larger sister at all times. One of the reasons for the nadir of the seventeenth century is simply that chance and circumstances did not combine to produce a writer of the highest quality, from a relatively much smaller population.

That said, the Reformation was not, generally, a friend to drama in Scotland. The powerful classical tradition urged writers towards Seneca and the 'armchair theatre movement', while James VI showed no sustained interest in plays and, certainly in the Edinburgh part of his reign, was anxious not to follow English dramatic fashions. Later, when the court had moved to London, the major audience for theatrical performances was no longer in Scotland, all of which must have been rather discouraging to any budding native playwrights.

For all genres the increasing pressure to write in English posed further problems, for not all writers made the transition with Drummond's ease. This movement began prior to the Union of the Crowns but that event certainly acted as a catalyst. James, for example, began anglicising while still based in Edinburgh but his motivation for so doing almost certainly lay in his vision of what the future held for him. For poetry I still feel that a more important factor was the general loss of confidence in a specific Scots identity; the loss of the vision of the 'Golden Age' in which the Union, being led by a Scottish king, would predominantly mirror Scottish values. However unrealistic such a view was, it was widely held. In fact James became an absentee monarch and although he did encourage Scots writers in London, they felt outsiders and mostly turned to pale imitation of the movements just about to go out of fashion in London. In this context it is no coincidence that Drummond is above all an imitative writer, building any originality by modifying the ideas of others rather than striking out boldly on his own.

For Prose, as David Reid notes, ecclesiastical writings dominated on both sides of the Tweed but two major differences stand out. First, Scottish writers in general preferred the plain style. Elaborately mannered writing, for Scots, was very much the exception. Also, ecclesiastical writings were more or less the whole story. Where on earth is Scottish prose fiction? Where, above all, is the Prose Romance? One could draw Urquhart in, I suppose, or move just a little beyond 1660 and mention George Mackenzie's *Aretina*. But Urquhart is so much a law unto himself and *Aretina*'s date in fact serves painfully to highlight the length of the earlier silence. The naked fact is that we missed out on the most exciting advances in all three genres and the reasons we can adduce for this provide at best part accounts. In short, a volume which contains some of the finest Scots writing of any time does end with a whimper rather than a roar. Further research is necessary to explain precisely why this is so but no amount of further research will alter the conclusion itself.

Finally, there are one or two practical points to be explained. At an initial meeting of contributors we decided on the best texts to follow. We also agreed that for a work of this sort quotations would usually follow certain principles of normalisation and modernisation. As a result we have substituted y for ȝ (yogh) and th for þ (thorn) and for y where y has that value. We distinguish i from j and u from v or w in accordance with modern practice. Punctuation and capitalisation are editorial. Where linguistic arguments demanded a different practice deviation from these norms has been clearly indicated.

The editors have tried to maintain consistent forms for titles and for key words. Thus we always refer to *Ane Satyre of the Thrie Estaits* although other forms are possible, and we use Mediaeval rather than Medieval, mediaeval or medieval. In a Volume of this size we were also anxious to be as economical as possible in presenting bibliographical material. To this end we adopted certain abbreviations which are listed before this Introduction. Where, as in Matthew McDiarmid's chapter, all the necessary Bibliographical material was contained in the Notes, no section of Further Reading was added. Elsewhere, no references are duplicated in Notes and Further Reading. The General Bibliography, having been compiled from texts (both Primary and Secondary) which were mentioned by a number of contributors, has also allowed us to shorten the Further Reading sections for particular chapters. We hope that these decisions will help those readers who wish to use the volume as a guide to further study.

Finally, I would like to take this opportunity to thank J Ramsay Brand, without whose valuable editorial assistance this volume would have taken much longer to produce. Ramsay and I in turn would like to thank all the contributors for the speed with which they produced their Chapters and the patience with which they responded to our interminable letters asking for clarification, often on the most pernickety of points!

NOTES

1   *Longer Scottish Poems, Vol. I, 1375–1650*, Priscilla Bawcutt and Felicity Riddy (eds) (Edinburgh, 1987), p. xxi.
2   Robert Cummings, 'Drummond's *Forth Feasting*: A Panegyric for King James in Scotland', *The Seventeenth Century*, 2, 1987, 1–18.
3   Leonard Foster, *The Icy Fire* (London, 1969), p 83.
4   *See* R D S Jack, 'Mary and the Poetic Vision', *Scotia*,1, 1979, 34–48.

GENERAL BIBLIOGRAPHY

This Bibliography contains major works and collections as well as general secondary works and collections of essays. They have been cited again under FURTHER READING only where special reasons existed for so doing.

PRIMARY WORKS

Bawcutt, Priscilla (ed), *The Shorter Poems of Gavin Douglas*, STS (Edinburgh and London, 1967)

Buchanan, George, *Opere Omnia*, Ruddiman, T (ed), 2 vols (Edinburgh, 1715)

Coldwell, David F C (ed), *Virgil's Aeneid Translated into Scottish Verse by Gavin Douglas*, STS, 4 vols (Edinburgh and London, 1957–64)

Craigie, W A (ed), *The Maitland Folio MS*, STS, 2 vols (Edinburgh and London, 1919–27)

—— *The Maitland Quarto MS*, STS (Edinburgh and London, 1920)

—— *The Asloan MS*, STS, 2 vols (Edinburgh and London, 1923–25)

Fox, Denton (ed), *The Poems of Robert Henryson* (Oxford, 1981)

—— and Ringler, William (eds), *The Bannatyne Manuscript* (facsimile), (London, 1980)

Hamer, Douglas (ed), *The Works of Sir David Lindsay*, STS, 4 vols (Edinburgh and London, 1931–36)

Kinsley, James (ed), *The Poems of William Dunbar* (Oxford, 1979)

Kittredge, George L and Sargent, Helen (eds), *The English and Scottish Popular Ballads* (Boston and New York, 1905)

Ritchie, W T (ed), *The Bannatyne MS*, STS, 4 vols (Edinburgh and London, 1928–34)

Scot, Sir J (ed), *Delitiae Poetarum Scotorum Huius Aevi Illustrium*, 2 vols (Amsterdam, 1637)

Stevenson, George (ed), *Pieces from the Makculloch and the Gray MSS* [etc], STS, (Edinburgh and London, 1918)

SECONDARY WORKS

Aitken, A J and McArthur, Tom, *Languages of Scotland* (Edinburgh, 1979)

—— McDiarmid, M P and Thomson, D S (eds), *Bards and Makars* (Glasgow, 1977)

Bawcutt, Priscilla, 'Middle Scots Poets', and Craigie, James, 'Scottish Literature', in *The New Cambridge Bibliography of English Literature*, Watson, George (ed), vol I (600–1660) (Cambridge, 1974)

Blanchot, Jean-Jacques and Graf, Claude (eds), *Actes du 2ᵉ Colloque de Langue et de Litterature Ecossaises* (*Moyen Age et Renaissance*) (Strasbourg, 1978)

Buchan, David, *The Ballad and the Folk* (London and Boston, 1973)

Collinson, Francis, *The Traditional and National Music of Scotland* (London, 1966)

Donaldson, Gordon, *Scotland: James V to James VII* (Edinburgh, 1965)

Duncan, A A M, *Scotland: The Making of the Kingdon* (Edinburgh, 1975)

Farmer, Henry, *A History of Music in Scotland* (London, n.d.)

Geddie, William, *A Bibliography of Middle Scots Poets*, STS (Edinburgh and London, 1912)

Grant, Alexander, *Independence and Nationhood: Scotland 1306–1469* (London, 1984)

Jack, R D S, *The Italian Influence on Scottish Literature* (Edinburgh, 1972)

Kinsley, James (ed), *Scottish Poetry: a Critical Survey* (London, 1955)

Kratzmann, Gregory, *Anglo-Scottish Literary Relations 1430–1550* (Cambridge, 1980)

Lyall, Roderick J and Riddy, Felicity (eds), *Proceedings of the Third International Conference on Scottish Language and Literature* (*Medieval and Renaissance*) (Stirling/Glasgow, 1981)

MacRoberts, David (ed), *Essays on the Scottish Reformation 1513–1625* (Glasgow, 1962)

Mill, Ann J, *Mediaeval Plays in Scotland* (Edinburgh and London, 1927)

Nicholson, Ranald, *Scotland: The Later Middle Ages* (Edinburgh, 1974)

Ridley, Florence H, 'Middle Scots Writers', in *A Manual of the Writings in Middle English 1050–1500*, Hartung, A E (ed), vol IV (New Haven, 1973)

Scheps, Walter and Looney, J Anna, *Middle Scots Poets: a Reference Guide to James I, Robert Henryson, William Dunbar and Gavin Douglas* (Boston, Mass., 1986)

Simpson, Grant G, *Scots Handwriting 1150–1650* (Aberdeen, 1977, repr 1986)

Speirs, John, *The Scots Literary Tradition* (London, 1962)

Wormald, Jennifer M, *Court, Kirk and Community: Scotland 1470–1625* (London, 1981)

Chapter 1

Middle Scots as a Literary Language

ALEX AGUTTER

It will become obvious from later chapters in this volume that Middle Scots was not the only language spoken or written in Scotland during the Mediæval and Renaissance period. However, Middle Scots became the dominant language and its dominance coincided with a period of intense activity in Scottish literature. As a result, this language was used by some of the best writers Scotland has produced.

Scots is a Germanic language, closely related to English. It first reached Scotland from England as a result of northward raiding and eventual colonisation by people from the Anglo-Saxon kingdom of Northumbria. Initially, of course, it must have been indistinguishable from the English dialect spoken in Northumbria, but it developed differences over time. Scots is, therefore, related to British Standard English much as American or Australian English are, except that Scots has developed at least semi-independently from English, especially from the southern dialects, for more than thirteen centuries. The period of greatest independent development for Scots was from the fourteenth to the sixteenth century, and it is therefore in the literature of this period that the greatest differences between Scots and English can be seen.

Somewhat ironically, one of the first indications that a dialect of English had arrived in Scotland is contained in a Mediæval poem written in a Celtic language akin to Welsh. This poem, *The Gododdin*, gives an account of the arrival of Anglo-Saxons in Scotland, and of their capture of a place with the Celtic name Din Eidyn, now known in its English translation as Edinburgh. Clearly, this dialect of English must have ousted the Welsh-type Celtic language as well as the unknown language of the Picts. Both these languages were indigenous in the seventh century, but were under threat not only from Old English but also from another recent arrival, a Celtic language that was a dialect of Irish not of Welsh. This language, Gaelic, was becoming firmly established in the West, and in the eighth to thirteenth centuries was commonly found not just in what we now consider the Gaeltachd but in most of the areas of Scotland where English was also in use. It seems likely, then, that quite a number of people at this period were bilingual in Gaelic and Scots, and if this were so we would expect to see a lot of Gaelic influence on Scots (and vice versa). The conventional view is that there is very little in Scots that can be attributed to Gaelic, whether in vocabulary, grammar or

13

the sound system. Recently, this view has been challenged so that it is now an open issue. There is no doubt at all, however, that Scots, not Gaelic, developed into the national language of Mediæval and Renaissance Scotland.

A later arrival than either Gaelic or Scots was Old Norse, the language of the Viking raiders. This language was spoken in the far north and west of Scotland, but had little or no written tradition in Scotland; it had little direct influence on Scots, which was never spoken in the areas where Norse was strongest. The Norse words and sounds which were and still are current in Scots have mostly come via the language of immigrants who spoke the heavily Scandinavianised dialects of northern and midland England, areas which had been part of the Danelaw.

We know that the dialect of English which developed into Middle Scots gained dominance over the earlier indigenous languages of Scotland, as well as over other incoming languages, and so became the national vernacular. This happened for social, economic and political reasons, and not through any inherent linguistic superiority.

The emergence of Middle Scots as a literary language from the fourteenth century onwards must be seen in the context of the European trend towards secularisation, which included the increasing use of the vernacular as opposed to Latin for official as well as recreational purposes. The influence of Latin is seen in Scots as in English, primarily in the vocabulary. This influence will be discussed further in relation to stylistic variation in Middle Scots.

THE LINGUISTIC CHARACTERISTICS OF SCOTS

Vocabulary

The vocabulary of Middle Scots overlapped to a very large extent with the vocabulary of southern English. Obviously, the majority of words were of Anglo-Saxon origin. Even here, however, there were differences between Scots and southern dialects in that some words survived in the north long after they had died out in the south, e.g. *bairn* (child), *ken* (know), *neb* (nose). This is also true of some words borrowed from Old Norse. Although many of these loans from Old Norse are still shared by all the dialects of English, e.g. *they*, *egg*, others have survived longer in Scots, *nieve* (fist), *skayth* (harm), *gate* (road). French and Latin have also been rich sources of vocabulary in Scots just as in the other dialects of English. Again many loan words were shared, but some appear to be only or mainly found in Scots, e.g. *disjune* (Fr. (petit) déjeuner—breakfast), *gairding* (Norman Fr.—garden), *cherarchy* (Fr.—hierarchy); *compeir* (L.—to appear formally, e.g. before a Court of Law), *propiciant* (L.—favourable), *intitulit* (L.—entitled).

Although Old English provided the basic vocabulary of Middle Scots, and although Old Norse, French and Latin were the main sources of loan words, there were other minor sources including Middle Dutch, e.g. *dub* (puddle), *cuit* (ankle), *craig* (neck); and Gaelic. Gaelic was the source of a number of Middle Scots words (as well as many place and personal names), e.g. *clan, bledoch* (buttermilk), *drammock* (oatmeal and water mix), although many of the now familiar loan words from Gaelic are not recorded until the end of the Mediæval and Renaissance period (e.g. *garron, claymore*).

Although words which are only or mainly found in Scots occurred in all kinds of Middle Scots texts, there were differences of vocabulary between texts of different styles. Most obviously, and just as in Middle English, Early Modern English and present day English, a larger number of Latin and French loan words occurred in high style texts. This was presumably a legacy from the use of Latin as the sole written language until the fourteenth century, and also from the continued importance of Latin and French in the education of the clergy and the aristocracy respectively. However, the use of Latin and French loans in high style Middle Scots literature was not confined to the practice still familiar today. Certain words, usually of Latin derivation, appear to belong to texts of this style only. Examples of such words are: *visage* (face), *mansuetude* (meekness), *orient* and *aureate*. The last of these has given its name to the phenomenon of gilding the language of high style literature with these purely literary words. This phenomenon, 'aureation', is not confined to Scots, however, and often appears in the high style verse of English poets too, e.g. the first known use of *aureate* to mean 'splendid' or 'brilliant as gold' is by Lydgate; and the first known use of *mansuetude* is by Chaucer. The use of such terms, therefore, along with frequent references to figures from Classical mythologies—*Eolus* for the wind, *Aurora* for the dawn—may be seen as the language element of a literary tradition which extends far beyond Lowland Scotland.

In contrast to the aureate nature of high style Scots, the language used in low style Middle Scots literature had a greater proportion of Anglo-Saxon vocabulary items and of loan words from Old Norse and Middle Dutch. It is in this kind of literature that we find the greatest number of words with obscure etymologies, many of which survive only in a single text. From this we may deduce that the language of this style of literature was closer to the ordinary colloquial Scots of the day: it contained fewer 'educated' words, but more words and idioms which may have been slang and which may have been ephemeral, e.g. *get thy paikis* (get your just deserts), *swappit* (great big), *skaff* (to scrounge). Even though low style verse used colloquial vocabulary, it was still concerned with literary effect; e.g. 'sueir swappit swanky swynekeper' (lazy, big fat lump of a pig-herd) alliterates three colloquial forms and one idiomatic insult. The selection of vocabulary is obviously governed by the suitability of individual words to the style rather than simply by the idiosyncratic preferences of different authors, since all of these examples of both high and low style vocabulary have been taken from the works of Dunbar; the high style from *The Thrissill and the Rois* and *The Goldyn Targe*, and the low style from Dunbar's contributions to *The Flyting Betwixt Kennedie and Dunbar*.

The stylistically-motivated choice of vocabulary was so entrenched in Scots that it is possible to identify sets of words of very similar meaning which were distinguished principally by the stylistic level in which they appeared. For example, *visage* was used in high style texts, *face* was stylistically neutral, while *gane* was low style; similarly *hound*, *dog*, and *tyke*; and *pas*, *ga* (go) and *gang*. The association of a particular type of language with each style in literature was also evident in the grammar and in the spelling and sound systems of Middle Scots (see below).

Spelling and the sound system

Many of the initial difficulties faced by a reader of Middle Scots literature are caused by spelling practices which appear very different from those of Middle English and Early Modern English literature as well as very different from our own spelling system. The problems obviously fall into two categories: first, difficulties arise when an unfamiliar spelling practice was used for a perfectly familiar pronunciation of a word; and second, a word may have been spelt in a way that suggests an unfamiliar pronunciation.

To some extent the unfamiliarity of Middle Scots spelling conventions is lessened by the common practice of normalising the spelling (and the punctuation): a practice followed in almost all editions of texts other than facsimilies. Normalisation is usual not just for Middle Scots texts, but also for Middle English ones. Editors differ in the extent to which they normalise the spelling and punctuation in their texts, but at the very least they usually expand unfamiliar abbreviations found in the manuscripts, and replace letters no longer in use in English. For example, even in some manuscripts, and certainly in printed editions, the letter ⟨þ⟩ was replaced by ⟨y⟩ in words such as *the*, *that* but this change did not affect the pronunciation of these words at all: whether spelt with a ⟨þ⟩, a ⟨y⟩ or with ⟨th⟩ they should be pronounced as in present day English. Many texts also replace the letter ⟨ȝ⟩, which was pronounced as the first sound in *yes*, with ⟨z⟩, following the practice of the sixteenth and seventeenth century Scottish printers who had no letter ⟨ȝ⟩ in their founts. This explains some odd relationships between the spelling and pronounciation of certain words in modern use, e.g. *capercailzie*, or the two pronunciations of *Menzies* (/miŋəs/ and /menziz/) or *Dalziel* (/dijel/ and /dalzil/). The first of each pair developed naturally from the Middle Scots pronunciation but the second was influenced by the spelling.

Some editors do more than merely replace letters no longer used in English. For example, in Middle Scots it was possible to use ⟨u⟩ or ⟨v⟩ or ⟨w⟩ for any of the three sounds we now associate with these letters. Although there are numerous exceptions, the most usual pattern was to use ⟨v⟩ at the beginnings of words, ⟨u⟩ in the middle and ⟨w⟩ at the end, so that ⟨vp⟩ is *up*, ⟨diuinacioun⟩ is *divination* and ⟨thow⟩ is *thou*. Although all these letters are still current, many editors alter the spelling of the original text to conform to modern practice.

This level of normalisation and modernisation, coupled with the almost universal editorial practices of adding punctuation and dividing verse into separate lines (many early verse works were written continuously in their manuscript copies, as if they were prose), does of course destroy the original appearance of Middle Scots texts, but provided the editor explains what normalisation procedures have been carried out, we are still left with much information on the spelling and pronunciation of the original. On the other hand, little can be learned about the spelling and pronunciation of a text which has been fully modernised.

In Middle Scots, most of the consonant sounds were spelt as in English, but a few were spelt in a typically Scots way. For instance, the sound /x/ which many Scots speakers pronounce at the end of *loch* was spelt ⟨ch⟩ in Middle Scots, but ⟨gh⟩ in southern English texts, hence ⟨micht⟩, ⟨thocht⟩. ⟨lauch⟩ are equivalent to southern ⟨might⟩, ⟨thought⟩, ⟨laugh⟩ and would all have been pronounced with /x/ during the Mediæval and Renaissance period as they still are in many Scots dialects. The sound /hw/ which Scots speakers still have in words such as *where, white, what* was typically spelt ⟨quh⟩ in Scots but ⟨wh⟩ in southern texts. The normal Scots forms of these words were therefore ⟨quhare⟩, ⟨quhyte⟩ and ⟨quhat⟩. The initial sound /ʃ/ in such words as *ship, sheet, shoulder* was regularly spelt ⟨sch⟩ in Scots, but ⟨sh⟩ in English. The ⟨sch⟩ spelling was so regular in Middle Scots, that it should always be read as /ʃ/ even in words where this sound is not present today, e.g. we get ⟨schir⟩ for *sir* as well as ⟨schip⟩, ⟨scheit⟩ and ⟨schulder⟩. Conversely, where a word was not spelt with ⟨sch⟩ then it was not pronounced with /ʃ/, so *shall, should*, spelt ⟨sal⟩, ⟨suld⟩ really were pronounced with /s/.

Many words in Middle Scots were spelt with ⟨a⟩ and pronounced accordingly where the equivalent word in southern English would have been spelt with ⟨o⟩ and pronounced accordingly. Hence Mark Alexander Boyd rhymed ⟨evirmaire⟩ with ⟨in the aire⟩, and Dunbar rhymed ⟨aitis⟩ *oats* with ⟨debaittis⟩. The Scots pronunciation of these words, which still survives in Modern Scots dialects, is the older form; only southern dialects changed the sound in these words in the twelfth century, giving rise to the Standard pronunciation and spelling forms in present-day English.

The spelling of the examples above illustrates one of the most distinctive differences in spelling convention between northern and southern texts. Middle Scots could use the convention of a following ⟨i⟩ or ⟨y⟩ to mark a long vowel. In English a following ⟨a⟩ or ⟨e⟩ was used, or the vowel letter was doubled. These spellings were not normally used in Scots, so that a text with ⟨oa⟩, ⟨ea⟩, or ⟨oo⟩ spellings has some non-Scots influence; e.g. compare the Middle Scots and southern Early Modern English forms ⟨boitt⟩/⟨boat⟩, ⟨heid⟩/⟨head⟩, ⟨guid⟩/⟨good⟩. It is precisely these kinds of spellings as well as ⟨wh⟩ for earlier ⟨quh⟩, ⟨sh⟩ for earlier ⟨sch⟩ and ⟨gh⟩ for ⟨ch⟩ that increase in number from the early seventeenth century. Presumably the Scots authors and printers concerned are attempting to write in southern English Standard even if that involves using forms which were previously unacceptable in Middle Scots.

Occasionally a southern English pronunciation is apparently intended in a Scots text. Initially, this occurs only in high style texts, and is often represented by a Scots spelling convention, e.g. *whose* is written as ⟨quhois⟩ not as ⟨quhais⟩ in *The Thrissill and the Rois*. Occurrences such as these may imply the start of an association of southern forms with appropriate language for the most formal occasions; that is, it might be taken to imply that Middle

Scots was not considered sufficiently prestigious for such occasions. However, this view of Middle Scots seems unconvincing, since the use of southern forms was obviously only one option for marking formality: the majority of formal markers in Middle Scots texts are indigenous to Scots.

Spelling and pronunciation also show stylistic marking for low style texts. Two sound changes in particular are represented in the spelling of low style literary texts but not usually in high style texts. Many words in Middle Scots lost the sound /l/ after ⟨a⟩, ⟨o⟩ or ⟨u⟩. We know that this loss had occurred by the mid fourteenth century because spellings such as ⟨wawys⟩ *walls*, ⟨goud⟩ *gold* appear from that time. However, these spellings never completely displaced the original spellings with ⟨l⟩. In itself this would not be a problem; after all, we all spell *calm* as ⟨calm⟩ but none of us pronounces it with an /l/. However, in Middle Scots, spellings without ⟨l⟩ were very rare in high style texts whereas they occurred alongside ⟨l⟩ forms in low style texts. Was this merely a spelling convention which was stylistically marked or was it meant to imply a stylistically marked pronunciation difference? We face the same problem with the loss of /v/ in words such as *devil*, *even(ing)* and *harvest*. Although these are not stylistically marked in Modern Scots, spellings such as ⟨deil⟩, which clearly indicate the loss of /v/, are normally only found in low style texts in Middle Scots. That such words were normally pronounced without /v/ in low style texts can be shown by a rhyme from *The Wif of Awchtirmwchty* between ⟨evin⟩ *evening* and ⟨clene⟩ *clean*. The same poem also rhymes ⟨all⟩ and ⟨twa⟩ showing the same phenomenon for loss of /l/. We seem to be on fairly safe ground if we use the reduced pronunciations regularly in low style literature, but whether we should keep this pronunciation in high style literature or use the non-reduced form (i.e. pronouncing the /v/ or /l/) is a matter of taste so long as the rhyme scheme and metre leave the options open.

The desire to match appropriate linguistic forms with literary styles was common in European literature of the time and much was written on the subject. James VI wrote such a work for Middle Scots literature. In his *Reulis and Cautelis to be observit and eschewit in Scottis Poesie*, he exemplified the appropriate use of forms such as those discussed above. There was nothing haphazard or idiosyncratic about the stylistically-motivated use of language in Middle Scots.

Grammar

The grammar of Middle Scots was generally similar to that of English of the same period, although some forms that were in use in Scots had died out earlier in other dialects of English, or conversely, were introduced earlier into Scots than into other English dialects. The same can be said about the vocabulary and about spelling and the sound system (see above). In other words, although all the English dialects might eventually come to share a linguistic form, they may well have developed that form at different times. This can be true of both morphology—the marking of individual words to show, e.g. singular or plural in nouns, or tense, number and person in verbs—and syntax—the ways in which individual words can be grouped together to form acceptable sentences.

Among the characteristics of Middle Scots which can be accounted for in terms of different rates of development is the loss of a distinction between the forms representing the present participle and the gerund. The present participle in southern English had changed from its early form ⟨-ende⟩ to share the inflexion ⟨-ing⟩ with the gerund. In Scots, the forms representing the present participle ⟨-and⟩ and the gerund ⟨-ing⟩ were kept distinct until much later, e.g. 'Makbeth and Banquho war *passand* to Fores', a present participle from Bellenden's translation of Boece's *Chronicles of Scotland*; 'And gif sik trespassouris takis ony skaythe in ye *aresting* of yame' (if such lawbreakers are injured during their arrest), a gerund from a late fifteenth century copy of a 1424 Act of Parliament. These differences in rates of development need not affect a whole morphological category, but can relate simply to an individual word. For instance, for the plural of *cow*, Middle and indeed Modern Scots retain the Old English form *kye*, whereas southern English has adopted the weak plural form *cows*.

In these cases, Scots was more conservative than southern English. In other respects, however, Scots was in advance of southern English. For example, the present tense in Middle Scots could only be marked in two ways: by ⟨-s⟩ or by no ending. In southern English the endings ⟨-est⟩ (second person singular) and ⟨-eth⟩ (third person singular) lasted well into the seventeenth century, and ⟨-en⟩ (plural) into the sixteenth century, while no ending has been used for the first person singular from late Middle English to the present. In present day English we can only use ⟨-s⟩ or no ending to mark the present tense, so it is clear that the older southern system was replaced by the northern one, which has been modified and adopted as standard. In present day English ⟨-s⟩ marks the third person singular only. In Scots as in Northern Middle English the choice of ⟨-is⟩ depended on whether or not there was an adjacent personal pronoun subject. If there was, then the first person singular and all persons plural would have no ending; in all other circumstances the ending was ⟨-is⟩. This rather curious rule accounts for the many cases in Older Scots where a plural subject took a verb ending with ⟨-s⟩, e.g. 'Twa gods gyds me' (Mark Alexander Boyd Sonnet). This was not stylistically marked, but is found in all types of text. In no sense was it a grammatical solecism as it would be in present day English.

For the most part, however, the morphologies of Scots and southern English followed the same system, with apparent distinctions being explained as superficial differences in spelling conventions between the two dialects. So, plural nouns in southern English were (and are) normally marked by ⟨-es⟩ or ⟨-s⟩ whereas in Scots they were normally marked by ⟨-is⟩ or ⟨-s⟩: southern ⟨sisteres, sisters⟩ is equivalent to northern ⟨sisteris, sisters⟩. In all the dialects of English at this time there were more plurals in ⟨-n⟩ than have survived into present day English, so that the plural ⟨eyen⟩ for *eyes* may be found in any text of the period, whether southern English or Scots.

As with nouns, some of the differences between Scots and southern verb morphology were superficial. Past tense and past participles of weak verbs in southern English ended in ⟨-ed⟩ then as they do now. In Scots the same relationships were normally marked by ⟨-it⟩. This is one of the most obvious though trivial differences between northern and southern texts; it was largely a difference of spelling convention representing only a minor difference in pronunciation.

The grammar of all the English dialects was changing during the period that concerns us. In some cases this meant that the language was very flexible, so that authors could select from coexisting obsolescent and novel grammatical forms. Such options were exploited particularly in verse, where one alternative might fit the metrical pattern much better than another. An example of this would be the option of using either a modern simple conjunction (*when*, *if*, *where*, etc.) or the historically earlier complex equivalent, which had *that* following the conjunction: 'That I annone awoilk *quhair yat* I lay' (That I suddenly awoke where I lay) from Dunbar's *Thrissill and the Rois* and 'Bot *sen that* ye will husy skep ken' (but since you would learn a housewife's job—literally, 'housewife-ship') from the anonymous *Wif of Awchtirmwchty*. Since the former of these examples is from a high style, courtly verse, while the latter is from a low style, comic piece, it can be inferred that the use of *that* after a conjunction was not governed by this aspect of style. *That* was rarely used in this way in prose texts, which suggests that it was also rare in ordinary speech by the early sixteenth century. It may be an example of an obsolescent grammatical construction preserved in literary use because it offered an extra syllable which in no way altered the meaning.

Our knowledge of the grammar of this period of Scots is still rather sketchy, but it appears that in many cases the selection from the available options was governed by the stylistic level of the text. A characteristic of high style was the use of parallelism—the repetition of a grammatical structure especially within a stanza; for example

> '(Quhone) sabill all the hewin arrayis
> With mystie vapouris, cluddis and skyis,
> Nature all curage me denyis
> Off sangs, ballattis, and of playis.'
> (Dunbar's 'Meditatioun in Wyntir')

In this example, the syntactic structure: (conjunction) subject, object, verb, followed by a triple prepositional phrase; is followed by the structure: subject, direct and indirect objects, verb, and a triple prepositional phrase. Although the effect is offset in this case by the use of grammatical patterns which are unfamiliar in present day English, the use of this device often gives high style verse an apparent grammatical simplicity not found in low style verse, which uses a wider range of grammatical constructions some of which may be colloquial in origin. In *The Wif of Awchtirmwchty* there are a number of instances of informal grammatical constructions some of which could cause difficulty for a present day reader. The line 'Sayis Iok wil thou be maister of wark?' line 41, might be interpreted as the kind of structure found in reports in today's popular press, i.e. the verb followed by its subject, but in fact, it is not Jock who says 'Will you be in charge of the job?' but the woman (the 'wif' of the title) who says 'Jock, will you...'. The subject of the sentence could be carried over from the preceding main clause—a structure no longer allowed in written work but still heard in informal speech. In this case, Scots continued to use a construction which had been dying out in southern English from late Old English times.

Low style verse also frequently omitted grammatical links such as conjunctions, and this omission may also be seen in apparently sudden changes of topic. That this was related to style and was not an indication of an author's incompetence can be seen by comparing the high and low style verse of a single author.

Stylistic variation in the grammar of Scots was not confined to verse. Among the most common stylistically-motivated variations in the grammar was the choice of relative pronoun. Our knowledge of present-day constraints on relative pronouns can mislead us if we expect them to apply in Older Scots. For instance, we can no longer use *which* of a person, but this word, in its characteristic Older Scots spelling ⟨quhilk⟩, was the usual choice in a high style text whether it referred to a person or not. In very formal works the relative pronoun could even be inflected to show agreement with a plural referent, e.g. 'Quhat wemen be ye *quhilkis* bene sa unmerciful to me' (What kind of women could you be who are so...) from Bellenden's translation of Boece's *Chronicles of Scotland*. The use of *who* ⟨quha⟩ as a relative pronoun was not an option in Scots until well into the sixteenth century; before then it could only be used as an interrogative pronoun. The unmarked or stylistically neutral relative pronoun in Scots was *that* which was therefore not necessarily informal although we tend to think of it as informal now, e.g. 'Haill, Makbeth, that salbe sum tyme King of Scotlannd' from Bellenden. The least formal option was to reduce the relative pronoun from *that* to *at*, or to omit it altogether. It seems as though this stylistically motivated choice of relative pronoun reflects the non-literary use of Scots at the time: low life characters in Lindsay's *Ane Satyre of the Thrie Estaits* use more low style forms than the prestigious characters, and similarly, women's letters contain more low style forms than do men's letters to the same correspondent. The difference in usage by the two sexes is assumed to have been a result of different levels of education.

Although we cannot always tell why a particular grammatical form should be associated with a particular style, some such connections are clear. For example some grammatical constructions are found only or mainly in texts translated from a Latin original, and were clearly borrowed from Latin. This is true of the ablative absolute construction, e.g. 'Thir wourdis beand sayid' (These words being said = Having said these words) from Bellenden's translation of Boece's *Chronicles of Scotland*, and may be true of the accusative and infinitive construction in Scots, e.g. 'The pepill traistit yame to be werd sisteris' (The people believed them to be sisters with prophetic powers = the people believed that they were...). The retention of obsolescent marking of plural agreement between a relative pronoun and its referent (see above) might also be reinforced by Latin or French models.

The status of Middle Scots

It should be clear from the discussion of various aspects of the language of Middle Scots that many, but not all, of the characteristics which we think of as being distinctively Scots were also found in northern English dialects. This is a far cry from claiming that Middle Scots was indistinguishable from northern Middle English or the northern dialects of Early Modern English. Probably the major difference between Scots and the northern dialects of English was the acceptance of Middle Scots as a standard variety until the late sixteenth century or early seventeenth century when it began to be eroded by the competing southern English Standard. That is, Middle Scots during the Mediæval and Renaissance period was considered to be a suitable medium even for official records and high style literature; it was also the spoken and written variety of even those of highest social status in Lowland Scotland. There was no suggestion that Middle Scots was unsuitable for any of these purposes: there was no stigma attached to its use. Northern dialects on the other hand had never had the status of a standard variety, and so succumbed to the southern English Standard as it became established in the fifteenth century.

The erosion of the Middle Scots Standard by the southern English Standard is first apparent in late sixteenth century texts. Some non-Scots forms had occurred from the late fifteenth century, but they had only occurred sporadically in otherwise Standard Middle Scots texts, and only in high style literature. From the late sixteenth century non-Scots forms became more common; in some cases this was the result of deliberate translation of Scots forms into southern English forms until, in the seventeenth century, non-Scots forms predominate in high style texts and can even be found in texts of lower styles.

The process of translating Standard Middle Scots into southern Standard English can be seen very clearly in separate editions of works by James VI. In some respects, James's works show rather idiosyncratic applications of Scottish spelling conventions, but they are broadly within the range permitted by Standard Middle Scots. However, as his hopes for inheriting the English Crown increased, he prepared some of his earlier works for a British rather than a specifically Scottish readership, and the changes made were all in the direction of southern Standard. Two points should be emphasised: these changes begin before the Union of the Crowns although, of course, they continue after 1603; and some of them were made by James himself (in his own handwriting) although others were made by printers. Changes made in the text of *Basilikon Doron* include: in vocabulary—*thir* in the King's autograph manuscript was changed to *these* in the 1599 printed edition; and *kirke* to *Church*; in spelling—⟨lang⟩, ⟨na⟩ ⟨quhom⟩ and ⟨thaime⟩ were changed to ⟨long⟩, ⟨no⟩ ⟨whom⟩ and ⟨them⟩. Some of the changes do not correspond to our concept of southern Standard usage, but they are within the range permitted by that Standard at the time, e.g. ⟨heelande⟩ was changed to ⟨Hie-land⟩; ⟨uerrie⟩ to ⟨verie⟩; ⟨thefis⟩ to ⟨thieues⟩. The forms ⟨commounueill⟩ and ⟨common-weill⟩ were changed in the 1603 edition to ⟨common-weale⟩, and ⟨sen⟩ was changed at the same time to ⟨since⟩; the Scots forms ⟨obleishe⟩ and ⟨oblish⟩ for *oblige* survived these attempts to make the text conform to the southern English standard. It would appear then that James VI (and his printers) had a reasonable, if not a perfect, knowledge of southern Standard, but that despite this personal evidence of literacy in both dialects, he still felt it desirable to 'translate' his work into southern Standard. Whether this was because he felt that Middle Scots would be too difficult for a southern audience (a patronising attitude that is still found amongst both Scots and English) or whether he foresaw and wished to associate himself with the cultural dominance of southern English which gained momentum after the Union of the Crowns, it is hard to tell.

From this, it seems that the increasing influence of the southern Standard on Middle Scots in the late sixteenth and seventeenth centuries was effected by the abandoning of purely native Scots forms and their replacement either by forms which had always been shared by Middle Scots and southern Early Modern English or, more radically, by southern forms which had previously been unacceptable in Standard Middle Scots. However, it might be misleading to suppose that sixteenth century readers made the same assumptions about the language of the texts that we make. If mostly shared linguistic forms are used in a text, we (who are literate in English to the virtual exclusion of Scots) automatically read that text as if it were English. However, the literate population of sixteenth century Lowland Scotland (who could certainly read Scots as well as English) might well have read the same text as if it was Scots. Thus, although we perceive a rather sudden change from the use of Scots to the use of English in Scottish literature after the late sixteenth century, the change may have been perceived as much more gradual by Scots at the time.

As already stated, these changes initially took place only sporadically in high style literature and formal non-literary works; but by the mid seventeenth century many of these works have few Scots linguistic forms, and some non-Scots forms occurred even in low style texts. This process could be interpreted as a process of restandardisation: the change first affects the language in situations where, then as now, only a fully respected standard variety would be acceptable, suggesting that Scots was relegated from standard status to nonstandard dialect status. A Scottish national Standard which had had political, social and literary prestige was gradually replaced by a foreign Standard of greater prestige or utility. A similar process might soon be in operation in the erosion of British by American Standard English.

The claim that Middle Scots had its own Standard, independent of the southern Standard, raises the question of whether Middle Scots should be regarded as a separate language from English or only as a separate dialect. The answer to this question depends ultimately on the definition of a language. Throughout this period, Scots and even the southern dialects of English, let alone the northern dialects, remained too similar in their linguistic characteristics to support the claim that Scots was a separate language: they never diverged further than say, German and Austrian German, which are regarded as two separate dialects of a single language. However, if our definition of a language includes functional and social criteria, then there are good reasons for describing Middle Scots as a separate language: its use was not restricted to particular types of text or to particular situations, nor was its use restricted to a particular social group. It could even be used in diplomacy between countries (e.g. letters to English monarchs were frequently written in Scots although the replies came in southern English). As a result of its official status and widespread use, Middle Scots developed a range of stylistic variation clearly illustrated in literary texts. On the other hand, dialects are usually restricted in their range of uses, e.g. they are not used for the records of parliaments or for other official business; and nowadays they are usually restricted to particular social groups, although this restriction might not have applied to the Mediæval and Renaissance English-speaking world. Nor is the development of stylistic variation normally found in dialects, which tend to be monostylistic. In these terms, the situation of Middle Scots contrasts markedly with that of modern Austrian German which is not used for official purposes and does not display much stylistic variation; of course, it also contrasts with the position of Scots today.

(The principles of Normalisation outlined in the Introduction have not been applied in this Chapter. Editor)

FURTHER READING

PRIMARY TEXTS

(For Dunbar, Bannatyne MS see General Bibliography)

Chambers, R W, Batho, E C, and Husbands, H Winifred (eds), *The Chronicles of Scotland, Compiled by Hector Boece, Translated into Scots by John Bellenden 1531*, STS, 2 vols (Edinburgh and London, 1938–41)

Craigie, J (ed), *Basilikon Doron of James VI*, STS, 2 vols (Edinburgh and London, 1944–50)

SECONDARY TEXTS

Aitken, A J, 'Variation and variety in written Middle Scots', in *Edinburgh Studies in English and Scots*, Aitken, A J, McIntosh, Angus, and Palsson, Hermann (London, 1971), pp 177–209

—— 'How to pronounce Older Scots', in *Bards and Makars*, Aitken, A J, McDiarmid, M P, and Thomson, D S (Glasgow, 1977), pp 1–21

—— and McArthur, Tom, *Languages of Scotland* (Edinburgh, 1979)

Romaine, Suzanne, 'Contributions from Middle Scots syntax to a theory of syntactic change', in *Proceedings of the Third International Conference on Scottish Language and Literature (Medieval and Renaissance)*, Lyall, Roderick, J, and Riddy, Felicity (eds) (Stirling/Glasgow, 1981), pp 70–84

Chapter 2

The Metrical Chronicles and Non-alliterative Romances

M P McDIARMID

> Storys to rede ar delitabill
> Suppos that thai be nocht bot fabill
> (I, 1–2)

writes John Barbour (*c*.1320–95) in 1375–77, and it is their love of an extra-ordinary action that connects the early chroniclers with the romancers. Barbour values 'suthfastnes' but his 'suthfastnes', the fight of the few against the many, is for him a 'romans'. He can think it proper to compare Bruce with Tydeus, the hero of *Le Roman de Thèbes*, who fought and overcame the forty-nine who lay in ambush, and with Gaudifer, hero of the 'Foray of Gaderis' in *Le Roman d' Alixandre*. He will even give Bruce at Bannockburn a speech that owes something (if not its patriotic content) to one delivered by Alexander before the fictional battle of 'Ephesoun' in the same romance, and when the king is a fugitive show him reading 'romans of worthi Ferambrace'.

Perhaps no country ever lived with the conviction of so romantic a past. Its Gael-derived origin, the same with that of the royal House, was enshrined in a tale of odyssey.[1] About the time of the Israelite exodus a Greek prince Gadalos had married an Egyptian princess Scota, with his warriors sailed westwards, and from a mountain in Galicia fancied that, like another Moses, he saw his promised land from afar. Dying he bade his people always be true to 'the noble heart' and venture onwards. They settled for a time in Ireland and then from Ulster, in the fifth century, saw their destined home, Scotland. Some such romantic legend was needed to give a unifying history to the early kingdom, composed as it was of diverse peoples, Picts of the northeast, Bretts of the southwest, Angles of the Border and east coast.

Much fine story-telling must have been suppressed, lost, in the conflict of cultures, as is evidenced by the survival of the *Gododdin*, composed probably beside Dundee, by Neirin, about the year 600, the earliest extant of Europe's heroic poems in a vernacular tongue, and for sensibility the best[2] Only in our times has it been brought into Scots consciousness. One can still respond to the human voice in it, the universal appeal of the lament for young Ywain: 'it is a shame that he is under a cairn, I marvel in what land the slaying of the only son of Marro could come to pass'. Much too must have been lost in the Anglian speech while it slowly established its dominance over both Brett and Gaelic, not achieved till the twelfth and thirteenth centuries, and then only in southern (not southwest) and eastern Scotland. The Anglo-Scottish wars that did not cease till after the mid fourteenth century, and must have meant so many losses from church and castle, delayed still further the appearance of a considerable literary work.

Vacant as the Anglian centuries may appear Barbour writes with the ease of a man who is served by a tradition, so that one looks for evidences of the latter, at least in record. There seems to have been a lengthy verse narrative of the deeds of Malcolm Canmore (d. 1093), a few words describing his confrontation with a traitor being preserved by John of Fordun 1363, 'And thai wer hande for hande';[3] and from the same poem must have come Wyntoun's story of Macbeth that, as developed by Hector Boece would give Shakespeare the plot for his play. That nobles liked to hear romances recited is perhaps all that the early thirteenth-century visit of Guillaume le Clerc to Alan of Galloway, which produced his *Roman de fergus*, tells us, except that in his day as in Robert Burns's, Ayrshire lassies were the bonniest in the world (189–90).[4] In 1286 a Norwegian ambassador fetched home from the Scottish court an Anglian romance concerning a sadistic King Olif and his saintly and long-suffering queen. It is translated in the *Karlamagnussaga*.[5] At the same time the Border laird Thomas Rimour of Ercildoune was composing darkly prophetic sayings, on the model of those by Geoffrey of Monmouth, that would earn him a place in chronicle and ballad as Thomas the Rhymer. More interesting is the attribution to him of a romance on Tristan and Iseult, for he is most likely to be the Thomas to whom it is assigned in a somewhat later northern English reworking of this matter.[6] Certainly there were 'gret gestes' of Wallace and Bruce current in the first half of the fourteenth century. One of these must be the tale of Bruce outwitting a hostile boatman at Loch Lomond that is mentioned in Sir Thomas Gray's *Scalacronica*, begun in Edinburgh castle in 1355.[7] And one such 'geste', notably in French octo-syllabic couplets, is preserved by Wyntoun, of Wallace's night-time vengeance on the sheriff of Lanark for slaying his 'lemman' (wife in Hary's version).[8] Barbour, of course, though he gladly used such material, was much more than a retailer of popular 'gestes', yet it should be clear that he was born into a tradition that had naturalised its French indebtedness. Like the author of the *Buik of Alexander* (1438) he was able to give to his verse a wholly Scots spirit, more important, to turn it to a Scots purpose. It is this achievement that makes good his claim to be the father of Scots literature.

When one casts one's mind back to the very emotive, self-expressive Neirin, so concerned for the disaster at 'Catraeth' (more probably near Loch Macatterick where are the Hooden hills of the poem than Yorkshire's Catterick)—'my breath fails as if with strenuous running, and straightway I weep'—or forward to the equally involved Hary, the sobriety and self-effacement of Barbour become conspicuous. Yet he is no blandly recording Froissart, a careless comparison of Walter Scott's, but shows his vital concern with cause and characteristic action or utterance. Thus it is to his credit that he tells us of young Randolph's rebellious impatience with the battle-avoiding tactics of King Robert, to the credit of both Barbour and Edward Bruce, who forced the issue of Bannockburn on the king, that in the hour of victory Edward could stop by the dead body of a friend and wish, 'That journey wer/Undone than he sua ded had bene' (XIII 484–5), and to the credit of poet and king alike that in the retreat of the small Scots army from Limerick it should be halted while a woman was safely delivered of her baby, 'a ful gret courtesy' (XVI 270–86).

Barbour's national epic may be wanting in the images that make an arresting picture in Neirin—'a herd of red horses, the horseman fierce in the morning'—but affective detail supplies the want. On that hot June day we see, feel, the desperate labours of Randolph's schiltrum (defensive circle of spearmen), the sweat of men withstanding for hours the onset of cavalry, the hail of weapons. The poet may not himself openly respond to destruction and death, but he can break with convention enough to show men in tears, as when Bruce meets old comrades in like dire straits by Loch Lomond. Above all he can convey the full spirit of a heroic act, as when Nele Fleming cries, 'Quha dar fecht for his lord?', and falls before superior numbers, or in the escape of Randolph and his lieutenant Douglas from seeming entrapment by the army of Edward III, or the feeling in the momentous scene when the dying Bruce asks that his heart, 'Quhar-in consawyt wes that entent', be carried by way of atonement for the many dead to the Holy Land.

Still, a whole dimension of that terrible warfare that was known to Wyntoun and Hary is missing. It is from Wyntoun we have to learn it: at the English seizure of Berwick the burning of halls and houses, indiscriminate slaying of man, woman and child till the streets were wet with blood, and King Edward himself cried out in disgust, 'Laissez, laissez'. Bruce's equally terrible campaign in the north is noticed only for brave deeds, and almost *en passant* for the still remembered devastation of Buchan. It is plain, however, that the poet's heart is in the great descant, 'Ah, fredome is a noble thing', and that national right includes for him individual rights, that he believes, as he says, that free men fight best for freedom. He can say that yeoman and poor man fought just as well as did knight. He is not simply the voice of a ruling class defending position and inheritance. One good effect of the war, of which Barbour the archdeacon and lawyer would be well aware, was the disuse in Scotland, before other nations, of serfdom.

Two poems in the same metrical form could hardly differ more from each other in matter and spirit than the *Bruce* and the Scottish *Legends of the Saints*,[9] or Golden Legends, as they were sometimes called. The odd notion that the Legends as a whole, or at least those of St Machar and St Ninian which show a connection with Aberdeen, were written by Barbour has been dismissed conclusively elsewhere and need not be argued here.[10] One need only observe that the above-mentioned two cannot be separated from the others: they do not come together, the list of miracles is the same for St Alexis as for Ninian, they end with the identically worded prayer of all the Legends, and personal statements agree with what is said elsewhere. The author tells us that he was in 'gret eld', his eyesight failing, which means that he had a researcher for his Scots Lives and dictated them. He had written a Life of the

Virgin that was widely read, and a more worldly interest had been *The Romance of the Rose*. Clearly he is well acquainted with Old Aberdeen, as his 'St Machar' shows, and in his 'St Ninian' he mentions an Aberdeen landholder, Jac Trumpoure, a merry fellow, as an event in King David's time (d. 1371) showed. Jac was Carrick herald, and on the Borders one day, giving a cheerful blast with his horn, unknowingly scattered an English raiding party. The poet was also friendly with John of Balormy (at Elgin) and knew of John's 'kin'. The old writer was almost certainly one of Barbour's colleagues, William of Spyny (at Elgin), at Paris 1352–63, precentor at Elgin, canon and Dean at Aberdeen, bishop at Elgin where he died in 1406.

One Legend redeems the tedium conveyed by the others, 'Mary the Egypciane'. A prostitute who hired herself to a crew sailing to Israel, she had her call to grace in Jerusalem, penitent wandered the desert naked, sun-blackened, and one day met another penitent, the old priest Zosymus. They could only meet once in the year, and when they met they kneeled to each other. She asked for, and received, the sacraments, and next year he had to bury her, and died soon after. Perhaps the old priest-poet saw himself in Zosymus, for unlike all other versions this one affects as a spiritual love-story.

The *Original Chronicle* (*Cornykkyllys*) of Andrew Wyntoun (*c*.1350–*c*.1420) (his Chronicle of Origins) was written at St Serf's Priory in Lochleven, much revised, between 1407 and 1420. It is a history of Europe that soon centres on Scotland. Ever the conscientious historian Wyntoun criticises one fiction by another. Can the Celtic story and Barbour's (in his lost genealogy of the Breton Fitz Alans, Stewarts) both be right? Barbour says a Briton ruled all Britain from the south, a dangerous notion. But doubtless Barbour argued that the Fitz Alans were the true heirs of Britain. Perhaps a little weary he is happy to refer the reader to Barbour for an account of the first Brucean War, and for the second he gives place to a nameless author.

Yet there is interesting matter in Wyntoun, not only that account of the taking of Berwick but also his samples of the Canmore-Macbeth-Macduff saga and 'the gret gestes' of Wallace. From the saga comes his unique version of the Macbeth story in which the witches meet the latter only in a dream, and the usurper marries the wife of his murdered uncle. The 'geste' preserved by him gives to the hero a dramatic dialogue not equalled in Hary's version, yet the life in this belongs to the 'geste' and not Wyntoun. More life comes in with his unknown successor (surely known to him). I note that the 'Anonymous' uses *Li Abrejance*, a section of Jean de Meun's translation of Vegetius, to comment on Scots practice in war. We owe to him arresting scenes: Black Agnes of Dunbar, that good housewife, with her handkerchief flicking away the dust left on her castle walls by English cannon; the last defiant jest of David of Athol, his back to an oak, addressing the great stone by his side, 'Be Goddis face/We twa the flycht on us sal samyn ta'.

Romances of various dates are listed in *The Complaynt Of Scotlande* 1549, some of which had, some may have had, Scots versions.[11] The list includes these: 'ypomedon' (used for the three knights in *Roswall and Lillian*), 'the four sonnis of aymon', 'the brig of mantribil' (which features in 'romans of worthi Ferambrace' read by Bruce at Loch Lomond, the names of characters being Scoticised by Barbour), 'syr euan arthouris knycht', 'the seige of millan' (much used by Hary), 'lancelot du lac' (not necessarily the French text), 'floremond of albanye' (extant in a Scots fragment), 'the pure tynt' or 'the purs tynt' (if the latter reading, referring to *A Lord and His Three Sons*), 'arthour of litil bertangye' (phrasing and spelling do not suggest an English version), 'syr egeir and syr gryme' (a Scots romance), 'beuis of southamtoun'. Outside this list, used by Scots poets are these: *Otuell and Roland* (in *Wallace*, *Rauf Coilyear*, *Golagros*), *Perceforest* (for a connection of Alexander with Britain in *Golagros*), the two Alexander romances, and 'amadas' (in *Roswall and Lillian* and *Roland Furious*).

The earliest dateable romance in Scots is *The Buik of Alexander*[12] which remains to us in one copy of an Edinburgh edition of 1580. The date 1438 is worded carefully in the colophon. Its two Parts, the 'Foray' and the 'Avowis' or Vows of the Peacock are almost certainly the publisher's selection, of what he thought would be popular, from a much larger version of the *Roman d'Alixandre*. The Foray narrates a foraging expedition that encounters superior force, stands its ground manfully and is rescued by Alexander. Heroic attitudes are struck convincingly, the two main heroes being Aristé who is only persuaded by his many wounds to ride for help, and Gaudifer de Larys on the enemy side, splendid in retreat, whose bravery became a legend so that he is cited by both Barbour and Hary. The 'Avowis' deals with Alexander's defence of the city of Ephesoun against the covetous King Clarus. A main hero is Clarus's son Porrus.

Both narratives have movement and spirit beyond what one finds in the original. The Scots language gives a forceful simplicity to the characterisation that it did not possess before. This simplicity makes Alexander, who guides rather than dominates the action, seem to be a more likeably spirited and generous personality. Where the Scots writer is less happy is in his rendering of the very formal love-talk of ladies with their knights; he seems to escape with relief to the battlefield. And in the romantic 'Avowis' his two most affective moments concern the death of that determinedly cheerful old man Cassamus; the pure savagery of Porrus's outburst over the dead body of his father's slayer, and the search for and finding of the dead man by Alexander's knights:

> Thay socht him all day to the nicht
> And fand him with the evin licht.
> (10673–74)

The comic obsession of Scots scholars with discovering yet more achievements by Barbour has made them dismiss the worded date, ignore the different rhyming practice, and stress the many phrases, even lines, lifted from the *Bruce*. The direction of borrowing has not been considered; thus the Alexander poet speaks of the sweet-smelling flowers of the Ephesoun carpets because he has Barbour's description of the Irish fields in mind, and describes Porrus's fierce swordsmanship as producing a 'lardner' of bodies, a term obviously deriving from what Barbour tells us was the country tale of 'The

Douglas Lardner'. Yet more surprising is the wilful misreading of the epilogue to the 1499 translation in pentameters of the same romance. This whole later romance is claimed by the epilogue writer as his 'making'. The only previous translation, he says, was done by Sir Gilbert Hay who had lived twenty-four years in France. And this agrees with what we know of Sir Gilbert, apart from his being a translator of French prose treatises. He was knighted at Senlis in 1428, according to himself was chamberlain to the French king, and is last mentioned in the Scottish *Accounts* 1458–59, as receiving a gift from James II. He should have been born a little after 1400 and died a little after 1459. His ideal was to be a 'knycht-clerc', and he fulfilled it.

Perhaps the so-called Scottish Troy-book deserves a note here. It is what it appears to be, some Books of the *Historia Destructionis Troiae* translated into octosyllabic couplets, the language indicating a date about 1450, to supplement a defective MS of John Lydgate's 1420 version of the Latin work. The supplements have been hurriedly made, so that the matter is ill-ordered, the Books misnumbered, words untranslated, e.g. 'castres' for 'castra'. Yet an early sixteenth-century MS, Cambridge Kk.V.30, attributes these Scots verses to 'barbour'! One has only to observe that where the Scot comes in by contrast he speeds up and enlivens the drawling Englishman.

The reign of James III (1462–88) was troubled but full of stirring energies, and creative of great poetry, great story-telling. The young Dunbar may have begun to write, Henryson wrote his *Testament of Cresseid* in its last years, in alliterative romance there were *Golagros and Gawane* and the comic masterpiece *Rauf Coilyear*, and the most remarkable of all early stories in Scots was written, Hary's *Wallace* (1476–78). As the German critic Friedrich Brie says, this is one of the very few really original poems of its century.[13] It could still move Robert Burns and William Wordsworth in their times, and today leaves no reader indifferent. About Hary, probably a surname, we know only what his work indicates, his political stance, his reading of Latin chronicles, romances in the original and as translated, that he was not the '*Blin* Hary' lamented by Dunbar (1505–6) when he wrote his poem. He appears five times in attendance on James IV, always at Linlithgow in 1491–92, and that area is likely to have been his native area—though much of his work must have been written at Auchtermoonzie, an estate of the contemporary Sir William Wallace of Craigie near to that of Sir James Liddale of Creich also named at the close of the poem, and that of John Ramsay of Colluthie in the same parish who is complimented by him. The occasion for writing was the king's policy of dynastic alliances with England that, as Hary and his friends rightly feared, would one day lead to the loss of Scotland's independence.

The governing conception of the poem was not a new one, a national war that was a holy war, and of which the hero was the martyr, betrayed by one of what he calls the 'thrifty men', a Stewart who preferred the profits of peace to honour. War may be the circumstance, but one is never allowed to forget that the poet deals with a Life, a person, treated with astonishing inwardness, attention above all to the man who has cause for grief. As a youth he thinks on his father and brother slain, his flight with his mother from home, later the murder of his wife at Lanark, and revenge on the sheriff there, which begins his career as leader of a band of guerilla fighters. His losses are vividly narrated. We see with the eyes of the woman who tells of his beloved uncle's death by treachery in the Barns of Ayr:

> 'Nakit, laid law on cald erd me beforn.
> His frosty mouth I kissit in that sted,
> Rycht now manlik, now bar and brocht to ded!
> And with a claith I coverit his licaym   [corpse]
> For in his lyff he did nevir woman schayme...
>
> (VII, 278–82)

Grief or revenge, description always has the living touch. We see at the Barns how the swathe of fire 'had that fals blud ourgane'; recognise in Wallace's flight from English forces in Perthshire, which includes his imagination-heated vision of Fawdon slain by him, and his swim across the 'cheyle watter' of the Firth of Forth, the most felt conveyance of physical action in all Scots verse.

In Book XI of his twelve-book Life his picturing of scenes is at its best. At Falkirk Bruce, who has fought on the English side, is addressed by Wallace as 'Thou renygat devorar of thy blud', and the conceit is continued in the English king's tent where Bruce enters and eats with unwashed hands. English lords mock him and do not understand his reply, 'This blud is myne. That hurtis most my thocht' (540). Winning Bruce for the cause is the hero's greatest victory, but his quality as a leader is conveyed in retreat:

> Mekill he trowyis in god and his awn weid   [sword]
> Till sayff his men he did full douchty deid...
> Sic a flear befor was nevir seyn!
> Nocht at Gadderis off Gawdyfer the keyn
> Quhen Alexander reskewed the foryouris,
> Mycht tyll him be comperit in tha houris.
>
> (XI, 327–44)

But it is still on the man of sorrows that Hary's imagination fastens, as when the French queen of England is puzzled by his vehemence of feeling, and he speaks of his wife:

> 'Madem', he said 'as god giff me gud grace,
> In-till hir tym scho was als der to me,
> Prynsace or queyn, in quhat stait so thai be'.
>
> (VIII, 1383–85)

There is only space here to refer the reader also to the dirge-like march of the verse as Wallace seeks and finds his 'best brothir' Sir John the Grayme:

> Full weyll arrayit in-till thar armour clen
> Past to the feild quhar that the chas had ben,
> Amang the ded men sekand the worthiast...
>
> (XI, 559–61)

In that last line is the true ring of heroic verse.

And there is a further and related dimension to Hary's tragic study of greatness, the hero's feeling of the unreality of things. His youthful cry in the prison at Ayr (II. 189), 'O wariede suerd, of tempyr neuir trew!', is to life itself. When news of his mother's death comes (X. 853) 'He sies the warld so full of fantasie', a feeling that comes again at Falkirk as he watches Bruce fight against his own right (XI. 210), 'this warld is contrar-lik', and is uttered in his last moments, 'Maist payn I feill at I bid her our lang'.

The inherited tales about Wallace that as Wordsworth in his *Prelude* said grew like wildflowers throughout Scotland, the three or four mentions in chronicles, could not supply Hary with so well structured and impressive a creation. So great a figure, so inwardly conceived, had not appeared in European literature. Not till the tragedies of Shakespeare would one personage so dominate the stage of imagination.

None the less, another story-teller of genius appears only a decade later with the romance of *Sir Eger and Sir Gryme*,[14] first mentioned in the *Accounts* under 1497 with the name 'Graystiel', then with its Scots title in the *Complaynt*. An Edinburgh edition came out before 1577, but we have it only in anglicised, somewhat corrupted texts of 1669, 1711. Also there is a differing English version in the Percy Folio Manuscript as written about 1665. Whichever version is the earlier, the earlier named Scots one is an original poem. There are the formal differences, the Scots tale being twice as long, not ending in happy marriages all round, introducing new characters, a figure of warning for Sir Eger, a hospitable burgess, his wife (we enter her kitchen) with an obliging son, a Sir Hew. The name Gryme, that replaces the English 'Grin', is given in 1555 to a Sir Fergus Gryme, one of the Graemes about the Solway that won the lands of Garrieston and Alston (Sir Alistoun) in Cumberland, mentioned in the poem. Phrases, lines, are from Barbour and Hary.

A substantial difference, a stroke of genius, is the death of Sir Gryme, the true hero, in a tournament celebrating his marriage to the heroine Lillias, so that Sir Eger, standing with his wife Wynliane of Bealm above his friend's grave, is moved to confess to her that it was Sir Gryme and not he that slew the 'uncannand' (uncanny) Sir Graystiel; and she, who had proudly sworn never to wed a defeated knight, leaves him for a convent, while he goes to Rhodes to fight the invading Turk. When Wynliane dies he returns to share life with the also widowed Lillias.

The Scot's interpretation of characters through vivid conversation is much more arresting. They feel and speak more intensely, as does the humiliated Sir Eger,

> 'Then wot I well I must forgo
> Love-liking and manhood all clean'.
> The water rushed out of his een.
> (774–76)

Yet there can be a humourous touch, as when it is said of Sir Gryme's helmet after battle, 'With great knowledge it was written'. The contrasting unwholesome dark of Wynliane's Bealm where the sick Sir Eger hides his shame and the happier, brighter bower of Lillias, along with the frequent application of proverbs, makes the story seem to carry a generality of meaning. We are not in a timeless, placeless world, even if there is strangeness: a water that has to be forded to enter Graystiel's Land of Doubt (Dread), horses that themselves fight when their masters are unhorsed, an ancient sword that is needed against Graystiel. That worthy, sudden as his appearances are, is simply a lord forbidding entrance to strangers. What contributes specially to the sense of a dramatic action is the pace of both events and verse. These lines may have been chanted to James IV when fiddlers 'sang Graystiel':

> But where twa meetis them alane,
> And departs without company
> But one must have the victorie.
> Graystiel unto his death thus thrawes,
> He walters and the grass updrawes...
> A little while, then he lay still.
> Friends that him saw liked full ill.
> (1608–16)

After this well conceived, well written tale comes the onset of decadence in both versified history and romantic story-telling. Serious interest such as Gavin Douglas can take in rendering Virgil with the 'richt sapour' is quite absent. His *Eneados* reflects the new vital Humanism, but the heroic world had become merely the chivalric world and lost its reality. Thus the 1499 *Buke of Alexander the Conqueroure*[15] has nothing of the force and conviction of Sir Gilbert Hay's writing. Its style is slip-shod, commonplace. Perhaps the only notable individual lines in the *Buke* are these, 1071–76: 'For all this warld of law and labour levis,/And labour leving to all lordis gevis... Than gif thai keip na law to laborage/The labour aw nocht for to pay thair wage' (that is, not pay dues in kind or work, should have the right to strike!).

Decadence is plain in the equally end-of-century *Lancelot of the Laik*.[16] This has the same bright, smooth, uncharactered manner as has *The Quare Of Jelusy*, so apparently written by an Auchenleck, perhaps the James Afflek lamented by Dunbar in 1505–6. It is the only known version of the first section of the prose *Lancelot du Lac*, dealing with Arthur's conflict with Galehaut. Its unpopular Arthur, however, has made the same fatal error as James III, he has made no attempt to visit the various parts of his kingdom, to oversee justice, and so win the hearts of his barons. The author, with so recent a political lesson before him, did not need to cull his reforming counsels from Hay's idealising treatises on 'Knychthede' and 'Governaunce', but he did. Neither the repentant Arthur, the traditionally brave Sir Gawain, nor the love-dazed Lancelot, achieves a moment of convincing life.

The writer of *Clariodus* lives more in his romantic world, placeless, timeless, impersonal as it may be.[17] He lives mainly for the energy of his language, which goes to such an extreme of aureation at times that his romantic world becomes then a merely literary world. One cannot place such a style in the vital world of Henryson, Dunbar or Douglas; aureate as their language can be it is never merely aureate, so that a date of composition in the 1520s or 1530s seems required. The author tells us that he had two prose texts before him, *Le Livre de Messire Cleriadus...Et de Meliadice* and a version by an English lord. Despite this florid manner one is glad, for the occasional lyrical note, that the poet did versify.

The story is fairly interesting as it is developed. Briefly, Meliades is heir to England, the king's brother plots to have her killed, the intending murderers cannot do as ordered, and the separated lovers have their adventures abroad till a touching scene occurs; they meet at a well, he as a palmer, she as a servant, at first not recognising each other; from their reunion events proceed inevitably to their becoming the happy King and Queen of England. At the well even this rhetorician knew to let the lovers speak simply, but where there is the possibility he indulges his penchant for the merely picturesque, thus in a banquet scene love is reduced to such languishing prettiness as this:

> With easie sichis grundit on plesance,
> With law demandis of ladies by and by,
> With sweit love songs and cumlie minstrelly,
> With secreit blenkis and inwart beholding,
> With smylling loukis full of cherising.
> (II, 1860–64)

Alliterative lyricism in the lover's song makes him seem to be more in love with his language than with his lady:

> 'Lodstar of love and lampe of lustieheid,
> Blossome of beautie, and rose of gudliheid,
> Illustar lillie, and leime of my delyt'...   [light]
> (II, 365–67)

Clariodus is a readable and glossy fantasy. It belongs with those romances that at the end of the century a true if Puritanical poet, Alexander Hume, author of *Of the Day Estivall*, would rather harshly denouce as idle 'raveries'.

'Raveries' with a more serious intent appear in the early part of the last of Scotland's metrical histories, a translation of Hector Boece's *Historia* of 1526 written over the years 1531 to 1535.[18] The author, contrary to his editor's belief, was the William Stewart (*c*.1479–1545) who duly became bishop at Aberdeen, having previously been parson of Lochmaben, rector at Ayr, Dean of Glasgow. His displayed knowledge of the Glasgow diocese from the Solway and its tides to Inchinnan on the Firth of Clyde make the identification quite clear. He had studied at St Andrews in Arts and theology fourteen years, 'Suppois I brocht richt little awa with me'. He becomes more interesting than his history when he tells us that one great great-grandfather was 'the *vorax* Wolf of Badyenoch', and another the Dunbar who fought at Otterburn, so that he was probably an offspring of Stewart of Arthurlee and Dunbar of Mochrum. When he is not speaking of himself he is entirely tedious, only once braving the Solway-like tide of Boece's fluency and fictions, to prefer a statement in the Register at St Monans. His occasional eloquence does not make his story live; his very Latinate vocabulary does not help to make him a Scots classic. It would seem that the heroic concept of Scots history was no longer an inspiration.

One poem that is anti-romantic in spirit is significant here, Sir David Lindsay's *Historie of Squyer Meldrum* (1548–50). Meldrum, a friend of Lindsay, had modelled himself on the heroes of romance, he was like Tydeus, Roland, Oliver, Gawain, but not like that adulterer, Lancelot, this exception despite the ease with which he was seduced. He had suffered so many wounds for his lady that he learned the art of medicine on his own person. Having achieved his ideal, but lost his lady, he arranged his own funeral: no priests, churchbells, but merry musicians and a merry company to give him a good send-off. Romance had become amusing.

The romance had indeed been replaced with short tale, though it was still pastime reading, as is witnessed by the quite dull sixteenth-century fragment of *Florimond of Albanie* recently discovered.[19] This account ends, not with that mere list of marvels, *The History of a Lord and his Three Sons*, but with another short story that is truly romantic, the *Pleasant Tale of Roswall and Lillian*.[20] Dramatically improbable, of course, events have a rapid pace, the spirit of young love comes across, and the lyricism in the woodland scenes is delightful. The reference to *Amadas* puts it after 1550.

Possibly John Stewart of Baldynneis believed that in his *Roland Furious*,[21] 1583–84, better called his 'Angelica', since this very free translation of Ariosto concentrates seriously on the heroine's love for the shepherd Medoro, he was writing a romance; and indeed he refers to *Clariodus* and *Amadas*, but the reader has only to consider the scene in which the lovers unite 'As tender delicat daisies of delyt' to know that he is in a different literary world. And he is in a comic world with 'Patrick Gordon, Gentleman', able to supply the *recent* loss of King Robert's diary with 'remarkable Tales' from a Peter Fenton, monk at Melrose in 1369, that Ariosto, Tasso and Spenser would have found strangely familiar. The Tales were published at Dort in 1615.

NOTES

1   The tale is in John of Fordun's *Historia* and *Annals*.
2   Kenneth Jackson's prose version of 1969 is quoted. *See also* M P McDiarmid, 'The Gododdin And Other Heroic Poems of Scotland', in *Scotland and the Lowland Tongue*, J D R McClure (ed) (Aberdeen, 1983).
3   Fordun, V. cap. ix.
4   *The Romance of Fergus*, Wilson Frescoln (ed) (Philadelphia, 1983). He does not think Guillaume's knowledge of Scotland accurate but it is surprisingly good.
5   Bjarni Vilkhalmson (ed), 3 vols. (Reykjavik, 1934), I, 99–137.
6   Scott's preface to the ballad of Thomas the Rhymer has two charters concerning him. *Scotichronicon* X. cap. xliii knows him as 'ille vates ruralis'. See *Sir Tristrem*, G P McNeill (ed), STS (Edinburgh and London, 1886).

7   Sir Thomas Gray, *Scalacronica*, J Stevenson (ed), Maitland Club (Edinburgh, 1836), p 132.

8   *The Original Chronicle of Andrew of Wyntoun*, F J Amours (ed), STS (Edinburgh and London, 1902–14), V, 298–303.

9   For discussion of the attribution of this work to Barbour, as for all other such attributions noted in this chapter, *see* 'Barbour's *othir werk*' in M P McDiarmid's Introduction to *Barbour's Bruce*, M P McDiarmid and J A C Stevenson (eds), 3 vols, STS (Edinburgh and London, 1985).

10   *See* n. 9.

11   *The Complaynt of Scotlande*, J A H Murray (ed) (London, 1872), p 63; and by A M Stewart, STS (Edinburgh and London, 1979), p 30.

12   *The Buik of Alexander*, edited in 4 vols with parallel French text by R L Graeme Ritchie, STS (Edinburgh and London, 1925–29). Vol I. has a fantastic commentary. *See* n. 9.

13   Hary's *Wallace*, edited with Introduction by M P McDiarmid, STS (Edinburgh and London, 1968). *See* Friedrich Brie, *Die Nationale Literature Schottlands* (Halle, Saale, 1937), pp 201–3.

14   *Sir Eger and Sir Gryme*. Editions are David Laing's in *Early Poetry of Scotland*, 2 vols. (London, 1895) and J R Caldwell's in *Harvard Studies in Comparative Literature* (Cambridge, Mass., 1933). *See also* Mabel van Duzee, *A Medieval Romance of Friendship: Eger and Grime* (New York, 1963). Since the kingdom is Bealm she needlessly looks for place-names in Bohemia. Sir Fergus Graham or Grime, a Scot, got a patent of arms from Henry VIII *c*.1555.

15   This 1499 poem is studied in a thesis by John Cartwright, University of Toronto. Like Graeme Ritchie and so many others he carelessly assigns it to Sir Gilbert Hay.

16   *Lancelot of the Laik*, M M Gray (ed), STS (Edinburgh and London, 1912).

17   *Clariodus*, Edward Piper (ed), Maitland Club (Edinburgh, 1830). See the pleasantly lyrical lines on the nightingale, III, 515–18.

18   *The Buik of the Croniclis of Scotland*, W B Turnbull (ed), 3 vols (London, 1858).

19   *Florimond of Albanie*, J D R McClure (ed), *Scottish Literary Journal* Supplement 10, 1979.

20   The *History* (which tells of a bottomless purse, mantle of invisibility, fruits that give leprosy and cure it) and *Pleasant Tale* are in Laing's *Early Popular Poetry*.

21   *The Poems of John Stewart of Baldynneis*, T Crockett (ed), 2 vols, STS (Edinburgh and London, 1913).

Chapter 3

The Alliterative Revival

FELICITY RIDDY

When he had finished compiling his huge collection of poetry in the last months of 1568, George Bannatyne composed an epigraph for it which consisted of two eight-line stanzas, beginning like this:

> Ye reverend redaris, thir workis revolving richt,
> Gif ye get crymis, correct thame to your micht
> And curs na clark that cunnyngly thame wrait,
> Bot blame me baldly brocht this buik till licht ...
> (1–4)

As he goes on, the heavy alliteration dissolves, without ever quite disappearing, however: the very last half-line is 'I neid no moir narratioun'. The use of alliteration at the beginning of a poem in this way was a familiar means of establishing weight and formality: Bannatyne probably noticed when he copied Lindsay's *Ane Satyre of the Thrie Estaits* that Diligence's opening speech begins with a fully-alliterating thirteen-line stanza which never recurs thereafter.

In both these cases the alliteration is rhetorical, even though in Lindsay's stanza it is almost structural as well, in the sense in which the word is used of alliteration in Old English poetry. In that poetry there were no formal links between one line and the next as there are in stanzaic verse, where lines are related by a pattern of end-rhymes. Rhyme was hardly known in Old English; instead, links within, not between, lines of verse were created by repeating sounds at the beginnings, not the ends, of syllables. Each line fell into two halves, and each half-line contained two strong stresses. The two halves were held together by alliteration which crossed the divide between them: one or both of the stressed syllables in the first half-line always alliterated with the first stressed syllable in the second half-line, thus:

> héafunes hláford,   hǽlda ic ni dórstæ
> (45)

([I held aloft] ... the lord of heaven; I durst not stoop)

The Anglian speakers of southern Scotland in the Old English period knew and composed this kind of poetry: this line from *The Dream of the Rood* was inscribed in runes on the Ruthwell Cross in Dumfriesshire. However the later history of alliterative verse, in Scotland as in England, is obscure.

We know that after the Norman Conquest English writers became familiar with French principles of versification which they applied to the composition of poetry in their own language, in place of the old alliterative mode. Among these principles were syllable-counting, rhyme and the forms that go with rhyme: four-stress couplets, for example, and a variety of stanzas. We can see that the same thing happened in Scotland, where contact with French was also strong. The song quoted by Wyntoun, which he says was composed after the death of Alexander III in 1285/6, is written in an eight-line stanza (ababababab$_4$) that stands out from his staple four-stress couplets, and begins like this:

> Quhen Alexander our kynge was dede,
> That Scotlande lede in lauche and le,   [law and safety]
> Away was sons of alle and brede,   [abundance]
> Off wyne and wax, of gamyn and gle.   [play and gladness]
>   (1–4)

Two of the eight lines contain alliterative sequences: 'That Scotlande lede in lauche and le' and 'Off wyne and wax, of gamyn and gle'. The last of these phrases has a long history: it is the 'gamen ond gleodream' of *Beowulf* (3021), and one of its latest occurrences is in *Rauf Coilyear* (953) in the late fifteenth century. It looks as if both Scots and English poets had a residue of alliterative phrases to draw on, some of them very old, which furnished them with elements of a specifically poetic diction. And so this earliest Scots poem—if it really does hark back to the end of the thirteenth century—shows just what we would expect: the blending of two traditions of versification.

In England this blending seems to have stimulated the exuberant experimentalism of the lyrics in Harley MS. 2253, copied around 1330, in which heavy alliteration frequently combines with elaborate stanza forms. Such alliteration is no longer structural in the old way, since lines are now linked to one another by rhyme, and yet it is not rhetorical either. Later in that century, however, the unrhymed alliterative line was revived in England— how or why we can only guess—in a body of major poetry which includes *Piers Plowman, Sir Gawain and the Green Knight, Morte Arthure* and much else. The line used in these poems is looser than that of Old English, although generally still with four major stresses and, characteristically, a non-alliterating final foot. The pressure of alliteration encouraged the use of a characteristic poetic diction, some of it, like 'game and gle', very old. The recurrence of unrhymed alliterative verse was originally provincial: it seems to have begun in the west midlands, but spread rapidly to other parts of the country, especially northwards, at the same time as the development of the metropolitan poetry of Chaucer's school, which preferred French-style forms and principles of versification. If the fourteenth-century alliterative revival extended to Scotland, we have lost sight of it, with so much else. All the surviving Scottish poetry from before as late as 1440 is in four-stress couplets (if we except the poem on Alexander III which I have already quoted and the *Kingis Quair* which may not have been composed in Scotland): the *Bruce*, the saints' lives, the Troy fragments, *The Buik of Alexander*, Wyntoun. Nevertheless, it is, as a matter of common sense, surely inconceivable that no Scottish writer used any other metre for a hundred and fifty years while English poets were trying out a whole range of forms.

The first surviving alliterative poem in Scots belongs to the 1440s, by which time alliteration had largely been discarded in England. The Scottish alliterative phenomenon—as it appears to us now—is both later than the English and different in kind. Whereas most Middle English alliterative verse is in the unrhymed long line, there are very few unrhymed alliterative poems in Scots, and these few—Dunbar's *Tretis of the Twa Mariit Wemen and the Wedo* and some popular prophecies—are both, in their different ways, aberrant. It looks as if Dunbar's choice of the unrhymed alliterative long line for a poem which is in many ways his most Chaucerian—the Wife of Bath's prologue and the *Merchant's Tale* both lie behind the *Tretis*—is made in a spirit of emulation. Part of the point of the joke may lie in the Scottish poet's doing the kind of thing that Chaucer had done—dramatised ironic self-revelation—in the most un-Chaucerian of all verse forms. It is a response, in a way, to the well-known remark of Chaucer's Parson: 'But trusteth wel, I am a Southern man,/I kan nat geste 'rum, ram, ruf' by lettre'. It is left to the northern man—also, as it happens, a priest—to show him how. The prophecies are aberrant in a different way. 'Classical' English alliterative verse is not a popular mode; it is bookish, even learned, and often sophisticated. The cryptic fifteenth-century Scottish prophecies—'Quhen Rome is removyde into Inglande' and 'Quhen the koke in the northe halows his nest'—belong to a sub-literary outgrowth which flourished for centuries on both sides of the border. Prophetic poetry uses a variety of forms, and these two are in a mixture of rhymed and unrhymed long and short lines in which 'classical' patterns of alliteration are only fitfully maintained.

That Scottish poets should have favoured the more demanding combinations of alliteration and rhyme, in which they had to attend to both the beginnings and endings of words, is typical of the resourcefulness of the verse of this period. The exuberance which had marked the lyrics of the Harley MS., as English and French traditions came together, also characterises Scottish verse from the mid fifteenth century on. Confronted with English (and probably Scots) alliterative verse of different kinds, and with the new styles of Chaucer and Lydgate, Scottish poets responded with an eclectic freedom that is almost without parallel south of the border. We can see this eclecticism very clearly in Henryson, whose language is deeply imbued with habits of alliteration, and whose lyrics show him experimenting with different alliterative levels. In 'The Garmont of Gud Ladeis', for example, alliteration is decorative, but not merely so; it also weaves the lines together, contributing to the poem's graceful fluency:

> Wald my gud lady luf me best
> And wirk efter my will,
> I suld ane garmond gudliest
> Gar mak hir body till.   [Have made for her body]
>
>   (1-4)

In 'The Ressoning betuix Aige and Youth' alliteration is more insistent:

> Quhen fair Flora, the godes of the flouris,
> Baith firth and feildis freschely had ourfrete,   [ornamented]
> And perly droppis of the balmy schouris
> Thir widdis grene had with thair watter wete,   [woods]
> Movand allone in mornyng myld I mete
> A mirry man, that all of mirth couth mene,   [spoke]
> Singand the sang that suttellie wes sete:
> 'O yowth, be glaid in to thy flouris grene!'   [rejoice in]
>
>   (1-8)

For all its Lydgatean manner and metre—the opening line is very close to Lydgate's 'Mighty Flora, goddes of fresshe floures'—the alliteration in this poem is so pervasive as to be almost structural, as Denton Fox points out in his commentary on the text. Only five of its seventy-two lines do not alliterate; one of these is the third line quoted above. Alliteration binds together the long lines, which tend to divide on either side of a medial pause. Moreover Henryson also draws on traditional alliterative diction: 'firth and feildis', 'freik on fold', 'bird ... in bour', and so on, creating out of this marriage of styles a new mode for the moral debate poem.

Henryson not only brings new forms into the alliterative tradition, but he also uses old ones. Alliterative poetry in Scotland begins and ends for us with the thirteen-line stanza of 'Sum Practysis of Medecyne': Richard Holland had already used it for *The Buke of the Howlat* around 1448, and Montgomerie and Polwarth flyted each other in it in the early 1580s. This stanza did not originate with Holland. There are a number of alliterative poems in English, in a variety of versions of the form, from the late fourteenth century on, including 'Summer Sunday', *The Quatrefoil of Love* and *Susannah*. All of these, however, use a strikingly short bob of only one foot at the ninth line, marking the four-line tail off from the preceding octave. Oddly perhaps, given the later popularity of the standard Habbie stanza with its medial short bob, the form of the thirteen-line stanza favoured by Scottish poets has a long ninth line. This scheme—$ababababc_4dddc_2$—is used by Holland, by Henryson in 'Sum Practysis of Medecyne', by the authors of *Rauf Coilyear*, *Golagros and Gawane* and *The Gyre Carling*, by Douglas in his eighth Prologue and by Montgomerie and Polwarth, while Lindsay's stanza has a slight variation. In English only the early fifteenth-century *Awntyrs of Arthure*—apparently composed in the region of Carlisle—uses an identical stanza. But since there is no evidence that Holland knew the *Awntyrs* when he composed *The Buke of the Howlat*, or that Henryson drew on either the *Awntyrs* or the *Howlat* for the form of 'Sum Practysis', we can assume that

there were other poems in the *Howlat* stanza, known to both poets, which
have now been lost. We need not assume because the *Awntyrs* predates the
others that this particular stanza originated in England. It is just as likely to
have drifted southwards across the border into the *Awntyrs* as northwards.
And in trying to reconstruct the lost body of thirteen-line verse in Scots we
should not forget the drama. No Scottish play cycles survive, but various
thirteen-line alliterative stanzas occur quite frequently in the English mystery
plays.

The Buke of the Howlat was written around 1448 by Richard Holland
(*c*.1415–*c*.1482) who was a member of the earl of Moray's household in the
far north of Scotland. The variety of styles that Holland deploys with such
assurance provides better evidence than anything else of the extent to which
alliterative verse was known in Scotland by the mid-century. The poem tells
an old fable about an owl who demands to be refashioned because he is so
ugly and unpopular. A council of birds is summoned, presided over by the
peacock-pope and the eagle-emperor, at which a great banquet is held, and
Nature grants the owl a feather from each of the other birds in order to
improve his appearance. His new finery, however, makes him so obnoxiously
arrogant that Nature is obliged to restore him to his old ugliness, saying that
'My first making ... was unamendable'. Owls, that is, are irredeemably owls.
Summarised thus, this fable apparently expresses just the kind of conservatism
that seems designed to flatter a countess: in the final stanza Holland tells us
that he composed the poem for 'a dow [dove] of Dunbar .../Dowit [endowed]
with a Douglas—and boith war thai dowis—'. His pun on the first syllables of
the surname of his patroness, Elizabeth Dunbar, and her husband Archibald
Douglas, earl of Moray, places them neatly in the bird-world, but as gentle
doves, not despicable owls who do not know their place.

The place of the earl and countess is quite literally a place: we are told at
the end that the poem is set in the grounds of their castle at Darnaway in
Morayshire, and it opens with three stanzas of dream-vision pastoral into
which this country seat has been flatteringly transfigured:

In the myddis of May at morne as I ment,	[made (my) way]
Throwe myrth markit on mold till a grene meid,	[went on the ground]
The bemes blythest of ble fro the son blent	[colour] [gleamed]
That all brychtnyt about the bordouris on breid;	[all around]
With alkyn herbes of air that war in erd lent	[all kinds] [from] [bestowed]
The feldis flurist and fret, full of fairhed.	[blossomed] [where adorned]

(1–6)

English alliterative poets had used a similar style to establish the various *loci
amoeni* in which their dream-visions are set. Holland, however, blends the
concreteness and specificity of alliterative diction and its listing techniques
with an abstraction that derives from the Chaucer-Lydgate tradition:

The birth that the ground bure was browdin on breidis,	[growth] [brought forth] [adorned far and wide]
With gers gaye as the gold and granes of grace;	[plants] [beneficient seeds]
Mendis and medicyne for mennis all neidis,	[cure]

Helpe to hert and to hurt, heilfull it was.   [heart] [wholesome]
Under the cerkill solar thir savorus seidis
War nurist be dame Natur, that noble mastress . . .
                              (27–32)

There is an intellectual scheme underlying Holland's depiction of the idyllic landscape that distinguishes it from its English alliterative antecedents, and which in this sense looks forward to the landscape poetry of Gavin Douglas. The pleasingness of the scene is not merely pictorial but derives from the beneficence of God and Nature revealed in it. In the passage above, the scientific phrase 'cerkill solar', of the sphere carrying the sun on its course, seems to have been coined by Holland on the model, perhaps, of 'cercle celestial' which occurs in the Chaucerian *Tale of Beryn*. He constantly interweaves aureate, learned or specialist vocabularies with traditional alliterative poetic diction: 'blythest of ble', 'but resting or ruf', 'farly was fair', 'with lyking and luf', 'sekerly and sure', all from the opening stanza.

The style that Holland uses in the pastoral frame locates the source of this patronage in an order that is not only social but natural and divine. The other styles he uses at the centre of the poem in the excursus on the banquet (itself framed by the fable of the owl) also serve order and hierarchy: these are the heraldic, in stanzas 27–34; the heroic, in stanzas 35–42; the courtly, in stanzas 52–55; the devotional panegyric, in stanzas 56–58, all of which Holland handles with the confidence and panache born of deep familiarity. Much of the poem can be read as a skilful but nonetheless unctuous deployment of styles designed to flatter the branch of the Douglas family into which his patroness had recently married. Nevertheless, Holland was a churchman as well as a court man; the division of the birds in the poem into clerical and lay expresses his own dividedness. Another style at his command rejects the identification of the social order with the divine. Stripped of his finery at the end of the fable, the owl says: 'Now mark your merour be me, all maner of men,/Ye princis, prentis [disciples] of pryde':

Quhen ilk thing has the awne, suthly we se
Thy nakit cors bot of clay a foule carioun,
Hatit and hawless; qhuarof art thou hie?   [hated and destitute] [proud]
We cum pure, we gang pure, baith king and commoun.   [go]
                              (980–83)

This is not the voice of the court flatterer or the chivalric chronicler, but of the preacher, to whom we are all, with our loathsome flesh, hated owls. The homiletic style that Holland uses at this point is well-established in earlier English alliterative verse: for example, in *The Three Dead Kings* (written in the north of England in a variant of the thirteen-line stanza), the dead kings address the living with a similar self-disparagement:

Lokys on my bonus that blake bene and bare . . .   [look]
Thenkes ye no ferlé bot frayns at me ferys,   [marvel] [ask my companions]
Thagh ye be never so fayre, thus schul ye fare.
                              (106, 109–10)

'Makis your merour be me, my myrthus bene mene [poor]', confirms the third king. Henryson was to adapt the moralising alliterative style for the complaint of Cresseid:

> Now is deformit the figour of my face;
> To luik on it na leid now lyking hes.   [man]
>   (448–49)

She addresses the ladies of Troy:

> And in your mind ane mirrour mak of me:
> As I am now, peradventure that ye
> For all your micht may cum to that same end.
>   (457–59)

Owl, skeleton, leper: all serve the same purpose and draw on the same traditional stock. The preacher's reductive moral radicalism subverts the social hierarchies supported elsewhere in the poem by other styles.

This is still not the last voice, however. The poem does not rest here but returns in the last stanza to the complimentary manner with which it began. It is impossible, in the end, to know quite where Holland stands. The entertainments at the feast are an image of the poem itself, as the abusive Irish bard—the uncontainable outsider who speaks another tongue—disrupts the courtly display. The mixing of styles and genres, with the ironies this creates, means that the poem is peculiarly enigmatic in an almost Chaucerian way.

The Buke of the Howlat seems to contain the seeds of almost all the other alliterative poetry written in Scotland. The pastoral style is used, for example, in a love poem which begins 'In May in a morning I movit me one' and more extensively in the haunting *Tayis Bank*, which is written in the stanza which Henryson had used for 'The Bludy Serk':

> Quhen Tayis bank was blumyt brycht
> With blosomes blyth and bred,
> Be that rever ran I doun rycht:
> Under the rys I red.
> The merle melit with all her mycht
> And mirth in mornyng maid.
> Throw solace sound and semely sicht
> Alsuth a sang I said.
>   (1–8)

The language used to establish the idyllic landscape, in which is glimpsed the elusive figure of a beautiful woman, draws on both courtly poetry—it is tempting to think that the poet might have known the *Kingis Quair*—and alliterative verse, perhaps directly on the *Howlat*, of which there seem to be several echoes. It has been proposed as a source of Dunbar's *Tretis of the Twa Mariit Wemen and the Wedo*; whether or not this is the case, it is clear that by the turn of the century the conventions of alliterative pastoral were well enough known for Dunbar to ring the changes on them in the opening lines of his great poem.

The alliterative heroic style, which Holland had used in the *Howlat* to describe the death of the founder of the Douglas dynasty, forms the staple of the anonymous knightly romance, *Golagros and Gawane*. This poem, written towards the end of the fifteenth century, is translated from a French prose redaction of the thirteenth-century *Continuation Perceval*. Several other French romances were translated into Scots in the fifteenth and early sixteenth centuries, all into four- and five-stress couplets. In England, fifteenth-century translators of French romances, including Malory and Caxton, had begun to use prose; it is in these translations, in fact, that English prose fiction begins. Why their Scottish counterparts did not, so far as we can tell, do likewise is a mystery that is the concern of another chapter. The decision of the author of *Golagros and Gawane* to render his prose source into alliterative verse is exactly the opposite of what Malory did in Book Two of *Le Morte D'arthur*, and is an index of the divergence of English and Scottish tastes. Apart from *Piers Plowman*, which was caught up in the Reformation, the only alliterative work to reach print in England is *The Quatrefoil of Love*, which de Worde published in an attenuated form. The Scottish scene is very different. De Worde's contemporaries, Chepman and Millar, printed at least three alliterative works at the very start of their career, presumably in the expectation that they would sell; these were *Golagros and Gawane*, the *Howlat* and *The Tretis of the Twa Mariit Wemen and the Wedo*. *Golagros* was still being read in the mid sixteenth century, while *Rauf Coilyear*, of which there was probably at least one early print, was published as late as 1572. The *Howlat* was probably also reprinted, and George Bannatyne, whose manuscript contains several alliterative works, still thought it worth copying in 1568. *The Flyting of Montgomerie and Polwarth* was printed several times in the seventeenth century. In opting for an alliterative form, the author of *Golagros* was helping to mould a taste that would last for well over a hundred years.

The style into which *Golagros* has been translated reaches back, by whatever route, to Old English heroic poetry. It is a style in which an aristocratic military caste—that second estate who appear in the *Howlat* as 'fowlis of reif'—created its self-image, justifying its morality and masking the nature of its power. This is the second stanza of the poem:

Thus the royale can remove, with his Round Tabill,	[king]
Of all riches maist rike, in riall array.	
Was never fundun on fold, but fenyeing or fabill,	[earth] [without dissimulation]
Ane farayr floure on ane feild of fresch men, in fay;	
Farand on thair steidis, stout men and stabill,	[travelling]
Mony sterne our the streit stertis on stray.	[fierce (knight)] [moves in a new direction]
Thair baneris schane with the sone, of silver and sabill,	[shone]
And uther glemyt as gold and gowlis so gay;	
Of silver and saphir schirly thai schane;	[shone]
Ane fair battell on breid,	[formation all around]
Merkit our ane fair meid;	[made (their) way]

With spurris spedely thai speid
Our fellis, in fane.   [over] [joyfully]

(14–26)

Along with the heavy alliteration here goes a constant elaboration which is encouraged by the spaciousness of the stanza; the last twelve lines are an opulent enlargement of the first. They enact the image of Arthur's wealth while idealising his might. The brute force behind military strength is neutralised into decoration, even innocence: in line 18 the old metaphor of 'floure ... of fresch men' is momentarily charged with its pristine pastoral sense by the insertion of the usually empty phrase 'on ane feild'. The pastoral idyll is evoked again towards the end: 'merkit our ane fair meid', a phrase which Holland had used in the opening stanza of the *Howlat*. Meads, then as now, exist only in poems; we are not being asked to think of this army despoiling crops and ploughlands as they pass. That 'feild' in line 18 also suggests a heraldic field, or background, and points forward to the heraldic colours of the banners: these are painted horses, painted knights. Along with the expansiveness of this stanza there is a vacuousness which is the vice of the alliterative style, with its repetitions—'riches maist rike', 'spedely they speid', three occurrences of 'fair'—and fillers: 'but fenying or fabill', 'in fay', 'in fane'. This inertness diminishes the energy which the alliterative style is often felt to possess because of its insistent emphasis on stress, and so creates a pictorial rather than an active image, static rather than aggressive. But if we look briefly at the whole poem we can see that these effects of stasis are central.

In making his translation the poet has worked very freely, selecting only two incidents from a much longer work, omitting the love-interest in the original and so ensuring that the focus is entirely upon relationships of honour among men. It falls into two quite distinct sections. In the first Kay goes into a strange castle in search of victuals for the army and simply tries to take what he wants and so receives nothing, while Gawane defers to the lord of the castle and so is deferred to in return. In the second and longer part, Arthur demands tribute from Golagros, who refuses since he owes homage to no-one. There follow three days of fighting outside Golagros's castle, culminating in a single combat between Gawane and Golagros, which the latter loses. In order to preserve Golagros's honour in front of his followers, however, Gawane pretends to have been defeated and goes into the castle with Golagros, whose followers tell him they would rather have him alive and lord over them, even if he has to submit to a superior power, than dead. So Golagros submits to Arthur, who in turn renounces his claim to overlordship and leaves him 'Fre as I the first fand'. The two halves are linked by the way in which they set deference, self-abnegation and backing-off above aggressive self-assertion. They define the man who is 'lord of his aune' in a personal as well as a social sense.

The narrative thus seems to undercut the military ethos which the heroic style was developed to express, by using a tale of conquest to explore the notion of self-conquest. Its internalisation of the heroic places it alongside

The Porteous of Noblenes, which was also printed by Chepman and Millar. This is a prose translation by Andrew Cadiou of Alain Chartier's *Breviaire des Nobles*, and in it we can see the old aristocratic mores being redefined for the wider society that constituted the Edinburgh reading public.

Another narrative poem plays different styles off against one another, as the *Howlat* had done. This is *Rauf Coilyear*, which reads like a riposte to *Golagros and Gawane*, though it is unlikely to be by the same author, as has been suggested, because the alliterative and metrical patterns of the two poems are different. Whereas *Golagros* is an Arthurian tale, *Rauf* is loosely attached to the Charlemagne cycle. Like *Golagros*, *Rauf* falls into two parts (a structural feature which both poems may derive from *The Awntyrs of Arthure*): in the first half Charlemagne, lost in a storm, takes refuge incognito in the house of a collier where he finds that the deferential and self-effacing manners of the court (which Gawane epitomises in *Golagros*) no longer apply. When, for example, Rauf tries to get Charlemagne to sit down at the table and the latter politely demurs, saying 'That were unsemand, forsuith, and thyself unset', the king is rewarded with a blow on the ear that sends him to the floor. Being 'lord of my awin'—Rauf uses the phrase of himself—means, for Rauf, forcing your guests to do what you want them to.

The humorous clash between the mores of court and cottage extends to the poem's style: traditional alliterative diction is mixed with lively colloquial speech, and the heroic is constantly nudged at by the mock-heroic. For example, the meal of venison and boar poached from the king's forest which Rauf's wife serves up to Charlemagne is described as if it were a royal feast (which, in a sense, it is):

Thus war they marschellit but mair and matchit that nicht.   [placed at table]
                                                 [without delay] [set together]
They brocht breid to the buird and braun of ane bair   [table] [flesh] [boar]
And the worthyest wyne went upon hicht.   [on high]
Thay beirnis, as I wene, thay had eneuch thair,   [warriors] [believe]
Within that burelie byrnand full bricht;   [noble dwelling]
Syne enteris thair daynteis on deis dicht dayntelie.   [dais] [prepared]

(184–89)

This is the way Galeron is feasted in *The Awntyrs of Arthure*.

Thus thei served that knight
And his worthely wight,   [honourable]
With riche dayntes dight
In silver so shene.   [bright]

In silver so semely thei served of the best,
With vernage in veres and cuppes ful clene.   [wine] [glass]
And thus thes galiard gomes glades hour gest,   [valiant men gladden]
With riche dayntees endored in dysshes bydene.   [covered with yellow glaze] [indeed]

(452–59)

And in the second half of the poem Rauf (now forgiven and knighted) has a comic fight with a Saracen on a camel which is described in terms similar to those used by the poet of *Golagros* for the encounter between Golagros and Gawane, while other passages of heroic verse are mocked by their contexts.

The direction of this mockery is ambiguous. It looks at first as if we have in Rauf Coilyear an early user of the reductive idiom, or a fifteenth-century man of Crowdieknowe. But Rauf is as easily seduced to the court as the Saracen is converted: the latter ends up as Duke of Anjou, while Rauf becomes Marshall of France. Perhaps the poem is best read as a literary game or a playful spoof, with the pleasure lying in its incongruities of style and event; their point depends, of course, on the reader's familiarity with alliterative romance conventions. If it is a spoof, it is neither the first nor the last in the thirteen-line alliterative stanza: Henryson's 'Sum Practysis of Medecyne'—surely his most underrated poem—had burlesqued the medical recipes which every household seems to have collected, while Douglas was to satirise the alliterative dream-vision in his eighth Prologue.

'Sum Practysis' is a dramatic monologue in which the speaker, a testy quack doctor, is ostensibly rebutting charges of incompetence: 'Gife I can ocht [know anything] of the craft,/Heir it be sene', he says ambivalently, offering specimens of his mad cures in his own defence. The ailments he treats are obscure (the obfuscations of medical language are part of the target) but seem to include colic, impotence and hoarseness. Many of the wildly absurd ingredients of his recipes are *impossibilia* like red rooks, five ounces of a fly's wing or a grey mare's yawn, but others are close enough to contemporary medical practice for the satire to be clear. Henryson uses a constantly inventive mixture of technical jargon, colloquial language, reworked proverbs, and alliterative poetic diction: 'our the feild fure', 'suthfast seggis', 'I have no tome at this tyme'. Although there are other mock medical recipes in Middle English, the closest parallels to this comic doctor's monologue are in French plays, as Denton Fox shows. There is a genuinely dramatic construction of character: Henryson is not an unworthy predecessor of Browning. One element, however, seems to be native, and can also be traced in the *Howlat*. Early in the poem the speaker addresses his imaginary provoker thus:

> 'Ye wald deir me I trow, becaus I am dottit,   [harm] [believe] [stupid]
> To ruffill me with a ryme—na, schir, be the rude.   [treat me roughly] [by the cross]
> Your saying I hafe sene and on syd set it ...'   [aside]
>   (3–4)

This poem, then, is presented as a response to an attack in verse ('ruffill me with a ryme') of the kind that the bard-rook threatens in the *Howlat*. 'Raike hir a rug of the rost [Give her a bit of the roast meat],' he demands (muddling the first and third-person feminine pronouns in a way that is conventional in later parodies of Gaels trying to speak Scots), 'or scho sall ryme the!' Henryson's choice of form for 'Sum Practysis' perhaps derives, then, from a northern tradition of alliterating diatribe which includes both the abusive verses of the Yorkshireman Laurence Minot in the fourteenth century and Montgomerie's 'Ane Answer to ane Helandmanis Invective' in the sixteenth.

Douglas's eighth Prologue is also abusive and comic. It is a dream-vision in the consistently scolding tone which we have heard before in the Howlat's complaints about his appearance: first the 'selcouth seg' of the poet's dream rails at length against the evils of the age, then he and the poet fall to quarrelling, and when he has awoken the poet continues to complain about the untrustworthiness of dream-visions. Whereas in the Chaucerian tradition dream-visions tend to deal with love, most alliterative dream-visions are complaints on the times, like *Winner and Waster*, 'Summer Sunday', *Mum and Soothsegger* and *Piers Plowman*, which last Douglas knew. It is this tradition which is the target of his satire: there is, after all, a good deal of quarrelsomeness and 'teyn' in Langland's poem, and the dreamer of *Piers Plowman*, like the dreamer of the eighth Prologue, is querulous and unable to accept rebuke meekly. And behind Douglas's largely conventional complaints on the times ('Devorit with dreme' in the Bannatyne and Maitland Folio MSS. is another such) looms Langland's apocalyptic satire.

Compared with the dream-vision in the Prologue to book thirteen, or with Aeneas's dream in Book Eight to which this Prologue is an ironic inception, the dream-vision here is made to seem the product of a parochial and limited culture. This is how the dreamer falls asleep in the thirteenth Prologue:

Ontill a garth undir a greyn lawrer	[garden] [laurel tree]
I walk onon, and in a sege down sat,	[seat]
Now musyng apon this and now on that.	
I se the poill, and eik the Ursis brycht,	[pole-star]
And hornyt Lucyn castand bot dym lycht,	
Becaus the symmyr skyis schayn sa cleir.	[shone]
Goldyn Venus, the mastres of the yeir,	[mistress]
And gentill Jove, with hir participate,	
Thar bewtuus bemys sched in blyth estait:	[state]
That schortly, thar as I was lenyt doun,	[reclined]
For nychtis silens, and this byrdis soun,	[song]
On sleip I slaid, quhar sone I saw appeir	[I fell asleep]
Ane agit man ...	
(64–76)	

The same situation in the eighth Prologue is handled thus:

Of dreflying and dremys quhat dow it to endyte?	[incoherent thoughts] [profits]
For, as I lenyt in a ley in Lent this last nycht,	[field]
I slaid on a swevynnyng, slummyrrand a lyte,	[fell to dreaming] [sleeping]
And sone a selcouth seg I saw to my sicht ...	[extraordinary man]
(1–4)	

There are traces in the longer passage of the old alliterative diction—'On slepe I slaid', for example—but these are mere echoes in a delicate and allusive amplification. The terse opening of the eighth Prologue is like the way the dreamer falls asleep in *Piers Plowman*, Passus XVIII:

... I wex wery of the world and wylned eft to slepe,
And lened me to a Lenten-and longe tyme I slepte ... [laid down until Lent]
(4–5)

Douglas seems to be deliberately reining in his description here, denying it the elaboration possible in this style (as the poet of *Winner and Waster* shows), as if to point up the eccentricities and limitations of what is seen as a purely native mode. The chief spokesman in and for this mode is the 'selcouth seg', dream-visitant as angry local prophet, one of whose complaints is that there is too much learning around: 'Sturtyn study hes the steir, distroyand our sport.' He disparages Douglas's 'buke', and offers to extend the poet-dreamer's intellectual range by teaching him about the stars, but he knows them by their vernacular not their classical names: 'the Charl Wayn', 'Arthurus Hufe'. He cannot offer access to the culture which underlies the passage from Prologue Thirteen quoted above, with its poised allusiveness. In the end the dreamer awakes, scrabbling for pence in a molehill in a way that seems to symbolise the low and blinkered pursuit of what is hardly worth pursuing. The mockery of the Prologue turns back on itself, guying the 'poems on the times' of which *Piers Plowman* was the transcendant and most widely-read example. In it the humanist poet confronts a venerable vernacular tradition and judges it too narrowly provincial, too restricted in its outlook, too ignorant to carry authority. The Prologue can thus be seen as part of the poet's long meditation on his own poetic role.

Douglas's dialogue with himself is a version of the self-consciousness which characterises all these poems from the *Howlat* on. This is particularly true of the last work in thirteen-line stanzas, *The Flyting of Montgomerie and Polwarth*. It is not necessarily the case, as is often claimed, that by the time the *Flyting* was written alliterative verse had become associated only with low styles. Sometime in the first decades of the seventeenth century Alexander Craig used a ten-line, tailed stanza with marked alliteration in his allegorical dream-vision, *The Pilgrime and Heremite*, which was published posthumously in 1631. Here the alliterative mode is not low, but archaising; it goes along with the other mediæval paraphernalia—including the 'hoarse hoarie Heremite' of the title—which are strangely intermingled with elements of Renaissance pastoral. Montgomerie's choice of the alliterative stanza in the 1580s had made a different point. He and Polwarth flyted one another in a variety of metres and forms which were designed to demonstrate their versatility to the court audience for whom the whole exercise was presumably staged. The true subjects of their verses were, in a way, themselves. Montgomerie introduces the *Howlat* stanza in the last part of the *Flyting*, and Polwarth picks it up from him. Montgomerie uses it to tell, with great zest, the manic story of Polwarth's birth, begotten by an elf on a she-ape, and of his upbringing among witches, a topic which flattered a current preoccupation of the king. Three factors may have lain behind his choice of form: it was a narrative stanza, and this is the first point in the *Flyting* at which narrative is used; it is the stanza of two other comic poems featuring grotesque females, *Kynd Kittok* and *The Gyre Carling*, and the latter seems particularly close to the elrich spirit of the *Flyting*; and the listing techniques of alliterative verse were wonderfully appropriate, as Dunbar had shown, for cumulative insults and comic effects. The list of musical instruments that Holland gives in stanza 59 of the *Howlat*, for example, is a serious counterpart to several of Montgomerie's bravura displays.

To the last, then, Scottish poets treated alliterative styles as part of a wider repertoire. They used them for panegyric, scatology, romance, burlesque; they described visionary landscapes and expressed the pains of love; they conjured up grotesques and heaped abuse on one another; they were both deeply traditional and constantly experimental as they moved from one discourse—learned, courtly, colloquial, aureate, heroic, homiletic—to another. James VI gave the characteristic alliterative triple rhythm—which he calls 'tumbling verse'—royal approval in his *Reulis and Cautelis* of 1584, quoting Montgomerie. It is a measure of the narrowness of his range of reading in Scots, however, that he saw it only as a flyting metre: George Bannatyne could have told him better.

FURTHER READING

PRIMARY TEXTS

(For the texts of Douglas, Dunbar, Henryson, Lindsay and for the *Bannatyne MS* see the General Bibliography)

Amours, F J (ed), *Scottish Alliterative Poems*, STS, 2 vols (Edinburgh and London, 1892–97). (*Buke of the Howlat; Rauf Coilyear; Golagros and Gawane*)
—— (ed), *The Original Chronicle of Andrew Wyntoun* (Edinburgh and London, 1907) V, 145. ('Quhen Alexander our Kynge wes Dede')
Bawcutt, Priscilla and Riddy, Felicity (eds), *Longer Scottish Poems*, vol. I, 1375–1650, (Edinburgh, 1987). (*Buke of the Howlat; Rauf Coilyear*)
Hanna III, Ralph (ed), *The Awntyrs of Arthure* (Manchester, 1974)
Hughes, Joan and Ramson, W (eds), *Poetry of the Stewart Court* (Canberra, 1982). ('In May in a morning' and *Tayis Bank*)
Laing, D (ed) *The Poetical Works of Alexander Craig of Rosecraig*, Hunterian Club (Glasgow, 1873). (*The Pilgrime and Heremite*)
MacQueen, John (ed), *Ballatis of Luve* (Edinburgh, 1970). ('In May in a morning' and *Tayis Bank*)
Stevenson, G (ed), *Poems of Alexander Montgomerie*, Supplementary Volume, STS, (Edinburgh and London, 1910). (*Flyting of Montgomerie and Polwarth*)
Whiting, Ella K (ed), *The Poems of John Audelay*, EETS (London, 1931). (*The Three Dead Kings*)

New STS editions of *The Buke of the Howlat* and *Rauf Coilyear* by Elizabeth Walsh and Margaret A Mackay are forthcoming, as is a new EETS edition of *Golagros and Gawane* by W R J Barron.

SECONDARY TEXTS

Alexander, Flora, 'Richard Holland's *Buke of the Howlat*', in *Literature of the North*, Hewitt, D and Spiller, M (Aberdeen, 1983), pp 14–25
Bennett, J A W, 'Survival and Revivals of Alliterative Modes', *Leeds Studies in English*, NS 13/14, 1982–83, 26–43
Barron, W R J, 'Alliterative Romance and the French Tradition', in *Middle English Alliterative Poetry and its Literary Background*, Lawton, D A (ed) (Cambridge, 1982), pp 70–87
Craigie, Sir William, 'The Scottish Alliterative Poems', *Proceedings of the British Academy*, 28 (1942), 217–36
Fox, Denton, 'Sum Practysis of Medecyne', *Studies in Philology*, 49 (1972), 453–60
Mackay, Margaret A, 'Structure and Style in Richard Holland's *The Buke of the Howlat*', in *Proceedings of the Third International Conference on Scottish Language and Literature* (*Medieval and Renaissance*), Lyall, Roderick J and Riddy, Felicity (eds) (Stirling/Glasgow, 1981), pp 191–206

McDiarmid, M P, 'Richard Holland's *The Buke of the Howlat*, an Interpretation',
   Medium Aevum, 38 (1969), 277–90
Riddy, Felicity, 'Dating *The Buke of the Howlat*', *Review of English Studies*, 37
   (1986), 1–10
Smyser, H M, '*The Taill of Rauf Coilyear* and its Sources', *Harvard Studies and Notes
   in Philology and Literature*, 14 (1932), 135–50
Stewart, Marion, 'Holland's *Howlat* and the Fall of the Livingstones', *Innes Review*,
   26 (1975), 67–79
Turville-Petre, T, *The Alliterative Revival* (Cambridge, 1977)

Chapter 4

Poetry—James I to Henryson

JOHN MACQUEEN

By English and continental standards, Scots poetry until the end of the first quarter of the fifteenth century had been old-fashioned. The metrical range was limited, as a comparison of Barbour (*c.*1320–1395) with Chaucer (*c.*1343–1400) will show. Chaucer's earliest extended works, *The Book of the Duchess*, *The House of Fame*, and *The Romance of the Rose* (this last, of course, a translation) had been written in an English adaptation of the couplet used by such earlier French authors as Chrétien de Troyes (ob. *c.*1175) and Guillaume de Lorris (first half of the thirteenth century), that is to say, in a basic octosyllabic, often with feminine rhyme, and with a norm of four stresses. None of Chaucer's later poetry uses this metre; he turned almost exclusively to variations of the five-stress line, commonly in the form of the heroic couplet or stanzaic *rime royal*. His style changed with this change of metre; the date of *The Parliament of Fowls*, written in *rime royal*, is not much later than that of the other poems mentioned, but the structural clarity has much increased, and there is a greater richness of invention to accompany the new metrical form. Italian poetry, in particular that of Dante and Boccaccio, had become an important influence. Chaucer's older contemporary, Barbour, shows originality in the choice of a modern subject for his heroic romance, but metrically and stylistically the *Bruce* belongs to the older fashion, as does Wyntoun's later (before 1420) *Cornykkyllys* (the *Original Chronicle*). The first Scots poet to experiment with the newer style is James I (1394–1437).

There is an instinctive reluctance on the part of modern critics to allow that a king might play a significant role in the development of a literature. Such anachronistic feelings are not to be trusted; in Professor Alan Harding's phrase, they lack 'a true historical sense of the role of kings in the formation of European societies'.[1] Temperamentally, as shown by his political as well as his literary career, James was an innovator, and his kingly status allowed him to exercise a powerful effect on all the workings of the society which depended on him. His poetry, like that of Chaucer, sometimes gives a deliberate impression of *naiveté*, not usually to be taken at face value. Despite its relative brevity, the *Kingis Quair* is a complex, powerful, and above all, influential work of art.

The suggestion is sometimes made that during the fifteenth and sixteenth centuries it remained virtually unknown, and cannot therefore have been an influence on Scots literature in general. This seems improbable, even if one ignores the apparent verbal reminiscences which occur in later poets, the direct, if not always perceptive, references made by Walter Bower, John Major, John Bale, George Buchanan and Thomas Dempster, and the fact that the manuscript,[2] written c.1488 for Henry Sinclair, 3rd Earl of Orkney, is a wide-ranging collection, which included among much else a text of Chaucer's *Troilus and Criseyde*. This might lead one to the conclusion that the *Kingis Quair*, no less than Chaucer's poem, formed a part of the public literary domain. The MS did not remain in the exclusive possession of a single family; in the mid sixteenth century, for instance, it was for a time in the hands of a MacDonald chieftain, Donald Gorm of Sleat in Skye. Two poems, *Lancelot of the Laik* and *The Quare of Jelusy*, neither by James, appear to imitate the distinctive linguistic usage of the *Quair*. All fifteenth century poetry, finally, was a public rather than a private art, and it is not likely that a king of James's accomplishments would have confined a major work to a circle which he deliberately had restricted to a few intimates.

The poem is an idealised autobiography, based on James's kidnapping at sea in 1406 and his subsequent eighteen years of captivity in England, which came to an end soon after his marriage to Lady Joan Beaufort in February 1424. The *motif* of captivity is prominent in the two chief literary models which he used, *De Consolatione Philosophiae* of Boethius, and Chaucer's *Knight's Tale*. The first gave him the philosophic emphasis which characterises his poem, the second helped to combine it with a love interest which itself has strong philosophic overtones. James is unusual, although not unique, in the emphasis placed, by way of the speech of Minerva in the dream-vision, on the fulfilment of courtly love in marriage. He is almost hubristic in the confidence with which he offers his own experience as a counterpart and confirmation to that of Boethius, whose virtuous and well-trained youth enabled him to overcome, at least in his mind, the disasters of later life; correspondingly James's own early ignorance and misfortunes were transformed, he claims, by the philosophic miracle of love to set him finally in a position superior to all mischance. Reading this, one becomes uncomfortably conscious of the final scene at Perth, the brutal murder of the king only a few years after the completion of the poem, a murder, the very abruptness of which in a sense sets at nothing all the poetry and philosophy.

'Heirefter followis the quair Maid be King Iames of Scotland the first callit the Kingis Quair and Maid quhen his *Maiestie* wes in Ingland.' The sixteenth century rubric which in the MS precedes the poem recognises that the poem is an offshoot of James's captivity, but is wrong to assert that it was composed during that period. As Professor Norton-Smith notes, 'The evidence of the poem (11.1264–1351) shows clearly that the poem was written after a marriage had taken place, and after a release from prison had been obtained.'[3] The poem indeed suggests that several years had passed and had given the king the opportunity to develop the philosophic detachment exhibited. Metrically it belongs to the later, more ornate, tradition:

> Unto the impnis of my maisteris dere,   [poems]
> Gowere and Chaucere, that on the steppis satt

> Of rethorike quhill thai were lyvand here,
> Superlative as poetis laureate,
> In moralitee and eloquence ornate,
> I recommend my buk in lynis seven,
> And eke thair saulis unto the blisse of hevin.
>
> (1373–79)

Notably and curiously, James gives Gower precedence over Chaucer, while his own older English contemporary, John Lydgate (1370–1450), as a model at least as important as Gower, remains unmentioned, probably because he was alive when the *Quair* was composed. The reason for the position given to Gower may be that the central situation of *Confessio Amantis*, the appeal made by the Lover to Venus and Cupid, which is answered by the appearance of the priest Genius, runs parallel to the prayers made by the captive in the *Kingis Quair*, and the divine response which they obtain:

> Than wold I pray his [Cupid's] blisfull grace benigne
> To hable me unto his service digne.   [make worthy]
> And evermore for to be one of tho   [those]
> Him trewly for to serve in wele and wo.
>
> (270–73)

> O Venus clere, of goddis stellifyit,
> To quhom I yelde homage and sacrifise,
> Fro this day furth your grace be magnifyit,
> That me ressavit have in swich [a] wise,
> To lyve under your law and do servise.
> Now help me furth, and for your merci lede
> My hert to rest, that deis nere for drede.
>
> (358–64)

The dream-vision which forms a response to these prayers and which constitutes the greater part of the poem, is the dreamer's visit to the Zodiacal house of Venus and Cupid, and his subsequent journeys to the court of Minerva in the Empyrean, and the garden abode of Fortune on Earth. In a sense, the conversations which he has with these goddesses correspond to the Lover's confession in Gower. It is also, I suppose, possible that James intended the word 'moralitee' to apply particularly to Gower, 'eloquence' primarily to Chaucer, although he is unlikely to have intended an absolute distinction between the two.

C S Lewis noted that in the *Kingis Quair* 'the poetry of marriage at last emerges from the traditional poetry of adultery',[4] a point well-made if one ignores the *Franklin's Tale* as a special case, and confines oneself otherwise to literature in English. Gower's French poems, however, in particular the *Traitié . . . pour essampler les amantz marietz* and the opening group of *Cinkante Balades*, devote themselves to the same theme, and it is possible that this also may have led James to give Gower so prominent a position.

His long captivity in England and France had certainly made him

acquainted with the vernacular literatures of the southern courts, and with a
rhetoric more complex than anything yet produced in Scots. It is certainly
poetry of this general kind, emerging from a courtly life resembling that of
England and France, which he recommends, through the *persona* of Venus,
to the Scots nation:

> Say on than, quhare is becummyn, for shame,
> The songis new, the fresch carolis and dance,
> The lusty lyf, the mony change of game,
> The fresche array, the lusty contenance,
> The besy awayte, the hertly observance,   [attendance]
> That quhilum was amongis thame so ryf?   [once]
> Bid thame repent in tyme and mend thaire lyf.
>   (841–47)

C S Lewis noted that the Boethian prologue to the *Kingis Quair* is in effect
a literary manifesto, which lays strong emphasis on personal experience as
the basis for courtly philosophical poetry.[5] Although at first it may appear
an excrescence, the stanza just quoted adds a new dimension to this idea.
What has the complaint of Venus, or indeed the court of Venus, to do with
the poet's personal development, or with the development in terms of the
poem of a philosophic theme? The answer lies in the highest reaches of the
poetry of *amour courtois* exemplified, say, by the *Vita Nuova* of Dante, or
the *Troilus and Criseyde* of Chaucer. Love, the operation of Venus, was
central to the operation of the Mediæval universe. But as the universe was a
complex work of art, so the celebrations of the central power of the universe
must themselves be complex works of art, and the product of a complex and
ornate society. The philosophic subject which emerges from the personal experience of the *Kingis Quair*, is the part played by Fortune in

> luffis ordinance,
> That has so mony in his goldin cheyne.
>   (1277–78)

The sacrament of matrimony made the service of Venus transcend courtly
play, a serious make-believe, philosophically worked out in terms of literature
and music; it became something vitally related to the experience of Everyman.
The complaint of Venus is that the Scots court has omitted this kind of
observance; the remedy which she urges, and which is linked to the sacrament
by the homily of Minerva, is that the court should adopt a philosophy, a way
of life, and a literature embracing the kinds exemplified in the *Kingis Quair*.
This is not merely to say extended dream-vision. The poem incidentally
contains specimens of other kinds, most notably the songs which punctuate
the first autobiographical episode—stanzas 34, 52, 63 and 64–65. In my book,
Ballattis of Lufe I have tried to show how the Scots courtly lyric developed,
in part at least, according to James's example, an example which is strong in
the later fifteenth century poets Clerk and Mersar, and which had not entirely
lost its power when Alexander Scott (*c*.1515–*c*.1583) was writing for Mary of

Guise and her daughter Mary I, nor when Alexander Montgomerie (*c.*1545–1597) was James VI's master poet.

The *Kingis Quair* is the earliest Scots poem which we can describe with reasonable certainty as intended for the court, and intended to set an example, which others could follow, of the art appropriate to such poetry. It has long been recognised that this last appears, partly in the elaborate stanza used, partly in the level of diction, imagery and thematic development. Less well recognised, indeed until recently not recognised at all, is the importance of the formal structure, in which a total of 197 stanzas is made up of a Boethian prologue in 13 stanzas, the 60 stanzas of the first autobiographical section, 99 stanzas of the dream-vision, 24 stanzas of the second autobiographical section, and the single dedicatory stanza directed to Gower and Chaucer. The first line of the first stanza, 'Heigh in the hevennis figure circulere', is repeated as the last line of the penultimate 196th stanza, and gives a circular effect to the movement of the entire poem.

The effect is complicated by the fact that 196 which completes the circle, is also a perfect square ($14 \times 14 = 196$), and that 197 is a prime number. James draws a distinction between 'hevin', the Empyrean beyond the Primum Mobile, and 'the hevynnis', the 9 celestial spheres contained by the Empyrean, as may be shown in stanza 196, where he distinguishes between 'him that hiest in the hevin sitt' (God), and 'the hevynnis figure circulere', the 9 celestial spheres of the created universe. In the general context of Mediæval numerology, it may not seem extravagant to suggest that the circular structure of the first 196 stanzas is intended to correspond to that of the spherical created universe, while the extra stanza, which transforms circle and perfect square to a prime number, corresponds to the relationship between the unique Creator and his multiplex but orderly creation, an interpretation which agrees with James's idiosyncratic use of Boethius to illustrate relations between divine Providence, which directly governs the movements of the stars and planets, and Fortune, the apparently arbitrary mistress of affairs in the world below.

The number 99, one of those which tend to appear whenever a literary work deals with the Otherworld or Eternity, makes its appearance as the total number of stanzas (74–172; lines 512–1204) in the dream-vision in which three goddesses, Venus, Minerva and Fortune, advise the imprisoned poet on the progress and significance of his apparently hopeless love for the young woman whom he has seen from his tower window as she walks in the garden below. The vision is decidedly extraterrestrial; he is snatched up through the spheres to one of the Zodiacal houses of Venus; later he goes beyond the Primum Mobile to the palace of Minerva (Heavenly Wisdom—the Fronesis or Prudentia of Alan of Lille's *Anticlaudianus*) in the Empyrean, from which he is returned to the domain of Fortune, Earth—Earth however in an archetypal and symbolic form, which is itself Otherworldly.

Within the dream vision, 50 stanzas are devoted to Venus and her court. Fifty (5×10) is 5, the number of the senses, in a glorified form appropriate to the planetary goddess of love. Twenty-one (thrice the number of the body, seven) stanzas are devoted to Fortune and her realm, and (most significantly)

28, the second perfect number, to Minerva. The 99 stanzas which represent eternal experience, combine with other groups representing temporal existence; the 13 stanzas of the prologue representing the 13 spheres of the created universe (Primum Mobile, Fixed Stars, 7 Planets, 4 Elements), by the movements and relations of which time is measured; the first and second autobiographical groups of stanzas the 60 minutes of the hour and the 24 hours of the day. Other numerological felicities might be mentioned: here it is probably enough to say that such distinctive features of the text are always clearly and accurately pointed.

Although he never forgets eternal values, James's concern is more with the temporal creation, subjected to the whims of Fortune, but ultimately governed by a Boethian and benevolent Providence. His Otherworldly vision enables him to reconcile benevolence with apparent cruel whimsicality, and his ultimate meaning is conveyed by the structure, which subordinates the vision to the circle squared in 196 stanzas, and transformed in 197.

Insofar as the literary programme proposed by James was immediately carried out, it was by lesser men, often translators, working under royal or noble patronage, and continuing the process of naturalising courtly concepts to the Scots language and experience. Their work in verse is paralleled by the more or less contemporary prose translations of Gilbert of the Haye, the *Buke of the Law of Armys*, the *Buke of Knychthede*, and the *Buke of the Governaunce of Princis*, begun in 1456. Gilbert himself made a verse translation of the *Roman d'Alixandre*, an edition of which is at present under preparation by the Scottish Text Society. This is not to be confused with the work now known as *The Buik of the Most Noble and Valiant Conquerour Alexander the Grit*, completed in 1438, one year after James's death, and derived from the second Branch of the French *Roman d'Alixandre*, 'Li Fuerres de Gadres' ('The Forray of Gadderis'), and a late offshoot of the third Branch, 'Les Voeux du Paon' ('The Avowis of Alexander' and 'The Great Battell of Effesoun'). The translator keeps to the metrical pattern established by Barbour, to whom indeed his work has (quite erroneously) been attributed.

Second is *Lancelot of the Laik*, a substantial fragment (3484 lines) of a long poem based on parts of the anonymous thirteenth-century French prose *Lancelot del Lac*, and apparently composed during the reign of James III (1460–88), in all probability for the queen, or another lady of the court.

The figures of Alexander and Lancelot are each central to the courtly tradition. Each translator claims to have written only to assuage the pangs of a love which is obviously courtly. Both, in other words, write on the assumption of a Scots audience which itself could appreciate the skilled handling of such themes.

The strange linguistic forms found in the latter poem link it to a shorter piece, *The Quare of Jelusy*, preserved in the same MS as the *Kingis Quair*. It has been suggested that all three are by the same author, a suggestion which, so far as the *Kingis Quair* is concerned, Miss Gray long ago effectively refuted,[6] but which still stands for the remaining two. *The Quare of Jelusy* has a colophon which was read by David Laing as 'Quod Auchen...', and the poem has therefore been attributed to the Afflek (Auchinleck) mentioned as a poet in line 58 of Dunbar's 'Timor Mortis Conturbat Me', who in turn has been identified with James Auchlek, who graduated at St Andrews in 1471, who in 1494 was Secretary to the Earl of Ross and Precentor of Caithness, and who died in September, 1497. If this is so, we have a considerable body of verse attributable to him, verse also which displays some literary ambitions.

Both poems have fairly conventional seasonal prologues in which the author is presented as a lover who walks out to keep his May observance, during which he has an unusual encounter. His mind is thus turned towards the composition of a poetry, which is at once courtly and moral. The encounter in *Lancelot of the Laik* is the more fantastic. The sight of the daisy, which is the symbol of his lady, casts him into a trance, in which he is approached by a messenger from the God of Love, a bird, 'as ony laurare gren', by whom he is urged to action. Her advice is to make his sorrow known to his lady, not by conventional love lyrics, of which there are already too many in the world, but by way of more serious work:

> Sum trety schall yhoue for thi lady sak,
> That unkouth is, als tak one hand and mak, [unfamiliar]
> Of love, ore armys, or of sum othir thing,
> That may hir one to thi Remembryng brynge.
> (145–48)

Despite self-doubt, which he expresses at some length, he determines to accept the advice. The romance of Lancelot attracts him, but he is overwhelmed by its sheer scale:

> Bot for that story is so pasing larg,
> One to my wit It war so gret o charg
> For to translait the romans of that knycht,
> It passith fare my cunyng and my mycht,
> Myne Ignorans may It not comprehende.
> (198–213)

Despite his protestation, he skilfully overcomes the difficulty by the method which Chaucer had previously used in the *Knight's Tale* to reduce Boccaccio's epic *Teseida* to more modest proportions. He makes the rhetorical figure known as *occupatio*, 'the refusal to describe or narrate', cover the earlier parts of the action—the birth and upbringing of Lancelot, his various adventures, his love for Guenevere, and how finally he became the prisoner of the Lady of Melyhalt—all, as it were, in negative terms. He refuses to describe these episodes, which nevertheless he names. Some seventy-five lines (215–92) thus suffice to bring him to the situation with which the action opens, the sinister interpretation of Arthur's prophetic dreams, confirmed by the challenge which Galiot (Galehaut) delivers to Arthur, and the early stages of Lancelot's heroically ambiguous behaviour which eventually reconciles the two leaders. Galiot's admiration for Lancelot then turns him into the pandar, whose cunning brings about the consummation of Lancelot's love for the queen and gains for himself the love of the Lady of Melyhalt. Unfortunately, the MS breaks off well before this point, which nevertheless must be the conclusion towards which the complexities of the narrative are directed. The tale is one of the best-known love stories of the Middle Ages, the reading of which, for instance, is the cause of the sin of Dante's Paolo and Francesca (*Inferno*, v, 127–38).

The Scots poet is certainly no Dante, but the criticism which his work has received has in general been too harsh, provoked, I suspect, not least by the unhappy orthography of the form in which it has been preserved. It is difficult to believe that some of his more severe critics have read the poem; R W Ackerman, for instance, claims at one point that it is written in 'couplets of four-stress lines'.[7] He corrects himself a little later, but adds significantly that 'the metre is notably irregular and rough'. Any reader of fifteenth-century poetry in English, and even in Scots, will recognise that this is not so.

The poet has set himself a difficult task. His narrative, like its French original, is subtle in terms of the psychology of courtly love, for which Lancelot and Guinevere are prime exemplars. From this point of view, the poet's treatment of the motives for the strange behaviour of the Lady of Melyhalt is particularly interesting. With this he combines a political element, the conduct of Arthur in his kingship, which leads to the difficulties encountered by the king in the attempt to repel Galiot's invasion, and perhaps to the loss of his wife's loyalty. This in turn is combined with ideas about predestination and free-will, illustrated by Arthur's prophetic dreams, and complicated by the typically Scots hostility towards Arthur as a bastard who had usurped the throne which properly belonged to the family of his nephew, Gawain. The poet, finally, takes a straightforward pleasure in a story about arms and knightly deeds, a pleasure which he keeps in careful balance with the other elements of his design.

It would almost seem that his ambitions were epic. His prologue ends with an invocation of Virgil, author of the complete epic, the *Aeneid*, whom modesty forbids that he should name in his own work:

> Flour of poyetis, quhois nome I [n]il report;
> To me nor to non uthir It accordit,
> In to our ryming his nam to be recordit;
> For sum suld deme It of presumpsioune,
> And ek our rymyng is al bot derysioune,
> Quhen that remembrit is his excellens,
> So hie abuf that stant in reverans.
> The fresch enditing of his laiting toung
> Out throuch this world so wid is yroung,
> Of eloquens, and ek of retoryk,
> Nor is, nor was, nore never beith hyme lyk.
>
> (320–30)

There is some verbal evidence that Gavin Douglas made at least occasional use of *Lancelot of the Laik* when he wrote his translation of the *Aeneid*.

The Quare of Jelusy is shorter, but formally more elaborate. The prologue, in which the poet's sympathies are roused by hearing a lady complain of her jealous husband, and the brief epilogue, are both in heroic couplets. They are separated by four sets of rhyming stanzas, each of which denounces jealousy in a different way. The first and most lyrical, in nine-line stanzas rhyming aabaabbab, laments the victimisation of womanhood by marital jealousy. This is followed by the 'trety In the reprefe of Ielousye', written in *rime-royal* stanzas, and adopting a more philosophical approach, which includes many references to Biblical Wisdom literature and to *exempla*, drawn from the rare French *Livre de Sydrac le philosophe*, from the *Legenda Aurea*, and once apparently from contemporary Scots history. A distinction is made between a harmless and hurtful form of jealousy, the first shown by the courtly lover, the second by the churlish husband. A second group of nine-line stanzas, rhyming aabaabbcc, is devoted to the denunciation of such husbands. A single ten-line stanza, rhyming aabaabbcbc, comes immediately before the epilogue.

The Quare of Jelusy has received even less attention than *Lancelot of the Laik*, yet it too possesses a certain complexity and power. At worst, it is an interestingly elaborate specimen of fifteenth-century Scots literature which is feminist because it is courtly. If both pieces are the work of a single author, his contribution to the literature of courtly love was greater than has yet been allowed.

In much of the best fifteenth-century poetry, courtly ideals, although present, are modified and even transformed by another factor, the emergence in Scotland on however limited a scale of an educated middle and professional class. The foundation of the two oldest Scots universities, St Andrews in 1412 and Glasgow in 1451, the growth in social importance of lawyers and merchants as a class, and the lay endowment of collegiate churches in many burghs, are only some among the factors which testify to the increasing importance of this group. Another is the moral seriousness, sometimes approaching dullness, characteristic of much even among the predominantly courtly writing. In *Lancelot of the Laik*, for instance, Maister Amytans delivers a long homily on kingly duties to Arthur, a homily which is of some importance in terms of plot, and which is present, although not at such length, in the French original. The expanded version was obviously much to the taste of the Scots audience, and it may be significant that Amytans is not presented as someone in holy orders, but rather as a lay Master of Arts:

> Non orders had he of Relegioune,
> Famus he was, and of gret excellence,
> And rycht expert in al the vii. science;
> Contemplatif and chast in governance,
> And clepit was the Maister Amytans.
> (1299–1303)

All this appears to derive from a single phrase in the French original, *un preudons plains de mout grant savoir*. In general, the word *preudons* (*preudome*) means 'man of worth', but in this context Elspeth Kennedy[8] glosses it as 'applied to wise man, neither knight nor in religious orders'. Notable is the precision with which the author has grasped this meaning, and re-interpreted it in terms of fifteenth-century Scotland.

The *Prolog* to the *Morall Fabillis of Esope the Phrygian* by Robert Henryson (*c*.1420–*c*.1490) illustrates the same point from a different angle. Henryson makes a gesture towards the convention that literary works are written only at the request of noble patrons:

> I wald preif   [try]
> To mak ane maner of translatioun—
> Nocht of myself, for vane presumptioun,
> Bot be requeist and precept of ane lord,
> Of quhome the name it neidis not record.
> (31–35)

If such a lord ever existed, Henryson subjected him to fairly cavalier treatment. One suspects that he is a rhetorical fiction like the *uther quair* on which Henryson said he had based his *Testament of Cresseid*. The very stanza in which he mentioned the lord begins with an address to 'my maisteris', and such parallel phrases as 'worthie folk', 'freindis', once even 'my Brother', occur time and again in the *Fabillis*. This is not the language of the court, but rather, I suggest, of the professional man, reasonably well placed on the social scale, addressing a group of his peers. Throughout the *Fabillis* the vocabulary is similarly professional and popular rather than courtly. Henryson's extensive and precise use of legal language is well known, and his dialogue shows an easy command of colloquial usage. 'Lords' are directly addressed in the *moralitates* of *The Lion and the Mouse* and *The Wolf and the Lamb*, but not in a courtly manner; the poet speaks as the representative of ordinary people who suffer under the conduct of their superiors. The *Fabillis* are not courtly poetry, and seem intended for private reading rather than the public performance which all courtly poetry to a certain extent demands. Their market was the new reading public of the fifteenth century, the public which in its English manifestations has been discussed by H S Bennett[9] and whose demands were in part satisfied by Caxton. A L Brown and Jenny Wormald have made interesting studies of the Scots equivalent. Lesser works which seem likely to have been written primarily for this market are the alliterative *Rauf Coilyear*, *Ratis Raving* and the other moral pieces edited by Ritchie Girvan, *The Three Priests of Peebles*, *The Talis of the Fyve Bestes*, and *The Freiris of Berwick*. Although there is evidence that Hary's *Wallace* received royal patronage, the poem, which is ultimately based on the popular *Scotichronicon*, and centres on a hero who belonged to a social level well beneath that of the nobility, may have been primarily intended for the same bourgeois audience. In the end certainly it became the people's book.

Henryson is the central literary figure of the later fifteenth century. He was a university graduate in arts and law, probably of one or more continental universities, who in 1462 was incorporated in Glasgow University, perhaps to give lectures in law. He was thus a man of some learning, which was not confined to legal studies. During his residence in Glasgow, it seems probable that he wrote his *Orpheus and Eurydice*, drawing much of his material from the manuscript copy of Boethius's *De Consolatione* with the gloss of Nicholas Trevet, which in 1432 is on record among the books held by Glasgow Cathedral. He also made notable use of two other works by Boethius, *De Musica* and *De Arithmetica*, which may well have been included in the same MS, to produce the elaborate numerological structure of the poem. About 1468 he seems to have moved from Glasgow to Dunfermline to become master of the grammar school attached to the ancient monastery. Although during his period in Dunfermline he is on record (in 1477 and 1478) as a notary public, the change implies the abandonment of a legal in favour of a humanistic career. Dunfermline was a royal residence, and a cultural centre in which were produced several important Scots manuscripts of the fifteenth century. It was here that Henryson wrote most of his best poetry. The *Fabillis*, or at least those among them based on books printed by Caxton, probably belong to the 1480s; the *Testament of Cresseid*, with its hints of a Dunfermline background and reference to the poet's old age, may well be a work of the same decade. Nothing suggests that Henryson was still active during the reign of James IV, who came to the throne in 1488, and it seems likely that he was dead by 1490 at latest. His reputation among his near contemporaries is shown by the inclusion of two of his poems in manuscripts probably connected with St Andrews and the humanist William Schevez, archbishop from 1476 to 1496, by the presence of *Orpheus and Eurydice* among the Chepman and Myllar prints, and by the references in Dunbar and Douglas.

Henryson's subsequent standing as a poet has always in some degree been lessened by the pre-eminence accorded in the eighteenth century to Gavin Douglas, which more recently has been transferred to Dunbar. Henryson has nothing to compare with the translation of the *Aeneid*; in terms of Douglas's original work, however, there can be no question which poet has the greater range and weight of achievement. Dunbar's metrical and linguistic virtuosity, the total effectiveness of his best poems, has to some extent hidden his emotional and intellectual limitations. He misses the two great literary kinds—tragedy and the form of comedy which depends on interplay of personality and social and stylistic level—partly at least because he possesses no extensive coherent body of general principles and ideas from which his poetry may grow. Henryson's virtuosity with language and metre is less ostentatious than Dunbar's, and so to some extent has passed unnoticed. His greatness is most plainly to be seen in the range of general principles and ideas which informs his verse and allows it to encompass tragedy and comedy alike. Henryson is more Shakespearian than Dunbar.

As was suggested above, the *Fabillis*, his great achievement in comedy of the kind I have described, were written for a middle-class professional audience of private readers, much interested in the state of contemporary Scotland, an audience which we may assume to have been predominantly masculine. By contrast, his tragedy, *The Testament of Cresseid*, is written in a more public high style, for recitation to a more courtly audience formed at least partly of women with some consciousness of their own relatively precarious situation. The central figure is a woman, and twice Henryson, as narrator, addresses the women in the audience. Once he does so obliquely through the mouth of Cresseid:

> O Ladyis fair of Troy and Grece, attend
> My miserie, quhilk nane may comprehend,
> My frivoll fortoun, my infelicitie—
>
> (452–54)

(It is worth remembering that in the pseudo-historical tradition all the people of Britain were regarded as descended either from Greeks—the Scots—or Trojans—the Welsh and English.) A second time he speaks to the women in his own *persona* as narrator:

> Now, worthie wemen, in this ballet schort,
> Maid for your worschip and instructioun—
>
> (610–11)

The *Testament*, his greatest poem, and one of the great poems in any variety of the English language, is also his most Chaucerian in that it pre-supposes in the reader a knowledge of Chaucer's *Troilus and Criseyde* and, for the most part employs *rime royal*, which is also the *Troilus* stanza. But that is not to say that it is simply derivative of Chaucer, who, apart from anything else, is by no means the only *auctor* to influence the poem. More important is the way in which Henryson's imitation (in the technical rhetorical sense) conveys an implicit criticism and correction, as well as appreciation, of Chaucer's masterpiece.

Henryson makes five implicit points:

1. In the latter part of his poem Chaucer inartistically concentrates the reader's attention on Troilus to the exclusion of Cresseid, of whom he had previously drawn a sensitive and sympathetic portrait.
2. Chaucer avoids the realities of dirt, disease and death.
3. Chaucer's poem is long and over-diffuse in style.
4. Chaucer's attempt at a Boethian treatment of free-will and pre-destination is unsatisfactory and on occasion downright clumsy.
5. The Christian epilogue is inartistically related to the remainder of the poem, not because it is Christian, but because the earlier part of the poem does not establish the opposition of the pagan gods and Christ which the epilogue so powerfully emphasises.

Henryson's solution to the first three points is tolerably clear. The fourth and fifth he established in a more indirect way. He is unequivocal in his introduction of paganism by way of the planetary divinities who pass sentence on Cresseid in her dream. These also represent the destinal forces of the universe, the natural laws to which Cresseid, insofar as she is a material being, is subject. At the same time they are the pagan gods whom Chaucer set in opposition to Christ and Christian salvation. Henryson accepts physical determinism as exemplified by Cresseid's leprosy. Even after her affliction, however, she retains a rational free-will which is finally capable of bringing her to a recognition of her own spiritual responsibility.

The poem contains no specifically Christian reference to counterbalance the presence of the pagan divinities, but a Christian interpretation remains a possibility, indeed a probability, in terms, first, of Cresseid's progression from ignorance to self-knowledge by way of an act of grace for which Troilus is the unconscious agent, and secondly, of the narrative parallels between the *Testament* and the Gospel stories of the Prodigal Son, who returned to his father, and of Dives and Lazarus, the leprous beggar who attained salvation, when Dives, the rich man, was condemned. The combination of implicit Christian reference with a specific and historically appropriate pagan setting seems to me not only independent of Chaucer, but also a major triumph of controlled literary art.

In an earlier book I noted how the *Testament* falls naturally into eight sections.[10] Here I should like to make slight adjustments to the scheme and put forward the following divisions:

i.   Proem—70 lines (1–70)
ii. First narrative episode—70 lines (71–140)
iii. Dream-vision—203 lines (141–343)
iv. Second narrative episode—63 lines (344–406)
v.   'The Complaint of Cresseid'—63 lines (407–469)
vi. Third narrative episode—70 lines (470–539)
vii. Lament, testament and death of Cresseid—70 lines (540–609)
viii. Conclusion—7 lines (610–616).

The formal nature of this structure is at once evident. As a whole, the poem contains 86 stanzas, 616 lines. Seventy-nine of these stanzas are in seven-line *rime royal*, with each of the seven stanzas of 'The Complaint of Cresseid' containing nine lines. There is an obvious balance among the first seven parts, sections i and ii, for instance, corresponding to the later sections vi and vii, each containing 10 seven-line stanzas. Internally, section iv, which contains 9 seven-line stanzas, mirrors section v, with 7 nine-line stanzas. Section iii, as befits its other-worldly subject matter, stands somewhat apart, but its 203 lines make up precisely one-third of the 609 lines of the poem *minus* the single stanza of the conclusion, as do sections i, ii and iv combined, and sections v, vi and vii combined. (This in itself is evidence that the conclusion should be regarded as a separate eighth section.) The pattern is too perfect and too complex to be accidental.

The numbers which this structure emphasises are 7, 9, 10, 63, 70 and 8. The limitations of space imposed on this essay make it impossible to say more than that 7 is traditionally the number of the body, 9 of the mind, 10 is perfection, 63 the bodily climacteric, and 70 the natural life-span. Finally 8 is the Pythagorean number of Justice. Even when put in such a compressed form, the relevance of the numerical structure to the action of the poem is reasonably apparent.

This use of numerological construction is only one of the devices the use of which links Henryson to James I. Elsewhere I have written at some length on the use of numerological techniques in *Orpheus and Eurydice*.[11] For the rest, the example which comes readily to mind is Henryson's most extensive and complex Aesopic fable, *The Preiching of the Swallow*, which Professor Burrow has convincingly shown to be an 'ethical construction' on the theme of *Prudentia*, or Prudence, the Latin equivalent of Greek σοφία (sophia), a word which on one level might be used of the Divine Wisdom, on another might be applied to the group of mental faculties by means of which it is possible for the human mind or soul to achieve contact with the Divine Wisdom.[12] Minerva in the *Kingis Quair* represents both senses of Prudence.

The cardinal parts of Prudence are Foresight, dealing with the future, Understanding with the present, and Memory with the past. Prudence is often presented as a human head with three faces, one contemplating the future, one the present and one the past.

The 47 stanzas of *The Preiching of the Swallow* fall naturally into three divisions; a prologue containing 13 stanzas, the main narrative in 25 stanzas, and the *moralitas*-epilogue in nine stanzas. Forty-seven is a prime number. The 25 stanzas represent the appetitive realm of the five senses—in Trevet's sinister phrase, the *amena presentis vite* (the pleasant things of this life), which in *Orpheus and Eurydice* lead to the downfall of Eurydice. In this fable, the role of Eurydice is played by the birds other than the swallow, whose good advice they ignore to their own eventual destruction. They care only for immediate satisfaction; their relation to the present is governed solely by appetite. Prudence is represented by the swallow, whose primary concern is to exercise understanding on the deceitful *amena presentis vite*. Understanding cannot, of course, operate simply in the present; it implies both memory and foresight, and the swallow's concern for immediate action is based on past experience, and directed towards the avoidance of future evil, *nam leuius laedit quicquid praeuidimus ante* (line 1754—'For whatever we have foreseen harms us less severely'). The predominance of appetite limits the other birds to the present.

The 13 stanzas of the prologue represent the spatial and temporal features of creation; the constituent parts are four, expressed spatially and materially by the four elements, temporally by the four seasons, together with the seven planetary spheres, one stellar sphere, and one firmament or *primum mobile*, the combined movements of which mark the passage of time. Apart from the sequence of the seasons, mentioned later (stanzas 9–13), the whole is summarised in a single stanza:

> The firmament payntit with sternis cleir,   [stars]
> From eist to west rolland in cirkill round,
> And everilk planet in his proper spheir,
> In moving makand harmonie and sound;
> The fyre, the air, the watter and the ground—   [earth]

> Till vnderstand it is aneuch, I wis,   [enough]
> That God in all his werkis wittie is.   [wise]
> (Stanza 6: 1657–63)

The work of the six days is thus summarised in stanza 6, and the 13 spheres provide evidence for the four Attributes of God—goodness, beauty, wisdom and benevolence—which at their own exalted level bear a particular correspondence to the four elements and, in particular, the four seasons. The point is doubly emphasised by a reference to one of the great numerological texts, *Wisdom of Solomon* 11.20:

> All creature he maid for the behufe
> Off man, and to his supportatioun
> In to this eirth, baith under and abufe,
> *In number, wecht and dew proportioun.*
> (Stanza 8: 1671–74)

Notice too that eight is the number of Justice, and that this expression of divine equity comes appropriately in the eighth stanza.

The emphasis in the prologue is on the past, on memory, that is to say, as the repository of experience applicable to the present and the future.

The *moralitas* completes the scheme by looking to the future. The fowler is identified with Satan, and the birds with sinners, who think only of the *amena presentis vite*. The *moralitas* is a vision of the future, which only the swallow by the application of foresight can avoid. The 9 stanzas, I suggest, correspond primarily to the nine circles of Hell (as presented, for instance, by Dante), although there is a side-reference to the alternative enjoyed by the swallow in company with the nine orders of angels. Nine is also, of course, the number of the mind and so, in a special sense, the number of Prudence and the swallow.

The poem, one might say in conclusion, is governed by the fact that four, the number of the elements, the seasons and the Divine Attributes, is a reconciling number, the first to contain two means (three and two as intermediate between unity and four).

> 'Borrowing the means from this number the Creator of the universe bound the elements together with an unbreakable chain, as was affirmed in Plato's *Timaeus*: in no other way could the elements earth and fire, so opposed and repugnant to each other and spurning any communion of their natures, be mingled together and joined in so binding a union unless they were held together by the two means of earth and water.
> (Macrobius, *Commentary on Scipio's Dream*, 1.6.24.)

The prayer in the final stanza of Henryson's *moralitas* re-emphasises the number, and makes the final application less gloomy than some of the earlier stanzas might have led one to expect:

> Pray we thair foir quhill we are in this lyfe
> For four thingis: the first, fra sin remufe;
> The secund is to seis all weir and stryfe;
> The thrid is perfite cheritie and lufe;
> The feird thing is, and maist for oure behufe,   [fourth]
> That is in blis with angellis to be fallow.   [fellow]
> And thus endis the preiching of the swallow.
> (Stanza 47: 1944–50)

Elaborate numerological form is one aspect of Henryson's 'high style', and tends to appear only in poems with a strong philosophic or theological emphasis. *The Lion and the Mouse*, for instance, seems to contain nothing of the kind, although it is a sequel to *The Preiching of the Swallow*: with the action of both taking place in the same symbolic landscape dominated by a hawthorn tree. Aesop in the prologue puts it on a lower literary plane than *The Preiching of the Swallow*:

> For quhat is it worth to tell ane fenyeit taill,
> Quhen haly preiching may na thing availl?
> (1389–90)

As the import of the 'fenyeit taill' is political rather than philosophical, it calls for the middle style and there is no need for the complex structure of the earlier poem. In passing, it should be noted that the order in which modern editions present these fables shows a sad lack of critical judgement: despite all evidence to the contrary, *The Lion and the Mouse* invariably precedes rather than follows *The Preiching of the Swallow*.

Henryson's greatest achievement in 'low style' is *The Tod* ('The Fox'), a miniature beast-epic in three branches, which forms a kind of comic counterpoint to *The Testament of Cresseid*. Cresseid is eventually forced to realise that she bears the responsibility for her own physical misfortunes, and this realisation is her personal salvation. The major characters in *The Tod* have the same responsibility, but do not admit it. Chanteclere and the wolf-friar pay the penalty for allowing themselves to be blinded by self-conceit and flattery; the elder fox fails to keep the terms of his penance; the younger breaks the king's peace by killing a lamb: as a consequence, both are killed, one on the gallows. Admiration for the foxes' cleverness in satisfying their own selfish ends is counterbalanced by a realisation of the helplessness of their victims—'ane lytill kid' and the fattest of 'ane trip of lambis dansand on ane dike'. The stupidity as well as the cleverness of the foxes is emphasised—one stroking his belly as he basks in the sun, and saying

> Upon this wame set wer ane bolt full meit;
> (760)

the other forgetting himself a few moments after quoting the very apposite proverb, *felix quem faciunt aliena pericula cautum* (1033: 'Happy is he whom the dangers of others make cautious'). For the foxes in particular there is no possibility of urging mitigating circumstances and no recognition on their part of their own responsibility. Their punishment exemplifies both divine and human justice. Despite its severity, or even perhaps because of it, *The Tod* remains unequivocally comedy.

Neither comedy nor tragedy seems an appropriate term for the *Kingis Quair* and the remaining poetry discussed in the earlier part of this chapter. Henryson's eminence is best exemplified by the reconciliation in his work of the two extremes, tragedy in the *Testament of Cresseid*, comedy in *The Tod*.

NOTES

1   Alan Harding, 'Regiam Majestatem amongst Medieval Law-Books', *Juridicial Review*, 29 (1984), 110.
2   Bodleian MS, Arch. Selden B.24, Oxford.
3   James I, *The Kingis Quair*, John Norton-Smith (ed) (Oxford, 1981), p xix.
4   C S Lewis, *The Allegory of Love* (Oxford, 1936), p 237.
5   *Allegory of Love*, p 235.
6   *Lancelot of the Laik*, M M Gray (ed), STS (Edinburgh and London, 1912), pp xviii–xix.
7   R W Ackerman, 'The English Rimed and Prose Romances' in *Arthurian Literature in the Middle Ages*, R S Loomis (ed) (Oxford, 1959), pp 480–519 (p 482).
8   *Lancelot du Lac*, Elspeth Kennedy (ed), 2 vols (Oxford, 1980), II, 475.
9   H S Bennett, *English Books and Readers 1475–1557* (Cambridge, 1952).
10   John MacQueen, *Robert Henryson* (Oxford, 1967), pp 45–46.
11   John MacQueen, 'Neoplatonism and Orphism in Fifteenth-Century Scotland: the Evidence of Henryson's *New Orpheus*', *Scottish Studies*, 20 (1976), 69–89.
12   John Burrow, 'Henryson: "The Preaching of the Swallow" ', *Essays in Criticism*, XXV (1975), 25–37.

FURTHER READING

PRIMARY TEXTS

(For Henryson and the *Asloan* MS (*The Talis of the Fyve Bestes*) see the General Bibliography)

James I, *The Kingis Quair*, Norton-Smith, John (ed) (Oxford, 1971)
—— *The Kingis Quair*, McDiarmid, M P (ed) (London, 1973)
Lawson, Alexander (ed), *Quare of Jelusy* in *The Kingis Quair and The Quare of Jelusy* (London, 1910), pp 104–23
MacQueen, John (ed), *Ballatis of Luve* (Edinburgh, 1970)
Small, John (ed), *The Freiris of Berwick* in *Poems of William Dunbar*, STS, 3 vols (Edinburgh and London, 1893), pp 285–304
A new edition of Gilbert of the Haye's *King Alexander the Conquerour* (the Taymouth *Alexander*) is being produced by J Cartwright.

SECONDARY TEXTS

Brown, A L, 'The Scottish "Establishment" in the Later Fifteenth Century', *Juridicial Review*, 23 (1978), 89–105
Gray, D, *Robert Henryson* (Leiden, 1979)
Kindrick, Robert L, *Robert Henryson* (Boston, 1979)
MacQueen, John, 'The Literature of Fifteenth-Century Scotland', in *Scottish Society in the Fifteenth Century*, Brown, Jennifer M (ed), (London, 1977), pp 184–208
—— *Numerology, Theory and Outline History of a Literary Mode* (Edinburgh, 1985)

Chapter 5

William Dunbar and Gavin Douglas

PRISCILLA BAWCUTT

Although Sir Walter Scott was among the first to recognise the genius of Dunbar and Douglas, he termed their Scotland 'rude' and 'barbarous' (*Marmion*, VI.xi). Modern historians have corrected this image of the reign of James IV, noting the increasing wealth of the country, its artistic and trading links with northern Europe, the learning of John Major and other scholars, and the luxury, indeed extravagance, of the court. There now seems a risk of slightly over-glamorising James IV and his achievements as a patron of the arts. Yet his reign certainly witnessed a flowering of Scottish poetry, at a drab period in the literary history of England. Some poets are unfortunately no more than shadowy names; others, such as Walter Kennedy, have only a handful of poems extant; but there has survived enough fine work, much of it anonymous, to show that Dunbar and Douglas wrote not in isolation but within a flourishing tradition of vernacular literature. Their lives over-lapped: but Dunbar's dates (*c*.1460–*c*.1513) depend upon scholarly conjecture, whereas Douglas's birth and death (1476–1522) are established with more precision. Both were styled 'Maister', a sign that they were university graduates—Dunbar seems, like Douglas, to have been a student at St Andrews. Both came from families associated with East Lothian, the most prosperous region of late-Mediæval Scotland, and spent much of their lives in Edinburgh. More importantly, both were associated with the court: Dunbar addressed many poems to the king, and Douglas dedicated *The Palice of Honour* to 'our soverane, James the Feird'. Yet despite similarities of environment their social status and careers were strikingly different. Douglas was a nobleman, son of the fourth earl of Angus; as early as his thirteenth year he made a supplication to the Pope for permission to hold a canonry and two other benefices. By 1503 he was provost of the important collegiate church of St Giles, Edinburgh, and in 1516 he became Bishop of Dunkeld, with an unrealised ambition to become Archbishop of St Andrews. During the minority of James V he seems to have abandoned poetry for politics. His alliance with the Dowager Queen, through her marriage to his nephew, brought him into conflict with the Governor, Albany, and he died in exile in London. Dunbar's worldly career seems to have been much less spectacular, but the exact details, like so much in his life, remain mysterious. He too was a churchman (one document calls him a 'chaplain'), and his poems contain several requests for a benefice, although there is no evidence that he ever obtained one. The most definite biographical facts about Dunbar are that from 1500 to 1513 he received a generous 'pensioun', or annual salary, as a 'servitour', or member of the royal household. Dunbar was employed by the king—he was no leisurely gentleman-poet—yet we do not know precisely what he did, and there is no evidence that he was rewarded simply for being a poet. The likelihood is that, like some of his poet-friends, Patrick Johnston, John Reid, or Quintin Schaw, he served in the royal secretariat, perhaps as an envoy or scribe.[1]

As poets Dunbar and Douglas had many important things in common, such as an orthodox religious faith and an unquestioning acceptance of the hierarchic society in which they lived. They shared the same cultural inheritance. An education conducted in Latin gave them access not only to the usual curricula of a late-Mediæval Arts course, with its stress on logic, but to the wealth of Latin literature, Classical, Mediæval and Humanistic. Yet both were keenly interested in vernacular poetry, and paid far from perfunctory tribute to Chaucer and the revolution he effected in English poetry. Their own writing demonstrates a lively awareness of their Scottish predecessors, such as Henryson, Holland, or the anonymous author of *Rauf Coilyear*. Nonetheless as poets Dunbar and Douglas could not be more contrasted. Perhaps the most obvious sign of this is that Dunbar wrote a number of fairly short poems, whereas Douglas's two main works are large and ambitious, one a dream-poem extending to over 2,000 lines, the other a translation of Virgil's *Aeneid*. (The canon of neither poet is established with certainty. Approximately eighty poems are attributed to Dunbar; although his authorship of most has never been seriously questioned, there are doubts, dating from the sixteenth century, as to his responsibility for some poems. There are also problems about Douglas's canon: he, like Dunbar, probably wrote poems that are no longer extant, but his authorship of *King Hart*, an excellent moral allegory once attributed to him, is now thought unlikely.)[2] Yet the differences between Dunbar and Douglas extend very much further, to their sense of themselves as poets, and the fictive worlds they created. Dunbar, 'the makar', did not take himself as seriously as do many of his modern critics. But Douglas held an exalted notion of the poet, and aspired to be a great one. Dunbar's most distinctive poems, though shot through with humour and fantasy, are concerned with actual people, 'heir at hame' in Scotland. Douglas is imaginatively more at home in remote or idealised landscapes, peopled with figures from ancient myth or legend. Dunbar's poems are so varied that critics have found it difficult to form a coherent image of their elusive, protean author. Douglas, however, is a strikingly consistent poet; despite flashes of sardonic humour, he is as 'sage and serious' as Spenser.

Dunbar has left nothing as critically interesting or self-revealing as Douglas's Prologues to *The Eneados*, yet his view of himself as a poet emerges from various scattered remarks. In *The Flyting* (23) he dissociates himself humorously but firmly from the Gaelic poetic tradition, exclaiming 'wondir laith wer I to be ane baird'![3] He styles himself a 'makar', and speaks of his writing as 'making'. These terms were by no means peculiarly Scottish; although not undignified, they seem not to have had quite the same lofty status as *poet* and *poetry*, with which they were roughly synonymous.[4] Commenting on Spenser's April Eclogue, E.K. said: 'in this word making, our olde Englishe Poetes were wont to comprehend all the skil of Poetrye...' Dunbar is clearly a maker in this sense; he is not a profoundly original thinker, but he excels in the shaping of his poems, and his metrical and stylistic versatility. No other early Scottish poet is so sensitive to the connotations of words and phrases, or deploys them so effectively. At the close of *The Goldyn Targe* (10) Dunbar praises Chaucer as 'rose of rethoris all', and continues

> Thy fresch anamalit termes celicall
> This mater coud illumynit have full brycht:
> Was thou noucht of oure Inglisch all the lycht,
> Surmounting eviry tong terrestriall
> Alls fer as Mayes morow dois mydnycht?
>   (257–61)

Dunbar does more here than voice a justified modesty about his poem in comparison with Chaucer's achievement; he also ignores the political boundaries between England and Scotland, and embraces their shared language and poetic traditions—for which Kennedy comically chides him in *The Flyting*. Writing in the Mediæval tradition by which poets are equated with 'rethoris', he distinguishes 'mater' (subject matter) from the gorgeous decorative language in which it is clad. The finished poem is seen as a brilliant artefact. The passage from which these lines come is justly famous, yet has recently received almost too much attention, as if it were Dunbar's sole pronouncement on his art. It is best seen as celebrating one particular kind of poetic excellence, to which he undoubtedly aspires in some but not necessarily all his poems.

Elsewhere Dunbar says other things about his poems. In 'Schir, yit remember as befoir' (42) he is ironically self-mocking—'Allace, I can bot ballattis breif [write]'—and he often refers to his poems as 'ballattis'. A *ballat* at this time could have almost any form, and deal with any subject. The term appears almost as flexible as *poem*, yet it seems to have possessed certain connotations. A ballat tended to be short, and to retain its original links with singing, dancing and music. What is more, unless narrowly defined by a modifier (as in 'ballattis of moralitie'), it was commonly associated with light, secular subjects, especially love. Dunbar's Widow envisaged the reading of ballats as part of the ritual of courtship: 'Sum rownis [whispers] and sum ralyeis and sum redis ballatis' (14, 480). Although few love poems by Dunbar now survive, one is very fine (12), and he jocularly implies that he had a reputation as a love poet (see 33 and 55). Again, although no poem definitely written by Dunbar is accompanied by music, it is possible that some were originally intended to be sung or set to music (17 and 43 are carols). Critics may disagree as to whether Dunbar should be called lyrical; there can be no argument that, by the standards of the time, his poems tend to be short. Only three have more than 200 lines, and many are very brief indeed. Mediæval dream poems often contain thousands of lines; *The Goldyn Targe* has no more than 279. Kennedy's *The Passioun of Christ* has 1,715 lines; Dunbar's poem on the same subject (3) is considerably shorter. Again and again his handling of a specific genre contrasts with the leisurely manner of his contemporaries. In another poem Dunbar comments interestingly on his earlier one (29), containing a comic portrait of a fellow-courtier. Addressing the queen, he says

> Thocht I in ballet did with him bourde
> In malice spack I nevir ane woord
> Bot all, my dame, to do yow gam.[5]
>   (30, 5–7)

Dunbar here represents his poetry-making as social, recreative and playful; it draws members of the court together into a relationship that is common in life—a *bourde* [jest] at one person's expense provokes *gam* [amusement] in others. Many of Dunbar's poems were written, in the first place, for a small group who knew each other well, king, queen, and courtiers, several of whom, like Dunbar, were both 'clerkis' and poets. Poetry is treated as an extension of conversation—'in ballet did with him bourde'—and poems like 'Schir, for your grace bayth nicht and day' (25) or 'The wardraipper of Venus boure' (29) are characterised by their intimate tone and high degree of colloquialism. But we should not trust the disclaimer of malice; cruel and vulgar practical jokes were sometimes termed *bourdes*, and cruelty and vulgarity are not wholly absent from Dunbar.

The court provided Dunbar not only with an audience but with much of his subject-matter. He writes of the great festive occasions—*The Thrissill and the Rois*, for instance, celebrates the wedding of James IV and Margaret Tudor. He employs two favourite courtly genres, panegyric and elegy: greeting the arrival of the distinguished knight, Bernard Stewart, in one poem (35), and lamenting his death in another (36). But he also writes, more informally, about more trivial events. He devises comic squibs about fellow-servitors, fools, or alchemists who seek the quintessence, but merely (in his punning phrase) 'multiplie in folie' (44). Dunbar displays a journalistic interest in the recent and the topical. He is apparently the first vernacular writer in Britain to mention the Voyages of Discovery (39); and a poem about a black girl 'that landet furth of the last schippis' (33) reminds us how novel was the presence of black people in Scotland. The entertainments of the court, such as dicing and falconry, supplied some of Dunbar's imagery. James IV's well-known interest in fire-arms perhaps suggested to him the violent conclusion of one dream-poem (51) by the shooting of a gun 'on Leith sandis'. A court-dance is the literal subject of one poem (28), and provides the metaphorical structure for another (52A), in which the Seven Deadly Sins perform modish dance-steps, 'That last came out of France'. Dunbar writes, sometimes with delight, sometimes with disgust, of what he sees 'Daylie in court befoir myn e [eye]' (44). His satiric stance towards court life is hardly novel, but he well conveys its uneasy atmosphere of envy and distrust. A portrait of a boorish churchman is dramatically presented through the eyes of a more learned nobleman, who sees the upstart

Sa far above him set at tabell	
That wont was for to muk the stabell—	
Ane pykthank in a prelottis clais	[flatterer] [clothes]
With his wavill feit and wirrok tais,	[twisted] [bunioned toes]
With hoppir hippis and henches narrow	[haunches]
And bausy handis to beir a barrow;	[clumsy]
With lut schulderis and luttard bak	[bowed] [?crooked]
Quhilk natur maid to beir a pak.	
(45, 51–58)	

Dunbar was no friend to upward social mobility.

Scholars have sought, without much success, to establish Dunbar's indebtedness to earlier poets, whether French or English. It has often proved easier to demonstrate the genres to which his poems belong than to identify precise sources or influences. Although intelligent and well-read, he was not a learned poet. The great tradition of classical poetry that meant so much to Douglas was of far less significance to Dunbar. To him the most important Latin tradition was that associated with the Church, in the Scriptures, hymns, and liturgy. Dunbar's acquaintance with popular and often anonymous forms of writing, in both Latin and the vernacular, tends to be under-valued. His comic poems are often treated as if they were literary 'sports', curiously isolated from the long-lived but not very respectable forms to which they are akin—bawdy love poems, drinking songs, prophecies, or doggerel invectives. The fifth and sixth stanzas from 'Schir Thomas Norny' (27) reveal Dunbar's interest in ballad and popular romance, and he alludes to a well-known method of oral transmission, 'Wyvis ... spynnand on rokkis [distaffs]' (34). In formal poems, such as *The Goldyn Targe*, he enriches the verse-texture by classical allusions, but his more down-market references to popular beliefs and customs often puzzle readers or pass unrecognised. His account of the Tailor with a banner, 'all stowin [stolen] out of sindry webbis' (52B), alludes to a jest with an international currency, although it is first recorded in an Italian *facetia*. It is important to recognise this popular strain in Dunbar, and his appeal to an audience with wide and omnivorous tastes. The court of James IV was no narrow aristocratic élite. Its entertainments were sometimes elegant and refined, sometimes robust and unsophisticated. We should not form too restricted a notion of the court poet at this time.

The prevalent critical view of Dunbar applauds his brilliant craftsmanship, yet often seems curiously reductive: he is seen as a virtuoso, a skilled technician, a writer who supplies, in response to the demands of patrons, poems framed in accordance with the rules of a genre. This is far from being the whole truth. Some poems, such as those on Bernard Stewart (35, 36), are likely to have been commissioned; and the fine religious poem, 'Done is a battell on the dragon blak' (4), is public and occasional (in no trivial sense), designed to celebrate a great feast of the Christian year. Yet for many others no such explanation can be devised. Their origin may well lie in Dunbar's spontaneous response to some experience in his own or others' life. Again, some of his poems, usually his least interesting, can be described by a single generic label. 'Now of women this I say for me' (72) uses topoi, arguments, and images that were commonplaces of the numerous late-Mediæval defences of women. Dunbar clearly enjoyed experimenting with different types of poem—he even tried his hand at a beast fable (37)—but many poems partake of several kinds, and others defy easy categorisation. To what genre does his short poem on a head-ache (21) belong? Other poems break the rules, or transcend the conventions. Dunbar often teases his readers, arousing and then subverting their expectations as to what will follow. One poem (63), which begins with a standard complaint on the times, ends with a powerful vision of the Last Judgement.

Much of the pleasure of reading Dunbar's most ambitious poem, *The Tretis of the Twa Mariit Wemen and the Wedo* (14), is indeed formal, and derives from its inter-weaving of different literary kinds. On the surface its structure is deceptively simple: three women recount their experiences of marriage. Yet in its small way this is as much a framed tale-collection as *The Decameron*. A rich, idle group, briefly isolated from society, entertain themselves by telling not fictions but fragments of life-history—the Widow exclaims, when her turn comes, 'my taill it is nixt'. But the narrator is outside the group—the framework (as is often noted) resembles both the *chanson d'aventure*, and *chanson de mal mariée*. Much ironic comedy springs from this basic device: the women speak indiscreetly, because they think they are alone and (in the Second Wife's words) 'ther is no spy neir'; the eavesdropping poet, however, hears no good of his own sex, since the husbands are represented as old, impotent, and jealous. The poem is not strictly a debate (though sometimes so termed), since there is no disagreement between the women. But the Widow, as befits her experience, takes the leading role. She is catechist, confessor and preacher, and her speech amusingly travesties several types of improving literature, one of which is the saint's life: 'Ladyis, leir thir lessonis.../This is the legeand of my lif, thought Latyne it be nane' (503–4). Dunbar also glances at the didactic treatises aimed particularly at women, with such self-explanatory titles as *How the Good Wife Taught her Daughter*. The poem purports to show how women really learn from other women, and *what* they learn—not the virtues of submission and modesty usually prescribed, but 'lessonis' in duplicity and the domination of men. The conversation is initiated by the questions, put by the Widow to the Wives, concerning the 'blist bond' of marriage. The poem concludes with another question, put by the poet to his 'auditouris':

> Of thir thre wantoun wiffis that I haif writtin heir,
> Quhilk wald ye waill to your wif gif ye suld wed one?   [choose]
> (529–30)

Mediæval love-poems often ended with questions, usually termed *demaundes d'amour*. But *demaundes* figured in real life as a social pastime, just as in the poem they are a merry 'game', with which the women entertain themselves. The final mocking question might suggest a poet in knowing complicity with male listeners. But Dunbar too is playing a game, and with an audience of both sexes, for whom the poem clearly furnishes a provocative talking-point.

Dunbar's finest poems almost all contain some tinge of comedy. His range of tone is wide: predominantly sardonic, mocking and derisive, yet also flippant, bantering, and even genial. His comic targets are varied. He does not simply mock deviants and outsiders, traditional comic butts, such as the friars, or those low in the social hierarchy; he sometimes makes fun of himself, notably in 'Schir, lat it never in toune be tald' (43), and is often disrespectful to the king. Dunbar delights in exploiting areas of social tension, between men and women, clerics and laymen, seculars and friars, lowlanders and highlanders. He still retains a remarkable power to startle and amuse readers, whose minds hover between shock and laughter, embarrassment and delight. Certain comic modes seem particularly congenial to Dunbar. He is a master of 'flyting', or invective, and grotesque portraiture. He has a keen eye for the absurdity and ugliness of life, and the physically 'misfassonit' [mis-shapen]— the 'knowll tais' [swollen toes] of one man, or the rheumy eyes of another. The image of the corpse upon the gallows often figures in his poems. Dunbar excels in parody of various kinds: two poems, 'Schir Thomas Norny' (27) and 'The Turnament' (52B), are mock-chivalric; two others spring from the central tradition of Mediæval Latin parody. 'The Testament of Andro Kennedy' (38) is modelled, in form and language, on real-life wills; and 'The Dregy' (22) is a small comic masterpiece, drawing upon the Office for the Dead, in order to celebrate the good things of life, such as fine claret. This light-hearted poem is irreverent, but not as blasphemous as earlier scholars found it, nor as solemn as it appears to some modern ones. Dunbar early announces

> We sall begyn ane cairfull soun,
> Ane dirige devoit and meik.
> (22–23)

Nothing could be less 'devoit' [pious] than the poem that follows, or less 'cairfull' [sorrowful] than its dancing, tripping verse. Such local verbal irony is highly characteristic of Dunbar; in some poems it is pervasive. C S Lewis remarked how often in Dunbar 'the comic overlaps with the demoniac and the terrifying';[6] this is particularly true of a cluster of dream-poems, the most famous of which is *Fasternis Evin in Hell* (52A–C).

I do not concur with those critics who see morality as the key to Dunbar. Yet a large number of his poems are didactic, and explicitly so, in a way that rarely appeals to modern readers. Poems like these were extremely popular in his own time, however, and were long copied into anthologies and commonplace books. They possessed an appeal similar to that of fables and proverbs, or the Wisdom books of the Bible. They encapsulated popular

morality on a range of topics; their approach was authoritarian, and promoted acceptance of the established social order:

> Thank God of it is to the sent,
> And of it glaidlie mak gud cheir:
> Aneuch he hes that is content.   [enough]
>   (66, 13–15)

Their tone is characteristically impersonal—the speaker in one poem is a
disembodied voice (81)—and the implied audience is equally universal. It is
a trademark of this type of poem to contain, usually in the opening lines, an
address to 'man' or *homo*. The syntax is simple, and often hortatory; the
diction plain, embellished chiefly by proverbs and proverbial similes. Commonly the refrain embodies the theme—e.g. 'All erdly joy returnis in pane'
(59). Several of these poems belong to recognised didactic genres. 'To dwell
in court, my freind' (77) resembles Polonius's advice to Laertes: precepts for
conduct, couched in the form of parental advice to a son. Behind it lies an
ancient tradition, best exemplified in the popular and influential pseudo-
Cato's *Disticha de Moribus ad Filium*. Many of these pieces could have
been written by any competent poet of the time; indeed some of the poems
attributed to Dunbar in one manuscript are elsewhere assigned to another
poet or anonymous. This uncertainty as to authorship is symptomatic of their
high degree of conventionality. Yet one or two of Dunbar's moral poems are
outstanding, notably 'In to thir dirk and drublie dayis' (69) and 'I that in
heill wes and gladnes' (62), better-known as 'The Lament for the Makars'.
They spring from the same tradition, yet have far greater individuality of
thought and expression. 'I that in heill wes' may be seen as a meditation on
Death the Leveller, an elegy on dead poets, and a re-writing of the Dance of
Death, but it also has great psychological truth. As the poem proceeds it
mirrors the way in which many experience the meaning of death; at first a
well-known but distant commonplace, only after the death of 'fallowis', or
friends, does it become a personal and poignant reality. This poem is partly
about the stages by which we come to understand a general truth—death is
perceived very differently at the end of the poem from the way it is perceived
at its beginning.

The exact degree of self-expression in Dunbar's poems is difficult to assess.
It is easy to make fun of earlier scholars who read every poem as a fragment
of autobiography, believing that in 'My hartis tresure' (12) Dunbar finally
abandoned thoughts of love, or that 'This nycht befoir the dawing cleir' (55)
reveals that he was once a Franciscan. We are better informed now about
the degree of convention in these and other poems. Yet it is ludicrous to
divorce all that Dunbar wrote from his own life. When he spoke of his
'pensioun', this was fact not fiction; and his oft-voiced desire for a benefice
was far from imaginary. It is desirable, though not easy, to discriminate
between poems wholly shaped by convention and those which use the conventions to say something relating to his own experience. The 'I'-figure of
some poems (e.g. 64 and 66) is merely a mouthpiece for orthodox morality;

the 'I' of 'I that in heill wes' speaks for Dunbar himself as well as Everyman. There is clearly some role-playing—as of a melancholy clown—even in the petitions to the king, yet it is in these that we hear Dunbar's most intimate and private-sounding voice. When he says in one of them (42), 'In sum pairt of my selffe I pleinye', we should believe him.

Douglas is exceptional among early Scottish poets for his learning. He abounds in references to other writers, telling us whom he likes and dislikes, praising Virgil's 'maist excellent buke' (Prol I, 80), or castigating Caxton's 'febil proys' (Prol V, 51). He bids us read some authors (such as Boccaccio), but to cast others (such as Caxton) contemptuously to the floor. Characteristically, when he wishes to praise his patron, he calls him a bibliophile. Henry, Lord Sinclair, is a 'fader of bukis', who

> Bukis to recollect, to reid and se,
> Has gret delyte as ever had Ptholome.
> (Prol I, 99–100)

Respect for the written word informs all Douglas's poetry. In *The Palice of Honour* he celebrates the power of literature to teach, to delight, and to preserve a knowledge of the past; but he also recognises its destructive power—there is a quirky but revealing episode when Catiline tries to sneak into the Palace of Honour through a window, and 'Tullius' strikes him down 'with ane buik' (1772). The invention of printing did not cause Douglas's love of books, but may have fostered it. He reveals an impressive awareness of new publications, consulting recently printed editions of Ovid and Virgil, and reading John Major's *History of Britain* almost as soon as it appeared.[7] Despite occasional pedantry there is great liveliness in his response to what he reads. He flytes with 'Inglis' books, translating his scorn into physical manifestations–spitting 'for dispyte', 'bytand my lip' (Prol I, 150, 252). Yet he also communicates wide and generous enthusiasms, for poetry, epic and, above all, Virgil.

Douglas had a learned circle of friends, and was aware of the passionate scholarly debates taking place on the continent. Although not strictly a Humanist (he did not read Greek, nor teach *studia humanitatis*), he shared many of the Humanists' values: an antipathy to some aspects of scholasticism, a respect for the text of ancient authors, and a belief in the high importance of the classics. He was fired by a missionary zeal, not simply to translate one particular great poem but to teach and educate his countrymen, and also to transfer to his native 'Scottis' tongue something of the richness and felicity of 'fair Latyn,/That knawyn is maste perfite langage fyne' (Prol I, 381–2). He was a translator in the widest sense—a transmitter of ideas and values. Douglas saw vernacular poetry not as something wholly divorced from that written in Latin, but as inheriting the same rich tradition. The central section of *The Palice of Honour* is dominated by the Muses and their procession.

Symbolically placed at the very end appear three English and three Scottish poets (one of whom is Dunbar); beside the multitude of Latin authors their number is small, yet they are all equally followers of the Muses. Douglas also puts himself there, half-comically and half-seriously, as an aspirant poet, who has much to learn. Douglas often represents himself as a follower of Virgil, which is true in a double sense: as a translator he follows Virgil's words closely; as a poet he sees Virgil as a model, and aspires to write in that great tradition which Chaucer introduced to Britain and which flowered in Spenser and Milton. Douglas had high ambitions. At the beginning of his career he represented poetry as his personal road to honour; at its end he proudly claimed that his work would bring him immortality, and that he would be read 'Throw owt the ile yclepit Albyon' (*Conclusio*, 11). He saw his poetry as having public importance, of value to Scotland as well as to himself.

The Palice of Honour (*c*.1501) employs an ancient form, the allegorical dream, to explore the nature of honour, its connection with love and poetry, and its distinction from fame, or glory. This was a topic that had long interested moralists, but peculiarly fascinated poets from the fourteenth to the sixteenth century, who frequently deified Honour, and placed him in temples, castles and palaces. (At this time, as Francoise Joukovsky remarks, 'les séjours d'Honneur sont toujours pleins. C'est l'hôtellerie du siècle'!)[8] In November 1501 elaborate pageants welcomed Katherine of Aragon to London; in one, placed upon a throne, the figure of Honour declaimed that many pursued him but failed through lack of virtue. Honour was Virtue's reward.[9] Douglas makes a similar point, at greater length, but far more imaginatively. The dreamer encounters three processions, led by Minerva, Diana, and Venus, who are making their way towards the palace of Honour. He joins a fourth procession, that of the Muses, and learns eventually that virtuous Honour, which is immortal, must be distinguished from 'eirdlie gloir', which is vain and transient. Yet such a brief summary fails to do justice to the poem's complexity. Douglas's notion of honour has caused some puzzlement. At times he seems to equate Honour with the Christian God, and his abode with heaven. But Honour's palace accommodates Venus, the Muses, Hercules, Robert Bruce, and—more surprisingly—Medusa and Semiramis. Douglas here follows a tradition that regarded Medusa and Semiramis, along with the Amazons, as heroic representatives of women; according to one contemporary French poet, they defended 'a l'espee l'honn-eur des dames'.[10] In thus peopling the inmost court with heroes of both sexes Douglas gives pre-eminence to heroic honour, won by martial virtue, or valour. This is fore-shadowed in earlier parts of the poem, which is studded with 'knichtlie deidis', tournaments, and 'battellis intestine'. Among the Muses Douglas gives priority to Calliope, who inspires epic poets to write of heroes, 'in kinglie style, quhilk dois thair fame incres' (878). Douglas's great contemporary, Erasmus, wrote on a theme more congenial to many modern readers—*dulce bellum inexpertis*. But the ideas here expressed by Douglas were probably more acceptable to his own age. The king to whom he dedicated the poem delighted in tournaments, and by a sad irony his own fame largely rests upon his courageous but foolhardy death at Flodden.

At a climactic point, when the dreamer first sees the palace, his guide promises him 'fouth of sentence' (1401).'Fouth', or a rich copiousness, of words and things, is the most striking feature of *The Palice of Honour*. Douglas characteristically uses words like 'repleit' or 'pleneist' to signify approval. He likes to be all-inclusive—the Muses' court contains 'Everie famous poeit men may devine' (850). The poem abounds in lists, of sages and lovers, rivers and mountains. The palace itself well illustrates his descriptive technique—idealised, glistening with precious metals, outdoing Troy or Solomon's Temple, and crowded with small architectural details:

Pinnakillis, fyellis, turnpekkis mony one,	[finials] [spiral stairs]
Gilt birneist torris, quhilk like to Phebus schone,	[?towers]
Skarsment, reprise, corbell and battellingis . . .	[horizontal ledge] [stone indentation]
(1432–34)	

But this modish late-Gothic edifice is set in a timeless landscape, recalling the earthly paradise:

I saw ane plane of peirles pulchritude
Quhairin aboundit alkin thingis gude,
Spice, wine, corne, oyle, tre, frute, flour, herbis grene,
All foullis, beistis, birdis and alkin fude,
All maner fisches, baith of sey and flude,
War keipit in pondis of poleist silver schene,
With purifyit water, as of the cristall clene.
(1414–20)

Douglas's favourite verbal ornament is *repetitio*, yet he is also mindful of another rhetorical category, *dispositio*. *The Palice of Honour* is a carefully composed and remarkably patterned poem. Douglas delights in symmetry, both in small features (the English trio of poets matching the Scottish one), and in large, such as the series of processions, all led by divinities. Yet again and again such parallelism highlights differences: the scantiness of Diana's court humorously contrasts with the multitude that follows Venus; and the dreamer's response varies significantly—mingled fear and delight at the sight of Venus, unqualified joy at the arrival of the Muses. Despite its symmetry *The Palice of Honour* is full of surprises. The basic pattern is that of the quest, Honour being the 'finall end' (1248), to which all, including the dreamer, are travelling. But it is a journey with many detours and interruptions—the digression on the properties of sound, for instance, where we learn that fish cannot hear, 'For as we se richt few of thame hes eiris' (377), or the comical incident, when the poet angers Venus and fears metamorphosis into 'a beir, a bair, ane oule, ane aip' (741). The poem abounds in odd, freakish, and sometimes terrifying images. The presiding deities (with the significant exception of the Muses) are often wrathful. As a dream *The Palice of Honour* hovers between celestial vision and nightmare.

The story of Aeneas was extremely popular in the Middle Ages, but to those who could not read Latin *The Aeneid* was known only through partial or abridged versions, in which the characters of Dido and Aeneas were distorted and striking changes of emphasis occurred. In the early 1500s no major classic had yet been translated into English. Douglas's *Eneados* (1512–13) was thus a pioneering work: it was a translation, not a loose paraphrase, of the whole *Aeneid*; and it was based directly on Virgil not on some intermediary version. Douglas was aware of both novelty and the magnitude of his undertaking, and voiced pithy criticisms of the perversion of the *Aeneid* published by Caxton:

> It has na thing ado tharwith, God wait,
> Ne na mair lyke than the devill and Sanct Austyne.
> (Prol I, 142–3)

He proudly asserts his own fidelity to Virgil: 'Rycht so am I to Virgillis text ybund' (Prol I, 299). But in the sixteenth century 'Virgillis text' was rather different from that we read today. The edition that Douglas used, almost certainly that published by Jodocus Badius Ascensius in 1501, differed from a modern one in wording as well as in spelling and punctuation; it omitted or inserted whole lines, and completed some of the famous half-lines. Any assessment of Douglas's accuracy as a translator must take account of this. Many apparent blunders or barbarisms originated not in his ignorance but in the peculiarities of his Latin text. Much else in *The Eneados* that might seem extraneous is modelled on the lay-out and contents of contemporary editions of Virgil, such as the marginal commentaries or the *monosticha argumenta* (twelve one-line summaries of the different books). Douglas's decision to translate the so-called Thirteenth Book, written by the Italian humanist, Maffeo Vegio, might well seem inconsistent, but we should remember that it formed a regular supplement to *The Aeneid* in almost all editions from 1470 to the seventeenth century.

Douglas's scholarly zeal also affects his style. His undoubted diffuseness springs partly from his innate love of 'fouth', partly from an intense desire to convey Virgil's 'sentence', i.e. to draw out the full implications of even the smallest word. When Virgil calls the treacherous Sinon *turbatus* and *pavitans* (*Aeneid*, II, 67 and 107) his dissimulation is largely contextual; but Douglas leaves us in no doubt, translating as '*semyng* ful rad [terrified]', and 'quakand...*as it had bene* for dreid' (II, ii.18 and 88). Again and again he thus explains Virgil's hints and ambiguities, making explicit what is implicit in the Latin. He gains clarity and introduces vivid details of his own, but often loses Virgil's brevity and rich suggestiveness. The relationship between *The Eneados* and *The Aeneid* has been much discussed, and Douglas's achievement compared to that of later translators, such as Surrey and Dryden. But critics sometimes ask us to consider *The Eneados* as a work of art in its own right. This poses a difficult question. How do we divorce *The Eneados* from *The Aeneid*, when story, larger structural features, and major themes all derive from Virgil? Douglas took great pride in retaining the proportions of his original, and invited his detractors to compare his work to Virgil's. His own contribution is essentially a matter of expression—he gives us Virgil 'in the langage of Scottis natioun' (Prol I, 103). In fact his language is inventive and remarkably wide-ranging: sometimes he uses harsh onomatopoeic words, of storms or bird-cries, sometimes he anticipates Milton in his use of sonorous Latinisms. Not surprisingly he is most successful when given an opportunity to do what is most congenial to him—descriptions of the natural world, for instance, or portraits, such as that of Venus, disguised as 'a wild hunteres/With wynd waving hir haris lowsit of tres' (I, vi.25–6), and Charon:

Terribil of schap and sluggart of array,	[slovenly]
Apon his chyn feil cannos harys gray,	[hoary]
Lyart feltrit tatis; with burnand eyn red,	[grizzled] [matted tufts]
Lyk twa fyre blesys fixit in his hed.	[brands]
(VI, v.9–12)	

Douglas provided each book of *The Eneados* with a Prologue, and paid a leisurely farewell to it in a series of epistles and epilogues. Anyone new to Douglas should start with these Prologues; designed chiefly to introduce readers to Virgil, they form an excellent introduction to Douglas himself. Their variety is startling: one Prologue contains only three stanzas, but many run into hundreds of lines; metrically, they range from the elaborate thirteen-line alliterative stanza of Prologue VIII to the five-beat couplet adopted for the translation itself. Their tone and contents are so varied that critics debate how closely they are integrated with the translation, whether some were written for a different purpose, and whether it would be better to regard them as independent poems. Some indeed, such as Prologues X and XI, form virtually self-contained essays on moral or theological themes. Yet many other Prologues, particularly the first six, are highly relevant to the books they introduce. Subtle attempts to fit the Prologues into a pre-meditated, over-all scheme, calendric or thematic, are not convincing. What unity they possess seems more casual and organic, proceeding from Douglas and his pre-occupations—in particular his enthusiasm for Virgil and his view of translation as a great and creative enterprise. One persistent theme arises from the tension in Douglas between poet and churchman; almost every Prologue touches on this in some way. Prologue I opens with a magnificent eulogy of Virgil, 'of Latyn poetis prynce', but corrects this significantly with a later prayer:

Thou prynce of poetis, I the mercy cry,	
I meyn thou Kyng of Kyngis, Lord Etern,	
Thou be my muse, my gydar and laid stern	[load star]
. . . .	
In Criste is all my traste, and hevynnys queyn.	[trust]
(Prol I, 452–54; 462)	

For the Christian, Virgil and his pagan inspiration are ultimately transcended by Christ.

Since the eighteenth century the so-called 'Nature Prologues' (VII, XII and XIII) have been particularly admired. In the past it was claimed that they sprang from Douglas's direct experience of nature. But books were an important element in Douglas's experience. It does not detract from his originality to note how these Prologues were partly shaped by his reading of Chaucer and Henryson, as well as Virgil's *Georgics*, Ovid's dawn descriptions, or the storm scenes of alliterative poetry. No vernacular poet before Douglas (or for long afterwards) described the natural world so well, or devoted so much space to it. Grand panoramic vistas are combined with accurate observation of tiny details. Long before Hopkins Douglas delights in dappled things—flowers, 'depart in freklys red and quhite' (Prol XII, 111), or the 'dapill grey' of a lawn, powdered with daisies (Prol XIII, 177–8). Prologue VII opens with a vivid but composite image of winter: the eye is led from the heavens down to earth, from mountain tops, 'slekit with snaw', to muddy roads and the activity of 'Puyr lauboraris and bissy husband men'. Yet the final focus is upon the poet, preparing for bed and later awakening:

Fast by my chalmyr, in heich wysnyt treis,	[shrivelled]
The soir gled quhislis lowd with mony a pew:	[red kite]
Quhar by the day was dawyn weil I knew,	[dawned]
Bad beit the fyre and the candill alyght,	[kindle]
Syne blissyt me, and in my wedis dyght,	[blessed] [dressed]
A schot wyndo onschet a litill on char,	[hinged window] [ajar]
Persavyt the mornyng bla, wan and har	[livid] [frosty]
. . . .	
The schot I closit, and drew inwart in hy,	
Chyvirrand for cald, the sesson was so snell,	[Shivering] [cold]
Schupe with hayt flambe to fleym the fresyng fell.	[Attempted] [banish]
(124 ff.)	

The subject might better be termed 'Poet in a wintry landscape' than 'winter'. So too with Prologue XIII—the description of a June night, beautiful though it is, is primarily a frame for the dreaming poet. (It has striking parallels of structure with Prologue VIII, including the topos of the weary poet, anxious to finish his 'buke'.) Douglas's chief purpose is to justify his inclusion of the Thirteenth Book, which he accomplishes, skilfully and humorously, in the dream-dialogue with its author, Maffeo Vegio. Prologue XII is dominated by the splendid image of the sun as monarch, making a triumphal progress, and receiving the homage of his subjects, who hail him as 'master and rewlar of the yer'. It celebrates 'dame Nature' at her most fecund and benign, the month is 'hailsum May', and the season not spring (as repeatedly stated) but the first day of summer (Douglas speaks of the 'lang symmyris day' in line 93; cf. also 204). Of the three, Prologue XII is the most whole-heartedly a 'nature poem'.

The 'after-life' of these two poets has been as contrasted as their poetry. Douglas's works were printed in the sixteenth century, in England as well as Scotland, and clearly influenced later poets, notably Surrey and Sackville. From then to the present day there has been continuous critical awareness of 'the learned bishop of Dunkeld'. Dunbar had a very different fate. Although Lindsay testified to his contemporary fame, there is almost complete silence about him in the later sixteenth century, and throughout the seventeenth century. Dunbar's re-discovery was initiated by the publication of some of his poems in Ramsay's *Ever Green* (1724); thenceforth there was ever-growing critical interest and admiration. Scott called him 'the darling of the Scottish Muses'; to Crabbe he was the 'giant' fore-runner of Burns. What is the present standing of these poets? Douglas's name has always been linked with that of Virgil; although this once aided his reputation, sadly this is no longer true. Today there is increasing appreciation of him not just as a translator but as an original poet, with wayward slightly eccentric gifts. It is perhaps revealing that his greatest twentieth-century admirer was Ezra Pound.[11] Dunbar is probably better-known, and to a wider range of modern readers. His admirers include Eliot and Auden, as well as Hugh MacDiarmid, who—when he sought a sophisticated, unsentimental and non-English model for Scottish poets—chose as his rallying-cry, 'Not Burns—Dunbar!'.[12] But it is a measure of Dunbar's remarkable variety that he seems to mean strikingly different things to different critics, who concur chiefly on the energy and brilliance of his language.

NOTES

1   R F Green, *Poets and Princepleasers* (Toronto, 1980) is enlightening on the condition of authors in the households of late-Mediæval kings.

2   *See* Priscilla Bawcutt, 'Did Gavin Douglas write *King Hart*?', *Medium Aevum*, 28 (1959), 31–47; Florence Ridley, 'Did Gawin Douglas write *King Hart*?', *Speculum*, 34 (1959), 402–12.

3   Quotations are from Kinsley's 1979 edition of Dunbar. Poems are identified by their number in this edition, and by their first line, except in the few cases where the title is well-established.

4   *See* G Olson, 'Making and Poetry in the Age of Chaucer', *Comparative Literature*, 31 (1979), 272–90.

5   Kinsley, following the Maitland text, reads ȝour, but the Reidpeth MS preserves the correct ȝow.

6   *English Literature in the Sixteenth Century* (Oxford, 1954), p 94.

7   *See* Sandra Cairns, '*The Palice of Honour* of Gavin Douglas, Ovid and Raffaello Regio's Commentary on Ovid's *Metamorphoses*', *Res Publica Litterarum*, 7 (1984), 17–38; and Bawcutt, 'The "Library" of Gavin Douglas' in *Bards and Makars*, A J Aitken *et al.* (eds) (Glasgow, 1977), pp 107–26.

8   *La Gloire dans la Poésie Française et Néolatine du XVIᵉ Siècle* (Geneva, 1969), p 527.

9   S Anglo, 'The London Pageants for the Reception of Katherine of Aragon', *Journal of the Warburg and Courtauld Institutes*, 26 (1963), 53–89.

10 *La Chasse d'Amours* [1509], M B Winn (ed) (Geneva, 1984), p 373.

11 *See* Ronald E Thomas, ' "Ere he his goddis brocht in Latio": on Pound's Appreciation of Gavin Douglas', *Paideuma*, 9 (1980), 509–17.

12 *Albyn, or Scotland and the Future* (London, 1927), p 35.

FURTHER READING

PRIMARY TEXTS

Dunbar

Kinsley, James (ed), *The Poems of William Dunbar* (Oxford, 1979)
Mackenzie, W Mackay, *The Poems of William Dunbar* (London, 1932); revised by
    B Dickins (1960)
Small, John, with Gregor, W, and Mackay, A J G (eds), *The Poems of William Dunbar*,
    STS, 3 vols (Edinburgh and London, 1884–93)

Douglas

Bawcutt, Priscilla (ed), *The Shorter Poems of Gavin Douglas*, STS (Edinburgh and
    London, 1967)
Coldwell, David F C (ed), *Virgil's Aeneid Translated into Scottish Verse by Gavin
    Douglas*, STS, 4 vols (Edinburgh and London, 1957–64)
—— (ed), *Selections from Gavin Douglas* (Oxford, 1964)
Small, John (ed), *The Poetical Works of Gavin Douglas*, 4 vols (Edinburgh, 1874)

SECONDARY TEXTS

General

Aitken, A J, 'The Language of Older Scots Poetry', in *Scotland and the Lowland
    Tongue*, McClure, J D (ed) (Aberdeen, 1983), pp 18–49
Durkan, John, 'The Cultural Background in Sixteenth-Century Scotland', in *Essays
    on the Scottish Reformation 1513–1625*, McRoberts, David (ed) (Glasgow, 1962),
    pp 274–331
Fox, Denton, 'The Scottish Chaucerians', in *Chaucer and Chaucerians*, Brewer, D S
    (ed) (London, 1966), pp 164–200
Kratzmann, Gregory, *Anglo-Scottish Literary Relationships 1430–1550* (Cambridge,
    1980)
MacQueen, John, 'Some Aspects of the Early Renaissance in Scotland', *FMLS*, 3
    (1967), 201–22

Dunbar

Bawcutt, Priscilla, 'Aspects of Dunbar's Imagery', in *Chaucer and Middle English
    Studies*, Rowland, B (ed) (London, 1974), pp 190–200
—— 'The Text and Interpretation of Dunbar', *Medium Aevum*, 50 (1981), 88–98
—— 'The Art of Flyting', *SLJ*, 10(2) (1983), 5–24
Baxter, J W, *William Dunbar: a Biographical Study* (Edinburgh, 1952)

Fox, Denton, 'Dunbar's *The Golden Targe*', *ELH*, 26 (1959), 311–34

—— 'The Chronology of William Dunbar', *Philological Quarterly*, 39 (1960), 413–25

McDiarmid, M P, 'The Early William Dunbar and his Poems', *SHR*, 59 (1980), 138–58

Morgan, Edwin, 'Dunbar and the Language of Poetry', *Essays in Criticism*, 2 (1952), 138–58

Reiss, Edmund, *William Dunbar* (Boston, 1979)

Ross, Ian S, *William Dunbar* (Leiden, 1981)

Roth, Elizabeth, 'Criticism and Taste: Readings of Dunbar's *Tretis*', *SLJ*, suppl. 15 (1981), 57–90

Scott, Tom, *Dunbar: a Critical Exposition of the Poems* (Edinburgh, 1966)

Douglas

Bawcutt, Priscilla, 'Gavin Douglas and Chaucer', *Review of English Studies*, New Series 21 (1970), 401–21

—— 'Gavin Douglas and The Text of Virgil', *Edinburgh Bibliographical Society Transactions*, IV.6 (1973), 213–31

—— 'Douglas and Surrey: Translators of Virgil', *Essays and Studies*, 27 (1974), 52–67

—— *Gavin Douglas: a Critical Study* (Edinburgh, 1976)

Blyth, Charles, 'Gavin Douglas's Prologues of Natural Description', *Philological Quarterly*, 49 (1970), 164–77

Ebin, Lois, 'The Role of the Narrator in the Prologues to Gavin Douglas's *Eneados*', *Chaucer Review*, 14 (1980), 353–65

Fowler, Alastair, 'Virgil for every gentil Scot', *TLS* (22 July, 1977), 882–83

Nitecki, Alicia K, 'Gavin Douglas's Rural Muse', in *Proceedings of the Third International Conference on Scottish Language and Literature* (*Medieval and Renaissance*), Lyall, Roderick J, and Riddy, Felicity (Stirling/Glasgow, 1981), pp 383–95

Norton-Smith, J, 'Ekphrasis as a Stylistic Element in Douglas's *Palis of Honour*, *Medium Aevum*, 48 (1979), 240–53

Starkey, Penelope, 'Gavin Douglas's *Eneados*: Dilemmas in the Nature Prologues', *SSL*, 11 (1973–74), 82–98

Chapter 6

Religious Poetry in Middle Scots

ALASDAIR A MACDONALD

INTRODUCTORY

To a very large extent, Middle Scots literature is the creation of churchmen. In the period of roughly two hundred years which stretches from Barbour's *Bruce* to the deposition of Queen Mary, the number of known poets not in at least minor orders is small: of these James I (if the author of the *Kingis Quair*), Blind Hary (?), Sir David Lindsay and Sir Richard Maitland are the most important. One may therefore be surprised that religious verse does not occupy a more prominent position in that literature. The pre-Reformation cleric poets, of course, were usually writing to commission, thereby placating the secular tastes of their respective patrons. And in the post-Reformation age secular subjects once again predominate; but this is only to be expected, since, under James VI, poet-clergymen—such as Alexander Hume and James Melville—were now the exception. Only during the two decades in the middle of the sixteenth century did religion become the principal theme of Scottish verse, albeit that much of this verse is marked by Reformation propaganda and polemic. Neither is the religious verse of Mediæval Scotland vivid in the modern memory: if the *Oxford Book of Scottish Verse* may be taken as an indication of the received impression today, the only significant religious poems of the period are a couple of lyrics by Dunbar, and a few items from the *Gude and Godlie Ballatis*.

There is, however, more. The large manuscript collections—Selden B 24, Asloan, Arundel 285, Bannatyne, Maitland Folio and Quarto—contain a sizeable amount of anonymous religious verse, and this forms an essential context for the productions of the named masters. Also contributing to this context are Scotticised versions of English religious poems by authors known (e.g. Lydgate) and unknown. Moreover, there are several lengthy religious compositions which, though generally ignored by critics, deserve to be rescued from the penumbra: the collection of saints' legends once attributed to Barbour; the *Contemplacioun of Synnaris* of the Franciscan William of Touris; Walter Kennedy's *Passioun of Crist* in Arundel 285; and *Ane Schersing Out of Trew Felicitie* of John Stewart of Baldynneis. With these works included, the corpus of Middle Scots religious verse becomes not inconsiderable; and this is still to leave out of account the bulk of moral verse which in practice is often difficult to distinguish from poetry of the purely religious sort.

Religious poetry habitually consists of expressions of, or exhortations to, devotion, and the most profitable critical approaches are functionalistic and generic. From the literary viewpoint, distinctions of doctrine are of minor importance, and the following discussion brings both Catholic and Protestant poetry together in a single conspectus. Though the framework of belief was modified by the Reformation, the literary modes continued: the dream allegory used by Stewart of Baldynneis in *Ane Schersing* has a long ancestry, and affective piety may be found in both the Catholic poems of Arundel 285 and in the Protestant *Gude and Godlie Ballatis*. Nonetheless, the Reformation did have two important effects upon Scottish religious verse: there was a reduction in the range of potential subject-matter (most obviously in that which related to Mary), with a compensatory development of poems declaring the contrite sinner's anxious hopes of salvation; and there was also a change in the characteristic expression, whereby plainness of style came to be prized more highly than traditional colours of rhetoric. Both before and after the Reformation, however, one can find exceptions to this generalisation, and in any case such changes are matters more of emphasis than of essence.

The Reformation impinges upon another quite different, but most important, problem—that of texts. Large numbers of Middle English religious lyrics are preserved in the marginalia of monastic manuscripts, in collections made by friars, and in the pages of sermons; one would therefore naturally suppose this to be true of Scotland also. However, to take the example of one very common Mediæval form—the carol—there is nothing in Scotland to compare with the multitude of English specimens, and the lacuna must be presumed to be the consequence of the Reformers' wilful destructiveness. The same iconoclastic zeal was responsible for the total loss of the texts of the Scottish vernacular religious drama, the popularity of which now has to be inferred from record sources alone. In the late fifteenth and early sixteenth centuries there was a fashion for Books of Hours, and for similar compilations of devotional texts in the vernacular (perhaps an indication of the growth of lay literacy). Arundel 285 is a representative of this kind of text, but it is impossible not to believe that there were many more. To the extent that the losses of texts were great, the resulting picture of Middle Scots religious verse must be commensurately distorted. Distortion may also be seen in the detail of the surviving texts. Dunbar's penitential poem, 'To the, O marcifull salviour myn, Jesus' (K6), found in Arundel 285, is also included in two post-Reformation anthologies—the Bannatyne (twice) and Maitland Folio manuscripts. While the Maitland scribe first began to copy out two lines of a stanza on the seven sacraments, until he realised the danger and simply scored the lines out, Bannatyne (more subtly) revised Dunbar's verses so that only two sacraments should appear. In the cases of other poems also—most extensively with his excerpt from the *Contemplacioun of Synnaris*, itself perhaps the first work of Middle Scots verse to be printed (Westminster, 1499)—Bannatyne anticipated hostile reactions to doctrinally-sensitive lines, and made many fascinating alterations. While such censorship is deplorable, the scribe may nonetheless be commended for his efforts to preserve the best religious poetry of the past in changed circumstances.

Furthermore, while the essentially retrospective collections of Bannatyne and Maitland have preserved religious poetry of a high level of literary artistry, there is a striking lack of the humbler, more utilitarian kinds—such as versifications of standard prayers. With the exception of the Scottish saints' legends (CUL Gg.II.6) and Arundel 285, all the extant manuscript anthologies of verse are known to come from secular circles, and it is unsafe to assume that these collections necessarily provide a fair reflection of the totality of religious verse existing at the time of compilation. Thus, although we are fortunate in still having the short, brilliant religious poems of Dunbar, there is almost no trace of the brief, anonymous lyrics so common in England in the thirteenth and fourteenth centuries. What survives, therefore, is the part which must be taken for the whole; yet, while awareness of the state of affairs with contemporary literatures (English, French, Latin, Gaelic) may encourage extrapolation, the *argumentum ex silentio* must be used with caution.

BACKGROUND

Though churchmen produced the Middle Scots religious poetry, they were not the intended audience. The Prologue to the saints' legends attacks the sin of idleness on the part of those who administer state and church, and a reference to the *Roman de la Rose* suggests that the author had the court in mind. These legends, as a mirror of holy life, had a strongly didactic purpose, and one may imagine them as being read aloud by a churchman in the king's hall or chapel. In view of the official position of Latin in the church, religious literature in the vernacular almost automatically implies (a) extraliturgical use, and (b) a lay audience. Almost automatically, because there is some evidence that in the late Middle Ages certain groups, such as houses of female religious, were permitted to follow the services in translation. Dunbar's Wedo (K14), who took to church an illuminated volume (probably manuscript, and big enough to spread on her knees), may supply, if incidentally, testimony to a similar practice among the rising bourgeoisie; one will recall that she seems to be familiar with saints' legends, the genre of which she declares her marital torments and triumphs to be a parody. Although the use of vernacular in the canon of the mass was impossible, it was an option in certain other situations: for example, in sermons destined for non-clerical ears, and in substitutes for specific set-phrases, such as 'benedicamus domino' (one reason why these phrases abound in Middle English lyrics). Vernacular religious verse could also lend itself to such occasions as outdoor preachings, banquets in the halls of the king and the nobility, Yule morning salutations in the king's bedchamber, ceremonial royal entries (such as those of Margaret Tudor into Edinburgh and Aberdeen), religious drama, and launchings of ships. (In 1506 minstrels were paid at the launching of the *Margaret*; it is possible that a poem in honour of the saint would have been sung.) Historical records confirm the occurrence of such public events: evidence is lacking, however, for the use of vernacular religious verse in the home devotions of private individuals—an activity to be assumed in many God-fearing house-holds, and especially in those (like that of the king) provided with chaplains. For this kind of worshipper the texts in Arundel 285 would have been eminently appropriate; indeed, these coincide to a large extent with the normal contents of Books of Hours—of which the one owned by James IV and his consort (Austrian National Library, codex 1897) is such a splendid specimen.

The cultivation of religious verse in late-Mediæval Scotland is both a token and a consequence of the heightened piety generally prevalent in the late fifteenth century. Observant Franciscanism arrived from the Low Countries in the 1450s, in the wake of James II's bride, Mary of Gueldres, and it retained the royal favour of Jameses III, IV and V. By the end of the century there were some dozen foundations organised in a Scottish province; coexisting with these were the older Conventuals, and the other orders of friars. The preaching activities of the mendicants, especially the Observant Franciscans and the Dominicans, were invaluable in spreading the word to—almost literally—the man in the street, but they had just as much success with the nobility and the royal family: James IV and James V drew their confessors from the Observant house in Stirling (founded 1494). Parallel to this was the influence of the *Devotio Moderna*, the movement associated with Geert Grote, Thomas à Kempis and Jan Standonck. This movement had a spiritually quickening effect originally upon the population of the towns along the Yssel valley, but it subsequently spread to the rest of the Low Countries, and thence to Louvain and Paris, where it was experienced by Scottish clerics such as Alexander Mylne, Abbot of Cambuskenneth, and Robert Richardson (Robertus Richardinus). Other contributory factors were the omnipresent and ever-increasing *Mariaverehrung* of the fifteenth and early sixteenth cen-turies, and the development of new liturgical feasts (e.g. in honour of the Five Wounds, the Crown of Thorns, the Holy Name). Religious guilds, a phenomenon of the late Middle Ages, could, with their own altars, chaplains and cult of saints, bring the laity into close co-operation with the ecclesiastics, and the new religious fervour could find public outing in spectacular processions with vestments, relics and banners (of which the Fetternear Banner is a solitary survival), and private expression in the devotion of the Rosary, as well as in the regular celebration of the votive mass for the dead. This was also a remarkable period of church construction—as witness the university and collegiate churches of St Salvator (St Andrews) and St Mary (King's, Aberdeen), the highly decorated chapel of St Matthew at Roslin, and the refoundation of the Chapel Royal at Stirling (1501). Several non-university collegiate churches (e.g. Biggar) were founded, and other humbler churches raised to collegiate status. All this bespeaks a vigour of religious life hard to imagine for anyone subscribing to the traditional view of the etiolated con-dition of the pre-Reformation church.

If Mediæval Scottish culture was church-inspired, it was also court-centred, and, as far as literature is concerned, there is not much that does not emanate from the royal (and ecclesiastical) centres of Edinburgh, Stirling, Dunfermline and St Andrews. The obvious reason for this is the sovereign's near monopoly of patronage (although, especially in the fifteenth century, a few members of the nobility also played that role). Relative prosperity, after all, was a precondition of literary production—the works of Dunbar providing the most telling illustration of this nexus. Where religious literature could voice or direct the piety of the monarch himself, circumstances were most propitious, and this was particularly the case during the reign of James IV, who would seem to have been smitten by sincere, if intermittent, guilt at his part in the rebellion which overthrew his father in 1488. In expiation of this and doubtless other offences, James went every Easter on retreat to his favourite convent—the house of the Observants in Stirling. Dunbar's facetious parody of the *Officium Defunctorum* (K22) clearly arises from this custom of the king's; it has recently been argued that the (altogether serious) *Contemplacioun of Synnaris* of William of Touris is likewise to be connected with the days spent by the king among the Stirling Franciscans. Moreover, it is also quite likely that Walter Kennedy's *Passioun of Crist* was intended for royal ears. In the Prologue the author complains that men are keener on literature dealing with the Crusades, the Trojan War, or the conquests of Alexander than on religious subjects. While there may be an element of convention here, Kennedy is unquestionably aiming his sights at courtly literature, and this in turn probably implies a courtly audience for his own poem. One might, moreover, wonder for whom Dunbar composed his 'Tabill of Confessioun' (K6): for the same youthful James IV for whom John Ireland (Johannes de Irlandia), author of a prose 'Table of confessioun' in the Asloan MS., composed his *Meroure of Wysdome*? Later in the sixteenth century, Stewart of Baldynneis certainly intended his long religious poem, *Ane Schersing*, for the delectation of James VI. As a general rule it may be said that nearly all the long works of religious verse in this period would have been composed to order, and/or in the hope of incurring royal favour (whether of king or queen).

With the shorter poems it is a little different. The Protestant collections of the 1560s—Robert Norvell's *Meroure of an Christiane* and the *Gude and Godlie Ballatis* (with its verse Commandments, Creed, Sacraments, Psalms, etc.)—were obviously not intended for the court. Indeed, the preface to the third edition of the latter speaks of reaching 'young personis, and sic as ar not exercisit in the Scriptures'. What of the short religious lyrics now preserved in the first section of the Bannatyne MS? These are not, it must be stressed, the spontaneous outpourings of powerful feelings on the part of their creators: like other works of Mediæval art, they would be devised to do, rather than to be, and it is the critic's task to disover a context and a function which may account for them.

Most of these poems have been grouped by George Bannatyne in three classes: 'ballatis of the nativitie'; 'cantilenae de passione'; and 'cantilenae de resurrectione'. Such an arrangement, under christological headings, suggests a literary sequence on the life of Christ, a structure highly suitable for post-Reformation circumstances. Several factors, however, deter one from too readily assuming this to have been the original function. Not a few of these poems, to judge from their forceful expression ('Jerusalem, rejos for joy'; 'Done is a battell on the dragon blak'; K4), seem peculiarly apt for public delivery; several use the words of Latin antiphons as refrains; the average length—around forty lines—is compatible with performance (where texts are to be read silently, length is immaterial); one or two allude to singing, and the choice of imagery may be surmised to be an indicator of the function. All these features may be seen in Dunbar's Nativity lyric, 'Rorate celi desuper' (K1), and the other poems of this type may be tentatively assigned to the same period—the age of James IV—and may have been intended for performance on any of the public occasions mentioned above. However, it is even more likely that their function was connected in some way with the Chapel Royal. James was proud of this institution (in Stirling Castle), which maintained forty choristers, and which was deliberately designed as a counterpart to the English Chapel at Windsor. It is altogether probable that music and public performance were essential dimensions of the Scottish religious lyric verse which burgeoned at the beginning of the sixteenth century. James's Chapel Royal furnishes an obvious social context for those poems, providing a motivation for composition and opportunities for artistic treatment in a courtly milieu. Such lyrics would in no way have competed with the Office hymns and psalms, but, as anthems, would have served as additional attractions on certain occasions. It should not be forgotten that music, as part of the *quadrivium*, played an important role in the education of the time (in Song Schools and College), and James's reign was a high-point in the history of Scottish church music, with the polyphonic style which, slightly later, was to be unfavourably contrasted by Robert Richardson with the ancient, Gregorian simplicity.

The music inside the Chapel Royal may be assumed to have been solemn and highly contrived. Outside, there would have been the partsongs typical of the Renaissance, and the simpler melodies of carols, dance-songs, and folksongs. It became the fashion in mid century to adapt religious verse to such melodies—as is seen in Maitland's 'Ballat of the creatioun of the warld' (Bannatyne, II, 26–32), set to the tune of the 'Bankis of Helicon', and in a large number of the *Gude and Godlie Ballatis*. To these may be added the tunes (French, English, and some Scottish) used for the singing of vernacular psalms in and out of Protestant churches. In sum, even where specific evidence is lacking one should consider music, both before and after the Reformation, to be a likely—and at least possible—dimension of almost any shortish religious poem, especially if composed in stanzas. Needless to say, this information is not recoverable from the manuscript verse anthologies, which preserve words alone (an exception is the so-called 'St Andrews Psalter' of Thomas Wode, which records much of the courtly musical culture of the age of Mary and later). It is surely no accident that it is the musical quality of certain Middle Scots religious lyrics which has impressed the critics.

THE POETIC PRACTICE

A multitude of classifications and subdivisions is possible within such a subject as religious verse, but for the Middle Scots specimens a simpler approach may suffice, involving a pragmatic trichotomy of poems of meditation, of celebration, and of argument. These categories, however, which are rhetorically based, are not 'watertight', and many poems could be ranged under more than one.

The works in the first group pose a challenge to some post-Romantic notions of the nature of poetry. Here the essential thing is the concept of the poem as exercise, by means of which the soul of the meditator may be brought into better condition. The devout recitation of familiar prayers is a direct way of attaining this result, and here, therefore, belong versifications of the *Pater Noster*, *Ave Maria* and *Credo*, such as those jotted down on one folio of the Makculloch MS. The style here is plain, and such works aim at little more than the adequate rendering of the Latin originals. One may contrast the economical version of the *Magnificat* in the *Gude and Godlie Ballatis* (pp 143–44) with the one in the Bannatyne MS. (II, 60–63); the latter, for which no author's name is given, is in fact taken from Lydgate's *Life of Our Lady* (this section may have circulated independently, however), and is in the English poet's typically expansive style. One reason for the popularity of prayer texts in pre-Reformation days is that they not infrequently carried an indulgence. Thus the second of the Middle English prayers to the Holy Name in Arundel 285 (the first being a well-known poem of Richard de Caistre) could come graced with an indulgence of 'Pope Innocent'; the poem, 'Ave, cuius concepcio'—rendered in Arundel as 'Haill, Mary, quhais concepcioun'—could, when said with other prayers, provoke 11,000 years of indulgence; and the poem, 'I pray yow, lady, Mary deir', is a Scottish version of the prose prayer, *Obsecro te, domina sancta Maria*, which regularly promised more than 500 years of pardon and an appearance of Our Lady before death (Arundel, pp xviii, xx–xxii).

Reiteration of such prayers, though mechanical, can only increase the beneficial effect. The best illustration of this procedure is the devotion of the Rosary, which, because of its great popularity in late-Mediæval Scotland, even makes an appearance in the visual arts. No Middle Scots versification is extant, but the Gaelic lyric, 'A phaidrín do dhúisg mo dhéar' [Thou rosary that hast waked my tear], in the Book of the Dean of Lismore, is eloquent testimony to the power of the Rosary to stimulate the emotions. A Marian application of the Rosary structure is evident in the Arundel prose texts, *The Three Rois Garlandis* and *The Lang Rosair*, and Dunbar's ornate, seven-stanza elaboration of the Angelic Salutation ('Ave Maria, gracia plena': K2) should probably be associated with such texts (pp 299–321, 322–34, 4–7). The iterative technique is seen in the remaining Arundel prose texts, and also in the verse *XV Ois* (pp 170–81), of which Lydgate also composed a version. Such texts—like the pilgrims' labyrinth in Chartres cathedral—operate by setting mental (or physical) tasks for the individual, whereby the erratic mind may learn to concentrate upon the divine purpose.

Other texts used for this kind of meditation are Dunbar's 'Tabill of Confessioun' (which is comprehensive in its listing of sins in order to be applicable to every reader), and the poem, 'O Lord God, O Crist Jesu', which is a versification of a prose prayer in honour of the Seven Words (Arundel, pp

1–6, 259–61). Still others make an imaginative linkage with liturgical practice, such as the Hours of Our Lady ('Quhat dollour persit our Ladyis hert') and the Seven Hours of the Cross ('Compatience persis, reuth and marcy stoundis': pp 234–36, 255–57). In different ways, this also applies to the two long works: William of Touris's *Contemplacioun of Synnaris* and Walter Kennedy's *Passioun of Crist*. The seven sections of the former correspond to the days of the week (as with the influential *Meditationes Vitae Christi* of pseudo-Bona-ventura, and with the Arundel *Remembrance of the Passion*), in which the Passion falls, appropriately, on Friday; the latter disposes the events of the end of Christ's life on earth according to the Office Hours, and the unique, Arundel text is equipped with rubrics, so that, whenever one reads the poem, it is impossible to forget the church's celebration of Holy Week.

These works confront the reader with memorable subjects from *Heilsge-schichte*, they invest all their rhetorical energy in arousing strong emotional reactions to those subjects, and they lead to an imprinting of those subjects upon the memory. The meditation may be triggered by the sight of a crucifix (as in Dunbar's 'Amang thir freiris within ane cloister': K3), or by the reproaches of the crucified Christ (as in two English 'complaints of Christ' in Arundel 285, of which the first is by Lydgate, while the second appears also in the Towneley Plays: pp 266–69, 270–74, 261–65). In visual art, the Image of Pity (*imago pietatis*) and the *Arma Christi* had a comparable effect, and the Friday section of the *Contemplacioun of Synnaris*, as the first lines imply, begins with an illustration of the Passion (the other sections also have illustrations to stimulate meditation upon their respective subjects: the world; man; death; judgement; [the Passion]; hell; heaven—the general eschatological focus is notable). The following lines reveal precisely how the reader's imaginative reaction is to be aroused, directed and applied:

> Be divers maneris into thi mynd revolf
> How till imprent his pietuous passioun,
> And ask at God thi herd hert to resolf
> In teris of volabill lamentacioun,   [copious]
> To taist the rute of that confectioun;   [medicinal preparation]
> And, in thi hert, with devoit deligence,
> Graif deipe his dede be trew intencioun,   [death]
> And of his panis have inlie compassioun.
>
> (937–44)

In Middle Scots verse perhaps the most powerful expression of such a reaction is the lyrical passage in the *Passioun of Crist*, wherein the reader/spectator, at the moment of Christ's death, bursts into a moving threnody, each stanza concluding with the poignant word, 'allace'.

Although Arundel 285 is the richest Scottish source of such verse meditations, there are several similarly conceived poems in the Bannatyne MS. ('My wofull hairt me stoundis throw the vanis' of 'Clerk'; 'O man, remember and prent in to thy thocht' of 'Stewart'; 'O creaturis creat of me your creator' of pseudo-Lydgate: II, 77–79, 90–95, 105–08), in the *Gude and Godlie Ballatis*

('Till Christ, quhome I am haldin for to lufe'; 'Rycht sore opprest I am with panis smart': pp 59–61, 62–63), and elsewhere: one of the most accomplished is Henryson's poem on the Annunciation, which takes its text from a paradox of Solomon's (Cant. 8:6) 'Forcy as deith is likand lufe'. The following Arundel lyric (p 298) is sufficiently short to be quoted in its entirety:

> Haill, quene of hevin and sterne of blis,   [star]
> Sen that thi sone thi fader is,   [since]
> How suld he ony thing the warn,   [reproach]
> And thou his mothir and he thi barne?
>
> Haill, fresche fontane that springis new,
> The rute and crope of all vertu,
> Thou polist gem without offence,
> Thou bair the lambe of innocence.

The whole poem—which, formally considered, comprises a prayer for the reader, who is in a position to rehearse and share the devout thoughts of the original, anomymous author—redounds to the praise of Mary. The first stanza wittily but decorously plays with the relationships within the Trinity and the Holy Family, and the images listed in the second stanza emphasise ideas of purity, fertility, beauty and innocence, all of which find in Mary their summation. Novelty has no place in such a work of art; rather, familiar motifs are felicitously recombined in the interests of devotion. In works such as this, the mental habits and literary techniques of meditation have produced some of the best poetry in Mediæval Scotland.

Under the label, 'poems of celebration', one may group the works which take certain important episodes in the life of Christ as their starting-point, and which record the joy of the poet at those events. The majority deal with the Nativity and the Resurrection—themes which link the Catholic and Protestant periods. Poems with Marian connections, however, were liable to suppression—for example, the Resurrection lyric preserved in Arundel 285: 'O mothir of God, involat virgin Mary' (pp 274–75). Again, the two opening poems in the Bannatyne Draft MS. (I, 3–10) have the Annunciation as their subject: the first, by John Bellenden, is in the main Bannatyne MS. given the innocuous title of 'The Benner of Peetie', although in the Mitchell Library *Scotichronicon* MS. it is headed, 'Ane ballat of the cuming of Crist and of the annunciatioun of Our Ladye'; the second is, oddly but discreetly, banished to the very end of the first section of the main Bannatyne MS.

Characteristic of this kind of poem is the use of a public, exclamatory tone in the speaking voice, a regular use of exhortations and imperatives, and a resort to aureate vocabulary. These features appear in such splendid poems as: 'Now glaidith every liffis creature'; 'Rorate celi desuper' (K1); 'Jerusalem, rejos for joy'; 'Omnipotent fader, sone and haly gaist'; and 'The sterne is rissin of our redemptioun' (all in the group of Bannatyne's Nativity lyrics: II, 63–64, 65–66, 66–68, 75, 76–77); 'To the hie potent blisfull trinitie'; and 'Eternall king that sittis in hevin so hie': II, 95–96, 100–01). The poet's sense of exultation can become infectious, and may even appear to lead to an anachronistic participation of the audience in the events of the Biblical narrative:

> Al follow we the sterne of most brichtnes,
> With the thre blisfull orientall kingis,
> The sterne of day, voyder of dirknes,   [dispeller]
> Abone all steiris, planeitis, speiris and singis,   [spheres] [signs (of zodiac)]
> Beseiking him fra quhome all mercy springis
> Us to ressave with mirth of angell soun
> In to the hevin quhair the imperiall ringis: [reigns]
> The stern is rissin of our redemptioun.

Other Bannatyne poems dispense with aureation, while retaining Latin refrains ('Haill, Goddis sone, of mychtis maist'; 'We that ar bocht with Chrystis blude'; 'Surrexit dominus de sepulchro'). For its part, Dunbar's Resurrection lyric, 'Done is a battell on the dragon blak' (K4), exploits to the full the rhetorical possibilities of alliteration and parataxis (II, 68–71, 71–74, 87–88, 88–89).

Mutatis mutandis, the celebratory poems in the *Gude and Godlie Ballatis* strive for essentially similar effects, albeit usually with shorter lines, simpler stanza forms (deriving from popular songs, the melodies of which continued to be used for religious *contrafacta*), and homely diction. Several are translations from the *Geistliche Lieder* of Luther, or from other German sources, and artfully suggest the simple piety found also in the Middle English carols, but which has otherwise vanished from the Scottish record:

> My saull and lyfe, stand up and se,
> Quha lyis in ane cribbe of tre: [wood]
> Quhat babe is that, sa gude and fair?
> It is Christ, Goddis son and air.
>   ('I come from hevin to tell' 25–28)

This collection contains the earliest version of 'In dulci jubilo' (p 53) in any form of English, and in this poem, with its juxtaposition of the ecclesiastical and vernacular languages, we see a happy transmission of fifteenth-century Catholic verse into the new age of Reform.

Vernacular renderings of psalms, although not unknown in Mediæval times, enjoyed an extraordinary vogue among Protestant sympathisers, for whom they became a staple of public worship. The first Scottish examples are those found in the *Gude and Godlie Ballatis* (pp 85–131, 136–37, 161–62), and three (whereof two by Alexander Scott) find their way into the Bannatyne MS. (II, 33–34, 38–42). Among the Castalians, the Catholic Alexander Montgomerie (in his *Mindes Melodie*) and King James VI continued the practice. The impetus here came from the Protestants' enthusiastic return to the Scriptures—an inspiration responsible also for the new genre of Biblical paraphrase, seen in the songs 'of the Scripture'/'as it is writtin in ... Sanct Luc'/'of the Evangell' in the *Gude and Godlie Ballatis*, and in George Makeson's halting attempts at versifying Genesis (this from 1554). The 'Ballat of the creatioun of the warld' by the courtly poet, Sir Richard Maitland of Lethington, however, which is itself grounded upon part of Lindsay's lengthy poetic outline of world history, *The Monarche*, shows that Biblical paraphrase and elegant expression were not necessarily incompatible. The Scottish vernacular psalms on the whole exist at a higher level of artistry than those of the Englishmen, Sternhold and Hopkins; unfortunately, however, they were not simple enough to gain wide currency.

'Poems of argument' is a portmanteau term chosen to cover the remaining sorts of verse, which mostly lack the controlled subjectivity of meditation and the loud exuberance of celebration. Here may be grouped articulations of doctrine, recommendations to the life of faith and virtue, confessions of the troubled conscience, and comments on contemporary religious politics. However, I omit from discussion here the spate of satirical ballads which poured from the pen of Robert Sempill and others in the quarter-century after 1560. As an exposition of the teaching of the church, it would be hard to better the grave, latinate dignity of Bishop Gavin Douglas, whose Prologue to the tenth book of *The Eneados* is incorporated as a religious 'lyric' by George Bannatyne (II, 20–26):

> Thy maist supreme, indivisible substance
> In ane natur—three personis but discrepance
> Rignand eterne—ressavis nane accidence:
> For quhy thow art, richt at this tyme present,
> It that thow wes, and ever sall, but variance.
>
> (21–25)

On the other hand, when, in the *Gude and Godlie Ballatis*, Calvinistic theology is set to verse and technical terms suddenly oust aureate expression, the result can be poetically grotesque:

> Remember, Lord, my greit fragillitie,
> Remember, Lord, thy sonnis Passioun;
> For I am borne with all iniquitie,
> And can not help my awin salvatioun:
> Thairfoir is my justificatioun
> Be Christ, quhilk cled him with my nature,
> To saif from schame all sinfull creature.
>
> ('Rycht sore opprest' 22–28)

Indeed, the temptation to dogmatise is all too seldom resisted in post-Reformation verse: among the rare successes, however, one might mention Stewart of Baldynneis's *Ane Schersing Out of Trew Felicitie*, in its rather antiquated dream-vision mode, and Alexander Hume's hymning of nature as the beautiful handiwork of God, in 'Of the Day Estivall'.

Throughout the sixteenth century one can find poems which urge the reader to be devout: Dunbar's 'O synfull man, thir ar the forty dayis' (K5), the anonymous 'Thow that in prayeris hes bene lent' (Arundel, pp 257–59, 275–

76), and a host of edifying verses in the *Gude and Godlie Ballatis*. The same observation applies to poems voicing an awareness of sin (often in the proximity of death). These range in style from the tautness of 'O hicht of hicht and licht of licht most cleir' (Bannatyne, II, 52), through the lumpish phraseology of Robert Norvell's translations (in which the shrill expression of Protestant doctrine makes an unfortunate contrast with the poetic grace of his model, Clément Marot), to the emotionalism of 'With weippin eis and face defigurat' (Maitland Quarto, 251). While Protestant religious verse excluded many traditional subjects, this one theme flourished, and continued into later centuries: no post-Reformation poet, however, was able to bring to it the verbal craftsmanship of Henryson's 'Prayer for the Pest', and the proliferation of such confession poems imparts a gloomy tone to much of the religious verse of the later sixteenth century.

This survey may be concluded with a brief notice of poems—an innovation of the mid century—which discuss the state of the church, although these really take one from the religious to the historical. Here belong such vigorous squibs as 'With huntis up', 'The bischop of Hely brak his neck,' 'Of the fals fyre of purgatorie,' 'God send everie preist ane wyfe,' and the egregious propaganda-piece, 'The Paip, that pagane full of pryde' (*GGB*, pp 174–77, 180–82, 186–87, 188–89, 204–07). Though the success of such pieces of invective cannot be gainsaid, their hectoring tones should not be allowed to drown out the voices of poets who refused to prostitute their muse to faction. Alexander Scott, for example, deals out even-handed criticism to both Catholics and Protestants in his New Year (1562) greetings to Queen Mary (Bannatyne, II, 235–42), and William Lauder does likewise, in his *Godlie Tractate or Mirrour* (1567). Such exceptional works, however, could not vie with the *Gude and Godlie Ballatis* in the ability to ingratiate popular taste, and it was that very successful collection, with its many editions between 1565 and 1621, which stamped itself upon the memories of three generations of Scottish readers.

FURTHER READING

PRIMARY TEXTS

(For Dunbar, Henryson, *Asloan MS*, *Bannatyne MS*, *Maitland Folio and Quarto MSS*, *Makculloch MS*, see General Bibliography)

Bennett, J A W (ed), Arundel MS. 285 in *Devotional Pieces in Verse and Prose*, STS (Edinburgh and London, 1955)
Cranstoun, James (ed), *Satirical Poems of the Time of the Reformation*, STS, 2 vols (Edinburgh and London, 1891–93)
Crockett, Thomas (ed), *The Poems of John Stewart of Baldynneis*, STS (Edinburgh and London, 1913)
Furnivall, F J (ed), *The Minor Poems of William Lauder*, EETS (London, 1870)
de Irlandia, Johannes, *The Meroure of Wysdome*, MacPherson, Charles, and Quinn, F (eds), STS, 2 vols (Edinburgh and London, 1926–65)
Makeson, George, *see* Hans H Meier, 'A Pre-Reformation Biblical Paraphrase', *Innes Review*, 17 (1966), 11–23
Meditationes Vitae Christi, see Love, Nicholas, *The Mirrour of the Blessed Lyf of Jesu Christ*, Powell, L F (ed) (London, 1908)
Metcalfe, W M (ed), *Legends of the Saints*, STS, 3 vols (Edinburgh and London, 1896)
Mitchell, A F (ed), *The Gude and Godlie Ballatis*, STS (Edinburgh and London, 1897)
Norvell, Robert, *The Meroure of an Christiane* (Edinburgh, 1561)
Richardinus, Robertus, *Commentary on the Rule of St Augustine*, Coulton, G G, SHS (Edinburgh, 1935)
Schipper, J (ed), *The Poems of Walter Kennedy* (Vienna, 1901)
Stevenson, T G (ed), *The Sempill Ballates* (Edinburgh, 1872)

SECONDARY TEXTS

Literary Studies

Beattie, William, 'Some Early Scottish Books', in *The Scottish Tradition*, Barrow, G W S (ed) (Edinburgh, 1974). On Norvell
Bennett, J A W, *Poetry of the Passion* (Oxford, 1982)
Gray, Douglas, *Themes and Images in the Medieval Religious Lyric* (London, 1972)
MacDonald, Alasdair A, 'The Middle Scots Religious Lyrics', PhD diss. (Edinburgh, 1978)
—— 'Poetry, Politics and Reformation Censorship in Sixteenth-Century Scotland', *English Studies*, 64 (1983), 410–21
—— 'Catholic Devotion into Protestant Lyric: the Case of the *Contemplacioun of Synnaris*', *Innes Review*, 35 (1984), 58–87

—— 'The Bannatyne Manuscript—A Marian Anthology', *Innes Review*, 37 (1986), 36–47

Woolf, Rosemary, The English Religious Lyric in the Middle Ages (Oxford, 1968)

Religious Background

Bryce, William Moir, *The Scottish Grey Friars*, 2 vols (Edinburgh and London, 1909)

Carter, Charles, 'The *Arma Christi* in Scotland'. *Proceedings of the Society of Antiquaries of Scotland*, 90 (1956–57), 116–29

Cowan, Ian B, *The Scottish Reformation* (London, 1982)

—— and Easson, David E, *Medieval Religious Houses: Scotland*, 2nd edn (London, 1976)

Donaldson, Gordon, *The Scottish Reformation* (Cambridge, 1960)

Durkan, John, 'Education in the Century of the Reformation', in *Essays on the Scottish Reformation*, McRoberts, David (ed) (Glasgow, 1962)

—— 'The Observant Franciscan Province in Scotland', *Innes Review*, 35 (1984), 51–57

McRoberts, David, 'The Rosary in Scotland', *Innes Review*, 23 (1972), 80–86

—— *The Fetternear Banner* (Glasgow, n.d.)

Pfaff, R W, *New Liturgical Feasts in Later Medieval England* (Oxford, 1970)

Post, R R, *The Modern Devotion* (Leiden, 1968)

Ross, Anthony, 'Some Notes on the Religious Orders in Pre-Reformation Scotland', in *Essays on the Scottish Reformation*, McRoberts, David (ed) (Glasgow, 1962)

Music

Elliott, Kenneth and Shire, Helena Mennie (eds), 'Music of Scotland 1500–1700', *Musica Britannica* XV, 3rd edn (London, 1975)

Gilchrist, Anne G, 'Sacred Parodies of Secular Folk Songs', *Journal of the English Folk Dance and Song Society*, 3 (1936–39), 157–82

Harrison, Frank L, *Music in Medieval Britain* (London, 1958)

le Huray, Peter, *Music and the Reformation in England 1549–1600*, revd edn (Cambridge, 1978)

MacQueen, John, Introduction to *Ballattis of Luve* (Edinburgh, 1970)

Murdoch, Brian, 'The Hymns of Martin Luther in the *Gude and Godlie Ballatis*', *SSL*, 12 (1974–75), 92–109

Patrick, Millar, *Four Centuries of Scottish Psalmody* (London, 1949)

Shire, Helena Mennie, *Song, Dance and Poetry of the Court of Scotland under King James VI* (Cambridge, 1969)

Chapter 7

Sixteenth-Century Secular Poetry

GREGORY KRATZMANN

For Scottish secular poetry of the sixteenth century the years 1513 and 1584 have come to acquire a kind of symbolic status, just as they have for the history of the period. What most would regard as the most ambitious poem of the later Middle Ages in Scotland—Gavin Douglas's translation of *The Aeneid*—was completed only a matter of weeks before the traumatic defeat of the Scots at Flodden. The reign of James IV, often described as Scotland's 'aureate age', is coeval with the poetry of Douglas and Dunbar, whom literary historians have generally regarded as the premier poets of the sixteenth century. If 1513 has been seen as the *terminus ad quem* of the finest period of Scots poetic making, 1584 has been seen as a new *terminus a quo*, when at the outset of James VI's personal rule the young king's *Reulis and Cautelis* was written as part of a programme aimed at the establishment of a poetic Renaissance in Scotland, one intended to graft the styles of Ronsard, du Bellay and du Bartas upon the stock of native tradition.

What, then, of the seven decades between these *termini*, the one delimiting the high innovation and rich variety of Henryson, Dunbar, and Douglas, the other pointing forward to the copious if sometimes bombastic rhetorical glories of Montgomerie, Fowler, Stewart of Baldynneis and the king himself? Even after allowance has been made for the distortions and simplifications which may result from literary history's passion for schemata (such as classifying very different kinds of poetry on the basis of the reign in which they were written) and for vague designation (Mediæval/Renaissance), most readers would agree that the secular poetry of these seventy years falls short of the achievements of the earlier part of the century, at least when the evaluative criteria of originality of thought and originality of expression are simultaneously applied. Yet the middle years of the sixteenth century are not a poetic desert, and the effort of trying to comprehend the poetry on its own terms is one well worth making. I do not intend to undertake a chronological survey here, but rather to focus upon the poetry and collections of poetry associated with the years 1567 and 1568. Within the most turbulent century of Scottish cultural and political history this is a particularly turbulent time, its events both dramatic and decisive. For however unequivocal the enactments of the Reformation Parliament of 1560 may have seemed, it was not until seven years later, when Mary had been compelled to flee from Scotland as the result of the chaotic web of events involving the murder of Darnley, the precipitate marriage to Bothwell, and her capture by the Confederate Lords, that the reformed church attained the status of legal establishment. In poetry, the events of 1567–68 evoked a stream of highly articulate polemical poems (generally underrated by modern commentators), which can be read as a secular, political counterpart to the new strain of devotional poetry represented by the *Gude and Godlie Ballatis*, also printed in 1567. Before looking at some of these political poems, though, I intend to comment on two extremely significant literary phenomena of the year 1568, which in their different ways both reflect an impulse to conserve the poetry of an earlier generation: the first of these is the 1568 Edinburgh edition of Lindsay's *Warkis*, printed by John Scot for Henry Charteris, the second the vast 'ballat buik' completed by George Bannatyne 'in tyme of pest' during the last three months of 1568, although probably begun at least three years earlier.

Lindsay's poems were written during the reign of James V and part of the subsequent regency (c.1528–52). They had been printed before, whether singly or in collections, but in 1568 the time was clearly opportune for a publisher who was both astute entrepreneur and committed Protestant to bring out such an ambitious volume as the *Warkis*.[1] Charteris's *Preface* and its pendant 'Adhortatioun of all Estatis' (the latter showing him to be a competent poet in his own right) reflect a keen critical appreciation of at least part of Lindsay's appeal. One aspect of this is the accessibility of Lindsay's poetry, which although capable of rising to impressive rhetorical heights when the occasion requires (and one such occasion is parody), inclines more to a middle style of eloquence than the verse of the predecessors whom he admired so greatly. In Lindsay's last, longest, and most ambitious poem, *Ane Dialogue betwix Experience and ane Courteour* (1548–53), the elaborate rhetoric of the *locus amoenus* dream prologue (itself an essay in a tradition inherited from Douglas and Dunbar) gives way quite dramatically to a style of Gowerian plainness when the Dialogue itself begins. The stanzaic opening of Book I comments upon this mode, in its spirited defence of the 'vulgair toung' as a medium for poetic edification. Lindsay's address to an audience of unlearned folk suggests something more deeply-felt than the usual modesty topos (as he employs it himself in *The Testament of the Papyngo*, which is addressed to 'rurall folke' and 'landwart lassis')[2]

> Quharefore to colyearis, cairtaris, & to cukis,   [colliers]
> To Jok and Thome, my Ryme sall be diractit,
> With cunnyng men quhowbeit it wylbe lactit.   [condemned]
>
> Thocht every commoun may nocht be one clerk,
> Nor hes no leid except thare toung maternall,   [language]
> Quhy suld of God the marvellous hevinly werk
> Be hid frome thame? I thynk it nocht fraternall.
>   (549–55)

The plainness of Lindsay's language is, no doubt, one of the reasons which explain the continued popularity of his verse for the next two centuries, but more important is the broad sweep of its socio-political reference. He is, *par excellence*, the Scots estates satirist, and Charteris's 'Adhortatioun' reflects a judicious appreciation of the range of Lindsay's address. Poems such as the *Dreme*, *The Testament of the Papyngo*, and *Ane Dialogue* are studded with passages of direct address, and Charteris's invitation to the potential readership of the *Warkis* is an extension of Lindsay's own practice: the 'Adhortatioun' addresses princes, lairds, flatterers, idolators, lawyers, craftsmen, merchants, and courtiers, but the most memorable stroke of all is directed at the professionally uncommitted: 'Cum, nouchtie newtrallis with your bailfull band!' (50). Charteris's eagerness to claim Lindsay as a Reformer is apparent throughout his Preface: while recognising the force with which the poetry attacks the irregularities of the temporal estates, Charteris's main emphasis falls upon Lindsay as satirist of the spiritual estate, 'being sa bludie, & cruell boucheouris'. The *Warkis* are offered to the readers of 1568 in the hope that God 'will rais and steir up mony David Lyndesayis' whose writings will be 'ane prik and spur to the verteous and godlie'.

This interpretation of Lindsay's work by the values of a newly secure reformed faith is not accompanied by the degree of distortion which marks mid-sixteenth-century English reformation readings of *Piers Plowman*. Lindsay (1490–1555) was for the readers of 1568 a poet of the recent past, and the poetry offers a great deal which is congenial to the spirit of the reformed kirk—particularly *Ane Dialogue*, where the account of the five empires or monarchies of universal history is carefully pointed towards the flagrant abuses of the present age—in particular, the materialism and sensuality of the prelacy, who have been corrupted by a degenerate papacy. The poem, unlike anything he had written before (including *Ane Satyre of the Thrie Estaits*) attacks belief in 'that marvelois monstour callit Purgatorye', which is now seen as a popish confidence trick (4771–98): with this should be compared the much more muted criticism in the *Dreme*, written two decades earlier (337–50). Pilgrimages and the devotion paid to images are also condemned from the mouth of Experience:

> Off Edinburgh the gret Idolatrye
> And manifest abominatioun,
> On thare feist day, all creature may se...
> (2501–03)

The difference in spirit between *Ane Satyre* and *Ane Dialogue* is epitomised in the different characterisations of the friars: in the play, Flatterie's wiles are the subject of a satire which is at times almost genial, but in the poem most of the Doctor Friars are condemned as 'memberis of the Antichrist' and 'auld bosis of perditione' (2573, 2579).

Charteris's Preface invites a response to Lindsay's poetry as something more than trenchant and wide-ranging satire, however: it recognises his very considerable achievement as the successor to Douglas and Dunbar as a master of poetic language (both are mentioned, along with Kennedy, in Charteris's 'Adhortatioun'). A taste for wit, craft and originality is evinced by reference to 'plesand and delectabill versis', 'craftie and ingenious poeticall inventionis' and later by praise of 'ornate style', 'plesand proverbis', and 'weil waillit wordis, wyse and familiar,/of queynt convoy'.) This challenges the standard view that Calvinist readers were interested exclusively in what was sententious and improving, even though there is probably some truth in Sir Walter Scott's generalisation that the Reformation's 'tendency . . . to polemical discussion discouraged lighter and gayer studies'. Readers of Charteris's *Warkis* were treated again to what is arguably Lindsay's most delightful poem, *The Testament of the Papyngo*, which had been printed several times before, both in Scotland and in England. Written in about 1530, the poem is a superbly crafted melange of genres practised by Lindsay's predecessors in secular poetry: introduced by a first-person vision style prologue, the poem alludes to the interrelated traditions of *speculum principis*, *de casibus*, verse epistle, national history, and satire. Lindsay's gift for dramatic fable suggests a lesson well-learned from Henryson. After the aureate polysyllables of the *locus amoenus* opening, the bathos of the narrator's address to his royal charge is richly entertaining:

> Sweit bird, said I, be war, mont nocht ouer hie;
> Returne in tyme; perchance thy feit may failye;
> Thou art rycht fat, and nocht weill usit to fle;
> The gredie gled, I dreid, scho the assailye.   [kite]
>
> (157–60)

The 'gredie gled' figures prominently as a friar in the second half of the poem, where he shows a Lowrence-like capacity for *double entendre* in answering the papyngo's charges of chicken-stealing:

> I grant, said he; that hen was my gude freind,
> And I that chekin tuke, bot for my teind.   [tithe]
>
> (680–81)

The poem's concern for reform is manifested in several poetic modes: through direct address in the dying papyngo's epistle to James V, a combination of direct address and historical exempla in the address to the nobility, and finally, through fable, where the reader might have expected a similar epistle directed to the spiritual estate. This final part of the poem is a compelling dramatic satire on the decadence of the church, which manages to invite both a measure of sympathy for the papyngo's false spiritual custodians (for example, in the raven-monk's accusation of the 'temporall Prencis', 980 ff.) and a sense of pathos in the account of the overweight and overweening courtier's end. The subjects of Lindsay's anticlerical satire are similar to those of *Ane Dialogue*, but it would seem by 1550 he felt that it was inappropriate for a poem about universal reformation to employ anything but the barest superstructure of poetic fiction. Not all of Lindsay's writing was, of course, motivated by reformist impulses. *The Historie and Testament of Squyer Meldrum*, which belongs to the same period as *Ane Dialogue* but which was not included among the *Warkis*, is a verse biographical romance, an essay in the tradition of the *Bruce* and the *Wallace*. It remains one of the most undeservedly neglected poems of the sixteenth century, a tale of chivalric and romantic action which shows a new development of that gift for dramatic impersonation which is so memorably embodied in *The Papyngo* and *Ane Satyre of the Thrie Estaits*. The bold mixture of pagan and Christian frameworks in the 'Testament' section of the *Papyngo* is repeated in Meldrum's testament, but here the blend of humour and pathos has a new ingredient of personal reminiscence, notably in the character's address to his 'freind Sir David Lyndsay of the Mont' and his farewell to the ladies of Craigfergus and Stratherne. Although Charteris may well have known the as yet unprinted *Squyer Meldrum* (he alludes to Lindsay's 'frutefull and commodious Historyis, baith humane and divine, baith recent and ancient') it is hardly surprising that he could not accommodate it within a *Warkis* which was to support the cause of reform.

The omission of *Squyer Meldrum* from that other great literary monument of 1568, the Bannatyne manuscript, is perhaps more surprising, even if one does not share Sir Walter Scott's view of the young George Bannatyne's altruistic grand design (Scott wrote of Bannatyne's 'courageous energy to form and execute the plan of saving the literature of a whole nation'). It seems likely that Bannatyne did not include any other of Lindsay's poems because of the appearance of Charteris's *Warkis* in the same year that his own anthology, which had been in preparation for several years, was completed. The old view that Bannatyne prepared his collection with a view to having it printed has recently been interestingly revived by Alasdair MacDonald, who suggests that the manuscript was originally conceived as a collection appropriate to the years of Mary's personal reign (stemming from a collection of courtly poems), but no longer suitable for the press in 1568, despite its careful assembly and its subsequent 'fascinatingly devious accommodations to the deteriorating political and religious climate of the last two years of Mary's reign'.[3] Bannatyne, at a late stage in the preparation of his manuscript, did however include 'interludes' from *Ane Satyre of the Thrie Estaits* in the 'ballettis mirry' section. The most radical aspect of his editing is his omission of most of the topicality and specificity of the play as we know it in the printed text of 1602. Discussion of the manuscript's text of Lindsay's play is beyond the scope of this chapter, although it may be noted that Bannatyne's practice in minimising topical and controversial matter seems consistent with his general principles of selection and design.[4] Although several poems of quite recent date (for example, works by Scott, Montgomerie, Maitland and Baldwin) are included, the collection in its 1568 form has a strongly retrospective and moderate complexion. Of the political satire associated with the name of Robert Sempill (1530–*c*.1595), for example, there is no sign, although from the inclusion of three pieces to which the name Sempill is attached, it may be inferred that Bannatyne had no objection to broadside verse *per se*. These 'Sempill' items in the 'ballettis mirry' section of the manuscript are clever and entertaining pieces of bawdy, which deserve to be freed from the censures of nineteenth-century editors. One of them, 'The Defence of Crissell Sandelandis',[5] is a spirited address to the hypocritical magistrates of the new kirk who have confined a woman on suspicion of adultery with a minister. It is regrettable that the identity of the men named in the poem (including a sympathetic lawyer called James Bannatyne) cannot be established. The language has a sexual explicitness reminiscent of the Wedo's speech in Dunbar's *Tretis*, combined with the kind of topical directness found in some of Lindsay's addresses to James V; the malice would appear to owe less to literary convention than to the writer's personal sense of grievance:

> In your tolbuth sic presouneris to plant
> Wilbe ressavit weill, ye may considder;
> Gud Captane Adamsone will nocht lat thame want
> Bedding, howbeit thay sould lig all togidder.   [lie]
> As for his wyf, I wald ye sould forbid hir
> Hir eyndling toyis: I trow thair be no denger,   [jealous]
> Because his lome is larbour grown and lidder,   [penis] [worn out] [impotent]
> But undirstanding now to treit ane strenger.
>
> (89–96)

Perhaps one may be excused for wondering what was in Bannatyne's mind when he included Scott's 'Ane New Yeir Gift to the Quene Mary, quhen scho come first hame, 1562' among a group of *speculum principis* poems in the 'wisdome and moralitie' section. The other poems in the group address rulers in general, non-personal ways, and the arrangement of such a large number of them at the end of this section of the manuscript may suggest that 'in making the compilation, he was thinking in the first instance of the royal patron and a court audience'.[6] The poem has been praised, justly, because of its adaptation of familiar Mediæval conventions of occasional poetry to meet the needs of the particular, and complex, political situation of Mary's return to Scotland to begin her personal reign. As a poem of 1562 'Ane New Yeir Gift' is remarkable for its even-handed attitude to present realities; the young Catholic queen is reminded of the superstitious turpitude of the old clergy which it is her duty to keep at bay ('To ordour this the office now is thyne'), but at the same time she is to suppress that new graven image 'callit cuvatyce of geir' which is worshipped by too many of those who call themselves reformers:

> Protestandis takis the freiris auld antetewme,   [text]
> Reddie ressavaris, bot to rander nocht;
> So lairdis upliftis mennis leifing ouir they rewme,   [realm]
> And ar rycht crabit quhen thai crave thame ocht.
>
> (145–8)

The young widow is reminded of her duty to 'gett ane gude man' so that the old prophecy about the ruler of a united Britain may be fulfilled. Bannatyne may have copied the poem in 1565 or even earlier, but the fact that he did not excise it in 1568 is striking: Mary's first 'gude man' had recently been murdered (Bannatyne includes at least one love poem by 'King Hary

Stewart'), she had been forced to flee in the company of a second for whom little 'gude' was said, and so retrospectively Scott's optimism for the future of the reign seems sadly ironic ('So salbe welth and weilfaire without wo'). Does the poem remain because the anthologist approved of its sentiments, as the record of a hope that was never fulfilled? Was there still some topical value—for the infant king—in the prophecy about the 'berne sould bruke all Bretane be the see'? John and Winifred MacQueen describe *Ane New Yeir Gift* as 'the most memorable expression of moderate hopes before the medieval world-order began its final disappearance'.[7] It survives only in this manuscript, and Bannatyne's inclusion may reflect an appreciation of Scott's intelligent conservatism. A similar conservative, mediating emphasis is to be detected in Bannatyne's editing of *Ane Satyre*, and also in the combination of clearly Catholic material in 'ballatis of theoligie' (Dunbar's 'Tabill of Confessioun' and the strongly Marian Nativity hymns) with devotional poetry which would appeal to Reformation sensibilities. Bannatyne's text of Henryson's *Fabillis*, in the manuscript's final section, shows some expurgating tendencies (notably in the moralitas of *The Trial of the Fox*, where it can be clearly seen how the line 'O Mary myld, mediatour of mercy meik' has been cancelled), but Bannatyne's text contains many references to Catholic forms of belief and practice which were considered unsuitable by Charteris and Bassandyne, both of whom printed the *Fabillis* only two or three years later.

If Charteris could show in his Preface to Lindsay's *Warkis* an appreciation of poetry for more than its polemical value, we should hardly wonder that a shrewd conservationist like Bannatyne should have shown in his selection and methods of arrangement such an astute understanding of the diverse nature and function of poetry. This can be very clearly seen in the final section of the manuscript, devoted to 'fabillis', notably ten parts of Henryson's Aesop and *Orpheus and Eurydice*, Holland's *The Howlat*, Dunbar's *The Thrissill and the Rois* and *The Goldyn Targe*, *The Freiris of Berwick*, and *Colkelbie Sow*. Perhaps Bannatyne observed a major deficiency in his four-part book, a deficiency of narrative material with a patently fictional cast. What these poems demonstrate, as a group, is the potential of poetic fable to encompass an extraordinary range of effects, from the sombre gravity of *The Preiching of the Swallow*, to broad comedy of manners in *The Freiris of Berwick*, and a highly sophisticated burlesque of several conventional genres in *Colkelbie Sow*. Considered together these works are a *coda* which recapitulates through narrative and allegorical means the broad thematic emphases—doctrinal, ethical, entertaining and amatory—of the preceding books, which were originally to have formed 'the haill four pairtis' of the manuscript. Most of these poems were at least half a century old when Bannatyne transcribed them afresh, and although the cultural milieu of 1568 was a vastly changed one, Bannatyne felt that they were still interesting and relevant to a post-Reformation audience. High comedy gets the last word in the collection. *Colkelbie Sow* (which I have discussed at length elsewhere)[8] is a compendium of forms and genres which had long been practised by Scottish secular poets, the mock 'low-life' tournament, the romance, the experience-innocence advisory dialogue, and of course the *exemplum*. Like so many other Scots works of the sixteenth century, it is both eclectic and reflexive, depending for a now incalculable part of its appeal upon its audience's knowledge of the conventions upon which it draws and which it intermittently parodies. Its longest piece of moralising comment concerns the proper use of one's 'fyve wittis' (728–817), but here the didactic commonplaces of such works as *Ratis Raving* and *The Thewis of Gudwemen* are comically undercut by the narrator's graphic account of his authority figure Gurgunnald ('heavy-jowelled', 'bowel-rumbling):

> In to her heid I trest was nocht a tuth.
> Thairfoir grwew most gredely eit sche   [gruel]
> And laking teith famulit hir faculte   [mumbled]
> That few folk mycht consave hir momling mouth   [mumbling]
> Bot I, that was expert thairin of youth.
>
>   (701–05)

A similar effect is created by the tendency of the Proheme to slide away from reflection on the recreation appropriate to a courtly audience to a bold claim for the indulgence of personal 'fantesy': certainly the Proheme does nothing to prepare the noble audience towards which it gestures so grandiloquently for the 'cais' of a poor man who sold his 'simple blak sow ... For penneis thre'. Play is the *raison d'être* of all three parts of the poem, and not simply the pell-mell tale of the first penny: the poet invites his audience to share his 'hirdy dirdy' fantasy of verbal revel in a fictional world where anything is possible. Although there are several early sixteenth-century references to something like the 'feist' material of Part I, the poem as preserved by Bannatyne may well be a later reworking of a familiar tale. (It is suitably placed before the equally sophisticated but more restrained pastoral comedy of 'Robene and Makyne', attributed to Henryson.) When Bannatyne appended a fifth part to his 'ballat buik' he may have been all too aware that his own generation had nothing comparable to offer in the venerable Scots tradition of the fable, and that there was a particular need for the preservation of these works.

The fourth part of the Bannatyne manuscript—'ballattis of luve'—contains a larger number of poems than any of the other four. This section of the manuscript has received most scholarly and critical attention, and it is hardly surprising that this repository of attractive short poems should have been drawn upon by anthologists over the last two centuries. Helena Shire's comment on the manuscript as a whole is particularly apposite to its fourth part—'It resembles a two-way mirror, reflecting in one direction the courtly making of the past, in another the age of change'. She goes on to remark upon the impossibility of recovering anything like a clear picture of the state of love poetry in the age prior to the Reformation, since Bannatyne's choice which 'itself conditions our idea of the scope of what had once existed' was probably itself influenced both by the disappearance of material and by the need to accommodate a shift of sensibility.[9] Bannatyne's arrangement of his material is particularly suggestive: the introductory verse offers an invitation to the reader to choose at will, immediately followed by an admonition to godliness, and the implication of this is strongly reinforced by the placing of the 'songis of luve' in the context of three sections of 'contempis' and 'remeidis'. Alexander Scott (*c*.1515–*c*.1583) is beyond doubt the major single figure of part four, and its most modern, and were it not for Bannatyne's enterprise Scott would be as shadowy as most of the poets named in 'The Lament for the Makaris' and *The Testament of the Papyngo*. Although John MacQueen's hypothesis about the development of Scott's poetic career—a development which is said to illustrate a pervasive cynicism 'merging into the religious rationalism of the Reformers'—is open to dispute,[10] it is tempting to identify a poem such as 'Quha lykis to luve' (Bannatyne CCCLXXIV) with a specific historical moment. Even if the poem was not written as late as 1568—and here the comparison of the lover's life to 'the pest and plaig that ringis' is surely suggestive—the admonition of the final stanza signals disapproval of love as a pastime which encompasses the act of poetic celebration:

> My brethir deir, we most forbeir,
> and fra this sinfull life evaid us.
> Lat Ressoun steir your hairtis inteir
> and nocht thoill lathly lust to leid us,   [endure] [loathsome]
> quhilk is the verry net
> that Satane for us set
> to caus us quyt foryet
>   the Lord that maid us.
>   (42–49)

Yet there is a tension between this lesson of forbearance and the poem's formal structure: like other Scott poems, it is patently a song, although no music survives for it. In stanzaic form, rhyme and metrical pattern, 'Quha lykis to luve' corresponds exactly to an anti-romantic song whose text is reproduced in Forbes's *Songs and Fancies* (1682): this text would seem to be the 'godly' substitute of a lost complaint to Venus, the music for both of these sets of words also being the setting for Scott's 'Lament of the Master of Erskine'. Helena Shire, who discusses the latter poem but not 'Quha lykis to luve', observes that 'the emotions or attitudes associated with a tune can be important factors in the whole meaning and effect of a song'.[11] (In this context one wonders to what extent the *Gude and Godlie Ballatis* had a residual element of secularity for their first audience.) It is impossible for us to recover a clear sense of the social realities (of audience, nature of performance) which are the subtext of the sixteenth-century lyric, but it is quite likely that even Scott's most cynical and apparently disengaged love poems should be received as exercises in the game or debate of love, 'poems . . . written to order, exercises in a mode, art poetry'.[12] The moral emphasis of Bannatyne's carefully arranged selection of poems to do with love may well have resulted in the exclusion of celebratory poems in the vein of Scott's 'Up, helsum hairt', 'Rycht as the glas', and 'Quha is perfyte'. (In this context it may be worth recalling that Bannatyne decided not to include in his anthology Montgo-

merie's 'Lyk as the dum solsequium', one of the most popular of all Scots
lyrics: it appears only in a draft MS.) 'Up, helsum hairt' is full of exultant
celebration of fully shared sexual consummation, and it draws heavily on the
imagery of centuries of poetic tradition in its presentation of the lover as
Cupid's liege, rewarded for his service by the 'heritage' of the lady's heart for
which the nominal rent of 'one sallat every May' is payable. What is most
memorable about this piece is its synthesis of high rhetoric and simple colloquialism to create the illusion of a speaking voice:

> In oxteris clois we kis and cossis hairtis,   [armpits] [exchange]
> brynt in desire of amouris play and sport,
> meittand oure lustis. Spreitles we twa depertis.
> Prolong with lasir, lord, I thee exhort,   [leasure]
> sic time that we may boith tak our confort,
> first for to sleip, syne walk without espyis.
> I blame the cok. I plene the nicht is schort.
> Away I went. My wache the cuschett cryis,   [watch] [wood pigeon]
> wissing all luvaris leill to haif sic chance
> that thay may haif us in remembrance.

But for the note of self-abegnation in 'I coft hir deir, bot scho fer derrer me'
(in the preceding stanza) the poem would invite comparison with Donne's
dramatic songs.

A clear intertextual strain runs through these love-lyrics (the counterpart
to that play with the vocabulary and thought forms of aureate style which
links Dunbar and Douglas, and then Bellenden and Lindsay, or of William
Stewart's echoes of Dunbar), which goes beyond the obvious relationships
of 'paired' poems such as 'Haif hairt in hairt' (Bannatyne CCLXXV) and its
'Answeir' (Bannatyne CCXCI), and 'Hence, hairt' (Bannatyne CCXC) and
'Returne thee, hairt' (Bannatyne CCCXXVI). For example, in close proximity
to two of Bannatyne's own amatory exercises in the first part of 'ballattis of
luve' there is the very attractive lyric 'My hairt is heich aboif' (CCLXXXV).
Despite formal differences, this poem bears an affinity to 'Up, helsum hairt'
which is close enough to suggest either common authorship or clever
imitation. It illustrates the same kind of transition from rhetorical to colloquial lyricism, and the verbal parallels are close. With the stanza quoted
above we may compare:

> We interchange our hairtis in utheris armis soft,
> spreitles we twa depertis, usand our luvis oft;
> we murne quhen licht day dawis, we plene the nycht is schort,
> we curs the cok that crawis that hinderis our disport.
> I glowffin up agast quhen I hir mys on nycht   [glance]
> and in my oxster fast I find the bowster richt.   [armpit] [bolster]
> (31–40)

Such self-conscious echoing by one poem of another suggests the existence
of a cohesive and confident lyric tradition, and although the time was not

congenial to the *printing* of love poetry, it is unlikely that the troubled political and religious climate of the mid century could have entirely destroyed the taste for this kind of secular verse. The author of the *Complaynt of Scotlande* (*c*.1550) includes a number of love songs in his 'Monologue Recreative', and the very fact that a lengthy catalogue of secular tales, songs and dances should occupy such a prominent place in a work devoted to serious political and social commentary should make us wary of generalising about a *zeitgeist* which was uncongenial to non-polemical poetry. The Reformation itself should not be blamed too heavily for the apparent decline in 'courtly' poetry in the two decades after 1560: a more probable explanation is to be found in the instability of the court itself during the years of James's minority. Montgomerie's lyrics illustrate not so much a new beginning as an inventive re-interpretation of the poetic traditions represented in Bannatyne's 'ballattis of luve'.

The new poetry which was being written at the time Bannatyne completed his 'buik' and Charteris his edition of Lindsay could fittingly be labelled 'ballattis of despyit'. This kind of verse with which the name of Robert Sempill is so closely associated was printed in great quantities by the reformer Lekpreuik: so influential was it that an act of parliament was passed 'anent the makaris and upsettaris of plackardis and billis' in April 1567, in an attempt to stamp out the 'sclander, reproche, and infamye' being done to 'the Quenis Majestie and diverse of the Nobilitie'. The poems of 1567–68 take as their subjects the murder of Darnley and the Queen's marriage to Bothwell: later there is a series of laments for the death of Moray, which are followed throughout the 1570s by an exchange of invectives between Queen's and King's men. It is, presumably, the authors of these topical verse invectives (not all of whom were Protestants) that Richard Maitland (1496–1586) deplored in his 'Of the Malyce of Poyetis' (Folio MS. CV):[13]

> Dispytfull poyettis sould not tholit be   [endured]
> In commoun weillis or godlie cumpanie,
> That sorte ar ay to saw seditioun
> And putt gude men in to suspitioun.
> (39–42)

There is nothing particularly subtle about this large body of 'applied', polemical poems, but many of them deserve to be much better known, not only for their verbal dexterity but also for the way in which they (like so much other sixteenth-century Scots verse) interpret native literary conventions. They are popular literature in the sense that they attempt to address the widest possible audience, and it would be wrong to assume that their currency was restricted to the estate of kail-markat Maddie, Sempill's favourite *persona*. Many of them take the form of exhortations to the lords, and it may be assumed from Maitland's allusion to the 'mantenaris' of satirical poets that some system of patronage did exist. Most of these poems are written in styles which reflect a thorough grounding in the craft of Scottish poetry, and it may come as a surprise to see how frequently the ornate rhetorical mode occurs. One of the poems which deplores the murder of Darnley, 'To Edinburgh about vi houris at morne' (Cranstoun, III)[14] is set in the form of the *chanson d'aventure*, as the speaker listens to an elaborately rhetorical praise of Darnley's accomplishments ('In pulchritude to Paris perigall') followed by an enrolment of Mary in the legend of wicked women. The poem, which is enlivened by occasional descents into colloquialism,

> War I ane hund, o gif sho war ane hair,
> And I ane cat and sho ane lyttil mous,
> (177–78)

concludes with a dialogue between the narrator and his interlocutor which conveys a belief in the efficacy of this 'sweit figureit' style of poetry to motivate vengeance. One of the speakers declares himself to be a poet who sits beneath a hawthorn tree to write the poem which his fellow, 'ane menstrall', is to sing. A poem on the same subject, 'The Testament and Tragedie of umquhile King Henrie Stewart' (Cranstoun, IV) reflects a knowledge of the testament genre as it is employed by Lindsay. Close stylistic parallels with Lindsay's *Tragedie of Cardinall Betone* are to be found in a somewhat later poem called *The Bischoppis Lyfe and Testament*, which vigorously attacks the recently dead Archbishop Hamilton. 'Ane Exhortatioun derect to my Lord Regent and to the Rest of the Lordis Accomplisis' turns to the plainer mode of *speculum principis* discourse that is illustrated by the group of poems at the end of Bannatyne's 'wisdome and moralitie' section, as it advises its audience to 'mark the sentence rather nor the style'. This work is more general in its mode of address than some of the others, which makes the sudden specificity of the attack on the theologians of St Leonard's College very effective:

> Bot, principallie, I pray you to eject
> Ane cursit byke that cheiflie dois maling,   [swarm] [plot]
> In Abirdene, of Sophistis the welspring,
> And in thair place put learnit men of God.
> (123–26)

At the opposite end of the stylistic spectrum from the two pro-Darnley poems mentioned above is Sempill's vigorous flyting of a pro-Marian poet who had dared to attack the Regent (Cronstoun, VIII). The courtly pastime as practised by Dunbar, Lindsay and Scott is turned here to political purposes, though the flyting's conventional association with play is maintained in the ingenious internal signature advertised by the final stanza.

If there is any single broadside which deserves to be rescued from oblivion, it is *The Lamentatioun of Lady Scotland*, printed in 1572. Cranstoun dismisses it as 'one of the most tedious' works in his collection, but *The Lamentatioun* has an interest which he is not prepared to allow. The poem is an extended monologue spoken by Lady Scotland, the wife of John the Commoun-weill, driven from home by the Satanic forces of Sedition and Discord. The echo of Lindsay's Jhone the Comoun Weill, who appeared first in the *Dreme* of 1528, is unmistakable: he too wears ragged raiment, and has been driven

from Scotland by the manifestations of civil and religious disorder. The
unifying discourse is late Mediæval complaint, skilfully handled to accommodate considerable variety of style and mood. The first section (to line 148),
which begins and concludes with a sonorous high-style apostrophe to the
waters, is an allegorical account of the difference between Lady Scotland's
past and present conditions: the description of the garment here (19–28, 81–
90) recalls the mode of Henryson's 'Garmont of Gud Ladeis' and its imitation
in the Bannatyne manuscript (CCLXXVI). In the account of her children,
there is a shift towards topical allegory, as she laments the deaths of Lennox
and Moray and the subversion of Mary by 'sum curst Kittie unsell'. The
salutation to the Earl and Countess of Mar, guardians of the young king, is
expressed in terms of homely and even amusing familiarity ('gud Lord Deddy'
and 'Lady Minnie'). The second part of the poem consists of a series of
addresses to the Estates: not only the form, but also the particularity of the
language, recall Lindsay's practice in *The Papyngo*. The well-documented
problem of adapting the material structure of the old church to the pressing
needs of the new (particularly in rural parishes) receives memorable
expression in Lady Scotland's spirited criticism of the Kirk, her 'Faithfull
Mother deir':

> The parische kirkis, I mene, thay sa misgyde
> That nane for wynd and rane thairin may byde:
> Thairfoir na plesure take thay of the tempill;
> Nor yit to cum quhair nocht is to contempill   [contemplate]
> Bot crawis and dowis cryand and makand beir,   [noise]
> That nane throuchly the minister may heir;
> Baith fedders, fylth, and doung dois ly abrod,
> Quhair folk suld sit to heir the word of God.
>
> (163–70)

The address to the Commounis contains an entertaining speech from a
lawyer's wife which reflects something of Lindsay's talent for dramatic impersonation. There are some lively variations on the Lindsayan allegorical technique of lodging the vices among different occupational groups, in the account
of the burgess wives' attempts to outdo their sister's achievements as a hostess:

> Then wox the Lawers wyfe richt proud in hart;
> Bot yit hir cummers callit scho apart,   [gossips]
> Saying, 'Cummers, quhat is the caus, and quhy,
> That, in dispyte of me, ye treit Invy?'
> 'Becaus', quod thay, 'that ye alone tuik Pryde,
> And thocht that we suld not marche yow besyde;
> Thairfoir we thocht in that point ye did wrang us.'
> 'Aggre,' quod scho, 'and ludge thame baith amang us.'
> Quhilk thing thay did, and all did condiscend
> To treit and keip thame to the warlds end.
>
> (327–36)

Of all the satirical broadsides of these years, *The Lamentatioun* shows the
strongest appreciation of Lindsay's variety and lightness of touch: the little

vignette with which the poem concludes—about a sexually and gastron-omically replete prelate—owes more to the spirit of *Ane Satyre* than to that of the antipapist satire of the 1560s and 1570s. The Reformation did not fulfil Charteris's pious hope that the Lord would 'rais and steir up mony David Lyndesayis', but the broadside prints of the years after the publication of the *Warkis* show that there were some who were capable of learning from his example.

Among the political poetry of the post-Reformation period there are several works which answer the charges made by others. The events surrounding the delivering over of the captive Earl of Northumberland to the English authorities in 1572, for example, provoked an attack upon 'the Scottisch gyse' by an English pamphleteer, in terms which recall the spitefulness of Skelton's denigration of the Scots some sixty years before. This work (Cranstoun, XXXIV) provoked two Scots answers, which are very temperate by compari-son. One is epitomised by the couplet 'Althocht sum tratoris be among us,/In blaming all, forsuith, ye wrang us', while the second launches a fierce attack on those (including the earls of Mar and Morton) who had brought dishonour on their country by selling their noble captive (Cranstoun, XXXVI). All three poems were preserved in the manuscript anthologies of Sir Richard Maitland, one of them being ascribed to his son John, the 'maikles Maitland' who was to become the chancellor of James VI. Sir Richard Maitland's practice as an anthologist is to this extent unlike that of his younger contemporary George Bannatyne who, as we have seen, excluded contemporary polemical poetry from his collection. The Maitland manuscripts (not surprisingly) include some poems which were also transcribed by Bannatyne, but their emphasis is rather different. Most of the contents of the earlier Folio manuscript, for example, which was begun about 1570, could be subsumed under Bannatyne's rubric 'ballatis full of wisdome and moralitie', although there is a substantial group of 'ballettis mirry' which include *The Dumb Wife*, *The Freiris of Berwick*, *Peblis to the Play*, Roule's *Cursing* and Lichtoun's *Dreme*. Mait-land's reputation as an anthologist (and here principally as a recorder of poems by Dunbar) has tended to obscure his reputation as a poet in his own right. Although his manuscripts are not nearly so varied as Bannatyne's, Maitland was an incomparably better poet, whose work certainly repays closer attention than C S Lewis's comment—'Most of his poems are very like Dunbar and by no means contemptible'—would suggest.[15] As social criticism, his poetry reflects the same kind of temperance and concern for universal justice that one associates with Lindsay and with the Scott of 'Ane New Yeir Gift', discussed above. Maitland's own 1562 poem, 'Of the Quenis arryvale in Scotland' (Folio MS. XIX), offers dignified good counsel from a senior statesman who had served the Queen Regent. There is nothing comparable with Scott's trenchant attack on the excesses of both kirks, but Maitland sees no inappropriateness in a gibe at the friars:

> And amang uther servandis think on me.
> This last requeist I lernit at the freiris.
>
> (55–6)

A poem which invites closer comparison with Scott's is Maitland's 'O gratious God almychtie and eterne', which the colophon dates 1570 (Folio MS. XXII). Although a prayer, its emphasis (like that of the earlier 'Ane Prayer for the Pest' attributed to Henryson) is secular: plague, famine, and crop failure are seen as the workings of divine justice upon a commonwealth which has been failed by both temporal and spiritual governors. Like Scott, Maitland draws no distinction between the excesses of the papists and those of self-styled Reformers who

> callit ar the fleschlie gospellaris
> Quha in thair wordis apperis rycht godlie
> Bot yit thair warkis the plane contrair declaris.
>
> (62–65)

Here, as elsewhere, in his poems of a similar kind, Maitland's poetic style complements his political and moral attitudes in its avoidance of extremes. It is not verse of startling originality, but metrical craft (which may be a product of his interest in Dunbar) enlivens his exercises in the traditions of fifty years before. The poem which has become known as 'Satire on the Age' (Folio MS. XXI), which bears a close generic affinity to 'A General Satyre' (attributed by Maitland to James Inglis) is a spirited lament for the passing of the conviviality of a former age, which quickly moves to an attack on the abuses of the present:

> The kirkmen keipis na professioun,
> The temporale men committis oppressioun,
> Puttand the pure from thair possessioun;   [poor]
> Na kynd of feir of God have thai,
> Thai cummar bayth the court and sessioun   [trouble]
> And chassis cheritie away.
>
> (55–60)

This kind of satire, succinct and metrically pleasing, is no less effective than the more specific reference of 'Aganis the Theivis of Liddisdaill' (Folio MS. XCV). Some of Maitland's works are personal, in an unusually introspective way. Like the poem addressed to Mary on her return from France, 'The Blind Baronis Comfort' (Folio MS. XXIII) alludes to Maitland's blindness, but here in the context of his response to the despoiling of his 'landis of the baronie of Blyth' by his political enemies in 1570. The poem, which plays on the name of Maitland's lands,

> Blind man be blythe thocht that yow be wrangit,
> Thocht Blythe be hieriet tak no malankolye
> Thow salbe blythe quhane that thay salbe hangit
> That Blythe hes spulyeit sa malisiouslie,   [plundered]
>
> (1–4)

puts the conventions of *contemptus mundi* (exemplified in Dunbar's 'Best to be Blyth') to the ends of self-consolation. Maitland's 'Solace in Age' (Folio MS. CIX) returns to the theme of his dispossession, but here the tone is a highly individual combination of lament and sardonic amusement at his physical infirmity, as Maitland rejects the stereotype of the *senex amans*:

> Off Venus play past is the heit
> For I may not the mistiris beit
> Off Meg nor Mald;
> For ane young las I am not meit,
> I am sa ald.
>
> (26–30)
>
> . . .
>
> My wyff sum tyme wald telis trow
> And mony lesingis weill allow   [lies]
> War of me tald;
> Scho will not eyndill on me now   [be jealous]
> And I sa ald.
>
> (36–40)

It is hardly surprising that a poet who could write in this vein should, on the one hand, have included some fine comic poems in his anthology, and on the other, that he should have excluded from it any courtly love lyrics.

William Lauder is an inferior poet to Maitland, but his unrelievedly didactic verse shows that like Scott and Maitland he found verse a fitting medium in which to castigate the shortcomings of the Reformation church, of which he was himself a minister. His 'Lamentation of the Pure' (another work written in 1568 in the old form of the general satire with refrain) launches a vigorous attack on hypocritical Protestants.[16] It comes as a surprise to find that a poet who is so critical of Catholic religious observances and the pomp of prelacy ('Ane Godlie Tractate or Mirrour') can find good words to say for the charity and compassion of Catholics:

> The reuth that Papistis hes, I saye,
> On thame that beggis frome dure to dure,
> Sall us accuse on Domesdaye:
> How lang, Lord, wyll this warld indure?
>
> (33–36)
>
> Yit Papistis bearis ilke ane to uther
> More liberall luife, I am most sure,
> Nor dois sum minister to his Brother: [than]
> How lang, Lord, wyll this warld indure?
>
> (69–72)

For Lauder, verse was purely functional, a medium in which to articulate moral lessons without pretence at entertainment or adornment: he is confident that any exhortation to reform will be 'sweit and delicius' to the hearts of the godly by virtue of its subject matter alone ('Ane Prettie Mirrour or Conference', 1–4). This is the Calvinist aesthetic at its most extreme, and it comes as a pleasant surprise to find that there is not more of this kind of verse in mid-sixteenth-century Scotland.

Another minor poet of the mid century whose work deserves brief mention here is John Rolland, whose two lengthy poems *The Court of Venus* and *The Sevin Seages* had both been written by 1560, though they were not printed until 1575 and 1578. *The Court of Venus* is an encyclopaedic courtly vision allegory, whose closest relatives are Douglas's *The Palice of Honour*, the Chaucerian *Court of Love*, and Gower's *Confessio Amantis*. The poetry is old-fashioned, even self-consciously so, and eschews any kind of topicality. Rolland mentions in the Prologue to the later poem that the *Court* was sponsored by Lindsay, Bellenden, Stewart and Bishop Durie, but from Lindsay and Bellenden he seems to have learned little but a veneration for vision allegory: *The Palice of Honour*, written at least fifty years before, would seem to have been Rolland's prime Scots exemplar. *The Sevin Seages* is an even more backward-looking poem: it is a compendium of moral tales loosely framed by narrative, and is closely related to an English translation printed by Wynkyn de Worde in 1515. Although there are signs of anti-papist sentiment, and although the work is dated by a colophon which refers to the siege of Leith in 1560, Rolland obviously saw no need to write verse which would reflect contemporary political realities. That there continued to be a taste for this poetry 'of the auld fassoun' is clearly demonstrated by the printing of both works in the 1570s. *The Sevin Seages* was still being printed in Scotland until well into the seventeenth century, ample testimony (if any were needed) that a Mediæval taste for moralising with a modicum of narrative defied fashion or period.

The attitude which Lindsay expresses to his poetic forbears in *The Testament of the Papyngo*,

> Thocht they be ded, thar libells bene levand,   [living]
> Quhilkis to reheirs makeith redaris to rejose,
> (20–21)

would undoubtedly have been shared by the two great anthologists of four decades later, but it may be unwisely romantic to infer that Bannatyne and Maitland undertook their enterprises of conservation with an awareness that their changing culture would be inimical to the literary achievements of Catholic Scotland. Scottish publishers, whose market was small compared with that of their English counterparts, were slow to undertake the printing of poetry, and so most earlier poetry survived only in manuscript. Bannatyne may well have been prompted to undertake his great scribal project as much by what he knew of time's effects on paper ('My copeis auld, mankit and mutillait') as by any awareness he may have had of living in the shadow of a cultural revolution. If secular lyric and song, the genres to which Calvinistic attitudes were most strongly opposed, continued to be written in the two decades after 1560, it is hardly surprising that other non-polemical kinds of poetry should have been contemporaneous with poetry that had its *raison d'être* in politico-religious controversy.

When we compare what was being written in 1567-68 and the adjacent years with what was being conserved then (by Bannatyne, Maitland, and

Charteris), it is clear that there was little to rival the great achievements of Scottish secular poetry in the earlier sixteenth century. But when we compare the Scots poetry of the mid century with what was being written and read in England (where religious reformation had been accomplished and where there was a much more stable political situation), what do we find? In the shorter forms of poetry, Tottel's *Songes and Sonettes* were at the height of their popularity, yet even if the work of Wyatt and Surrey is excluded, there is little in this miscellany to rival the love poetry of Scott. Although it is doubtless true that there was more love poetry being written in England at this time, we can hardly lament the absence of a Scottish Googe or Turberville. In didactic verse, the popularity of the *Mirror for Magistrates* and the Baldwin-Palfreyman *Treatise of Morall Philosophye* testifies to a taste for sententiousness which is probably identical to George Bannatyne's. In England there was a vogue for translation of the classics, illustrated by the Ovidian works of Golding and Turberville (both in 1567). The great example of Gavin Douglas seems to have inspired no similar enterprise in Scotland, and the absence of large-scale verse translation constitutes the major difference in the state of secular poetry between the realms. Yet although there is no wide-ranging innovative impulse in Scottish poetry until the Renaissance fostered by the young James VI, the best of the secular poetry of the mid century shows that a respect for native craft and tradition was not incompatible with originality.

NOTES

1   For an account of Charteris's career, *see R Dickson and J P Edmond, Annals of Scottish Printing* (Cambridge, 1890), pp 348–76.
2   Quotations are from *The Works of Sir David Lindsay*, Douglas Hamer (ed), STS, 4 vols (Edinburgh and London, 1931–36).
3   'The Bannatyne Manuscript—A Marian Anthology', *Innes Review*, 37 (1986), 36–47 (44).
4   Joan Hughes and W S Ramson, *Poetry of the Stewart Court* (Canberra, 1982), provide the most elaborate account of the manuscript's design. Quotations from the manuscript, unless otherwise indicated, refer to the STS edition. (*See* General Bibliography.) The Introduction to the Scolar Press facsimile (London, 1980) prepared by Denton Fox and W A Ringler, is indispensable.
5   *Satirical Poems of the Time of the Reformation*, James Cranstoun (ed), STS, 2 vols (Edinburgh and London, 1890–93).
6   Hughes and Ramson, op. cit., p 97.
7   *A Choice of Scottish Verse 1470–1570* (London, 1972), p 27.
8   *See* the Introduction to my edition of the poem, *'Colkelbie Sow' and 'The Talis of the Fyve Bestes'* (New York and London, 1983), pp 8–25.
9   *Song, Dance and Poetry of the Court of Scotland under King James VI* (Cambridge, 1969), pp 12 and 21.
10 In his edition *Ballattis of Luve* (Edinburgh, 1970), p lvii, from which quotations are taken here.

11 Shire, op. cit., p 59.
12 Hughes and Ramson, op. cit., p 145.
13 *The Maitland Folio Manuscript*, W A Craigie (ed), STS, 2 vols (Edinburgh and London, 1919–27).
14 Quotations are from the STS edition (n. 5, above).
15 *English Literature in the Sixteenth Century* (Oxford, 1954), p 107.
16 Quotations are from *The Extant Poetical Works of William Lauder*, Fitzedward Hall and F J Furnivall (eds), EETS, 2 vols (London, 1870), reprinted as one volume by Greenwood Press, 1969.

FURTHER READING

SECONDARY TEXTS

Cowan Ian B, and Shaw, Duncan, *The Renaissance and the Reformation in Scotland: Essays in Honour of Gordon Donaldson* (Edinburgh, 1983)

Daiches, David, *Literature and Gentility in Scotland* (Edinburgh, 1982)

Jack, R D S, Introduction to *A Choice of Scottish Verse, 1560–1660* (London, 1978)

MacQueen, John, *Alexander Scott and Scottish Court Poetry of the Middle Sixteenth Century* (Warton Lectures on English Poetry, 1968)

Mapstone, Sally, ' "The Talis of the Fyve Bestes" and the Advice to Princes Tradition', in *Scottish Language and Literature, Medieval and Renaissance*, Strauss, Dietrich, and Drescher, Horst (eds) (Frankfurt, 1984), pp 239–54

Chapter 8

Poetry under King James VI

R D S JACK

What makes the period from the early 1580s until 1603 unique in the History of Scottish Literature is the character and literary ambitions of James himself. Tutored by the great Latinist George Buchanan, he came to regret the classical bias in his learning, lamenting that 'They gar me speik Latin ar I could speik Scottis'. Feeling this way, he was ready to fall under the cultural influence of his father's cousin Esmé Stuart with his knowledge of the French literary world. Another older man, the established poet Alexander Montgomerie also impressed the young king with his vernacular verses, which drew mainly from French and earlier Scottish sources.

What began as part game, part tuition led to James composing verses and having them published in two collections *The Essayes of a Prentise in the Divine Art of Poesie* (1584) and *His Majesties Poeticall Exercises at Vacant Houres* (1591). More importantly, the king's interest resulted in the gathering round him of men of like mind. Gradually James became the accepted leader/patron of a group of poets and musicians styled the Castalian band.

In seizing this role so enthusiastically he knew it allowed him to exert control over the more influential poets. The many eulogies on the monarch which characterise this period are in part due to the self-interest of the Castalians. They also provide a sharp contrast to the preceding reign and the fate of his mother at the hand of vitriolic Protestant poets. James had not forgotten this and used his role as patron to guard against any repetition. He also occasionally wrote politically-motivated verses including a lengthy paraphrase of Lucan's brief advice to subjects not to rebel against their King.

The major Scottish member of a band which attracted the talents of two English brothers, Robert and Thomas Hudson, was Montgomerie himself (*c.* 1545–1597). He belonged to the cadet branch of the powerful Ayrshire Eglinton family and was created 'maister poete' of the group after defeating Patrick Hume of Polwarth (d. 1609) in a flyting. He was the most gifted poet of the period, although he was to be exiled and eventually outlawed because of his Catholic activism. James's regret for this is expressed in 'An Epitaphe on Montgomrie', where he urges the Castalians to keep the poet's fame alive. William Fowler (1560–1612) was another prominent member. Born into an Edinburgh burgess family, he was a staunch Protestant and after a University education in Scotland and France became secretary to Anne of Denmark. John Stewart of Baldynneis (*c.* 1550–*c.* 1605) also hoped for political advancement and gifted the manuscript of his poems to the king. He was, however, the son of one of James V's mistresses and had earlier been imprisoned by James VI in the wake of bitter divorce proceedings resulting from his mother's late second marriage. Stewart may have gained royal forgiveness but he remained a shadowy figure at court, convinced that he had been passed over unjustly.

On the fringes of the group were William Alexander, Earl of Stirling (1567–1640) and Robert Ayton (1569–1638) both of whom made their literary reputations after the Union of the Crowns. Alexander Hume (*c.* 1557–1609) on the other hand wrote his best verse in the Castalian period and was an active courtier during the 1580s. But he was not one of the inner circle and his poetry is best considered along with that of another Protestant poet, John Burel (fl. 1590).[1]

In this Chapter I shall assess the nature and quality of the Castalian Renaissance. Was it in fact so forward looking that it deserves the title 'Renaissance' at all? How did it relate to the strong tradition of Scots poetry which preceded it and what sort of base did it provide for Scots poetry after the Union?

Certainly James intended his movement to align itself with the latest advances in Europe. *The Essayes of a Prentise* included his own critical treatise setting out *Some Reulis and Cautelis to be observit and eschewit in Scottis Poesie*. In it he urges that writing must move with the times. 'As for them that wrait of auld, lyke as the tyme is changeit sensyne, sa is the ordour of Poesie changeit.' Now, he claims, it has reached 'mannis age and perfectioun'. The treatise itself is clearly indebted to the critical writings of the Pléiade, especially those of Du Bellay and Ronsard. Even James's terminology relies on French forms. Instead of 'alliterative' he coins 'literall' based on the French *lettrisé*. There is also English influence from Gascoigne. But, drawing from such examples, the king nonetheless wants to produce critical guidelines which will be relevant to Scotland's verse specifically. That is why he writes at such a youthful age on a subject thoroughly dealt with by more experienced men:

> ... there hes never ane of thame written in our
> language. For albeit sindrie hes written of it in   [different people]
> English, quhilk is lykest to our language, yit we
> differ from thame in sindrie reulis of Poesie, as   [various]
> ye will find be experience.
>
> (*Reulis and Cautelis*, Preface)

In the work he pays special attention to Scottish modes (e.g. flytings) as well as encouraging distinctive stylistic features such as alliteration. It is clearly meant to be the trumpet call for a Scottish literary Renaissance.

The *Reulis and Cautelis* were very influential. Despite James's youth he had read widely and used the verse of experienced authors (e.g. Montgomerie) as models in his treatise. Above all he was a king already acclaimed as an amalgamation of David and Solomon. Although he would in practice contradict some of his own rules—actively encouraging translation, an activity whose limitations are stressed in the treatise—the major aims of the essay remained sacrosanct for most Castalians. It is therefore fair to measure the achievements of the group against their king's youthful hopes.

If the championing of a form intimately connected with the Renaissance and original use of it formally and thematically is accepted as a valid sign of forward thinking, then among Castalian lyrical verse, the sonnet merits first examination. To those who know only one Scottish sonnet from the period—Mark Alexander Boyd's poignant description of amorous servitude, 'Fra banc to banc, fra wod to wod, I rin',—it may come as a shock to learn that between the early 1580s and 1630 more than seven hundred Scottish sonnets were composed. This indicates that although the form gained popularity later in Scotland than in England, so it maintained that popularity longer.

Within the Castalian period four major features distinguish the Scottish sonnet from the English movement. First, the major Castalians (except William Fowler) do not compose long love sequences. They prefer shorter, thematically linked groupings. Montgomerie, for example, links many of his sonnets but the longest of these groupings contains only five poems, while of the sixty-nine sonnets generally agreed to be his, only twenty-seven at most deal with love.

This anticipates the second distinction. In the *Reulis and Cautelis* James warned against using the form solely for love. He preferred a wider thematic range. 'For compendious praysing of any bukes, or the authouris thairof, or ony argumentis of uther historeis, quhair sindrie sentences, and change of purposis are requyrit, use *Sonet* verse.' The Castalians, then, might employ the sonnet for courtly eulogies, for moral or theological argument or for personal petitions. The 'change of purposis' might be confined to a single sonnet or advanced in linked groups where the fourteen line form became part of a larger unit. Love as a topic remained important but was not emphasised so strongly as in other countries.

Source preferences also distinguish the Scottish Castalian sonnet from its English counterpart. Again with the exception of William Fowler, Scottish writers preferred to imitate French rather than Italian models.[2] James follows Desportes and Saint Gelais in particular while the former is also the strongest influence on Stewart. Montgomerie follows Ronsard in seven sonnets. The interrelationship may be close as between 'Heureuse fut l'estoille fortunée' and 'O happy star at evning and at morne' or merely the sharing of rhetorical features and the echoing of one line as in 'Oeil, qui portrait dedans les miens reposes' and 'Bright amorous ee whare Love in ambush [lyes]'. But Montgomerie clearly admired a poet whom the king distrusted both for his high-handed attitude to monarchs and for his championing of Mary.

The last distinguishing feature is formal. The ababbcbccdcdee rhyme-scheme, often thought to originate with Spenser, was used in Scotland prior to the *Amoretti* and in a sense became the trademark of Castalian sonnet-eering. All of James's sonnets in *The Essayes of a Prentise* use it; it accounts for thirty-two of Stewart's thirty-three sonnets and a hundred and eight of

Fowler's hundred and twenty-nine. Montgomerie experiments more widely and uses seven different rhyme schemes, mostly based on an abbaabba octet, but more than half of his sonnets still adopt the interlacing pattern.

Although some of the sonnets of David Murray (1567–1629) and William Alexander were probably written during the Castalian period, they were not published until after the Union of the Crowns. I have therefore focused on the four writers mentioned above. Of these, James is the most determined to follow his own advice both in terms of thematic range and adopting a novel attitude to love. His sonnets of praise and dedication are addressed to men as different as Sir Philip Sidney and Chancellor Maitland, Tycho Brahe and John Shaw, the master stabler. Usually they are carefully ordered works relying heavily on classical learning. They do not surprise the modern reader as his love sonnets (*Amatoria*) do. There, James's philosophical belief in the 'via media' permits him to argue for and against writing in the Queen's praise while the desire for realism produces not only the incongruously homely imagery of the king's blood boiling as if in a bed pan but singularly unamorous lines like the following:

> O womans witt that wavers with the winde
> When none so well may warie now as I   [curse]
> As weathercocke thy stablenes I finde
> And as the sea that still can never lie.
> > (*Amatoria* 5f, 1–4)

John Stewart also employs the sonnet form for a wide range of topics including an interesting group on moral themes and some ingenious complaints against life at court. He does not, therefore, disobey the king's rules by allowing love to be the major theme of his sonnets. But he does treat the passion in all its aspects from lust to the highest spirituality, leading on to love of God. Most noteworthy are 'In Going to his Luif', based loosely on Desportes' 'Contre une Nuict trop claire' and two bawdy hostess sonnets. The former, the first courtly love sonnet in Scots, skilfully evokes an atmosphere of doubt and hostility while the latter use the metaphor of host and guest to tell the witty tale of a whore and her impotent client.

But Montgomerie has the greatest range of all. He can use the sonnet form variously to argue out theological problems, to preach, to praise other writers, to present riddles for courtiers or merely to parade his own rhetorical virtuosity. He does not always handle his courtly love sonnets with his usual originality. Many of them do read like dutiful efforts from a laureate's pen. But when he is pleading for his pension or for re-instatement at court, his complete command of late Middle Scots allows him to move effortlessly from balanced argument directed at the king:

> Help, Prince, to whom, on whom not I complene,
> But on, not to fals fortun, ay my fo,
> > ('To his Majestie, for his Pensioun' I, 1–2)

to the depths of flyting reserved for the advocate who unsuccessfully presented his case:

> A Baxters bird, a bluiter beggar borne,   [babbler]
> Ane ill heud huirsone lyk a barkit hyde.   [baptised bastard]
>   ('Of M J Sharpe' II, 1–2)

If Montgomerie is the finest of those poets who embodied the old Castalian definition of the sonnet, William Fowler in his Petrarchan love sequence *The Tarantula of Love* anticipates the direction Scottish sonneteers would follow after the Union. The first line of *The Tarantula* echoes the first line in Petrarch's *Rime*; the rather shocking title is drawn from Castiglione's *Il Cortegiano*, where the tarantula's bite is identified with madness in verse, music and love. In a rather uneven sequence Fowler traces the lover's gradual ascent of the ladder of love as outlined in Book 4 of *Il Cortegiano* until at the end he sees his warlike lady, Bellisa, leading him to God. *The Tarantula* therefore ends on a religious note:

> As I IN ONE GOD EVER ay haith trust,
> So ar his promeis steadfast, trew and just.
>   ('Lord quha redemes the deid', 13–14)

Later Scottish writers including Alexander and William Drummond of Hawthornden will follow him in taking over the metaphysical implications of Petrarchism, as well as the more obvious ideas of the temporal love quest.

The Castalians produced a large variety of other lyrical forms, developing from the ideas of the Grands Rhétoriqueurs and the earlier practice of Scottish, English and European writers. Stewart in particular experiments with stanzas demanding both rhyming and rhetorical virtuosity. In 'Ane new sort of rymand rym' the last word of each line anticipates the first in the following one, while 'Ane man, ane beist, ane plant' proves to be an extended exercise in 'underwriting':

> The bone, the flesche, the bluid,
> Dois faill, dois feid, dois swage,   [abate]
> With tym, with cair, waxt ruid,
> In graif, in erth, in age.
>   ('Ane man, ane beist, ane plant', 5–8)

His love for coinages and for heavy alliteration produces virtuosic diction as well as complexities of rhyme and form. If the Renaissance encouraged linguistic adventure, then Stewart was determined to be part of that particular game.

The lyric was also used for a wide range of topics and purposes—eulogies (especially to the king), courtly love verse, riddles, brief moral debates and philosophical outpourings often concerning time and fortune. Given James's desire to align himself with the religious side of the Pléiade, it is also not surprising to find lyrical versions of the Psalms along with penitential verses and those praising God rather than one's mistress.

The importance of music in all this must not be underestimated, as Helena Shire has demonstrated.[3] One of James's major achievements was the passing of an act which urged burghs to reorganise and support the teaching of music. At his court he appointed the Hudson brothers to lead this musical revival and the accounts also record payments to Italian and French minstrels. Even the people practised music for in 1587, when the king left the mercat cross in procession from Holyrood, it is recorded that 'the people sang for myrth, and a great nomber of musicall instruments war employit for the lyk use'.

It is, however, important to get a balanced picture of the situation. An overview of lyricism among the Castalians confirms that they provided adequate verse forms consistent with James's idea of a Scottish Renaissance. But with the exception of Montgomerie none impresses as an outstanding lyricist. Even Stewart, whose talents are not inconsiderable, allows his interest in rhetoric to become an end in itself rather too often. And this over-concern with virtuoso manneristic effects is unfortunately a characteristic of much Castalian writing.

James's lyrics remain for the most part unimaginative, often threatening to become mere lists ('A Satire against Women') although 'A Dreame on his Mistris my Ladie Glammis' with its careful interpretation of the mystic gifts of tablet and amethyst does show originality. Fowler seldom uses lyrical forms other than the sonnet and Robert Ayton, who was later to compose polished verses which look forward to the wit of the Caroline lyricists, was still an apprentice at the Edinburgh court. A charitable mind may find a foreshadowing of his pastorals and love songs in the early 'Diaphantus' group but roughness of rhythm and diction are undoubtedly evident. Indeed, next to Montgomerie, William Alexander, whose *Aurora* imitates the varied lyrical forms of Petrarch's *Rime*, shows the greatest promise.

There are many reasons for not regarding Alexander as a fully committed Castalian. James poetically criticised him for writing 'harshe vearses after the Inglisch fasone' and, as has been noted, his *Aurora* was not published until the band had broken up. It is, however, certain that many of the verses in the collection were composed before the court moved south. Without attempting to vye with Montgomerie's forceful diction or Stewart's ambitious verse forms, he shows a sureness in handling songs, elegies, sestains and madrigals as well as sonnets. There is, however, a sense in which the newer forms are still used to convey old material, Renaissance stanzas preserving Mediæval conventions. Certainly Song 8, one of his best, is still essentially a very detailed Mediæval 'descriptio', moving relentlessly downwards and only losing descriptive accuracy where metaphoric indirectness is prescribed by modesty:

> There is below which no man knowes,
> A mountaine made of naked snowes,
> Amidst the which is Loves great seale.
>   (Song 8, 75–77)

This leaves Montgomerie. I accept that he has a tendency, especially in his commissioned verse to retreat rather often to favoured and conventional ideas expressed through favoured and conventional metaphors. But at his best he combines technical expertise and a keen sense of rhythm with a simplicity of vision which can sweep the reader into the excitement of a tournament:

The freikis on feildis	[soldiers]
That wight wapins weildis	[stout weapons]
With shyning bright shieldis	
At Titan in trone,	
Stiff speiris in reistis	[rests (for spears)]
Ouer cursoris cristis	[war horses' plumes]
Ar brok on thair breistis,	
The night is neir gone.	

('Hay, now the Day Dawis', Stanza 6)

or into sharing the melancholy of love through contemplating a single mari-gold:

Lyk as the dum	
Solsequium	[marigold]
With cair ou'rcum	
And sorow when the sun goes out of sight	
Hings doun his head	
And droups as dead	
And will not spread	
But louks his leavis through langour of the nicht.	[locks up]

('Lyk as the Dum Solsequium', 1–8)

Indeed this simplicity of vision provides welcome variety within an art which seeks to harmonise and modify three major influences, each in its own way capable of introducing complexities.[4] The rhetorical teachings of the Grands Rhétoriqueurs, the demands of music and of Humanism are all accepted by Montgomerie but in each case he emphasises those elements in the traditions which are also notable in more popular verse. The proverbs of the Grands Rhétoriqueurs become proverbs current in Scotland. His songs have a refreshing simplicity which reminds one of Herrick. Latin learning is recounted in ballad mode with scholastic argument becoming almost the question and answer technique favoured in that form.

Montgomerie's comparative simplicity is in part the necessary concomitant of mingling three traditions without developing any one in detail. But that is not all. His vision of life is a less complex, more democratic one than his adherence to the élite Castalian band might seem to imply. Himself an Ayrshire man, there is something of the Burnsian temper in carousing stanzas like the following:

I, Richie, Jane, and George are lyk to [dee];
Four crabit crippilis crackand in our crouch.   [gossiping] [crouching place]
Sen I am trensh-man for the other thri[e],   [spokesman]
Let drunken Pancrage drink to me in D[utch].
          ('The Old Maister', 9–12)

By combining popular vision with mannerised form, he establishes a unique voice. But his originality is founded on a new intermingling of accepted traditions. James may be right in seeing him as a poet of the Renaissance but he moves forward cautiously, ever aware of the strengths of earlier writing.

The king was also aware that his Castalian band would ultimately be judged neither on their lyrics nor their sonnets. The true test of the poet was his ability to compose a long poem. Once again, at least in terms of variety, the band did not let him down. The sustained vilifications of Montgomerie and Polwarth's *Flyting* and John Stewart's witty re-working of Ariosto's *Orlando Furioso* represent the lighter part of the offering but there were also the serious imitations of Du Bartas by King James and Thomas Hudson as well as William Fowler's re-working of Petrarch's *Trionfi*. More original works included James's elegy on Esmé Stuart, *The Phoenix*, and his celebration of the martial victory of Don John of Austria in *Lepanto*. They also embraced the most popular poem of the period, Montgomerie's lengthy allegory *The Cherrie and the Slae* and Stewart's pilgrimage in search of religious truth, *Ane Schersing out of Trew Felicitie*.

It is logical to begin with the *Flyting*, not only because it is an early composition but because it reflects the intense competition within the Castalian band. The contestants indulge in a battle of namecalling and vituperation for the benefit of a courtly audience who act as judges. The result in this case was Polwarth giving over his place as 'maister poete' to Montgomerie. The *Flyting* also provides a link with the lyrical section, for although a lengthy work it is made up of smaller sections (claims and ripostes) in which each poet tries to outdo the other with more complex lyrical verse forms. Polwarth and Montgomerie move from one type of stanza to another making mastery of versification a major criterion in determining superiority.

While it could be argued that Polwarth was the better debater, answering each charge explicitly, Montgomerie's poetic imagination gave him victory, fairly, in a contest where poetic rather than dialectic arts had higher value.[5] The new 'maister poete' reserves his most complex stanzas for later movements in the contest and his account of Polwarth's fantasy birth combines imagination with supreme verse control:

Into the hinderend of harvest, on ane alhallow evin,
Quhen our goode nichtbouris ryddis, if I reid richt,   [neighbours]
Sum buklit on ane bunwyd and sum on ane bene [fixed firmly] [stalk of ragwort] [beanstalk]
Ay trippand in troupis frae the twielicht;
Sum saidlit ane scho aip all grathit into grene,   [arrayed]
Sum hobling on hempstaikis, hovand on hicht.   [hempstalks] [staying stationary]
The king of pharie with the court of the elph quene,
With mony alrege incubus, ryddand that nicht,   [weird]

Thair ane elph and ane aip, ane unsell begate   [rascal]
In ane peitpot by Powmathorne   [place near Edinburgh]
That brachart in ane buss wes borne;   [brat] [bush]
They fand ane monstour on the morne,
War facit nor ane cat.   [worse looking than]
      (*Flyting*, Tullibardine MS, 268–80)

Here all the skills of the makar are on show—mastery over complex rhythms, rhymes, patterns of alliteration and, above all, over a vast vocabulary spilling on to the page with an enthusiasm anticipating Sir Thomas Urquhart.

In contrast with the energy of this work the king's serious poetry pales into insignificance. As Agnes Mure Mackenzie notes, he was 'at eighteen or at any age a better critic and patron than a poet'.[6] Both his *Furies* and *Uranie* demonstrate that intended modesty topoi may often be statements of bare fact. He *is* incapable of matching the subtlety of his model. Yet his proclaimed intention of following the religious writers in the Pléiade, of presenting for Scotland 'a holy hallowde work' is of historical importance. The Castalians might look to France for inspiration but James/David gave clear guidelines on the authors he preferred. The result was a heavy bias towards religious and philosophical works.

The *Lepanto* is James's only attempt at a heroic poem. What strengths it has were soon forgotten in the political furore it caused. The major hero, Don John of Austria, was a Catholic and Scottish opinion was horrified at seeing a Protestant monarch praising the other side. For those who had eyes to see, James had clearly made Don John an instrument of God and introduced an angelic choir whose comments provide a Protestant framework. But religious leaders were not impressed by such niceties and the poem became the centre of impassioned controversy. A much finer work is *The Phoenix*, where the governing conceit announced in the title, permitted James at once sympathetically to lament the death of Esmé Stuart and welcome as the new Phoenix his eldest son Ludovick:

      Let them be now, to make ane Phoenix new
      Even of this worme of Phoenix ashe which grew.
                (*Phoenix*, 273–74)

It will by now be obvious that while the long poems of the Castalians provided verse dedicated to almost every one of the seven Muses, some of them did not live up to the high hopes presented in the *Reulis and Cautelis*. Much was mere versifying, much uninspired translation or imitation. And James's desire for holy verse encouraged writers to return to Mediæval modes of thought, even if these were sometimes conveyed in new verse forms. William Fowler unfortunately did not improve the situation with his verse paraphrase of Petrarch's *Trionfi*. Fowler had admired the *Trionfi* for its 'stately verse', its 'morall sentences', 'goodly sayings', 'propper and pithie arguments' and 'golden freinyeis of Eloquence'. In fact his chosen heptameter form resulted in his making the 'stately verse' aureate and longwinded, explaining the 'morall sentences' at excruciating length, expanding interminably on the 'goodly sayings', losing the pithiness of the 'propper arguments' and elaborating the 'golden freinyeis of Eloquence' with such enthusiasm that often the sentence structure breaks down completely.

Stewart's two major poems are both designed for James. The *Roland Furious* aims to give him 'sport' while *Ane Schersing out of Trew Felicitie* is specifically written for the leader of a Renaissance in religious verse. Thus, although the latter depicts the pilgrimage of the Christian soul, following the guidance of Charity, Humility, Labour and others until it reaches the Heavenly City, and does so in a manner anticipated by many Mediæval poems, a line of kingly panegyric is woven into the established pattern. Notably Veritie leaves the pilgrim to serve James, as does Constancy. Even the final prayer to Holy Church focuses primarily on the king as 'ane fair reflex of Phoebus' and God's 'anoyntit veschell'. Despite the implications of this last remark, it is difficult for modern readers to avoid finding this interplay between God and James at times comically incongruous. Also, although there are some magnificent descriptive passages, Stewart's pilgrim has few doubts, so that the intensity of the psychomachia is replaced by a steady and largely foreseeable progression, well visualised but lacking in dramatic conflict.

In contrast the *Roland Furious* is full of drama and deserves Matthew McDiarmid's assessment of it as 'the most brilliant and energetic poem of the brief Scots Renaissance.'[7] It is an 'abbregement', of Ariosto's *Orlando Furioso* and although Stewart has also used material from Desportes' *Angélique* and *Roland Furieux* as well as relying on at least one French prose translation, the originality of the final product disproves James's belief that all translation must be limiting. Stewart tries to highlight the comic events in the epic, using his tighter and more analytic scheme to show that characters as different as Roland and the Hermit, Sacripant and Rodger (Ruggiero) are all obsessed by the same desire to possess Angelique. Thus she survives the ludicrous impotence of the Hermit thanks to a hero on a flying horse, only to find that hero (Rodger) has identical intentions! Angelique's practicality provides further humour when set against the highsounding idealism of her suitors and much is made of the irony that after withstanding the combined efforts of almost every Christian and Saracen leader on her chastity, she easily submits to the unassuming shepherd, Medor. The work is even a comedy in the 'de casibus' sense because both Roland and Angelique finally find a higher happiness. The aim of providing merriment for the king is thus fully realised. At the same time in setpieces such as Roland's madness Stewart shows his mastery of rhetorical skills and of late Middle Scots, while behind the surface humour he remorselessly satirises the game of love as played by both sexes.

But the one major poem of the period which enjoyed continued popularity was Montgomerie's *The Cherrie and the Slae*. It went through so many reprints in the seventeenth and eighteenth centuries that then it ranked second in popularity only to the *Wallace*. That popularity mystifies many modern readers who find it a meandering work, lacking in drama and without any clear thematic focus.

Montgomerie certainly regarded it as his magnum opus, working on it throughout his life and James in his *Reulis and Cautelis* advocates its fourteen line stanza with bob and wheel (later used by Burns in the Recitativo of 'The Jolly Beggars') as one of the forms to be practised in his Renaissance. But in many ways the poem looks back rather than forwards. Most notably it is an allegory and although Montgomerie, I believe, uses that mode in a creative way its Mediæval inheritance is clear.

The story centres on the poet's quest for a fruit which will satisfy him: either the easily attainable but bitter slae or the almost inaccessible cherrie. We first meet him on a spring day watching a river plunge from a cliff into a 'pit profound'. Cupid appears and lends him wings but he soars too high and wounds himself rather than the vaguely delineated object of his search with Cupid's arrow. He falls to the earth and Cupid deserts him, whereupon he becomes aware that wilfulness and ignorance have caused his dilemma. At this point he sees the fruits for the first time, the cherrie beyond the river high on the crag, the slae beside him on a bush. There follows a lengthy debate with, broadly speaking, Hope and Courage arguing for the cherrie, Dread and Despair preferring the slae. Danger's position is more complex as, although the protagonists of the cherrie see him as an enemy, he argues rather for taking further counsel. He gains his wish and Experience, Reason, Wit and Skill broaden the discussion philosophically while Will urges a second attack. Finally Reason reconciles even apparent enemies such as Courage and Dread, Hope and Despair. Wit works out a way of climbing the cliff but, as they advance, the fruit 'for ripnes fell'. The dreamer feels refreshed and thanks God for his love.

Throughout his allegory Montgomerie does maintain an associative openness which encourages the reader to redefine the symbolic values of the cherrie and the slae as the poem progresses. As a result it has been valued and dismissed for very different reasons and assuming very different intentions. For the earliest critics it was valued as a storehouse of proverbs. C S Lewis and others have seen it as an erotic allegory stemming from *The Romance of the Rose*. This places it at the very end of a tradition which, in Lewis's words, 'has taken an unconscionable time to die'.[8] But most commentators point, I think rightly, to a wider moral and/or religious significance growing out of the earlier romantic experience. This links the poem with a newer, more flourishing tradition having Scottish precedents in Douglas's *King Hart* and Rolland's *Court of Venus*. The poem's most thorough critic, Helena Shire, sides with this group but stresses Montgomerie's Catholicism and the symbolism of cherrie and slae to argue for a more specific religious and political interpretation, involving an opposition between Catholicism (cherrie) and Protestantism (slae).[9]

My own view is that, like the Middle English elegy *Pearl*, *The Cherrie and the Slae* charts a spiritual progression. As the poet learns more the allegorical emphasis alters. Thus, while at the outset the fruits refer primarily to romantic oppositions between easily attainable and distant loves, the focus of debate widens with the introduction of Reason and the other counsellors. The earlier values are not negated but by the time of the final assault the context has become religious rather than erotic and we are encouraged to see the falling of the cherrie as the gift of grace for a pilgrim who has, after intense argument, reconciled the conflicts within him. This battle for the soul is a complex one with the poet advancing by stages of ignorance and confusion to final enlightenment.

Such an interpretation rescues the poem from charges that it represents the last echoes of an outdated tradition and explains why James was happy to present it as part of his Renaissance. He must also have been pleased that his literary role as 'David' along with his carefully balanced religious policies prevented staunchly Presbyterian poets from attacking him as they had done Mary. John Davidson (c. 1549–1604), who had described James's mother as 'Jesabell, that Monstour of Mahoun' in a poetic defence of Knox gave up what had been essentially a poetry of protest after those troubled days were past and many other religious propagandists followed his example.[10]

Other Protestant poets like John Burel wrote throughout his Edinburgh reign but only criticised the king in the most general and indirect way. In 'An Application concerning our Kings Majesteis Persoun', Burel uses James's sea journey to Denmark as proof of the monarch's love, but pauses to warn him and all sailors against forgetting the universal pilot (God). His two long poems do not concern themselves with those doctrines which separate Catholics and Protestants. *Pamphilus Speakand of Lufe* tells how Galathea is tricked by an old crone into giving her love to Pamphilus. *The Passage of the Pilgremer*, which uses *The Cherrie and the Slae* stanza, takes the poet-dreamer into limbo and Hell to prove the existence of Lucifer and evil spirits. Though neither poem is dedicated to James it is noteworthy that an old witch is at the centre of the first plot and the second concerns an apparently beautiful nymph who changes shape after leading the dreamer into the underworld:

> In monstrus maner, sche come thair,
> As Crusa did, that dame so fair,
> Efter sche wes deceist.
> (*The Passage of the Pilgremer*, II, Stanza 33, 1–3)

Both of these works might be expected to appeal to a king, interested in witchcraft and daemonology.

The finest of the Protestant religious poets is Alexander Hume. In 'The Triumph of the Lord after the Manner of Man' he celebrates the defeat of the Armada in a fiery, dramatic work which could have taught the author of *Lepanto* how to make God the unequivocal hero of any conflict no matter how bloody. Equally interesting is his Horatian epistle to Gilbert Montcreif, which advances from personal concerns to a prolonged attack on court and government. Even here it is admitted that James 'excells all uther Kings', a concession which does not prevent Hume from attacking the upholders of authority in Scotland with some fervour.

Even in the darker moods of satire Hume gains comfort from the belief that ultimately everything is the work of God:

I have delight in heart maist to behald,
The pleasant works of God sa manifalde.
('Epistle to Gilbert Montcreif', 378–79)

The argument that God's beneficent control is mirrored in Nature is a theme
he returns to in 'Of God's Benefites Bestowed Upon Man', in 'Of God's
Omnipotencie' and, most effectively, in 'Of the Day Estivall'. That poem in
particular reminds us that Presbyterian distrust of mythology, certain types
of imagery and aureate language need not always work against art. The
poem's power derives first of all from simple, vivid descriptions of the passing
phases of the day:

> Begaried is the saphire pend [ornamented] [vault]
> With spraings of skarlet hew, [streaks]
> And preciously from end till end
> Damasked white and blew.
> ('Of the Day Estivall', Stanza 17)

But the circular form of the poem, beginning and ending with God, also
reminds us that every one of these details is valued not in and for itself but
as proof that Nature is a statement of divine order and a test of faith through
perception.

When evaluating the writers at the court of James VI, critics have tended
to adopt either of two extreme viewpoints. Some have emphasised the best
of their work and the proclaimed 'Scottishness' of their movement, partly to
set it against a period after the Union, which they see as barren and anglicised.
In fact the movement from writing predominantly in Scots to writing in
English was much more complex and gradual than this. Most of the Castalians were already writing thinner Scots than their predecessors. Some were
already anglicising verse written in Scots before 1603, although the Union did
act as the major catalyst for such activities. Moreover the heyday of the
'band' itself was the 1580s and early 1590s. James did hold it together, partly
for political reasons, until the end of his Scottish reign. But his own earlier
enthusiasms were dulled by cares of state. Thus the final break-up of the
Castalians when he went south was the end of a period of worsening relations
among its members rather than the sudden extinguishing of a movement at
its brightest.

Other critics refuse to accept that there was such a thing as a Castalian
Renaissance at all. Despite the claims for innovation, they feel that the
late sixteenth century poets provide an inferior postscript to the powerful
movement begun a century earlier by Henryson and Dunbar. Often they seem
to be looking for a very obvious breach with earlier traditions, using England's
situation as a parallel. But the very strength of the Scottish tradition in
that period at once invalidates the parallel and gives good reasons for a
Renaissance building on rather than rejecting past models. Much of the
appeal of, say, *The Cherrie and the Slae*, derives from our awareness of earlier
traditions being creatively brought together.

In the last analysis and with the value of hindsight we may see that the poets under James were rather too small and select a group, overly concerned with mannerism and too heavily reliant on their king. Certainly a broader based Renaissance would have adapted more easily to the events of 1603. But the fact remains that this same group kept alive the vast variety of verse forms they had inherited, adapted others and adopted new forms such as the sonnet. Their work may have been uneven but they did have in Montgomerie one poet of outstanding ability; while Stewart's *Roland Furious* and Hume's 'Of the Day Estivall' show in very different ways how the Renaissance at its best could express itself. It may have fallen some way short of James's vision but it still provided a varied and at times innovative base on which later poets might build.

NOTES

1   Quotations from all the poets considered are taken from the editions cited under *Further Reading.*
2   See R D S Jack, 'William Fowler and Italian Literature', *Modern Language Review*, LXV (1970), 481–92.
3   Helena Mennie Shire, *Song, Dance and Poetry of the Court of Scotland under King James VI* (Cambridge, 1969).
4   R D S Jack, 'The Lyrics of Alexander Montgomerie', *Review of English Studies*, XV (1969), 168–81.
5   R D S Jack, *Alexander Montgomerie* (Edinburgh, 1985), pp 26–33.
6   'The Renaissance Poets I: Scots and English' in *Scottish Poetry: A Critical Survey*, James Kinsley (ed) (London, 1955), pp 33–67 (53).
7   'Notes on the Poems of John Stewart of Baldynneis', *Review of English Studies*, XXIV (1948), 12–18 (17).
8   C S Lewis, *The Allegory of Love* (Oxford, 1936), p 259.
9   Shire, pp 117–38.
10 R M Gillon, *John Davidson of Prestonpans* (London, 1938), p 195.

FURTHER READING

PRIMARY TEXTS

Burel, John, *Poems* (Edinburgh, *c* 1595)

Craigie, James (ed), *The Poems of King James VI of Scotland*, STS, 2 vols (Edinburgh and London, 1947–52)

Cranstoun, James (ed), *The Poems of Alexander Montgomerie*, STS (Edinburgh and London, 1887)

Crockett, Thomas (ed), *The Poems of John Stewart of Baldynneis*, STS (Edinburgh and London, 1913)

Davidson, John, *Poetical Remains*, Maidment, J (ed) (Edinburgh, 1829)

Gullans, Charles B (ed), *The English and Latin Poems of Sir Robert Ayton*, STS, (Edinburgh and London, 1956)

Kastner, L E and Charlton, H B, *The Poetical Works of Sir William Alexander, Earl of Stirling*, STS, 2 vols (Edinburgh and London, 1921–29)

Kinnear, T (ed), *The Poems of Sir David Murray of Gorthy*, Bannatyne Club (Edinburgh, 1823)

Lawson, Alexander (ed), *The Poems of Alexander Hume*, STS (Edinburgh and London, 1902)

Meikle, Henry W, Craigie, James and Purves, John (eds), *The Works of William Fowler*, STS, 3 vols (Edinburgh and London, 1912–39)

Stevenson, George (ed), *The Poems of Alexander Montgomerie*, STS (Supplementary Volume) (Edinburgh and London, 1907)

SECONDARY TEXTS

Borland, Lois, 'Montgomerie and the French Poets of the Early Sixteenth Century', *Modern Philology*, XI (1913), 127–34

Dilworth, Mark, 'New Light on Alexander Montgomerie', *The Bibliotheck*, IV (1965), 230–35

Jack, R D S, 'James VI and Renaissance Poetic Theory', *English*, XVI (1967) 208–11

—— 'Petrarchism in English and Scottish Literature', *Modern Language Review*, LXXI (1976), 801–11

Lewis, C S, *English Literature in the Sixteenth Century Excluding Drama* (Oxford, 1954)

McDiarmid, M P, 'John Stewart of Baldynneis, the Scottish Desportes', *SHR*, 17 (1915), 303–10

Nelson, Timothy, 'John Stewart of Baldynneis and *Orlando Furioso*', *SSL*, 6 (1968), 105–14

Ross, Ian, 'The Form and Matter of *The Cherrie and the Slae*', *Texas Studies in English*, XXXVII (1958), 79–91

Shire, Helena Mennie, 'Alexander Montgomerie. The oppositione of the courte to conscience . . .', *SSL*, 3 (1966), 144–50

Chapter 9

Poetry after the Union 1603–1660

MICHAEL SPILLER

Whoever writes on this period of Scottish literature must face C S Lewis's judgement, in his *English Literature in the Sixteenth Century* (p 113) that historians can fill their chapters only by dwelling on writers who in happier lands and ages would hardly secure a mention. A small and impoverished country which yet managed to produce the finest British Petrarchist, in Drummond of Hawthornden, and the greatest Renaissance translator, in Sir Thomas Urquhart, need not feel apologetic; but there is indeed a decline in Scottish poetry, a lull before Scotland again becomes a European cultural centre in the eighteenth century, while in social turmoil her ablest men recast their livelihoods and allegiances.

We must be careful, too, with the very term 'Scottish poetry', and avoid the temptation to think that, among so much political and financial south-seeking, it was by some act of linguistic treachery that Scotsmen wrote poetry, when they did, almost wholly in Southern English—or had it thus printed, however they may have spoken it. Literary nationalism is, indeed, a marked late Renaissance feeling, as the writings of Du Bellay, Webbe, Sidney and James VI (in his *Reulis and Cautelis...*) all show; yet far more important than the distinction between one native tongue and another, or between any of these and Latin, was the distinction between one level of style and another, the critical concept of *decorum*. What marks off the literature of the Renaissance from that of the Middle Ages preceding, or of the Age of Wit following, is a powerful conviction that literary voices are everywhere the voices of social hierarchies, proclaimed according to international, not national conventions.

No matter what the birth and fortunes of a poet, in Florence, Paris, London or Edinburgh, he was likely to accept that there were three levels of style, high, middle and low, corresponding roughly to court and aristocracy, bourgeois, and rustic. These styles were articulated in various lexes and genres, about which there was much critical debate; yet there was consensus that poetry was an eloquent speech—a 'speaking out' of the self into a social identity—that caught by its mimesis the rank and quality of the subject, kingly or clownish. What an Italian rhetorician would call *grave*, bespeaking statesmen and heroes in epic or ode, *piacevole*, for the passionate lover or relaxing bourgeois in sonnet or madrigal, and *aspro*, for the malcontent in satire or flyting or the peasant in clodhopping measures, passes over to James VI as three styles: 'heich, pithie and learned', 'commoun and passionate' and 'corruptit and uplandis'. Whatever the terminology, the result all over Europe for those who sought to dignify their vernacular with poetry, was an assiduous search for the equivalent of the Latin and Greek heroic registers for a high style; of the Petrarchan or pastoral registers for a middle style; and only on the low level, for purposes of mockery, flyting or patronising mimicry of the confusions of Hodge or Jocky, to admit the orthography or dialect items of the 'uplandis' speaker. Where these last intruded on a higher level, they were faults: so Patrick Gordon, attempting with fair success to place Scotland's hero, Robert the Bruce, in the canon of European epic, nevertheless apologises in his Errata for his and his printers' failure to standardise Scotland's words:

> Their is sindrie errours askepd, both in the Orthographe and want of single letters . . . This with sindrie other falts, as *but* whear it is teaine for without, (and uther *Scots* words, which I have rather chusd to pas, than loise a sound runing line) I dout not but the reader will excuse in respect that the Book was Printed in ane uther cuntrey wheir the setters did not understand the Langage.

Metropolitan printers in Britain, accustomed to the wild varieties of phonetic spelling in their copy, would normally iron out regional orthography; to insist on the preservation of regional features was to risk writing 'rude Scottis and hask' poetry (as Alexander Hume says) when one's poesis required a higher level. The issue was not patriotism, but propriety.

There was a distinctive Scots aureate diction that could never be thought low, and traces of that, with its close companion in rhetoric, alliteration, appear in most of the Scottish poets writing at the beginning of the seventeenth century. Yet while single aureate words or phrases can always be used to great effect (one thinks of Shakespeare's 'incarnadine' in *Macbeth* or Milton's 'enameld eyes' in *Lycidas*), aureation and alliteration gradually give way to a desire for balance and cleverness, for wit and ingenuity. The aureation of the Scottish courtly makars may be magnificent, but it is not witty nor concentrated: it is fundamentally a trope of intensification in the topos of praise (whence the alliteration that goes with it), and shows a kind of ceremonial extravagance that the seventeenth century began to distrust, whether in courts, churches or poetry. Committed to this kind of iteration, the self cannot recover poise:

> O Puissant Prince, and King Cunctipotent,
> Whose bodie rent, was on the rack or Rude,
> For mans great good, O Lord, they selfe was shent
> Of that intent, the *Devill* to denude,
> Us to seclude, from that fierce fierie flood
> Whilk reddie stoode, to drink up, and demain   [control]
> That thou had then, bought with thy blissed blood.
> (Alexander Gardyne, 'Invocation for seasonable weather', 1–7)

The seventeenth century preferred, even in ceremonial, a lighter and more ingenious movement of the speaking voice:

> Sonne, with thy Syre in yeares, in might,
> In all, co-equall: man's dimme sight
> Transcending; like thy paterne bright
>   An Other, and the Same:
> True God of God, mild Maid-borne wight,
> Blest Ladder, reaching earth aright,
> Co-apting things of greatest hight
>   With lowe: Light's glorious beame.
>
> Safetie of Soules, Sight of the blinde,
> Haven, where the shipwrakt shelter finde,
> End of all toyles, Ease of the minde
>   Press'd down with sinful loade;
> Reward of works due in no kinde
> To conflict past, the Palme assignde,
> Soul's cure, with sin's sore sicknesse pynde,
>   The banisht man's aboade.
> (Mure of Rowallan, 'A Spirituall Hymne', 33–48)

With the exception of Drummond, Scotsmen writing poetry at home or in England seem stylistically insecure: they inherit the Renaissance ideals of style, but can neither quite forsake them nor adapt them to a new poise and lightness. Shifting this perception from the aesthetic to the historical, one might suggest that there is in this period a double loss: loss of a court, and loss of a religious centre (or a quest for a new one)—the High Renaissance rhetoric of praise, whether of a prince or a paramour, involves an abasement of the self before an ideal, and its favoured tropes are hyperbole, aureation, classical parallelism and alliteration. This abasement becomes more and more difficult to sustain, though still deeply desired (witness the extraordinary profusion of formal grief on the death of Prince Henry, and the almost pathetic rush of Scotsmen to shower their absentee monarch with adulation on his return in 1617); and poets, whether Royalist or Covenanting, begin to work with modes and forms that allow themselves a more equivocal or independent stance: the witty lyric, the verse romance (where the poet merely recounts the passions of others), the heroic couplet. England has two exceptional poets who confront a similar shift of self in their own ways, Herbert and Marvell; Scotland has Drummond, who found his own retreat and distinctive voice. The discovery of an ethnic voice lay almost a century in the future: it was not, for any of these present writers, a possible choice.

If a majority of our poets belong to Court circles, that is a matter more of patronage than temperament; among those who do not, such as Alexander Gardyne, Zachary Boyd, Mure of Rowallan and Drummond, there is little in common. My treatment therefore is simply alphabetic, for ease of consultation, except that very minor writers with a tiny output are collected at the end.

The most prolific, and one of the most earnest, of the courtier poets was

Sir William Alexander, later Earl of Stirling (1567–1640), whose long and labour-filled court life brought him almost every reward except financial security and popularity in old age, but still left him time for considerable writings in lyric poetry, drama and epic. His dramatic works are dealt with elsewhere in this volume; his sequence of sonnets and lyrics in imitation of Petrarch's *Rime*, his *Aurora*, though published in 1604 in London, was written earlier than 1603. That is certainly the most readable of his works, and shows a young poet of lyric ease, melodiousness and remarkable metrical skill; but it was excluded by Alexander from his collected works, *Recreations with the Muses* (London, 1637), which represented him as a tragic dramatist and epic poet only.

The editors of his two large volumes in the Scottish Text Society's series (1921, 1929) describe him as 'a very solemn person with a rigorously commonplace mind' (1929, p xviii), and it does seem as though in moving from *Aurora* to the high style of his epic poem *Doomesday or, the Great Day of the Lords Judgement* (Edinburgh, 1614) and *Recreations*, he effectively repudiated his former self. Written in twelve books, called 'Hours', *Doomesday* is a comprehensive account of the Day of Judgement in about 10,000 lines of eight-line stanzas. The subject is certainly of the highest kind, and the *Book of Revelations*, from which the plot comes, provides suggestions enough of powerful visual effects and symbolism. Yet through more than 1,200 impeccably rhymed stanzas, Alexander does not once manage a clear visual description of any thing or person, or image precisely any sequence of events; the result is to make the experience of reading about Doomsday almost as disorienting as one might suppose the sensation of rising to attend it.

This is only partly ineptness; it is also the result of a deliberate but unfortunate style. Certainly he cannot control narrative—maintenance of voice, point of view and even tense is beyond him (as his other specimen of epic narrative, *Jonathan*, published in *Recreations*, confirms). But he also took three stylistic decisions that fatally clog his progress: first, to avoid classical imagery and allusion, as many Protestant writers upon sacred subjects did; second, to make each stanza end, where possible, with a generalisation or moral epigram—a curious but quite widespread trope in long stanzaic poems of the period; and third, to practise a very dense, elliptical and highly embedded syntax with chains of qualifying clauses (so too Milton, but he had the sense to work in blank verse). It is hard to believe that these two specimens come from the same hand:

> Once for her face, I saw my Faire
> Did of her haires a shadow make:
> Or rather wandring hearts to take,
> She stented had those nets of gold,   [spread]
> Sure by this meanes all men t'ensnare.
> She toss'd the streamers with her breath,
> And seem'd to boast a world with death:
> But when I did the sleight behold,

I to the shadow did repaire,
To flie the burning of thine eyes;
O happie he, by such a sleight that dies.
                    (*Aurora*, Madrigal 4)

That Queene whose name heavens register still beares,
What king they had the *Hebrews* so to teach,
Who came from farre (neglecting vulgar feares)
A mortals sight, and temporall ends to reach,
And as most happy envy did their eares
     Who might enjoy the treasures of his speech,
          She (whil'st wits wonders did her mind amaze)
          Damn'd liberall fame as niggard of his praise.
                    (*Doomesday*, Hour 5, st. 16)

With such large bounds to stray in, Alexander has no motive for conciseness, and nothing can be said without qualification, reflection, parentheses, parallels and generalisation. The result is a severe, dignified, impeccably moral and utterly diffuse epic—'More matter with less art!' The same vices of style confound his *Paraenesis to Prince Henry* (London, 1604), his *Elegie on the Death of Prince Henrie* (Edinburgh, 1613) and *Jonathan* (*Recreations*, 1637), thus marking a lifetime of lofty prolixity.

Though he travelled a very different path up Parnassus, Sir Robert Ayton (1569–1638) was as well fitted as his friend Alexander to succeed at the English Court of James VI and I, and worked his way up from Groom of the Privy Chamber to be Secretary to Queen Henrietta Maria. He lived, worked and intrigued among those who knew, as Donne puts it,

     When the Queen frown'd, or smil'd... and what
     A subtle states-man may gather of that,

and he hasted to an office's reversion with the foremost. Most of his Latin verse, written in stately Latin hexameters and elegiacs, is panegyric, and was printed in Ayton's lifetime in *Delitiae Poetarum Scotorum* (1637); his English verse was not collected, and survives for the most part in commonplace books. He wrote only three early poems in Scots, and for the rest, as he said of King James,

                    Scotisque relictis
          Tendi[t] ad affines Anglorum sedulus oras.
               ('Ad Jacobum VI... Panegyris', 204–05)

Ayton lacked entirely the moral earnestness of Alexander or of Mure of Rowallan: for him poetry was the articulation of the courtier's manner, used for gallantry, flattery and the elegance of fashionable passion in pastoral, sometimes in translation or paraphrase from Petrarch or Guarini or Tasso. In pursuit of this *sprezzatura*, Ayton rapidly discarded the aureate Petrarchism of his early poems:

Unhappy eyes, why did you gaze againe
Upon those Fatall, Loveing, fyring Spheires,
Know you not well, her fire flaughts would constraine   [flashes]
Your Cristall circles to dissolves in teares?
('Love's Provocation', 1–4)

and moved towards the witty, sensual, epigrammatic mode that we are apt
to think of as libertine, but which has its roots in Jonson and even the
Epicurean verse of the Pléiade:

What uthers doth discourage and dismay
Is unto me a pastime and a play.
I sport in hir deneyalls and doe know
Weman love best that does love least in show.
Two sudden favors may abate delight:
When modest coynes sharpes the appetite,
I grow the hotter for hir cold neglect
And more inflam'd when sho showes least respect.
('To his coy Mistres', 1–8)

He is at his best when his wit condenses; in short songs and epigrammatic
verse his skill in turning a neat antithesis shows to best advantage. He can
tread just this side of banality, as a good song requires, and his 'Valediction',
which has a fine anonymous setting, might well keep company with the court
airs of Henry Lawes:

Then wilt thou goe and leave me here?
Ah doe not soe my dearest deare.
The sunns departur clouds the sky
But thy departure makes mee dye.

Thou canst not goe but with my heart,
Even that which is my cheifest part,
Then with two hearts thou shall be gone,
And I shall rest behinde with none.
('A Valediction', 1–8)

Coming south from a literary culture which, though strong, was almost a
generation behind the English in matters of taste, Ayton sought, and quickly
found, a voice which proclaimed the seventeenth century courtier in his
English verse, and the graver humanist man of affairs in his Latin pieces. As
at the end of his life, making his will in 1637, he pondered the destination of
his 'Frenchbedd' and 'hatband sett with diamondes' he might well have felt
that his devotion to both court and Muse had been rewarded:

Thus have I liv'd, thus have I lov'd till now,
And find noe reason to repent mee yet,
And whosoever otherwise will doe,
His corage is as little as his witt.
('Upon Love', 37–40)

Equally eminent, but in the violently opposed sphere of Presbyterian politics and theology, was Zachary Boyd (c.1585–1653), who rose to be Vice-Chancellor of Glasgow University. Boyd was a pious and learned man, whose ideas of literary education are quite Platonic:

> Our Schooles and Countrey are stained, yea, pestered with idle Bookes, your children are fed on fables, love songs, badry ballads, Heathen husks, youths poison...

and in this spirit he issued *The Garden of Zion, wherein the life and death of godly and wicked men in Scriptures are to be seen* (Glasgow, 1644), in the preface to which, already quoted from, he urges the General Assembly of the Church to 'banish out of the land all the names of the pagan gods and goddesses'. This belongs to the crazier side of Puritan educational reform, in those heady days of the 1640s when clerical assemblies really did seem to be agents of the millenium; but its effect on Boyd's own poetical *Garden* was disastrous, for his avoidance not only of the pagan names but of all the metaphorical and symbolic richness of the classical world leaves a set of versified Biblical biographies of unrelieved plainness. Even plainness might be endurable, but Boyd seems to have embarked upon some eight hundred pages of sacred poems without ever having had it pointed out to him that a verse line is the better for some regularity in the placing of stress. When in the second part of the *Garden* he uses the metre of the Metrical Psalms, he is surer of his rhythms, which is just as well, since about one tenth of the 1650 *Psalter* is his; but when he turns to couplet verse, then, as James VI would have said, it 'flowis nathing at all'.

> This soulesse *Saul*, by *Doegs* villenie
> Was mov'd to slay at *Nob* with crueltie
> Fourscore and five servants of the great God,
> Who for armour had but linnen Ephod,
> Because to *David*, in hunger and need,
> They had vouchsav'd some peece of Gods shewbread.
> At divers times *Saul* fill'd with rage and strife
> Hunted *David* like a flea for his life...
> ('Saul', 127–134)

Boyd is not, as is sometimes said, uncouth or barbarous: he writes in a plain, colloquial style that any intelligent child of the time would understand, but if any man alive had a worse ear, he also had the sense to refrain from printing verse.

Not a faulty ear, but a stuffed head was the handicap of Alexander Craig of Rosscraig (c.1567–1627), who was one of that older generation for whom recondite classical allusion was 'the golden fringe of eloquence'. He referred to himself as 'Scoto-Britane' and 'Scoto-Banfa' (because he lived near Banff), and was one of the most assiduous Scots poets of his age, publishing four volumes of verse. His *Poetical Essays* (London, 1604) was followed by *Amorous Songs, Sonets and Elegies* (London, 1606); then, after he obtained a pension from the King, possibly but not certainly for the very heavy flattery of his poems, and had retired to his house of Rosscraig, he published two volumes of *Poeticall Recreations* (Edinburgh, 1609; Aberdeen, 1623). After his death, Robert Skene printed a curious pastiche of early alliterative verse, Langland crossed with Petrarch, *The Pilgrime and Heremite* (Aberdeen, 1631) which he attributed to Craig.

Craig's output is extremely miscellaneous, even disordered (as his titles hint), comprising praise poems dedicatory, celebratory and elegiac in profession, love sonnets, occasional pieces to his friends—who included Ayton, Alexander Garden and Patrick Gordon (q.v.)—and satirical epigrams. He is surely Europe's most promiscuous sonneteer, writing passionately to Idea, Cynthia, Lithocardia, Kala, Erantina, Lais, Pandora, Penelope, Lesbia and Kalatibia; one hopes that at least one of these names conceals a real woman who returned his affection, for there is good and even moving poetry in him, if the demon of classical pedantry will but hold off:

> Deare heart, dear heart, dear dear dear heart againe,
> More dear than writ can shew, or waxe can seale,
> O! if thou knew the care, the woe, the paine
> I felt since last I tooke from thee fairwell . . .

but then the fit returns, and

> The night in black chimerick thoghts I spend:
> Ere *Phlegon* rise, I wish the day to end.
> ('To his absent and loving Lesbia', 1–6)

He is dreadfully attracted to poulter's measure, but can write surprisingly light and fluent couplets:

> As I have lov'd, so shall I love thee still
> Unto the death, hap either good or ill,
> And now I sweare, by that true love I owe thee,
> By all the sighs which day by day I blow thee,
> By all the verse and charming words I told thee,
> By all the hopes I have for to beholde thee,
> By all the kisses sweete which I have reft thee,
> And all the teares I spent since last I left thee,
> That absence helps (not hinders my desire),
> And sets new force and Fagots to my fire:
> Each thing that chance presents and lets me see,
> Brings arguments, and bids me thinke on thee.
> ('To his Calidonian Mistris', 11–22)

A varied and (for all his pomposity) an unexpectedly moving poet for the reader with patience to sift much dross, 'kind cunning Craig', as Alexander Garden called him, deserves the tribute of some deft anthologising.

William Drummond of Hawthornden (1585–1649) is by so very much the

POETRY AFTER THE UNION 1603–1660 149

greatest Scots poet of his time that he deserves a chapter to himself: what follows is the merest gesture towards his merits. Rarely stirring from his beloved home of Hawthornden, a few miles south of Edinburgh, he avoided parochialism by the extraordinary range of his private reading, by which he absorbed the spirit and style of some of the best European literature in two or three languages, particularly Italian: he lifts his Scottishness into a European idiom. He is in some respects a very traditional poet: aureate, ceremonious and pastoral; Petrarchist (less indebted to Petrarch himself than to the master's Italian followers); classically learned, fond of archaisms and inversions; and little inclined to wit (his many epigrams have no snap or cleverness). But so too might one describe Milton; and it is the young Milton of whom Drummond is most apt to remind the reader. Like Milton, Drummond mastered syntactic fluency (as his friend Alexander did not), and he avoids thumping alliteration; he has a sense of sonority, which in him is a phonic manifestation of his preoccupation with transience and melancholy; and he shows a delighted reverence for the magnificence of creation that (if he were more philosophically minded) one might call neo-Platonic. For Drummond as for Milton, this marvellous universe will attire us with stars, and it is the constant impact of its beauty or terror on the mortal senses that he tries to convey: so God abides, he declares, in 'unaccessible and dimming light', and the Moon 'various in virtue, changing, light, With his small flame engemmes the vaile of Night'. But the argumentative and doctrinal earnestness that drives through most of Milton's verse is absent from Drummond's temperament, and his longer poems, sacred or secular, read as a loose set of decorative impulses, moving indeed, but not all together to one end—a fault discernible too in his long prose meditation upon death, the *Cypresse Grove* of 1623.

The bibliography of Drummond's works is extremely complicated, partly because he liked to make up preliminary issues of his works for giving to friends. This problem aside, his chief poetic works are *Teares on the Death of Meliades* (Edinburgh, 1613), his contribution to the obsequies of Prince Henry; *Poems: Amorous, Funerall, Divine, Pastorall* (Edinburgh, 1616); *Forth Feasting* (Edinburgh, 1617), a panegyric of welcome to King James on his Scottish visit; *Flowres of Sion* (Edinburgh, 1623), which contained also his *Cypresse Grove*; and a pastoral elegy, *To the Exequies of ... Sir Antonye Alexander* (Edinburgh, 1638) in memory of the untimely death of the son of his lifelong friend, Sir William Alexander, then Earl of Stirling. Editions of Drummond's works printed after his death, including the edition in two issues (London, 1656, 1659) by Milton's nephew, Edward Phillips, include further poems from such manuscript sources as were from time to time available. Drummond is also credited with an extremely funny macaronic poem, *Polemo-Medinia inter Vitarvam et Nebernam* (n.p., n.d., but possibly Edinburgh, 1642–50, reprinted Edinburgh 1684), which Drummond's very readable nineteenth century biographer, David Masson, renders as 'The Midden-Fecht between Scotstarvet and Newbarns'.

Drummond's *Poems* of 1616 consists of a chain of sonnets, madrigals, sestinas and songs arranged, as in Alexander's *Aurora*, after the Petrarchan pattern, followed by a reprint of the *Teares on the Death of Meliades* and a miscellany of madrigals and epigrams. The sonnet sequence is in three parts: the first, with sixty-nine poems, is in praise of a living woman; the second, with twenty, praises her after her death (again a Petrarchan division); and the third, in thirteen poems subtitled 'Urania', praises a state of spiritual peace. In the wake of an unsupported statement by an eighteenth century editor of Drummond's works, it used to be thought that these poems were occasioned by Drummond's love for Euphemia Cunningham of Barns, who died on the eve of their marriage; recent scholarship has discovered a date for Miss Cunningham's death, 23 July 1616, too late for the Second Part to have been written after it, and has thus cast doubt on the whole notion that the 1616 poems tell the story of a true and tragically ended love.

Drummond is one of the most intertextual of our poets, constantly weaving into his verse echoes of others'; and his poetry is unreadable on the assumption that sweet verse must be the private expression of a unique soul. The ghosts of half the love poets of Renaissance Europe whisper among his lines: from foreign poets he will often translate and adapt directly, masking them in the change of tongues; from his own countrymen he will take suggestions and echoes, chiefly from Sidney but also from Shakespeare, whose sonnets he may have known, and whose preoccupation with time and change is melodiously like his own. Sometimes he will dramatise a well known gesture or situation, as when, in the lovely Song that ends the Second Part, his dead love comes to his bedside to console him, irresistibly recalling (though without direct borrowing) the consolation of Laura in Petrarch's 'Quando il soave mio fido conforto'. In the sense in which one might properly say that Bunyan's *Pilgrim's Progress* is written by John Bunyan, but authorised by the English Bible, so Drummond writes verse authorised by the major love poets of Europe.

His weakness is to be diffuse, and to attitudinise, and his longer poems lose by their very extent. In the sonnet he is disciplined, and his touch in the difficult final couplet is more consistently sure than Shakespeare's. At his strongest, he can weave the classical learning and aureation that clogs and deadens the verse of Craig or Garden into erotic hyperbole, the style we call mannerist:

> Trust not sweet Soule those curled Waves of Gold
> With gentle Tides which on your Temples flow,
> Nor Temples spread with Flackes of Virgine Snow,
> Nor Snow of Cheekes with *Tyrian* Graine enroll'd.
> Trust not those shining Lights which wrought me Woe,
> When first I did their burning Rayes beholde,
> Nor Voyce, whose Sounds more strange Effects doe show
> Than of the *Thracian* Harper have beene tolde:
> Looke to this dying *Lillie*, fading *Rose*,
> Darke *Hyacinthe*, of late whose blushing Beames
> Made all the neighbouring Herbes and Grasse rejoyce,
> And think how litle is twixt Lifes Extreames:
>   The cruell Tyrant that did kill those Flowrs,
>   Shall once (*aye mee*) not spare that Spring of yours.

Drummond's *Flowres of Sion* of 1623, reissued in 1630, is the only really distinguished collection of religious poems to come out of Scotland in this century, and contains a wide variety of sonnets, short songs and long hymns, running the gamut of religious and moral attitudes from the ecstatic to the Epicurean. The effect is again, overall, one of diffuseness, for there is no driving conviction uniting these many moods, as there is in Herbert's verse; but the Marinesque sense of *meraviglia* is splendidly there, as no other Scots poet (and few English) could manage it:

> Bright Portalles of the Skie,
> Emboss'd with sparkling Starres,
> Doores of Eternitie,
> With diamantine barres,
> Your Arras rich up-hold,
> Loose all your bolts and Springs,
> Ope wide your Leaves of gold;
> That in your Roofes may come the King of kinges.
> Scarff'd in a rosie Cloud,
> Hee doth ascend the Aire,
> Straight doth the Moone him shrowd
> With her resplendant Haire;
> The next enchristall'd Light
> Submits to him its Beames,
> And he doth trace the hight
> Of that faire Lamp which flames of beautie streames.
> ('An Hymne of the Ascension', 1–16)

If he lacks theological coherence, he can still guide commonplaces into plangency:

> As doth the Pilgrime therefore whom the Night
> By darknesse would imprison on his way,
> Think on thy Home (my Soule) and thinke aright,
> Of what yet restes thee of Lifes wasting Day:
>   Thy Sunne postes Westward, passed is thy Morne,
>   And twice it is not given thee to bee borne.
> ('No Trust in Tyme', 9–14)

Passed indeed was his morn when he wrote that, and though his marriage, in 1632, and a numerous family were still to come, he was increasingly drawn into prose writing amid the gathering troubles of Scotland. A dutiful pageant for the visit of Charles I in 1633, lauding that shiftiest of monarchs for every virtue he did not possess, and an elegy for the Earl of Stirling's dead son, like enough to *Lycidas* to demonstrate the gulf between a very fine poet and a superlatively great one—these, and a number of cynical squibs fired off at the squabbling clerics and politicians, suggest that Drummond's energies turned at the close elsewhere than to the poetry of passion, in which, till Burns, he has no native rival.

The effects of that provincialism which Drummond avoided can be seen in Alexander Garden or Gardyne (*c*.1590–*c*.1642), advocate of Aberdeen, who can be set alongside his contemporary Patrick Hannay (*c*.1594–*c*.1650), gentleman, Master of Arts and soldier in the cause of the luckless Queen of Hearts, Elizabeth of Bohemia. Both Garden and Hannay wrote collections of short poems, sonnets, elegies and epigrams; both attempted longer works in the popular sixain stanza (rhyming ababcc, the form of *Venus and Adonis*). Hannay, with no great originality, is light, charming and eminently readable; Garden's platitudinous and morose reflectiveness seems quite untouched by anything in literature after about 1590, bounded as it is by a dry classical education on the one side and severe religion on the other ('To gather gear is good, I grant,/But godlie nocht therein to glore'). Garden had read Sidney, or a piece of him, as his dedicatory sonnet to his *Garden of Grave and Godlie Flowers* (Edinburgh, 1609) shows, but he seems unaware that the curious diction, wealth of allusion and letters 'running in rattling rows' is something at which Sidney pokes fun. For him the Muse is a mistress of inversion, alliteration and inkhorn terms:

> Convert your eyes unto this Voult, and view
> This *Sepulture*, or this *Spelunck* espie. . . .
> ('Epitaph upon . . . Walter Urquart', 1–2)

In later life Garden compiled two long poems, neither of which was printed in the seventeenth century: first, his *Theatre of Scottish Kings*, written between 1612 and 1628, and first printed by James Watson in Edinburgh in 1708; second, a parallel *Theatre of Scottish Worthies*, finished about 1628, which remained in manuscript until the Hunterian Club issued it in 1878. Both are very dull. His most readable poem is *The Lyf, Doings and Deathe of . . . William Elphinstone* (Aberdeen, 1619), a versification of the Bishop's life in Hector Boece's *Vitae Episcoporum Aberdonensium*. Resolutely looking backwards, Garden chose poulter's measure, but printed as it is in lines of 6 : 6 : 8 : 6, it has a kind of hirpling jauntiness, and he sensibly keeps to a plain narrative style, if sometimes a little put to it to generate excitement:

> The channons, clerks and all,
> Al wounderfullie proone,   [prone]
> Prayes, and for Pastor postulats
> Ane Williame Elphinstoune.
> (*The Lyf*, 5–8)

Patrick Hannay, from a Galloway family, probably had his education in England, and rather ambitiously published his poetical works in 1622, after which we have nothing from him except some commendatory verse in the works of others. He first broke into print in 1619 with two elaborate elegies in the manner of Donne on the death of Queen Anne, reprinted in his 1622 volume: their intellectual affectation quickly palls. Much better, and thoroughly typical of Hannay's secular gracefulness, is his long poem *Philomela, or the Nightingale*, a retelling of the Ovidian legend in 107 stanzas, for which he provided (and may have composed) a melody in the new *stilo recitativo*. Its first stanza so perfectly represents how voices mixed in the ear of a Scots writer in the south that I give it entire:

> Walking I chanc'd into a shade
> Which top-in-twining trees had made
>   Of many several kinds.
> There grew the high aspiring Elme,
> With boughs bathing in gum-like balme,
>   Distilling through their rinds.
> The Maple with a skarry skin
>   Did spread broad pallid leaves:
> The quaking Aspine light and thin
>   To th'ayre light passage gives:
> Resembling still
> The trembling ill
>   Of tongues of womankinde,
> Which never rest,
> But still are prest
>   To wave with every winde.
>   (1–16)

Backward looking to *The Cherrie and the Slae* for its stanza form, and to Spenser and Elizabethan georgic verse for its earnest catalogue of trees, with compound adjectives, this also has the casual elegance of Sidney or Morley in its phrasing and cadences; but the last six lines are flippant and worldly, breaking out of Arcady into the more ironic world of the seventeenth century courtier, from whose fashionable music the style of the melody also comes.

Hannay is quite ready to try other styles: after *Philomela* comes an Italianate romance, *Sheretine and Mariana*, in 223 sixains, in which we move into the world of conflicting passions and duties so favoured by the later seventeenth century; after that in the 1622 volume comes a sequel to Sir Thomas Overbury's *A Perfect Wife*, called *A Happy Husband*, full of colloquially expressed marital advice. But the last and best item in the 1622 *Works* is a collection of *Songs and Sonets*, a delightful and varied set that should be better known. The man is a good chameleon: with nothing much of his own to say, he can pick up the colours of others and mimic them: Ayton, for example,

> I can love, and love intirely,
> And can prove a constant friend,
> But I must be lov'd as dearely,
> And as truly to the end.
>   For her love no sooner slaketh,
>   But my fancie farwell taketh.
>   ('Song III', 1–6)

Or Drayton or Daniel, in a recherché simile:

> My Celia's love thus prov'd a Lizard right:
> I seene, it lived; it di'd, I out of sight.
>   ('Sonnet XIV', 13–14)

There are dialogue sonnets, paradoxes, religious pieces, cynical court airs: when he is not distracted by moralising or flippancy, he has a very good ear indeed. His 'Song IV', inviting his Celia to love as the birds do, has a delicate rocking rhythm that makes one realise how rhythmically unadventurous many of his fellow Scots poets were:

> He sweetly sings, and staies the nimble wings
>   Of her in th'aire,
> She hovering staies, to hear his loving laies
>   Which wooe her there:
> She becomes willing, heares him wooe,
>   Gives eare unto his song:
> And doth as *Nature* taught her doe,
>   Yeelds, su'd unto not long.
>
> But *Caelia* staies, she feeds me with delaies,
>   Heares not my mone:
> She knows the smart in time will kill my heart
>   To live alone:
> Learne of the birds to chuse thee a pheare   [peer]
>   But not like them to range:
> They have their mate but for a yeare,
>   But sweet, let's never change.
>   (9–24)

The distance between Aberdeen and Bohemia seems about fifty years.

Another engaging Patrick is Patrick Gordon (dates unknown, but supposed to be the same as Patrick Gordon of Ruthven (d. 1650?), author of a prose tract, *A Short Abridgement of Britains Distemper* (Aberdeen, Spalding Club, 1844)). He produced two strikingly good prentice attempts at epic, both published abroad at Dort in 1615; first, *The Famous Historie of the Renouned and Valiant Prince Robert Surnamed the Bruce*, which carries the imprimatur of the Archbishop of St Andrews, dated December 1613, and may be the earlier work. It is an Italianate martial epic with romantic trimmings—or at least the first book of one—written in seventeen chapters of eight-line stanzas, amounting to about 8,000 lines, and tells the story of Bruce from his meeting with Sir James Douglas to his victory at Bannockburn. Spenser is his immediate model, but a certain historical sobriety makes him reluctant to use the whole range of romantic fantasia. He does his best to romanticise the Scots landscape, as Scott was to do in *The Lady of the Lake*, and in much the same mood of chivalric nostalgia; and there are theatrical moments of decided power, as when (quite improbably) Thomas the Rymer encounters Bruce in the mountains:

'And so, fairweill'—this said, throu schaples air
Hee went away: a light, cleir, bright and schining
Enlightened all the Place, so cleir and fair
As *Phebus* seimd but *Phebe*, thence refining   [the moon]
His paill old Beautie spent with aige and cair,
The Prince his kneis and dasled eies enclining
  Doun fals he straight: lyf seemd to leave his statione,
  Stroke blind with light and dumb with admiratione.
                                        (*Bruce*, ch 5, st. 43)

Gordon's second epic attempt, *The First Booke of the famous History of Penardo and Laissa* (Dort, 1615) is quite free of any debt to history, and is a marvellous Spenserian romp in the world of dungeons and dragons. Like his *Bruce*, it is a First Book, written in seventeen chapters, but it is in the lighter sixain stanza, and is set in the never-never land of Greek romance, as the Renaissance knew it: the wizard Mansay, the evil Prince Sigismund, the treacherous Olinda, the unhappy Hungarian princess Vodiva, all crowd in with the Muses, giants and dwarves, to complicate the passionate love of Penardo for the warrior-maid Laissa. Many of the unskilfulnesses of the *Bruce* have gone, and the pastoral/fairy-tale world unrolls fluently in the manner of Spenser and Tasso. Gordon does not seem to have allegorical designs on his readers, though it is hard to tell from one book only (he clearly intended a sequel), but many of his folk motifs are suggestive of ampler things, and his phantasmagorical powers are considerable.

Drummond, contributing a complimentary sonnet to the volume, said of his Laissa that

      ... though thou after greater ones be born,
      Thou mayst be bold ev'n with the first to sitt,
      For whilst fair Juliett or the Farie Quene
      Do live, with theirs thy beautie shall be seen.
('Come forth, *Laissa*, spred thy lockes of Gold', 11–14)

Gordon's *Bruce*, indeed, was reprinted by James Watson in Edinburgh in 1718, and is not difficult to find; *Penardo and Laissa*, much the more enjoyable work, is extremely rare, and deserves a sympathetic modern reprint, to establish Gordon as one of Scotland's first fantasy writers.

Every age should have at least one poetic eccentric, and our specimen is William Lithgow (b. 1580–90. d. after 1660), Scotland's equivalent of John Taylor, the Water-Poet. Lithgow made his reputation as 'the Scotish Traveller' by roaming in Britain and abroad and writing up his travels, the first Scotsman to do so; most of his resulting work is in prose, and falls outside this chapter, but he was also an energetic versifier, writing political, religious and topical as well as topographical poetry. He came from a respectable but humble family (his father was a burgess of Lanark), and having no private means, had to sing for his supper: like Craig of Rosscraig, another favour seeker, he shows great ingenuity in composing dedicatory poems, and his *Pilgrim Farewell to his Native Countrey of Scotland* (Edinburgh, 1618) has eleven of them. One has to admire the casual flick of the pen that propels yet another possible patron into his verse:

> From Carlile unto Clyde that Southwest shore I know,
> And by the way, Lord Harreis I remembrance duelie owe.
>
> ('An Elegie', 35–36)

His most interesting poem is the long *Scotland's Welcome to her Native Sonne and Soveraign Lord King Charles* (Edinburgh, [1633]): after some routine adulation, he settles into the conversational style at which he was best, and gives a trenchant account of the distresses of Scotland, caused by an absentee aristocracy and gentry haemorrhaging money and power steadily south. His unhappy Scotland speaks to her King with a colloquial bite that has lost none of its relevance in 350 years:

> As for my *Trades*, they're ruind with decay,
> There few or none imploy'd: My *Nobles* play
> The curious Courtizan, that will not bee
> But in strange fashions; O! what Noveltie
> Is this? that *London* robbes Mee of my gaine,
> Whilst both my *Trades* and *Merchands* suffer pain
> ... Besides my *Nobles*, see my *Gentry* too
> Post up, post downe, their states for to undoe:
> Nay, they will morgadge all; and to bee breefe,
> Ryde up with gold, and turne againe with greefe.
> Who better far might stay at home, and live,
> And not their meanes to lovelesse labour give.
> It grieves Mee, I should yeeld them yeerely rent
> Whilst vainely it in Neighbour Lands is spent;
> But *ecce homo*, and behold the end,
> My Lands change *Land-Lords*, whilst my *Youngsters* spend.
>
> (*Scotland's Welcome*, 391–96, 405–14)

He lived to write in the age of Dryden, a tough, passionate and sharp observer of the times, whose direct and unpretentious verse lets the modern reader see how a humble Scot reacted to the stresses of the seventeenth century.

One who did indeed 'stay at home and live' was Sir William Mure of Rowallan (1594–1657), born too late to be sucked south among the place-seeking courtiers of James VI and I, who seems to have lived quietly all his life upon his estates near Kilmarnock. He went south briefly into military service for the Covenant, at Dunse Law, Marston Moor and Newcastle, where the worst that befell him was 'a sore blow upon my back with the butt of a musket'. His poetic output is almost a recapitulation of the development of poetry in the late Renaissance: he begins with a strongly Mediæval 'Conflict tuix Love and Ressoun' (about 1611) in the vein of Alexander Montgomerie (whose nephew he was); he moves through a phase of alliterative Petrarchism and elegant trifling:

> Must I unpittied still remain,
>   But regaird,
>   Or rewaird,
>   Nothing caird,
> Bot by my sweitest slain?
>   ('Must I unpittied', 1–5)

He shows both aspects of a godly humanist education in his 'Dido and Aeneas', a very competent reworking, sometime before 1617, of Books 1 and 4 of the *Aeneid*, and 'Doomesday' (1628), a passionate, oft-apostrophising evocation of 'hells horrour and Heavens happinesse'; and he ends within measurable distance of *Religio Laici*, with a series of earnest theologico-political poems in heroic couplets, a response to the religious conflicts which pestered his last two decades. There is a certain grim force in these, but he is fatally handicapped by diffuseness and prolixity, to both of which the heroic couplet is pitiless: it is one thing to lay aside, as he said, 'the whorish ornaments of affected eloquence'; it is quite another to acquire the deft arrangement of antitheses and unforced syntax that mark good mid-century argumentative verse. Yet when the gradient is with him, as it were, he can sometimes run pleasingly enough:

> Looke yet a little in this mirror rare,
> Predictions with accomplishments compare,
> With wonder ravisht, heere thou shalt behold
> All done, what earst was to bee done, foretold,
> Of Typs the clowdie Mysteries explaind,
> Shadows sequestred, reall Truths attaind,
> The legall rites, the ceremoniall lawe
> By Him abolisht, who the vaile did draw,
> Of Christ affording a more lively sight,
> A clearer knowledge, and a nearer light,
> So that the tenderest sight, the weakest eye,
> Him now unmasked in this glasse may see.
>   ('The True Crucifixe for True Catholiques', 355–366)

Perhaps he is happiest under external discipline: in the small frame of the sonnet, he need not be extravagant and cannot be diffuse, and his 'Adieu! my love, my life, my blisse, my being' has a neat and honest gallantry that is most winning.

While modestly admitting that he was 'pan to Apollo, if compaird in worth' with Montgomerie, Mure felt himself obliged by pedigree to be a poet, and has left us about eleven thousand lines of diligent verse (including yet another metrical version of the Psalms) in proof of it. Like so many of his contemporaries, he changed voices as the century advanced: shrugging off the rather threadbare Castalian mantle, he reacted to the now changing and confused relations between a gentleman and his Sovereign and State by embracing with a stronger faith not only 'a sword, a horse, a shield' but the rough, plain couplet verse that foreruns the witty clarity of the Augustan age.

Backward looking, though most creatively, was the courtier poet Sir David Murray of Gorthie (1567–1629), whose sonnet sequence *Caelia*, though published in 1611, is one of the most accomplished and attractive of the 1590s' imitations of Sidney's *Astrophel*. Unlike his friend Sir William Alexander, Murray thought well enough of the 'youthfull follies' of his 'unstay'd yeares' to publish them in his maturity; but they belong to the earlier age, and are mentioned in the previous chapter.

Well-nigh faultless as his sense of the sonnet's structure and movement is, he required different talents for his other poetical production of 1611, *The Tragicall Death of Sophonisba*. Written in 190 septains, the seven-line stanza of *The Rape of Lucrece*, the poem tells of the death of Sophonisba by poison at the unwilling direction of her husband, Massinissa; and it lies, like *The Rape of Lucrece*, somewhere between romance and tragedy—the action is curtailed, and great space given to the passionate self-communings of the protagonists. The resemblances between *Lucrece* and *Sophonisba* are marked, both thematic and stylistic: neither the young Shakespeare nor Murray has Spenser's command of a narrative line, and the tight stanza form pushes both of them towards the creation of a series of jewelled moments and epigrammatic reflections. But Shakespeare's extraordinary lexical richnes and feeling for the speaking voice, even then, lifts *Lucrece* above Murray's more diffuse poem; yet it has its moments, as when Sophonisba tries to argue herself out of her predicament with a foretaste of Comus' argument that 'beauty is Nature's coin, should not be hoarded':

> Beauty (God knowes) was not ordain'd to mone,
> Nor to live chastely at her first creation:
> For skilfull Nature, who hath made the Sunne
> To give us light, made her for procreation,
> Not Image like for ostentation,
>   But as choise fruites are made-of for choise seedes,
> And stately Stallions to breed stately steeds.
>
> As th'Apple to the taste, the Rose to smell,
> The pleasant Lilly to delight the eye,
> Gould for the touch, sweet Musick greefe to expell,
> So rarest beauty was ordained to be
> The mindes desired full satiety,
>   The treasure of the soule, the hearts delight,
>   Loves full contentment both by day and night.
>   (*Sophonisba*, stt. 93–94)

Like Hannay in his *Sheretine and Mariana*, and like Gordon in *Penardo and Laissa*, Murray had some sense, felt in the blood and felt along the heart by all those who had read Spenser and Tasso, of what one might call passionate nobleness—sought perhaps the more keenly in verse romance as it was less and less exemplified in the behaviour of their sovereign and his advisers.

A clutch of very minor writers remains. We may begin with two Grahams, at opposite ends of the period, and opposite in every other way as well:

Simion Grahame (*c.*1570–1614) is a gloomy and stridently bitter figure, better known for his Websterian *Anatomie of Humors* (Edinburgh, 1609), which contains a few poems, than for his single verse production, *The Passionate Sparke of a Relenting Minde* (London, 1604). This was dedicated to James VI and I, and very decoratively set forth, but its temper and quality are sufficiently indicated by the anagram which Grahame therein made of his own name:

> A pilgrim stille, my Oracle was so,
> And made my name, AH MISER MAN I GO.
> ('His Passionado', 47–48)

No such sullen gravity in the career of James Graham, Marquis of Montrose (1612–50), the *preux chevalier* of his day. He left only a handful of poems in the cavalier idiom, and the best known of these ('Great, good and just' on the death of Charles I and 'Let them bestow on every airt a limb', written, it is said, on his cell window the night before he mounted his thirty-foot scaffold) owe more to the romance of their composition than to the skill of it. Two perfect stanzas of his 'Love Verses', that find their way into every anthology of Scots poetry, show the wit, urbanity and grace of that tragic prodigy:

> My dear and only love, I pray
> That little world of thee
> Be governed by no other sway
> Than purest monarchy,
> For if confusion bear a part,
> Which virtuous souls abhor,
> I'll call a synod in my heart,
> And never love thee more.
>
> As Alexander I will reign,
> And I will reign alone:
> My thoughts did evermore disdain
> A rival on my throne.
> He either fears his fate too much,
> Or his deserts are small,
> Who dares not put it to the touch,
> To win or lose it all.
> (1–16)

Robert Ker, Earl of Ancrum (1578–1654), might from his very successful court career have acquired the wit and will to be another Ayton, but all that survives, apart from some psalmody, is a sonnet upon the life of retirement, not as good as Ayton's whimsical adaptation of Saint-Amant, 'Upon Tobacco'. Another ardent Royalist, who like Ker died in exile abroad, was Sir Thomas Urquhart (1611–60), who attempted one volume of verse early in his career, his *Epigrams Divine and Moral* (London, 1641). No literary form could be more alien to the genius of the translator of Rabelais than the epigram, and Urquhart's are uniformly dull and dated, oscillating feebly between the obvious and the trivial.

Less dull, but also less polished, is the verse of John Lundie (d. 1652?) who belonged to the 'Aberdeen Doctors', a group of academic Latinists who kept classical learning and verse alive in Northern Scotland in the first part of this century: Lundie was Professor of Humanity at Aberdeen University. His vernacular verse is occasional: verse letters, elegies and ceremonial pieces arising from a placid professorial career, and stuffed full of rough pedantry and heavy politeness.

The Sempills of Beltrees, James (1566–1626) and his son Robert (1595–1669), were responsible for a crude anti-Catholic poem, *The Packmans Pater Noster*, printed by James in Edinburgh before 1640, and enlarged and reprinted by his son in Edinburgh 1669. But Robert's name is chiefly associated with the poem which put the 'Burns stanza' into currency, *The Life and Death of the Piper of Kilbarchan*, written, probably, within our period, though not printed until the end of the century. The Piper's name was Habbie Simson, and when Allan Ramsay and Hamilton of Gilbertfield rediscovered the stanza form, at once so colloquially suited and so close to Horace's favourite verse form, they christened it 'standard Habbie'.

Aberdeen may also be allowed to provide a wry, and final contribution to this survey of poetry after the Union with the publication in the city in 1662 of what was, astonishingly, the very first collection of secular songs in Scotland: the printer John Forbes' *Songs and Fancies* (often known as *Cantus: Songs and Fancies* from its title page, though 'Cantus' of course refers to the part, the only one published). The contents seem to have been the repertoire of the flourishing sangschule of Aberdeen, and are shrewdly chosen to offer something to every taste, from the frivolous pastoral fa-la to the serious penitential song. But what is really remarkable is that almost nothing in the collection postdates 1620, and two-thirds of it is English, drawing heavily upon the songbooks of Dowland, Bartlett, Jones and others. The third that is Scots has texts mostly anonymous (some of which may be English in origin) and the poet most frequently represented is Alexander Montgomerie. Since the golden age of British Renaissance song lies indeed between 1588 and 1620, Forbes' poetic retrospection is musically excusable; yet the manuscript song collections and music books (such as Mure of Rowallan's) surviving from the seventeenth century show us a considerable interest in native texts and airs, particularly folk song, and of this virtually nothing appears in *Songs and Fancies*. For all its vaunted musical independence, Aberdeen closes our period with an anthology that once again stresses the dominance, in matters of art, of the Southern idiom.

FURTHER READING

PRIMARY TEXTS

Boyd, Zachary, *The Garden of Zion* (Glasgow, 1644)

Forbes, John (compiler), *Cantus: Songs and Fancies*, 3rd edn (Aberdeen, 1682, repr Paisley, 1879)

Gardyne or Garden, Alexander, *A Garden of Grave and Godlie Flowers, The Theatre of Scottish Kings*, Turnbull, W B D D (ed), Abbotsford Club (Edinburgh, 1845)

—— *A Theatre of Scottish Worthies*, Laing, David (ed), Hunterian Club (Glasgow, 1878)

Gordon, Patrick, *The Famous Historie of...Robert...the Bruce* (Dort, 1615), Watson, James (ed) (reissued Edinburgh, 1718)

—— *The First Booke of the Famous History of Penardo and Laissa* (Dort, 1615)

Graham, James, Marquis of Montrose, in *Scottish Poetry of the Seventeenth Century*, Eyre-Todd, G (ed) (London and Edinburgh, n.d.)

Grahame, Simion, *The Passionate Sparke of a Relenting Minde* (London, 1604)

Gullans, Charles B (ed), *The English and Latin Poems of Sir Robert Ayton*, STS (Edinburgh and London, 1963)

Kastner, L E (ed), *The Poetical Works of William Drummond of Hawthornden*, 2 vols (Manchester, 1913) (repr for STS)

—— and Charlton, H B (eds), *The Poetical Works of Sir William Alexander*, STS, 2 vols (Edinburgh and London, 1921–29)

Ker, Sir Robert, in *Scottish Poetry of the Seventeenth Century*

Kinnear, T (ed), *Poems of Sir David Murray of Gorthy*, Bannatyne Club (Edinburgh, 1823)

Laing, David (ed), *The Poetical Works of Alexander Craig of Rosecraig*, Hunterian Club (Glasgow, 1875)

—— *The Poetical Works of Patrick Hannay, 1622*, Hunterian Club (Glasgow, 1875)

—— *Miscellaneous Poems of John Lundie*, Abbotsford Club (Edinburgh, 1845)

Lithgow, William, *Poetical Remains*, Maidment, J (ed) (Edinburgh, 1863)

Stirling, S D (ed), *Works of Sir Thomas Urquhart of Cromarty*, Maitland Club (Edinburgh, 1834)

Tough, W (ed), *Works of Sir William Mure of Rowallan*, STS, 2 vols (Edinburgh and London, 1897–98)

SECONDARY TEXTS

Fogle, F R, *A Critical Study of Drummond of Hawthornden* (Oxford, 1952)

Jack, R D S, 'Drummond: the Major Scottish Sources', *SSL*, 6 (1968), 36–46

MacDonald, R H, 'Drummond, Miss Euphemia Kyninghame and the Poems', *Modern Language Review*, 60 (1965), 494–99

—— *The Library of Drummond of Hawthornden* (Edinburgh, 1971)

McGrail, T H, *Sir William Alexander* (Edinburgh, 1940)

Masson, David, *William Drummond of Hawthornden* (Edinburgh, 1873)
Roberts, W, 'Saint-Amant, Ayton and the tobacco sonnet', *Modern Language Review*, 54 (1959), 499–506
Wallerstein, Ruth, 'The Style of Drummond of Hawthornden in its relation to his translations', *PMLA*, 48 (1933), 1089–1107

Chapter 10

Vernacular Prose before the Reformation

R J LYALL

By comparison with the rich poetic tradition of the Makars, Older Scots prose was slow to develop and sparse in its achievements. There was, in contrast with fourteenth- and fifteenth-century English, little in the way of religious prose; no Malory emerged to create a Scots prose romance; no More or Elyot transposed the elegance of humanist Latin into the vernacular. The historians almost all wrote in Latin, like Fordoun in the fourteenth century, Bower in the fifteenth, and Major and Boece in the sixteenth, or in vernacular verse, like Wyntoun. Significantly, when in the mid fifteenth century an unknown Scot came to translate the French prose *Lancelot* into Scots, he wrote in pentameter couplets. Only in the second half of the sixteenth century did vernacular historians and religious controversialists emerge in any numbers, and their language shows increasingly the influence of contemporary English: in the fifteenth century, anglicisation is principally evident in poetry, but the influence of the English Reformation and of the English Bible in particular ensured that it was in prose that the greatest degree of erosion occurred after about 1550.[1] Not until the middle of the seventeenth century, and then in English, do we find, in Sir Thomas Urquhart's *Jewel*, a Scottish writer attempting imaginative, fictional prose in the way that Malory had developed a vernacular prose romance and Nashe and others had experimented with prose fiction in the age of Elizabeth.

Yet it is not true that there were no prose writers in Middle Scots, nor even that there were no significant ones. At least by about 1450, some writers were beginning to turn their hands to the composition of works in prose. As with verse, many of these comparatively early works were translations from French or Latin; the prevalence of translation should remind us of the fact that late Mediæval Scottish culture was part of a tradition common to Western Europe as a whole, and that the most obvious way of enriching vernacular culture was by making available in Scots works which were already popular in Latin or in another, well-established vernacular such as French. Nor did this preoccupation with translation quickly die out: as late as 1549 the author of *The Complaynt of Scotland* turned to the *Quadrilogue Invectif* of the fifteenth-century French writer Alain Chartier as a basis for his own work, and the writings of the early Reformers in the 1530s and 1540s are frequently translated or adapted from Luther and his Continental followers. As we shall see, this heavy reliance upon foreign sources had a clear effect upon the development of Middle Scots prose style.

Latin models had a profound influence upon the earliest prose texts we find in Scotland, the charters and other legal documents which began to be written in the vernacular in the last quarter of the fourteenth century. These items are, of course, in no real sense literary, but they do provide the first glimpse of Scots prose; and it is evident that they were closely modelled upon the Latin forms which had been current for three hundred years or so. The common opening formula 'Till al that thir lettres herys or seis', for example, derives directly from the Latin 'Universis presentes literas visuris vel audituris', with an interesting reversal of the verbs which perhaps suggests that the construction of even such functional prose as this might be influenced by an ear for an effective cadence. Both the terminology and the construction of much of what follows in such documents are similarly straightforward renderings of familiar legal phrases, often preserving a complexity of syntax which is unaided by the inflections characteristic of the Latin models:

> ... I ber witnes lele & suthfast [truthful] that Richart Jonsoun, whilum lard of a quarter of Colstoun, befor the witnes undirwrytin resignit and up gaf of his awin gude wil, quytly and frely, be staf and bastoun [staff and cudgel (symbols by which land was resigned)], al the rycht that he had or mycht haf of the forsayd quarter of Colstoun liand within the Schirrefdome of Fyf in my handis for to gif to Michel Rony, lord of ane othir quarter of Colstoun, til his ayris and his assignes [appointees (legal)], for a sum of silvir, the whilk the forsayd Michel payt til Jhon Martyn, lard of Brigland for the lyfe of the forsayd Richart, quytly boucht fra the forsayd Jhon Martyn for mysdede he had done to the forsayd Jhon, for the whilk him behuvit [ought] til haf deit [died] ...[2]

The complexities of lawyers' syntax are fully apparent here: the detachment of the adverbial phrase 'in my handis' from the verbs 'resignit and up gaf' is particularly striking, and the draftsman is not afraid to string together relative clauses when dealing with the legal intricacy of Richard Johnson's payment of compensation to John Martin for his unstated misdeed. The fairly rapid rise in the incidence of these vernacular documents over the last two decades of the fourteenth century demonstrates an advance in the status of Scots which parallels developments in England, and which is almost exactly contemporary with the emergence of a substantial body of vernacular Scots verse.[3]

By the same token, the beginning of the fifteenth century sees the first occurrence of the laws themselves in Scots: new statutes were not recorded in the vernacular until the reign of James II, but the collections of ancient laws which were made and transmitted from about 1425 frequently contain some Scots items, usually translations of Latin laws. The earliest such manuscript to survive, which was written in 1424 or earlier, includes a Scots translation of the *Leges Burgorum*, an early compilation of legislation relating to burghs, and one of two versions of *The Law of Schippis*, known to Continental lawyers as the *Laws of Oleron*. The translator shows himself to be altogether competent to deal with the pithiness of the original, with its decidedly participatory approach to labour relations:

A schyp is in to a havyn and abydis his tyme: and he be redy to sayle, the maystyr aw [is obliged] to ask consaile at his falowis, and he aucht to say, 'Lordis, we hafe this weddyr.' Sum sais the weddyr is gude, and sum says nay; the maystyr aw to acorde wyth the mast part, and gyf he dois uthir-gatys [otherwise] and oucht cum to the schip bot gude, the maystyr aw to pay the skathys [damages], gyf he hafys quhar-of.[4]

Although the sentence structure is fairly loose, the argument here, with its various contingencies, is clear enough, and the practical-minded vigour of the translation, which is generally shared by these early legal texts, reflects the functional purpose of the prose.

The syntactic characteristics of these legal texts become clearer when we compare two early translations of the *Laws of Oleron*, that in the Bute manuscript and another preserved in part of Cambridge UL MS. Kk.i.5 (4), in a fragment which can be dated *c.* 1460–75 but which may contain texts which are rather earlier:

Bute MS.

A schyp passys fra Burdews or fra vthyr placis; chance cummys that he may nocht eschew castyng of gudes. Thai aw to schaw to the chepmen the perel, and the chepmen aucht to say thair entente to the maystyr and aw to grante to the castyng thrw aventure, for than is the maystyr the clerar hw-euer it fal eftyr. And gyfe thai grant nocht to the castyng the maystyr aw nocht to let thar-for to cast als mykyl as hym thunk gude, and he sal swere wyth thre of his falows on Goddis halydome qwhen he is commyn to saufte to the land, that he ne dyd it bot in saufte [protection] of the schyp and of the men.

(p 133)

Cambridge MS.

Gyf a schip passis fra Burdeows or fra ony vthir stede, cas cummys scho castis gudis throw stormys; thai aw til tel the schipmen the case how it standis, and than the schipmen aw to grant to the casting throu auentour, and than is the maistir cler. And gif the schepmen grantit nocht the maistir sal cast it neuir the les, als mekil as him thinkis gude at his awyn wyl. Bot the maistir sal suer on Goddis hallowis that he kest yat gude for na caus bot for ye sanite of his schipe and of the guddis.

(f. 2ᵛ)*

The Bute version contains several details which are omitted by Cambridge, but we cannot be sure that these differences are due to the translators rather than to their sources. What is clear is that the compiler of the former version is more confidently in control of his syntactic structures: the translator of the Cambridge version loses track of his opening conditional clause, for example, and 'than is the maistir cler' is somewhat lame by comparison with Bute's 'than is the maystyr the clerar hw-euer it fal eftyr'. The fairly numerous Scots versions of legal texts which were evidently produced in the middle decades of the fifteenth century all share, in varying degrees, this idiomatic vigour,

* [Editor's Note: The passages used for this comparison have not been normalised.]

expressing complex legal principles in the everyday language of burgesses and notaries.[5]

The same vernacular confidence is apparent in the third group of early Scots prose texts, the letters which were written in that language from about 1390 onwards. While there is no significant corpus of vernacular letters to compare with those produced by the Pastons, Stonors, Celys and other English families, there is evidence that some Scottish households began to use Scots, at least for certain purposes, by the end of the fourteenth century. The formal epistolary language was still Latin, and the clerks of the royal household continued to use French for some diplomatic correspondence until about 1400; but some purely domestic items, and correspondence with recipients in England, began to be composed in Scots before the turn of the century. Apart from isolated instances in the royal household, the Dunbar earls of March and the earls of Douglas appear to have been pioneers in this regard, partly no doubt because of their particular political involvements with England. The earls of March, for example, were brought into contact with the monastic house at Durham through their patronage of the latter's daughter-house at Coldingham, and it was in this connection that the third earl wrote to the prior of Durham in 1392:

> For gyf yhe do in the contrarie of our intent at this tyme, we ar litille holdyn to be tendir, or travaille for any thynge that langes yhowe in tyme to come, syn sa lytill a thynge and, as us thynke, resonable and profytable, bothe for yhou and the house of Coldynghame, may noght be spedde anente yhoue for oure request and oure counsaille, the whilke we desire for the profytte of the hous.[6]

Here the rhythms of spoken idiom, though formalised and a few degrees elevated, come through clearly enough to give a subtly-modulated menace to March's argument of his case. In a somewhat different vein, Sir James Douglas similarly addresses Henry IV of England in forthright language:

> Anence the quhilkys, hee and excellent prynce, quhar yhe say yhu mervalys gretly that my men be my will and assent has brennede the toun of Berwik, the quhilk is wythin Scotlande, and other places in Inglande in brekyng fully of the sayde trewis [truce], I understand that giff yhour hee excellent war clerly enfourmyte of the brennyng, slachtyr and takyng of prisoneris and Scottis schippis that is done be yhour men to Scottys men wythin the saide trewis in divers places of Scotlande befor the brynnyng of Berwike, the quhilk skathis [damages] our lege lorde the kyng and his liegis has paciently tholyte in the kepyng of the said trewis and chargit me til aske and ger be askyte at dayis of marche and nane has gotyne, me think o resoune yhe sulde erar [sooner] put blame and punicioun to the doarys of the saide trespas done agayn the trewis in swilke maner, and callys thaim rather brekaris of the trewis than me that has tholyte sa mikylle injure so lang and nane amendis gottyn.[7]

As befits a magnate writing to a monarch, albeit a foreign one, Douglas is circumspect in his phrasing, but the tone of offended innocence is consistently maintained through these thirteen clauses, and the author has on the whole managed the complex patterns of subordination with admirable lucidity. Only towards the end of the passage, where the inverted phrase 'nane has gotyne' is attached awkwardly to the preceding clause and the verb 'callys', somewhat remote from its subject, appears to be in the wrong tense (it is syntactically parallel with 'put' in the previous line) does the argument start to crack under its own weight.

The categories which we have so far considered, legal documents, vernacular translations of legal texts, and personal letters, are in essence functional rather than literary. But even those kinds of Mediæval prose which come closer to literature as it is usually defined are characterised by functional rather than aesthetic considerations. Most of it is in some sense instructional, whether it offers moral, political or chivalric advice or provides a model for popular devotion. The manuscript evidence is sparse and derives almost entirely from the last decades of the fifteenth century, but it tends to suggest that the audience for works in vernacular prose, whether in noble or genteel households or in the growing population of townspeople, was for the most part interested entirely in works with this practical emphasis. It is, therefore, not surprising to find a group of them occurring along with legal texts in the miscellany which is now Cambridge UL MS. Kk.i.5, written in the latter part of the century but clearly preserving texts which are considerably earlier. The central sections of the manuscript are principally in verse, but there are also three prose works: *The Craft of Deyng*, a summary of the Book of Ecclesiastes entitled *Dicta Salamonis*, and *The Vertewis of the Mess*. None of the these works, of course, is entirely original, and all appear to be aimed at that group of pious, literate laypeople whose numbers were, it may be presumed, steadily increasing in the fifteenth century. The style is appropriately straightforward, employing simple rhetoric and basic syntactic structures:

> For God at ordanyt ded ordanyt it fore the best, ande He is mare besy fore our gud than we our self can ore may be, sen we ar his creaturys and handewerkis, and tharfore almen that wald weill de, suld leir to de, the quhilk is nocht ellys bot to have hart and thocht evir to God, and ay be reddy to resave the ded [death] bot ony murmur, as he that baide the cumyne of his frend ...[8]

Such works are the equivalent of the catechetical and other devotional texts in verse, often in octosyllabic couplets, which are common to England and Scotland at this period, some of which are found alongside the prose pieces in MS. Kk.i.5. They have few stylistic aspirations, but they are carefully tuned to their instructional purpose. We have no evidence of any other kind of Scots prose at this period, and it follows that prose writing was devoid of the influence exerted on verse by Chaucer, Gower and Lydgate and by such anglicised works as the *Kingis Quair*. Despite the obvious influence of its direct sources, Scots prose remains closer to its vernacular roots than much contemporary verse, at least until the end of the fifteenth century.

Both this basic vernacular simplicity and the influence, in some respects, of French sources are apparent in the translations of Gilbert Hay (floruit *c*. 1419–60). The most substantial of these, *The Buke of the Law of Armys*, is dated 1456, and it is likely that the other two, *The Buke of Knychthede* and *The Buke of the Governaunce of Princis*, are approximately contemporary. Similarly, it is only the first which is stated to have been translated 'at the requeist of ane hie and mychty prince and lord, William Erle of Orknay and Caithnes', but it is natural to suppose that all three treatises, with their related subject-matter, were intended for the same patron. Taken together, the three provide a comprehensive guide to chivalric principles, emphasising a knight's responsibilities to Church, lord and people.[9] *The Buke of the Law of Armys* is a translation of Honoré Bonet's *L'Arbre des Batailles*, originally composed in the later fourteenth century, and it seems probable that Hay's other sources were likewise French: although Ramon Llull's *Libre de Caballeria* was originally composed in Catalan, Hay most probably encountered the text in its French translation,[10] while the *Secreta Secretorum*, the source of *The Buke of the Governaunce of Princis*, had by the middle of the fifteenth century been translated into many vernacular languages, including French.[11] Hay certainly served in France for much of his life, and it is scarcely surprising that he should have drawn his texts from French exemplars.

Often a rather cautious translator, Hay nevertheless gives his Scots versions their own distinctive character. He sometimes appears to misunderstand the original, but we cannot always be sure that he is not rather changing the emphasis. Thus, when the French *Livre de lordre de Chevallerie* states

> Car se le bon chevallier amy de chevallerie estoit vaincu, ce seroit grant pechie et contre lhonneur de chevallerie,

> [For if the good knight, friend of chivalry, were defeated, this would be a great sin and against the honour of chivalry]

and Hay, dropping the conditional to translate

> Bot the curage of a lele knycht, that for a lele caus debatis, may nocht be our cummyn, bot gif it be for sum syn agaynis the ordre of knychthede,

converts the idea of sinfulness from a comment upon the impossibility of a chivalrous knight's defeat to an occasion for that defeat, it is difficult to determine whether this stems from a misreading of the French or a conscious change of direction. In either case, the comment becomes the stimulus for an elaborate and original excursus upon delinquent chivalry, illustrating the vigour of Hay's own prose style:

> For gif a knycht wald reve [steal] fra the small peple the gude that God has gevin thame, and geve it till otheris that he aw nocht to, that war agayne the office of knychthede, to tak fra lawar na [than] himself outhir moble [movable] gudis or possessiouns, and hald it as heretage till him, nocht gevand na restorand agayn; he may be lyknyt to the wolf that the lord gave the schepe to kepe to, as till a familyar faa; or he may be lyknyt till a fule lorde that left his faire wyf in keping till a yong traytour knycht; or he that left his stark castell and his gudis till a bitter cuvatous knycht, untrew knycht; and thus is he mekle to

wyte [blame] that gevis his castell, or his wyf, or his schepe, in syk governaunce. Or how ane othir suld traist his governaunce in him that governis nocht wele him self! For thir ar thingis that men suld nocht put in misgovernaunce of fule men, his faire wyf, his castell, and his moble gudis; for commonly syk men that begylis thair lordis may never be refourmyt na redressit till lautee, na till honour of knychthede.

(Prose Works, II, 31)

The individual elements of this passage are perhaps more convincing than the argument as a whole, for Hay seems to shift the terms of his comparisons in the middle of the sequence. The subject of the wolf analogy is certainly the recreant knight whose depredations upon the poor form the link with the French original; but the foolish disposal of wife and castle presumably refers to the misguided trust of such a knight's hypothetical lord. Logical blemishes of this kind are not uncommon where Hay breaks away from his originals, reinforcing the reader's impression that he worked quickly and without much revision. The force of his prose style is thus rather uncontrolled, contributing to the low critical esteem in which he has generally been held.[12]

Structurally, Hay's style is marked by informal, paratactic patterns of syntax which show little influence of his French originals. There is more evidence of their contribution to his diction: even in the passage quoted above, we can detect the French background ('bons meubles') of the phrase 'moble gudis', and the abstract vocabulary of chivalric discourse naturally pervades all three works whether or not it is derived directly from the phrasing of the original. Hay is perhaps the first Scots prose writer in whom we can observe the stylistic trait of the 'binary phrase' or doublet, the pairing of synonyms which was a widespread and distinctive feature of late Mediæval style. Often, the two (or even three) words so deployed have complementary meanings; and at times one may suspect that the device is a translator's way of capturing the full nuance of his source. But it is manifestly a decorative device as well, and one which extends beyond the paired phrase to the balancing of phrases and even whole clauses, producing effects such as the following:

For rycht as realmes are *destroyit and heryit* [plundered] throu *rebellioun and disobeysaunce* of subjectis, rycht sa ar thai *maid riche and haldin* at *honour and worschip* throu obedience, and that is honour to the prince. And that makis him till have *durable lordschip and lestand regne*, thai till obeye to thair soverane and he to governe thame in justice, lufe and leautee.

(Prose Works, II, 79)

The tendency to link Romance and native words in such phrases is less marked in Hay than in many later writers, and no doubt the pairing of words derived from French is in many cases attributable to the source. In prose which is in other respects fairly loosely constructed, however, Hay's use of such patterning devices gives a welcome sense of coherence.

Both the predominance of French materials in Hay's work and his pre-occupation with moral advice are characteristic of his age. It is difficult to assess what currency his translations may have had: the unique manuscript dates from about 1490, indicating that they were being copied a generation after their composition, but it was owned by, and probably copied for, Sir Oliver Sinclair of Rosslyn, second son of Hay's patron, and there is no evidence that it or any other exemplar passed out of the hands of the Sinclair family. Nor can we chart with any confidence the development of a continuous prose tradition, which might have owed something to Hay's pioneering efforts, during the second half of the century. Of the several prose texts included in John Asloan's early sixteenth-century anthology, only one can be dated with any accuracy: *The Spectacle of Luf*, translated from an unidentified Latin treatise, was composed 'at the cyte of Sandris' [? St Andrews] in 1492. The title is misleadingly voyeurist: 'spectacle' is an unusual way of translating the Latin *Speculum* (mirror), but the work itself is impeccable in its insistence that the son to whom it is addressed should 'abstene fra sic fleschely delectationis quhilk you callis lufe'. The translator is usually believed to be the 'M[aster] G Myll' named in the scribal colophon, but since this text is the only part of the manuscript not in Asloan's own hand,[13] it is equally probable that Myll was the scribe rather than the translator. (Since nothing is known about him in any case, it may not make much difference.) Similarly concerned with moral improvement is *The Porteous of Noblenes*, printed by Walter Chepman and Andrew Myllar in 1508 and also included by Asloan, which was translated by the Aberdeen notary and burgess Andrew Cadiou from the French of Alain Chartier. As a general chivalric guide, this work is closer to Hay's, and it is characterised by the same paratactic syntax and fondness for binary phrases.

Other works which can be ascribed to the fifteenth century are similarly instructional. Some are encyclopaedic, like the Asloan treatises *The Cart of the Warld*, a topographic handbook, and *The Sex Werkdays According to the Sex Agis*, harmonising the Old and New Testaments with the history of the world; the former work, in particular, reflects an awareness of and interest in the exotic which is also apparent in the fifteenth-century Scots translation of *Prester John's Letter* preserved in the British Library Royal MS. 17 D.xx copy of Wyntoun. Again, the middle of the century sees the first vernacular chronicles, whether the summary version of the history of the Scots found in the same manuscript and elsewhere, or the more topical annals covering the years 1428–55 which are somewhat inaccurately known as the 'Auchinleck Chronicle'. As so often in texts of this period, these annals consist of little more than a string of main clauses linked by conjunctions, and yet they make up in vigour what they lack in syntactical subtlety:

> The yere of God i^m iiij^c, lij°, the xxvij day of Merche, Schir James of Douglas, Erll James' secund son, for the foule slauchter of his brother, Erll William of Douglas, come on Sanct Patrikis Day in Lentryn to Striuling & blew xxiiij hornis attanis apon the king and apon all the lordis that war with him that tyme, for the foule slauchter of his brother; and schew all thair seles at the Corss on ane letter and band it on ane burd [board] and cuplit it till ane hors tale, and gart draw it throu the towne, spekand richt sclanderfully of the king

and all that war with him that tyme, & spulyeit [despoiled] all the toune and brint it; and thair was with him his brother the Erll of Ormond and the Lord Hammiltoun & na ma lordis, and thai excedit nocht of gud men vj^c. All this tyme the king was into Perth, passand to the Erll of Crawfurd.

(*Asloan* MS., I, 241)

Not until the middle of the following century do we find vernacular historical works which transcend this sparse style; for the present, the communication of simple facts and familiar ideas appears to have demanded little more than the simplest rhetoric and a few basic syntactic strategies.

I have argued that until the end of the fifteenth century Scots prose, founded upon vernacular speech and influenced to some degree by the patterns of its (largely French) sources, was stylistically homogeneous, governed by practical rather than aesthetic considerations. The change, when it came, seems to have been stimulated by the reception of alternative stylistic models, and to have paralleled in less extreme form and over a much longer timescale the stylistic diversification which appears to have affected the composition of verse around 1500. Within a generation or so, several different influences fell upon Scots prose, each implying a different stylistic norm. The first of these is apparent in the works of the theologian John Ireland (*c*. 1440–*c*. 1496), and particularly in his *Meroure of Wysdome*, written about 1490 for the young James IV. As a distinguished master of the University of Paris, Ireland was greatly experienced in the composition of complex Latin periods to express technical points of doctrine, and much of the *Meroure* is couched in a comparable form of Scots:

And tharfor, sene we ar in sa gret perell and has sa mony innemeis, as God has gevin us a gret licht in the hevin, the sone material, to direct us in this present waurld and wildernes, that we laubor nocht in the myrknes of the nycht without knawlage or distinccioun of the richt gait and peralus, bot in the bricht day, and in the nycht he has gevin us the mone and sternis and uthir planetis; richtswa God of his hie mercy, knawand the gret perell we ar in to cum to the realme of Paradice, has ordand for our direccioun and gyde the Halikyrk, that is the gret torche of licht and hevinly bricht sone in spiritualitie, that na way in the waurld may falye na falt in the faith and hevinly doctrine, that all maner of man and woman, gret and smale, mone & suld obey and trow to under the pane of dampnacioun eternale, for his Halykyrk is the verray spouse of Jhesu, and nouthir king, empriour, paip or pepill, be battale, be errour or ony uthir way may prevale na have victorye agane the Kyrk and haly spous of Jhesu; bot evir the mar that the Kyrk be invadit and ony lauboris in the contrar of it, evir the starkar it is, for than God schawis in the defence of it his strenth, his help and suple [support], and that he has promittit be the wourd of his blissit sone Jhesus, that has chosin this haly lady the Kyrk to his spous.

(*Meroure*, II, 67)

By comparison with the syntactic range of Ireland's predecessors, such prose is extremely elaborate, deploying a wide range of devices to expound complex ideas. There is a subtle balance between logical and rhetorical features: the fundamental comparison between the sun and moon on the one hand and the guiding light of the Church on the other is developed through a series of more detailed inferences, but this logical structure is matched by the persuasive rhetoric of such phrases as 'nouthir king, empriour, paip or pepill, be battale, be errour or ony uthir way may prevale na have victorye', where the cumulative rhythm of the exclusions suggests the characteristic voice of the preacher. Ireland's prose style in such passages is not remarkable for its immediate accessibility, although there is not much in the diction to extend the reader. Sentences as long and complicated as the above are, however, Ireland's stylistic norm.

Elsewhere, it is true, we find less demanding passages, closer, more consistently, to the language of the preacher than to that of the academic theologian. As might be expected, this is particularly evident where he adopts the homilist's strategy of exemplary narrative:

> As the woman in Parys, quhen sche knew that hir cosing [cousin] was drownit in the ryver of Sayn, cryit and said that it was his destany & he mycht be na maner evade it, for it was ordand for him, sche said, or evir cot or goune was schapin for him. Then come a clerk, as my self, and hard hir criand, sayand and affermand this, and be gret wisdome he thocht he wauld schaw hir foly, and gaf hir twa gret blawis and strakis in baith hir chekis, that sche was gretlie abasit of [dismayed at]. And sone sche turnit hir purpos and cryit agane the clerk quhy he had sa felony strikin hir without caus or ressoun, and that he suld be had to presoune and punyst for it. The wys clerk answerit sobirly and said: 'Lady, this God wist lang befor, that I suld fall in sic a rage and foly to strik you, and that ye suld thole and suffer this for your daft & wykit langage that ye have spokin agane his honour and wisdome; and sene this was destany and ordand for you, that ye suld nocht wyt [blame] me.' And thus the lady gat twa gret blawis, tholit gret scorne, and passit schamfully hir gait.
>
> (*Meroure*, II, 140–1)

Ireland manages such simple narratives with economy and energy, using a mixture of direct and indirect speech and keeping the sentences short. His diction, too, varies according to the context: here there is an almost total avoidance of elevated language, and the words of Romance origin are all well assimilated into Scots. Other features of Ireland's lofty style, such as the inversion of noun and adjective (note the phrases 'sone material' and 'dampnacioun eternale' in the passage previously quoted), also disappear from his more direct narrative passages. *The Meroure of Wysdome* is the first substantially original work of Scots prose, and its scope and manner are, despite the rather forbiddingly technical nature of some of its theology, not unimpressive.[14]

Ireland's circumstances, as a professional theologian returning as counsellor to a young prince, were unusual, and his ambitious project had no imitators in the early years of the sixteenth century. The generation of Scots who followed him in Paris and who outdid his achievements there seem never to have ventured out of Latin,[15] and the vernacular literature of the remainder of James IV's reign was composed in verse rather than in prose. Not until the end of the minority of his son, around 1530, are there surviving works of

Scots prose to compare with Ireland's *Meroure*, and then we can observe important, and to some degree contradictory, developments. On the one hand, there is a new kind of courtly prose, principally represented by the translations of John Bellenden (*c.* 1495–*c.* 1547), which is more self-con-sciously Latinate than anything Ireland produced. But there is also the first evidence of vernacular writing by Protestant sympathisers, publishing outside Scotland prose works drawn from Lutheran and other Reforming sources. Thus, prose style comes to be associated with the political and religious controversies of sixteenth-century Scotland.

Both in verse and in prose, Bellenden is a consistent proponent of a high, Latinate style. As far as his prose translations are concerned, he was no doubt influenced by the nature of his sources: Hector Boece, whose Latin chronicles of Scotland, published in Paris in 1527, he translated in 1531, was a humanist imitator of Cicero and Livy, while it was Livy's own Roman history which was the original for Bellenden's second major translation, produced in 1533. In both cases, Bellenden succeeds in assimilating some features of the Latin into his vernacular prose, extending the range of his Scots by means of judicious borrowings. Less felicitously, perhaps, he has a weakness for absol-ute constructions, rendering an ablative in the Latin with a past participle:

> *Sic thingis done* in Britan, Ostorius maid his army reddy ...
>
> > (*Boece*, I, 127)
>
> *Victoryne*, the Romane capitane, *aduertist* [warned] of thir tythingis, assemblit ane grete army ...
>
> > (ibid., I, 274)
>
> *Conrannus, maid* King of Scottis in this manere ...
>
> > (ibid., I, 353)

Such constructions, especially when they are frequently repeated, seem a little unnatural in Scots; but in general Bellenden achieves a fluent, dignified style, combining the native vigour of Scots prose with the copiousness of the Latin in a way which is reminiscent of Gavin Douglas' verse translation of the *Aeneid*:

> Skairslie war thir wourdis sayid, quhen boith the armyis ruschit to giddir. At the first junyng the Romanis war neyr disconnfist [overcome] throw huge noumer of arrowis and ganyeis, fleing with sick incredibill noumer in the aire that the lyftt [air] wes coverit with the samyn [same]. Maximiane, seing the first bront of Romanis in sik perplexite, send ane fresche legioun in thair support, throw quhilk followit ane bludy fecht, that the outewyngis [wings (of army)] of Romanis oursett thair inymeis with na les press than multitude of pepill.
>
> > (*Boece*, I, 283)

Such descriptive formulae do, of course, have a long heritage, and are wide-spread in Scots from Barbour's *Bruce* onward. But Bellenden makes effective use both of this indigenous tradition and the materials he derives from his Latin originals.

It is interesting to compare his methods with those of another translator of Boece, the anonymous author of the so-called 'Mar Lodge' version. Nothing is known of its early history, but it appears to be roughly contemporary with Bellenden's translation, and it is certainly quite independent of it. The extent of the divergence between the two versions can be seen from a comparison of the Mar Lodge text of the passage quoted above:

> Eftir the king had endit his harang to grete plesoure of the armye, he chargit at blast of trumpet thai suld jone the feild. The remanent chiftanis, using sic like exhortacioun to fecht, raissit thare folkis in ferme esperance of victorie. Sone thareeftir on athir partie scharplie was recounterit. At the first rusche Romanis fechting in the myddilwarde [centre (of army)] war nere ouresett be schott of cors bow, dart and arrow, sa thik that the hevin and lift [air] was obscurit. Maximiane, addverting the dangere, send haistelie ane legioun fresche and unfuleyeit [not worn out] to thare succouris; be quham the bargane was renewit with grevous strakis and woundis. The Romane wyngis stoutlie supprisit inemyis, quharethrow the feild was equale mare be corage than fortitude.
>
> (Mar Lodge *Boece*, I, 396)

In some respects closer to Boece's Latin, the Mar Lodge version does not have the narrative vigour achieved by Bellenden. The compression which Boece manages through the structure of the Latin is matched by Bellenden only through the omission of detail; by following the argument of the original more closely, the Mar Lodge translator becomes diffuse. When Bellenden expands a phrase, it tends to be for rhetorical effect: the Mar Lodge 'sa thik that the hevin and lift was obscurit' stays close to Boece's 'quibus obumbrabatur celum',[16] but Bellenden's 'fleing with sick incredibill noumer in the aire that the lyftt wes coverit with the samyn', despite its rather lame ending, gives a much more forceful immediacy. In his translations of both Boece and Livy, it is Bellenden's battle scenes which display the greatest command of narrative.

The Latinate tradition represented by Bellenden's translations reaches its apogee in the *Complaynt of Scotland*, published in Paris in 1550 and originally intended as a contribution to the propaganda war between Scotland and England. Its authorship is not absolutely certain, although its most recent editor has argued strongly for the traditional attribution to Robert Wedderburn.[17] Whoever he was, his initial attack on English ambitions in Scotland, written in the context of the war which had been continuing since 1542, seems to have been overtaken by the end of hostilities before it passed through the press, and the version which was finally published contains much additional material only loosely connected with the original political themes.[18] This change in purpose is reflected to some degree in the style, for the more overtly political sections, largely based upon Alain Chartier's *Quadrilogue Invectif*, are in a relatively straightforward, though always carefully structured, form of Scots:

> Ther is ane exempil of the trason that ane blac Jacopyne frere committit contrar Henry the Sevynt of that name: the toune of Florens wald nocht obeye to the

Empir, quhar for the said Empriour Henry brotht ane grit armye to seige the toune of Florens. Than ane blac Jacopyne frere gat ane grit some of moneye fra the Florentynis to tak on hand to sla the Empriour be cause this said frere was familiar witht the said Empriour. Than he trocht auereis: he poysont the Host of the Sacrament witht poyson. Ther eftir that nobil Empriour past to resaif the body of God undir the forme of brede, and as soune as he hed resavit it in his moutht his body began to swel and sa he decessit.

(Complaynt, pp 95–6)

The affinities of such narrative passages with Ireland's exemplary prose are clear enough, and support the author's contention that he has 'usit domestic Scottis langage, maist intelligibil for the vlgare pepil', avoiding 'oncoutht exquisite termis drevyn, or rather to say mair formaly, revyn fra Lating' (p 13). It is not invariably true, even in those sections of the work derived from Chartier, where vernacular simplicity is obviously appropriate to the propagandist purpose: there are many instances in which the Complayner uses Latinate diction, binary phrases and relatively complex syntax to produce an effective, Ciceronian rhetoric of lament and persuasion. These differences are still more marked in the 'Monolog of the Actor', in which the work is transformed through the traditionally poetic device of the dream vision. Here the influenceof Dunbar's aureate manner is reflected for the first time in Scots prose:

... there eftir I entrit in ane grene forrest to contempil the tendir yong frutss of grene treis, because the borial blastis of the thre borowing dais [last three days] of Marche hed chaissit the fragrant flureise of evyrie frute tree far athourt the feildis. Of this sort I did spaceir up ande doune but sleipe the maist part of the myrk nycht. Instantly there eftir I persavit the messengeris of the rede Aurora, quhilkis throucht the mychtis of Titan hed persit the crepusculyne [twilight] lyne matutine [morning] of the northt northt est orizone, quhilk was occasione that the sternis & planetis, the dominotours of the nycht, absentit them ande durst nocht be sene in oure hemisphere for dreddour of his awful goldin face.

(Complaynt, p 30)

Even here there are, apart from one or two deliberately ornate phrases, few real Latinisms; but the overall cast of the description clearly evokes the elaborate poetic style developed by Dunbar, Douglas and others around 1500. The effect derives from the imagery and the allusive patterns as much as from the lexis, a truth about the aureate tradition which has increasingly been recognised in the recent past.[19]

The elaboration of much of the prose in the *Complaynt of Scotland* is quite apparent when this work is compared with another manifestation of the propaganda conflict with England, *Ane Resonyng of Ane Scottis and Inglis Merchand* by William Lamb (*c.* 1494–1550). It, too, seems to have been overtaken by the end of the war, but unlike the *Complaynt, Ane Resonyng* was never completed or augmented. Lamb adopts the dialogue form, which he uses without much attention to verisimilitude or to the literary possibilities of his rather promising fictive framework, but with a considerable forensic verve. His vocabulary overlaps quite extensively with that of Bellenden, especially in Latin and French borrowings; in Lamb's case, however, there are few traces of Latinate syntax or of other more literary devices. Yet his Scots merchant, rebutting his English counterpart's arguments (all of which are drawn from the *Declaration of this present warre* which the English government had published in 1542), is often given vigorously scathing lines, as when he responds to the claim, based upon a statement of the Italian historian Sabellico, that Scotland is part of England:

> Nichtbour, can ony man in Ingland, beand nocht blind in witt, mynd and body (as, alace, ye be now), say that Scotland is or was evir a part of Ingland mair nor France ane part of Spanye; quharof gif ye pruif nocht be pretendit homagis bettir than Sabilicus previs Scotland ane part of Ingland, your fyre is bot ane smuke and your kyng and Counsell hes authorisate ane frevole buik and enterit ane inextingguabill [inextinguishable], injust weir [war] for sobir causis.
>
> (*Ane Resonyng*, pp 65–7)

Several coincidences of argument and imagery suggest that Lamb and the author of the *Complaynt*, both of whom were closely associated with the royal Council, were aware of one another's work as they proceeded along their separate lines during the summer of 1549; it is fascinating and instructive to compare the differences in style and approach between their respective treatises.

Well before these events, however, another tradition of Scots prose, which eventually supplanted the elaborate, Latinate style altogether, had begun to emerge. Its first exponent was probably John Gau (*c*. 1495–1553), who by 1533 had joined the small but significant number of Scottish Protestants who had sought refuge abroad. Gau seems to have taken up residence in the Danish city of Malmö, where there was a well-established Scottish community, and there he translated Christian Pedersen's *Den rette vey till Hiemmerigis Rige* as *The richt vay to the Kingdome of Heuine*, adding an 'Epistil to the nobil lordis and barons of Scotland' which is largely based upon Luther's preface to St Paul's epistle to the Romans. Printed in Malmö in 1533, these works are somewhat affected by their Danish compositors, but they nevertheless reveal that terse, unadorned style which was to become characteristic of Protestant prose:

> Trowis thou as the Halie Writ sais that thy sinnis ar forgiffine the with our Lord Jesus Christis word for his bluid, thane thay ar aluterlie [entirely] forgiffine the; bot trowis thou that thou wil dw satisfactione for thayme with thy awne guid warkis, thane thay sal notht be forgiffine to the, for causs thou lichtlis [insult] the passione of our Lord Jesus Christ.
>
> (*Richt Vay*, p 81)

This plainness, which is parallelled in such Protestant poets as Lindsay and the authors of the *Gude and Godlie Ballatis*, is a constant feature of Reforming prose, and is found in such later works as John Johnston's *Comfortable Exhortation* (1535) and Henry Balnavis' treatise *On Justification* (written 1548, printed 1568).[20]

Recognition of the early association between the plain style and the Protestant tradition is important, because it colours our attitude towards the most original and most important of Protestant prose writers, John Knox (1514–72). Discussion of Knox's prose has been dominated by the issue of anglicisation, which has frequently impeded a proper assessment of his importance as a writer in Scots. It is true that parts of Knox's corpus reflect relatively few distinctively Scots features, and that many of the texts also show a preference for English orthography. It is also true, as is often asserted, that the Scottish Reformers were influenced by English models for their prose style, not least because in the absence of a Scots Bible, they naturally acquired the cadences of sixteenth-century English translations. In fact, the only surviving evidence of an attempt to put the Bible into Scots is Murdoch Nisbet's version of the New Testament, but this is really no more than a Scots transcription of the Wycliffite version and in no way corresponds to the work which was done by English translators like Tyndale and Coverdale in the first half of the sixteenth century. Writing from exile, moreover, the early Reformers were evidently conscious of a dual audience, and no doubt addressed themselves not only to their own compatriots but also to the much larger number of English supporters of Lutheran, Zwinglian and Calvinist views.[21]

But it is possible to concede all this without accepting that the usual view of Knox as a generally anglicising influence upon Scottish prose is an accurate one. In the first place, as R D S Jack has recently demonstrated,[22] there is much of Knox's writing which is unambiguously in Scots. This includes *The Historie of the Reformatioun in Scotland* (1559–67), which contains both the best examples of Knox's skill in Scots and the widest range of style he ever attempted. It also includes the great majority of his letters, at least where we have reasonably reliable texts. David Laing's monumental edition, the only form in which many of Knox's works are readily accessible, does not always help us to discriminate immediately between texts based upon the writer's holograph, those where there is a reliable early authority, and those where the only evidence comes from seventeenth-century sources such as the historian David Calderwood. The result is that texts are often assumed to reflect Knox's own practice, when they have almost certainly undergone a process of anglicisation in the course of transmission.

Nor were Knox's writings immune from this process even within his own lifetime. It is instructive to compare the printed version of *A Comfortable Epistell sente to the Afflicted Church of Chryst*, dated 31 May 1554 and probably printed by Humphrey Singleton at Wesel about 1556, with the very similar opening of another letter to a similar English congregation, dated three weeks previously and copied in 1603 into a manuscript of Knox's letters which is now Edinburgh University Library MS. Laing III, 345:

Laing MS.

When I ponder with myself, rycht deirlie belovit brethrene, what was the estait of Chrystis trew Kirk imediatelie efter the deth and passioun of our Saviour Jesus, and what wer the changeis and greit mutationis in the commounweill of Judea, befoir the finall desolatioun of the same, as I can not but feir lyke plageis to stryke the realme of Ingland, and in feiring, God knawith, I lament and mvrne, sa can I not but rejose, knawing that Godis maist mercifull providence is na less ciarfull this day over his weak and feabill servandis, than he was that day over his dispersit and sair oppressit flock.
(p 313)

Printed text

When I ponder wyth myselfe, beloved in the Lord, what was the state of Christes true churche immediatlie after his death and passion, and what were the chaunges and greate mutacions in the commonwealth of Judea before the finall desolation of the same, as I cannot but feare that like plagues, for lyke offences shall strike the Realme of Englande, and in fearing, God knoweth, I lament and mourne, so can I not but rejoice, knowing that Godis most mercifull providence is no lesse carefull this day over his weake and feeble servantes in the Realme of Englande, than it was that day over his weake and sore oppressit flocke in Jurye.
(*Works*, III, 239)*

The manuscript version is, of course, itself rather late, and there is no guarantee that it preserves Knox's own orthography. In any case, it too reveals a number of anglicised features, such as ⟨wh⟩ rather than the normal Scots ⟨quh⟩. But the comparison reveals the consistency with which the printed version substitutes English forms for Scots ones; this may reflect Knox's preparation for the press, but it seems more likely, given the practice of sixteenth-century printers, that the changes were mostly introduced by the English compositors. In general, therefore, we should be wary about assuming that the extant texts of Knox's work are faithful to his own practice; in many cases, printers and scribes will have carried the process of anglicisation much further than he ever did. The same applies even to modern editors: the version of the Laing MS. printed by Laing himself in his edition of Knox is fairly inaccurate, and the inaccuracies consistently present a more anglicised text than is actually present in the original.

There are, moreover, good grounds, as we have already seen, for suggesting that Knox's style is characterised less by deliberate anglicisation than by a desire for lucidity which led him to prefer a plain vocabulary mingled with a relatively restricted range of well-established Latin borrowings. This is not to suggest that he altogether eschewed rhetoric; but his rhetoric is more akin to Lamb's scathingly persuasive arguments than to the elaborate, high-style diction and syntax of Bellenden or the author of the *Complaynt of Scotland*. His rhetorical devices are always directed towards a single end: the defence of his theological, moral and political positions and the castigation of his opponents. The structure of his sentences is often complex, but that complexity is always offset by the use of clear syntactical markers, balanced clauses, and similar aids to the reader:

* [Editor's Note: The passages used for this comparison have not been normalised.]

The will of God, plainly reveled in his holie Scriptures, we *do not onely* followe as a bright lanterne shining before us for the directing of our pathes walking in the darknes of this mortalitie, *but also* we affirme it to be *of such* sufficiencie *that if* an Angell from the heaven, with wonders, signes and miracles, *wolde declare* to us a will repugning to that which is alredie reveled, persuading us *upon that* to ground our faith, or *by that* to rule the actions of our lives, *we wold* hold him accursed and in no wise to be heard.

(*Works*, V, 312)

It is, however, for his *Historie* that Knox is principally to be remembered as a writer of prose. As a historian, even by sixteenth-century standards, he is overtly and unembarrassedly partisan, but it is that very commitment to his cause which enlivens his writing and gives it such immediacy. By comparison with the general formality and syntactical correctness of his pastoral and theological works, the *Historie* makes copious use of elision, inversion and unmistakable colloquialisms; where the diction of his other writings, with the exception of some of his personal letters, is for the most part tonally neutral, the *Historie* is coloured by the most vigorous display of informal as well as more elevated Scots. There is, no doubt, a sense in which Knox's absorption of the English Bible and his enforced dependence upon English printers contributed to that erosion of the Scots prose tradition which was part of the process by which, gradually throughout the sixteenth century and very quickly after 1603, Scots gave way to English as the accepted language of written discourse in Scotland. But passages such as the following, describing the St Giles' Day procession in Edinburgh in 1558, despite the evidence of some superficial anglicisation and rather less superficial bigotry, suggest that there is also a sense in which, in the *Historie* at least, he represents the fulfilment of a slow, erratic progress towards a confidently mature Scots prose:

Yit wold nott the preastis and freiris cease to have that great solempnitie and manifest abhominatioun which thei accustomablie had upoun Sanct Geillis day, to witt, thei wold have that idole borne; and tharefor was all preparatioun necessar deuly maid. A marmouset idole [grotesque figure] was borrowed fra the Gray Freiris (a silver peise of James Carmichaell was laid in pledge); it was fast fixed with irne nailles upon a barrow, called thare fertour [shrine]. Thare assembled preastis, frearis, channonis and rottin Papistes, with tabornes [shrine, reliquary], and trumpettis, banerris and bage-pypis, and who was thare to led the ring but the Quein Regent hir self, with all hir schaivelingis [tonsured ecclesiastics], for honour of that feast. West about goes it, and cumis doun the Hie Streat, and doun to the Canno Croce.

(*Works*, I, 259)

The riot which followed was a foretaste of the disorder to come; the prose tradition which Knox in part embodied was itself one of the victims of the changes which followed.

NOTES

1   For a summary account of this phenomenon, *see* M H Bald, 'The Pioneering of Anglicised Speech in Scotland', *SHR*, 24 (1927) 179–93; *also* Mairi Robinson, 'Language Choice in the Reformation: The Scots Confession of 1560' in *Scotland and the Lowland Tongue*, J D McClure (ed) (Aberdeen, 1983), pp 59–78.

2   This document is printed in facsimile, with a transcription, in Grant G Simpson, *Scottish Handwriting 1150–1650* (Edinburgh, 1973), no. 8.

3   *See* Basil Cottle, *The Triumph of English 1350–1400* (London, 1969), especially pp 15–27

4   This manuscript, formerly in the possession of the Marquis of Bute, is now NLS MS. 21246. The quotation is from p 131.

5   For the role of notaries public in Mediæval Scotland, *see* John Durkan, 'The Early Scottish Notary' in *The Renaissance and Reformation in Scotland*, Ian B Cowan and Duncan Shaw (eds) (Edinburgh, 1983), pp 22–40.

6   BL MS. Cott. Faust. A vi, f. 87^v.

7   BL MS. Cott. Vesp. F vii, f 17^v; printed in *Nat. MSS. Scot.*, II, no. 54.

8   *The Craft of Deyng*, printed in *Ratis Raving*, p 167.

9   Cf. Felicity Riddy, 'The Revival of Chivalry in Late Medieval Scotland' in *Actes du 2e Colloque de Langue et de Littérature Ecossaises (Moyen Age et Renaissance)*, J J Blanchot and C Graf (eds) (Strasbourg, 1979), pp 54–62, especially pp 57–58.

10   This text is available in Ramon Llull, *Obres*, I, M Obrador y Bennassar (ed) (Palma de Mallorca, 1906).

11   Cf. M Manzaloui, *Secreta Secretorum: Nine English Versions*, I, EETS (London, 1977), pp ix–xliv, especially pp xxii–xxiv.

12   *See* Agnes Mure Mackenzie, *An Historical Survey of Scottish Literature to 1714* (London, 1933), p 183; other writers are similarly dismissive, but cf. F Quinn (ed), *The Meroure of Wysdome*, II, STS (Edinburgh and London, 1965), pp xxii–xxiii.

13   This point is tentatively made by Catherine van Buuren-Veenenbos in her edition of *The Buke of the Sevyne Sagis* (Leiden, 1982), pp 9–10; careful analysis of the hands confirms that ff. 137^r–150^v are indeed by a different scribe, and the colophon might well refer to copyist rather than translator.

14   For assessments of Ireland's achievement as a vernacular theologian, *see* James H Burns, 'John Ireland and *The Meroure of Wysdome*', *Innes Review*, 6 (1955), 77–98, and Bro. Bonaventure, 'The Popular Theology of John Ireland', *ibid.*, 13 (1962), 130–46.

15   Cf. Alexander Broadie, *The Circle of John Mair: Logic and Logicians in Pre-Reformation Scotland* (Oxford, 1985), and *George Lokert, Late Scholastic Logician* (Edinburgh, 1983)

16   Hector Boece, *Scotorum Historiae* (Paris, 1527), f. 125^r.

17   *The Complaynt of Scotland*, A M Stewart (ed) STS (Edinburgh and London, 1979), pp vii–xx.

18   The textual history of the *Complaynt* is worked out by J A H Murray (ed), *The Complaynt of Scotlande*, EETS (London, 1872), pp xvi–xxii.

19   *See* Arne Zettersten, 'On the aureate diction of William Dunbar' in *Essays presented to Knud Schibsbye*, M Chesnutt et al. (eds) (Copenhagen, 1979), pp 51–68.

20   On Johnston's translations, *see* James K Cameron, 'John Johnsone's *An Comfortable Exhortation of our mooste Holy Christen Faith and her Frutes*: an early example of Scots Lutheran piety', in *Studies in Church History*, subsidia 2

(Oxford, 1979); Balnevis's treatise is in Laing's edition of Knox's *Works* III, pp 431–542.
21   *See* James K Cameron, 'Aspects of the Lutheran Contribution to the Scottish Reformation', *Records of the Scottish Church History Society*, 22 (1984), 1–34; Duncan Shaw, 'Zwinglian Influences on the Scottish Reformation', ibid., 119–39.
22   R D S Jack, 'The Prose of John Knox: A Re-assessment', *Prose Studies*, 4 (1981), 239–51.

FURTHER READING

PRIMARY TEXTS

(For *Asloan MS* see General Bibliography)

Chambers, R W, Batho, E C and Husbands, H Winifred (eds), *The Chronicles of Scotland, Compiled by Hector Boece, Translated into Scots by John Bellenden 1531*, STS, 2 vols (Edinburgh and London, 138–41)

Craigie, W A (ed), *Livy's History of Rome translated into Scots by John Bellenden*, STS, 2 vols (Edinburgh and London, 1901–03)

Gau, John, *The Richt Vay to the Kingdom of Heuine*, Mitchell, A F (ed), STS (Edinburgh and London, 1888)

Girvan, Ritchie (ed), *Ratis Raving*, STS (Edinburgh and London, 1939)

de Irlandia, Johannes, *The Meroure of Wysdome*, MacPherson, Charles and Quinn, F (eds), STS, 2 vols (Edinburgh and London, 1926–65)

Laing, David (ed), *Works of John Knox*, 6 vols (Edinburgh 1846–55)

Lamb, William, *Ane Resonyng of ane Scottis and Inglis Merchand betuix Rowand and Lionis*, Lyall, Roderick J (ed) (Aberdeen, 1985)

Law, T Graves (ed), *The New Testament in Scots*, STS, 2 vols, (Edinburgh, 1903–4)

Stevenson, J H (ed), *Sir Gilbert of the Haye's Prose Manuscript*, STS, 2 vols (Edinburgh and London, 1899–1908)

Watson, G (ed), *The Mar Lodge Translation of the History of Scotland by Hector Boece*, STS (Edinburgh and London, 1943)

Chapter 11

Prose after Knox

DAVID REID

If someone turned to the *Cambridge Bibliography of English Literature* eager to find out what Scottish prose after Knox consisted in, its twenty pages of double column would richly satisfy his curiosity. He might still wonder whether what it lists was literature exactly, especially since it promotes to its English sections Drummond of Hawthornden (1585–1649) and Urquhart of Cromartie (1611–60), the two authors whose writings an unspecialised twentieth century eye would most easily recognise as literature. What is left is overwhelmingly ecclesiastical: ecclesiastical controversy, at first between Catholic and Protestant, then between Episcopalian and Presbyterian; sermons and commentaries on the Bible; autobiographies, diaries and letters, most conspicuously by churchmen; histories of Scotland, frequently about its church; tracts on political theory, not all by churchmen, but naturally they made their mark there too.

English literature at this time has an even more voluminous ecclesiastical prose. What is striking about Scottish literature is that it has so little of other sorts. It has no popular journalism. This tells, even in ecclesiastical controversy. No Scot wrote against the bishops with the brutal animation and inventiveness of the Marprelate tracts. The prophetic Covenanting sermon comes nearest with its biblical invective, but however tumultuary, a sermon must take a fairly decorous form. Other sorts of popular writing are also missing, comedy and fiction. Edinburgh had no popular theatre and probably lacked the sort of social scene that liked to view itself in city comedy. But the absence of fiction, especially, as Priscilla Bawcutt has remarked, of the prose romance, is puzzling. It might be argued that *Gargantua and Pantagruel* is a sort of romance and that Urquhart's translation amounts to a work of original authorship. But then Urquhart is all the more a phoenix, for no one else wrote fictional prose. Indeed outside Urquhart there is little in the way of fun. Even the learned play of the mind (again outside Urquhart) lies under severe restraint. Scots rarely display curious learning or entertain strange thoughts. In comparison with Donne's *Biathanatos* or Browne's *Urne Buriall*, Drummond's 'Cypresse Grove' is a fairly conventional essay in melancholy, and there is nothing else of its kind. Curiosity in a more valuable sense is also missing. The Scots do not write philosophy. They have no Bacon or Hobbes. They neither turn their minds inwards upon their ways of thinking nor outwards upon the society or world they live in. They are content to work within received ideas, to draw on authorities, perhaps to systematise or adjudicate between them. As theologians or ecclesiastical controversialists, rather than philosophers, they aimed at authority, not inquiry, and forceful statements of dogmatic positions, not analysis.

Robert Bruce's sermons on the sacraments are instructive here. The sermon of 1598 on the communion is a grave and lucid exposition, which shows that the Protestants had a highly developed sacramental theory to meet Catholic attacks on the authenticity of their rite. And it must be said that Bruce's discussion of the absence or presence of the signified in the sign, not only sounds remarkably advanced, but genuinely opens up the topic to the understanding. It speaks highly for the intellectual appetite of his congregation that he could address them with a lecture such as this. But his ideas are all out of Calvin. Like the other sacramental writers on either side he is not in the least original.

One wonders why, when an extraordinary literary ferment was at work in England and France, Scottish intellectual culture should be solid, professional, but uncreative. The answer perhaps lies in its narrow institutional base. The court led a precarious existence till the 1580s and then in 1603 left the country, and no country house took its place as a leader of fashion, consumer of entertainment, or patron of learning. As a city, Edinburgh had too small a commercial life to release the anarchic popular energies that vitalised literary activity in London. Scotland did, however, possess a church and universities, and to them we owe the bulk of the prose written in the period. By itself, the church (and here we may include the universities) could produce only a restricted literary culture. Probably because it had so much the run of the country's intellectual life, churchmen themselves wrote in a more narrowly ecclesiastical way than they would have done if they had had to contend with robust centres of secular culture. No Scottish churchman addressed himself, like Bishop Hall, to a literary fashion, or, like Donne, preached to intellectual sensibilities unsettled by the currents of late Renaissance thought.

Buckle hoped his 'Examination of the Scotch Intellect During the Seventeenth Century' would enable his readers 'to understand why it is that so great a people are, in many respects, still struggling in darkness, simply because they live under the shadow of that long and terrible night, which, for more than a century, covered the land'. And he believed that it would 'also appear that their hardness and moroseness of character, their want of gaiety, and their indifference to many of the enjoyments of life are . . . the natural product of the gloomy and ascetic opinions inculcated by their religious teachers'. Buckle writes in a style in which, as Morley said of Macaulay's, it is impossible to tell the truth. Still he merely exaggerates the popular view of the effect of Calvinism on Scotland. And undoubtedly the Genevan discipline of the Scottish church was oppressive, socially and intellectually. Nevertheless, it can hardly be blamed for crushing the Renaissance in Scotland. The case is rather that it would have taken more than a church to make a Renaissance.

Besides the church did in a way institutionalise Renaissance learning. Buchanan, as well as Knox, was an inspirational figure with the radical party, and the ideal of humanistic, combined with religious, learning actuated Andrew Melville's reforms of the universities in the 1570s. The episcopal side had quite as much use for a learned ministry. By the late 1630s Scotland was able to sustain a full scale pamphlet war, such as had been entirely beyond its resources at the Reformation. That implies educational progress of a sort. I should add that throughout the period churchmen produced a lively historical literature and, amidst a pile of such reading as is never read, a small corpus of distinguished devotional pieces.

There remain two other topics bearing on the general character of prose after Knox, language and style.

Scots disappeared as the language of prose at the beginning of the seventeenth century. Some writers, like Drummond, took pains to write in English. Others wrote in Scots, but the printers anglicised their texts. The pieces in Scots that have come down to us are those that have survived in manuscript, and their Scots is thin. Even in the sixteenth century before the presses imposed an English Standard, anglicising had set in. The Catholic pamphleteer, Winzet, had jeered at Knox for having 'foryet our auld Scottis', implying that religious and national disloyalty went together. The Catholic party made a point of writing staunchly conservative Scots. But Protestant ministers such as David Fergusson (c.1523–98), Robert Bruce (1554–1631), or Alexander Hume (c.1560–1609), influenced perhaps by the English Bible and the stream of Reformation writing through England, diluted their speech when they wrote. An anglified style prevailed and took, even among James VI (1566–1625) and his courtiers. Their Castalian prose retains an agreeably Scottish flavour, but little more than a flavour.

We may regret the anglicising of Scottish prose culminating in the suppression of Scots forms by printers as the court left for England. But we should be cautious in supposing the English Standard inhibited Scots writers. David Fergusson at first sight looks like a case of inhibition. He was famous for his quick wit and pithy sayings and made a collection of *Scottish Proverbs*, some delightful: 'Fyre is ane good flour in winter'; 'All thingis helps (quod the Wran) when she pished in the sea'. People read such collections to season their discourse. But Fergusson did not season his own writing. His anglified Scots aims at clarity and decorousness; its occasional vivacities do not draw on Scots idiom. And yet the Catholic writers, for all their resistance to English, are equally restrained. The Scottishness of their prose lies in its spelling and its forms of words, not in specifically Scots vocabulary or turns of phrase. They do not draw, any more than the Protestants, on the rich communality of Scottish speech. And if their determinedly Scottish prose tends to educated restraint, we can hardly blame any narrowness of expressive range in others on the influence of English. Nor did that influence cramp the two writers who wrote with the greatest command of the resources of language after the Reformation. Knox was clearly entirely himself in an anglicised medium. Nor is there much sign of inhibition in this:

> [This] codpiece . . . , [Gargantua's] governesses did every day deck up and adorn with fair nosegays . . . , and very pleasantly would pass their time in taking you know what between their fingers, and dandling it. . . . Then did they burst out laughing, when they saw it lift up its ears, as if the sport liked them. One of them would call it her pillicock, her fiddle-diddle, her staff of love, her tickle-gizzard, her gentle-titler. Another, her sugar-plum, her kingo, her old rowley, her touch-trap, her flap dowdle. Another again, her branch of coral, her placket-racket, her Cyprian sceptre, her tit-bit, her bob-lady. And some of the other women would give these names, my Roger, my cockatoo, my nimble-wimble, bush-beater, claw-buttock, eves-dropper, picklock, pioneer, bully-ruffin, smell-smock, trouble-gusset, my lusty live sausage, my crimson chitterlin, rump-splitter, shove-devil, down right to it, stiff and stout, in and to, at her again, my coney-borrow-ferret, wiley-beguiley, my pretty rogue.
>
> (*Gargantua and Pantagruel*, Bk. 1, ch. 11)

Urquhart's translation expands Rabelais's mere thirteen endearments to thirty-six. It might be argued that Urquhart's polymorphous perverse pleasure in words, its very excess, was somehow symptomatic of a general Scottish unease with an alien tongue. But then the unease must have been rudely fecundating; why was Urquhart alone fecundated? Clearly Scottish writers were oddly placed towards English prose, but any theory of linguistic alienation would have to be refined considerably if it were to account satisfactory for what was going on.

As for style, the usual history of English pre-Restoration prose fixes on its luxuriance, and then various contributory tendencies are brought in to explain the emergence of a plain style in the 1650s and its establishment as the Standard after the Restoration. This does not hold for Scotland, where only three writers developed elaborately mannered prose. Drummond writes in a ceremonious fashion, intent on the balance of his clauses and the fall of his cadences. He is the only Scottish writer who seems to be listening to himself and indeed the only one who consistently cultivated the 'schemes', those patterns of words and syntax that give a rich auditory texture to prose. The other two examples of elaborate manner are eccentrics. I have given a specimen of Urquhart's ludic prose in the form of exhaustive catalogue. His other forms of display include sesquipedalian neologisms, syntactical labyrinths and whimsical rhetorical divisions. By contrast the extravagances of Samuel Rutherford (1600–1661) seem unselfconscious. His is an enthusiastic prose, language bent to convey religious excitement, images crowded thick with effects of visionary grotesqueness. Scotland produced only these three examples of highly evolved literary manner. Plainness was standard there from the start. There was little need to reform excess of artifice or of idiosyncracy.

It is true that many unpretentious writers worked up an ornate, often Ciceronian, paragraph when rhetorical occasion demanded. Covenanting pamphleteers might set a pompous exordium in front of tracts that continue in a workmanlike style suitable for close knit argument. It is also true that there is plainness and plainness. There is the plainness of the controversialists, at its best colourless and neat. There is a plainness that is no style at all; shapeless but often graphic, it is frequent in memoirs and journals. Finally

there is a plainness with literary grace, and here perhaps lies the real achievement of Scottish prose after Knox. I have in mind the sermons and commentaries of William Cowper (1568–1619), James's Bishop of Galloway,
Robert Leighton (1611–84), a Covenanter, though an increasingly reluctant
one, who became Archbishop of Glasgow after the Restoration, and Hugh
Binning (1627–53), also a Covenanter, but of the radical or Protester wing.
Their frequent imagery has the purpose of clinching points, not of decorating
thought or letting it ramify strangely. 'The ugly Death's head', writes Leighton
in his *Commentary on Peter*, 'when the light of glory shines through the holes
of it, is comely and lovely'. This surprises like a Herbert conceit, but in context
it is another Herbertian quality, conceptual grasp, rather than Metaphysical
strangeness, that counts. Though Leighton and the others are divines, their
plainness is expressive of men seeking to make their thought plain to other
men. And though Cowper is a disappointing and short-winded author, in
each of them natural and easy expression is pulled together by a certain
disciplined energy of thought. These writers do not fit into the development
of English prose according to the standard account, nor do they anticipate
it. They are too unworldly, too devoid of social tone, to sound like Restoration
divines. But they wrote well, and we should not let the history of English prose,
and with it the subsequent history of Scottish prose, hide the achievement.

I shall turn now to a descriptive survey of the most interesting writers,
sorting their works loosely into historical, controversial, devotional and
literary prose.

The historical prose is the most accessible to the general reader, partly
because the events of Scottish history are stirring and its characters appear
in bold outline. The best story tellers are the best historians, with an eye for
the telling fact, an ear for pithy dialogue and a feeling for strongly marked
character. These are especially the gifts of those who wrote memoirs, a sort
of writing in which Scots, since Knox's *History*, have excelled. Though none
equal Knox in rhetorical force, the single-minded subjection of events to one
point of view, many are successful in making what was going on vividly
present to the imagination.

The flourishing of various sorts of historical writing after the Reformation
is sudden and remarkable. But historiographically it remained primitive. No
Scottish historian could write, like Camden, of the sweat and dust that
covered him as he rummaged through confused rolls of parchment in a
disinterested pursuit of fact. Nor did Scots have developed ideas of political
life. Their narratives do not unfold complex chains of action; one thing leads
to another with the simplest explanations, or none. Instead of analysing what
was going on and why, they look for moral designs. Those not writing
presbyterian party history frequently say their accounts offer moral and
political instruction. They assume that history repeats itself and that its
characters and actions fall into exemplary types of virtue and vice. History
for them is a book of analogies. Presbyterian historians shape their accounts
according to religious, rather than moral, designs. They write to record God's
dealings with his church, or rather his party in his church and its enemies.
But they too think analogically, not analytically. They conceive of the history

of Scotland as a recapitulation of the history of Israel in its backslidings and returns to its covenant with God. Indeed they considered biblical history as a book, not just of analogies, but of precedents regulating action in the present. Binning, for example, argued from biblical history, such as the story of how Gideon turned away most of his volunteers, that God's party in Scotland should exclude all but the strictest Covenanters from fighting against Cromwell's invasion. This is fanaticism, the extreme development of reading the present in the analogy of the biblical past. Analogical history, however, could be used more critically. The Royalist pamphleteers John Corbet (1603–1641) and Drummond of Hawthornden, drew on their reading of Roman and European history to make analogies between what they saw as the misrule of Covenanting Scotland and the confusions brought on other kingdoms by priestcraft. There are inklings here of historical sociology in their discerning a recurrent theocratic pattern that cuts across the distinction between extreme Protestant and extreme Catholic. But they are only inklings. The apparent historical skepticism is harnessed to polemic, not inquiry.

But to return from pamphlets to histories, Robert Lindsay of Pitscottie's *The History and Cronicles of Scotland* shows how lively narrative may go with primitive historiography. His point of view is that of a Fife gentleman, a farmer, but a kinsman of Lindsay of Byres. His politics centre on the king. In his *Cronicles*, arranged by reign, good subjects serve their king staunchly and offer forthright counsel, while bad subjects offer him false counsel and conspire against him. Good kings distinguish between these subjects and make the good ones, often Lindsays, their servants. And they must guard against sensuality: God punished James IV's adultery with Flodden. Such ideas do not in themselves make a good history, though a good morality play like *Ane Satyre of the Thrie Estaits* may be made from them. Nor does Pitscottie's haphazard narrative, especially of his own time, convey insight into the workings of politics. But in the most readable part of his history, the reigns of James III to V, where he is retelling tales that have been told him, the frame of ideas stays in the background and the very absence of organisation allows circumstantial detail to stick vividly in the mind. The escape of James V from the Douglas faction, for instance, makes an excellent adventure story, the boy king in the hands of captors who pretend to be his friends, his own pretence that hunting fills his thoughts, his slipping from them while they sleep thinking he sleeps—here Pitscottie's shapeless prose pulls itself together and enters into James's resourcefulness and the astonishment of his captors with keen enjoyment.

Historiographically David Hume of Godscroft's *History of the Houses of Douglas and Angus* is as primitive as Pitscottie's *Cronicles*. He eulogises and defends the exploits of the chiefs of his clan with all the historical desultoriness and defective sense of fact that implies. Rhetorically, however, he writes an attractive humanistic history inspired by Buchanan, but, in retelling the splendid family stories, such as the Battle of Otterburn, with a narrative verve beyond Buchanan's classicising. His politics are Buchanan's, centred, not on the king, but on the overmighty subject. He records a dialogue between himself and the earl of Angus, in which he defends the liberty of aristocracy and church to resist tyrants. Other reflections in a sententious, mildly Senecan style encrust his narrative. These, though a substitute for political experience, are nevertheless interesting. He offers by far the most thoughtful formulation of how history teaches morality and some sombre observations on how power corrupts.

John Spottiswoode (1565–1639), Archbishop of St Andrews, wrote a much plainer sort of history. His narrative is in general unenlivened by the anecdotal particularity of Pitscottie or Hume, and the speeches that, imitating classical historians, he gives to important figures are not animating. *The History of the Church of Scotland* is an official episcopal account. Indeed speaking of the lessons of history, Spottiswoode instances how it teaches that the original Protestant constitution of the Scottish church was episcopal. James VI wished to encourage such views and had opened the state papers to his researches. These did not lead to awkward impartiality. Spottiswoode gets round the awkwardness of Knox's *History* by supposing it a forgery and the awkwardness of the Five Articles of Perth, where he thought James had gone too far in an English direction, by leaving them out. But though partisan, his narrative is temperate, ably summary on controversial points, only rather dull.

Like Spottiswoode's *History*, David Calderwood's *Historie of the Kirk of Scotland* is an official production, but a Presbyterian one, assisted by grants from the Covenanting General Assembly. Less a historian than editor of an enormous collection of constitutional documents and first hand accounts from a cloud of witnesses, Calderwood (1575–1660) has the vices and virtues of the Genevan or Presbyterian partisans he drew on, with an occasional vinegariness of his own. They assume that history is the revelation of God's plan, of a providence minutely regulatory of human affairs. Though they refer everything to God's will, they betray much egocentricity, egocentricity writ large in the belief that the Scots are a chosen people, writ smaller in the belief that their party are God's party, and writ in its own natural character in the belief that all things, including the disasters that befall others as well as themselves, have been arranged for the good of the narrators, this last a point of view more evident in the memoirs I shall discuss below than in Calderwood himself. Such beliefs could sustain only the narrowest comprehension of political life. And yet Calderwood has the virtues of the presbyterian school. Imitating Knox and James Melville (1556–1614), he inserts documents and eye witness accounts as evidence for his narrative. These, especially where he transcribes from Melville or Robert Bruce, display what Spottiswoode lacks, a gift for story telling. He contributes lively accounts of his own, notably of confrontations between Presbyterians and the authorities, often rendered as old-fashioned knock-about comedy of misrule to throw sarcastic reflections on the king and his bishops and their machinations.

It is indeed in memoirs that the Presbyterians excel as historians. James Melville's *Autobiography and Diary* reads men and events with all the intellectual narrowness of his party. But in association with his famous uncle, Andrew Melville, he was at the centre of the troubled relations between the Presbyterians and James VI. It would be hard for a first hand account of those matters to be dull. But Melville has, besides, in his uncle a character larger than life, a fiery and irrepressible zealot for Presbytery, whose outbursts against the king delight him and his readers, though perhaps for different reasons. To these materials he brought a certain naivety that goes with involvement in his story and a flair for Scots dialogue, dry or forthright. And story telling draws him to give more than his harsh ideas imply. A convivial sweetness comes through his accounts of his childhood, education and association in adversity with his fellow Presbyterians. This not only softens the unamiable impression his religious principles make; we see the author as human and so appreciate the clashes he records as differences, not just of principles, but of people and manners.

The Covenanters come nearest to producing a continuation of Melville's first hand history in the *Letters and Journals* of Robert Baillie (1599–1662). His most interesting letters are journals of his experiences as a leading figure among the moderate Covenanters, the Resolutioners. He sent these to friends, not just to keep in touch, but to supply them with a Covenanting news sheet. Nevertheless, he remembers he is writing a letter. As a divine he sometimes writes as if he discerned the hand of God behind events, most of all in the early triumphs of the Bishops' Wars, and as a church politician, he is concerned with solidarity and managing the right appearances. But at the same time he keeps his correspondents' natural curiosity in mind and entertains them with discreet gossip and lively observations of his journeyings, the highlanders, 'those unkannie trewesmen', at Duns Law, or the inns on the road to London 'all like palaces'. And as he writes, he gives a picture of himself, sociable, attached to the gentry, eager to promote the reputations of his friends, an insatiably political animal. In church politics his Covenanting principles hark back to the Melvilles, but in human temper, despite the vast changes in manners that come between him and men like Alexander Carlyle, we can already trace the lineaments of an eighteenth century Moderate.

Baillie does not record his spiritual experiences. Typically, presbyterian autobiographical writing turns to politics rather than the inner life. The *Autobiography* of Robert Blair (1593–1666), with its modest, exact account of his spiritual 'discoveries' in the 1620s is a partial exception, but was written, like other Covenanting memoirs, after the Restoration. Covenanting diarists, however, record their spiritual experiences, but their inner repertoire is banal, self-centred and canting. Some interest attaches to the wrestlings, tears and raptures of Archibald Johnston of Wariston (1611–63), partly because of his gross emotionalism and hunger for more than human greatness, partly because of his career as leader of the Covenanting extremists, the Protesters, and later as collaborator with Cromwell. His intensities went with theocratic politics: if God was to rule Scotland, he had to rule the hearts of his party. However crudely, Wariston's *Diary* suggests how Protester spirituality was the inner form of Protester politics and also shows how God-serving, party-serving, and as became clear, even to himself, self-serving, motives ran together.

Three memoirs, not closely connected with church politics, deserve mention. Sir James Melville of Halhill (1535–1617) served as a minor diplomat in Europe before returning to Scotland and attaching himself, first to Mary, then to the Regent Moray. He writes with the moral design of supplying his sons with a pattern of honest counsellor and servant of princes, namely himself. He was a rather unsuccessful courtier, and since he never won his way to the centre, his memoirs treat peripheral affairs. He aims, anyway, to show the neglect of his merit and good counsel rather than the workings of politics in the age of the Reformation. But despite his intellectual limitations, Melville, of all the historical writers of the period, has by far the sharpest appreciation of political character. His judgements of Buchanan and the Regent Moray are memorably shrewd and the account of the extraordinary interviews Elizabeth gave him, worthy of a life devoted to studying the ways of great ones.

The other two memoirs are by wandering Scots. In *The Totall Discourse* William Lithgow (1582–1645) records his nineteen years of 'Rare Adventures and Panefull Peregrinations' round the Mediterranean. He confirms many British prejudices about Abroad, but being a tough and slightly disreputable traveller, he experienced much of interest, including torture by the Spaniards. Robert Monro (1590–1647) was a mercenary in the Thirty Years' War. He divides his memoirs, *Monro, His Expedition*, into short accounts of actions, each followed by an 'Observation' in which he extracts a lesson of a moral or military sort, often embellished with the fruits of his classical studies. Those who relish the absurdities of Dugald Dalgetty will find his pedantry quite delicious.

Unlike the historical writing, the controversial prose makes dull reading. After the Reformation, the controversialists paid insufficient attention to tone or rhetorical character. Knox's opponent, Winzet, impresses because he projects himself as an honest, clear-witted Linlithgow schoolmaster. But the Covenanter, Baillie, who sounds agreeable in his letters, comes over peevishly in his tracts. Writers like him mismanaged not only their own characters but the attack on the characters of their opponents. The malicious imitations of the Reformers in the Reformation piece, Thomas Maitland's 'Pretended Conference', are far more damaging than all the indignant vehemence of later party writers. Only Corbet's *Epistle Congratulatorie* manages its adversaries with some subtlety. Actually a Laudian churchman, he pretends to be a Jesuit congratulating the Covenanters on their jesuitical principles and practices. He draws the similarities between Protestant and Catholic extremes ingeniously and maliciously, but also with a knowledge of their former controversies with the crown, solid enough to suggest that the extremes genuinely coincide in theocratic misrule.

But apart from Corbet and John Maxwell, Bishop of Ross, both Laudians and defenders of Charles's divine right against the Covenanters' divine right to oppose him, the religious professionals who wrote most of the controversial prose during the Civil Wars do not enliven their pamphlets even with malice. Their occasional scurrilities are dull, though fantastic. Among them, especially the Presbyterians, scholastic methods of disputation prevail. Issues are interminably subdivided into heads. Answers and answers to answers go point by point. Authorities are adduced and finessed upon, but evidence is not examined. The appeal is never to common sense or impartial inquiry.

Locked into adversarial positions, the controversialists aim to score points, and like Pope's schoolmen, 'none had sense enough to be confuted'. Such writing could not change anyone's mind, only provide material for further disputation. The most evolved product of this method, and the most unreadable, is Samuel Rutherford's *Lex Rex*, a theocratic defence of the subjects' right to depose a tyrant. The discipline and logic of Rutherford and other Covenanting pamphleteers is admirable. They never let themselves go with Milton's rhetorical violence. But neither do they express his human urge for liberty. They appeal to reason, but only to defend narrow orthodoxies. The open rationality of Winstanley, the English Leveller, lies quite beyond the scope of their tightly controlled revolution.

The poets' controversial writings are easier to read, if only because less closely argued. The Castalian, William Fowler (1560–1612), wrote *An Answer* to John Hamilton's early Counter-Reformation attack on the Protestant establishment. He begins with a preposterous invective, all parallelism and alliteration and other rhetorical schemes. But having shown what he can do in that line, he drops into plain Scots prose. Drummond is an infinitely finer artist, but his artistry seems misplaced in controversy. The rule of the Covenant drew some royalist pieces from him, notably *Irene* and *Skiamachia*. These he wrote, not for publication, but for an ideal audience of himself and his friends. Their highly wrought style distances them from real political engagement. Even their wisdom seems ornamental, more attentive to the choice apophthegm and balanced figure than grappling with actualities.

Drummond's ideas that the subject's duty is to obey and the king's, to keep order by holding the sectional interests of the three estates in balance receive plainer treatment in James VI's earlier *Basilikon Doron* and Lord Napier's 'Letter about the Soveraigne Power'.

Since the eighteenth century, the Scots literary tradition has been anti-clerical, certainly anti-Kirk. The seventeenth century English divines have Johnson, Coleridge and Eliot, to make them current reading. But without that sort of creative recovery, it is hard to write about Scottish devotional works as literature. Leighton has, however, Coleridge himself, whose *Aids to Reflection* consists largely of passages from Leighton's *Commentary on Peter*, the fine flower of Covenanting spirituality. Here then is an opening. What Coleridge found in Leighton was ideas of disinterested or spiritual ethics. Like all Calvinists, Leighton grounded himself on the paradox of the justified sinner, a paradox with political as well as ethical implications. If only Christ can justify, then no human institution can make one holy. Presbyterians thought this subverted the claims of Roman and episcopal church governments, but not of their own, which they imagined was under the immediate rule of Christ and free from worldly interest. The Covenanters went so far as to assert the right to resist a king who tried to overturn this rule of Christ. To these ideas, Leighton gave at most ambiguous commitment in this *Commentary* and later turned against them. It was the ethical, not political, implications of the paradox of the justified sinner that weighed with him. If only Christ can justify, attempts to justify oneself are vain. That might seem to encourage antinomianism, behaving as wickedly as one pleases since it makes no difference spiritually. But the Scottish divines are unremitting in their moral demands. They use the notion of unmerited grace to rule out the self-seeking inherent in attempts to acquire merit or a good character and then turn to the business of sanctification, the abolishing of the self and the acquiring of Christ as a new self. What distinguishes Leighton's treatment of this operation is the exact and practical application he gives it. He avoids theory and rhetorical expansion, aiming instead at transparency to the bearing of the biblical text on how to live. The wisdom of an ethic of self-effacement may be doubted. For all his disciplined practicality, Leighton is one of the great hunger artists of the seventeenth century with an alarming penchant for images of self-mortification, such as the crushing of spices in a mortar to make perfume. Again, for all their selflessness, Leighton's ideas, like most seventeenth century moral thought, ignore one's relation to other selves. He addresses the individual in relation to himself or alone with God. That said, however, Leighton's concentration on the effort to realise what Greville called 'a simple goodness in the flesh refined' is truly impressive.

Leighton's spirituality was not unique. I have mentioned Blair's *Autobiography*. Earlier Alexander Hume (*c*.1560–1609) had published 'Christian Precepts Serving to the Practice of Sanctification', a work that draws on Thomas à Kempis but bears the mark of lived principle. And Leighton influenced his contemporaries, notably Binning, whose *Treatise of Christian Love* shows some of Leighton's limitations and some of his moral keenness.

Leighton and Binning are credited with the introduction of a new style of preaching in the 1650s, though they are anticipated by the Jacobean preachers, Bruce and Cowper. The usual way was to stretch a text upon a scheme of doctrine, reason and use and subdivide these divisions, a method of invention useful for those who had to find something to say, but cumbersome—though dull books in this style, such as *Christ Crucified* by James Durham (1622–58) might be taken for wonders. A variant was the prophetic sermon, in which a scriptural figure was drawn out in heads and strained to glance allegorically at the times: lively examples are Andrew Cant's 'Sermon Preached at the Renovation of the National Covenant' and James Row's 'Redshanks Sermon'. In place of this method of forcing thought by division, Leighton and Binning introduced 'a discourse on some common head'. This assumes that the text has prompted a worthwhile train of reflection on a single topic and allows it to develop naturally. Like all Leightonian simplicity, it rests on an inward discipline of attention to what matters.

Scottish religion in its political and devotional forms was markedly christocentric. With Samuel Rutherford, one might speak of christolatry. In his controversial tracts he writes as a Presbyterian scholastic, but in his sermons and letters, as one who wishes 'to gather an earthfull and an heavenfull of tongues, dipped and steeped in my Lord's well of love, or his wine of love, even tongues drunken with His love'. In either character he runs to the sort of excesses the Leightonian mind concentrated itself against. He has one overriding theme: God's anger, felt in adversity or 'soul desertion' is the mask of his love; the gates of paradise open in the mouth of hell, or thereabouts. But whereas Leighton's treatment of the transformation of suffering into faith and hope has the weight of his sober moral effort behind it, Rutherford's seems inhuman. He is a mystic. No earthly blow could crush him. His letters of consolation and encouragement express little personal feeling. They are communications such as might pass between saints. One reads them and passages such as this from *Christ Dying and Drawing Sinners to Him* for their fitful imaginative brilliance:

> Jeremiah could prophesie no harder thing against *Pashur* but *Magor missabib* ...Thou shalt be a terror to thyselfe...Self-terrors are a Hell carried about with the Man in his Bosom, he cannot run from them. Oh! he lieth down and Hell beddeth with him; he sleepeth and Hell and he dream together; he riseth and Hell goeth to the Fields with him; he goes to his Garden, there is Hell...He goes to Church; there is a Dog as great as a Mountain before his Eye. (pp 41–42)

Someone who can write like that about wretchedness is an extraordinary force at least. There is, besides, enough strange speculation in *Christ Dying* to make up for its absence in the writings of most of Rutherford's Scottish contemporaries.

Some works by the two men of letters, Drummond and Urquhart, have escaped my historical, controversial and devotional categories.

Drummond's 'The Cypresse Grove' is in fact devotional, not, however, a sermon or a commentary, but a platonising Renaissance essay. He works the spoils of wide reading into this meditation on the vanity of earthly life and the joys of heaven with such art that it seems all of a piece, and his elaborate style gives a rich dye and an agreeable literary unreality to thoughts about death. His 'Conversations' with Ben Jonson are, by contrast, merely notes, never worked up into *Kunstprosa*, and fortunately, for their rough jotting catches Jonson at Hawthornden in all his gross and spiky vitality. Drummond's modesty is a strength: Jonson's vanity would have annihilated a vain man. Drummond had the wit to appreciate that Jonson was worth taking down minutely and the self possession to let Jonson spread his rather appalling self without interference.

Finally Urquhart, the uncategorisable. His whole career looks like a preparation for his last work, his translation of the first three books of *Gargantua and Pantagruel*, still the best way to read Rabelais in English. There his verbal exuberance, his display of curious learning and his jocular relation to the real world come into their own. But he pantagruelised outside the covers of his translation, with the result that his life was calamitous and his earlier writings puzzling, if entertaining. In *The Trissotetras* he displays himself as mathematical virtuoso, but in impenetrable Urquhartian, according to a mnemonic system no one could remember. He wrote his other works, a prisoner after the Battle of Worcester, to persuade the Cromwellian authorities that it was in the interests of the Commonwealth to release and reward so remarkable a man. He failed to persuade them, but his writings are indeed remarkable. *Pantochronochanon* traces the descent of the Urquharts from Adam. *Logopandecteision* and *Ekskybalauron* propose a scheme for a universal language.

Ekskybalauron also sets out to vindicate the honour of Scotland from the disgrace of Presbyterianism by running through all the eminent Scots Urquhart could remember or invent. Among them appears the Admirable Crichtoun, whom Urquhart pictures as a fantastic but triumphant version of himself, scholar, gentleman, soldier, cynosure, and whose self-display he matches with a display of all the verbal extravagance at his command. Urquhart's writing tends to self-reference and self-parody. He does not always seem in command of the eccentric personality he cultivated. But at his best he manages it successfully and appears as joker, perhaps absurdist, rather than bore and madman.

Urquhart's writing is a freak compound of all that Scottish prose after Knox is not. Where it is mostly clerical, his is the work of the gentleman amateur; where it is disciplined, his is fantastically improvised or systematised; where it rests on grave authorities, his delights in curious erudition and learned caprice. No one could take him seriously, but so far his is the only prose of the period that is generally accepted as part of the Scots literary tradition.

FURTHER READING

PRIMARY TEXTS

Baillie, Robert, *Letters and Journals*, Laing, David (ed), 3 vols, Bannatyne Club (Edinburgh 1841–42)

Binning, Hugh, *A Treatise on Christian Love* (Glasgow, 1743)

—— *An Useful Case of Conscience* (Edinburgh(?), 1693)

Blair, Robert, *Autobiography. The Life of Mr Robert Blair*, McCrie, Thomas (ed), Wodrow Society (Edinburgh, 1848)

Bruce, Robert, 'Narrative', in *Bannatyne Miscellany*, Bannatyne Club (Edinburgh, 1827)

—— *Sermons*, Cunningham, William (ed), Wodrow Society (Edinburgh, 1843)

Calderwood, David, *The Historie of the Kirk of Scotland*, Thomson, Thomas (ed), 8 vols, Wodrow Society (Edinburgh, 1842–49)

Cant, Andrew (1590–1663), *A Sermon Preached after the Renovation of the National Covenant* (Glasgow, 1638)

Corbet, John, *The Epistle Congratulatorie of Lysimachus Nicanor* (Edinburgh(?), 1640)

Cowper, William, *The Works* (London, 1623)

Drummond, William, 'Ben Jonson's Conversations', in *Ben Jonson*, 9 vols (Oxford, 1925), vol I

—— 'The Cypresse Grove' [1623], in *The Poetical Works of William Drummond of Hawthornden*, Kastner, L E (ed), STS, 2 vols (Edinburgh and London, 1913), vol II

—— *The Works of William Drummond of Hawthornden*, Sage, John (ed) (Edinburgh, 1711)

Durham, James, *Christ Crucified or the Marrow of the Gospel* (Edinburgh, 1683)

Fergusson, David, *Scottish Proverbs Gathered Together* [1641], Beveridge, Erskine (ed), STS (Edinburgh and London, 1924)

Fowler, William, 'An Answer to M. Io Hamilton' [1581], in *The Works*, STS, 3 vols (Edinburgh and London, 1914–40), vol II

Hume, Alexander, 'Christian Precepts Serving to the Practise of Sanctification' [1599], in *The Poems of Alexander Hume*, Lawson, Alexander (ed), STS (Edinburgh and London, 1944–50)

Hume, David, of Godscroft, *History of the Houses of Douglas and Angus* (Edinburgh, 1644)

James VI, *Basilikon Doron* [1599], Craigie, James (ed), STS, 2 vols (Edinburgh and London, 1944–50)

Johnston, Archibald, of Wariston, *Diary*, Paul, G Morison (ed), 3 vols, SHS (Edinburgh, 1911–40)

Leighton, Robert, *The Whole Works*, West, William (ed), 7 vols (London, 1869–75), vols II–VII

Lindsay, Robert, of Pitscottie (fl. 1523–78), *The Historie and Chronicles of Scotland*, Mackay, Aeneas J G Mackay (ed), STS, 2 vols (Edinburgh and London, 1899)

Lithgow, William, *The Totall Discourse of the Rare Adventures and Panefull Pere-grinations of Long Nineteene Yeares Travayles from Scotland* (London, 1632)

Melville, James, *The Autobiography and Diary*, Pitcairn, Robert (ed), Wodrow Society (Edinburgh, 1847)

Melville, Sir James, of Halhill, *Memoirs of his Own LIfe* [1683], Thomson, Thomas (ed), Bannatyne Club (Edinburgh, 1827)

Monro, Robert, *Monro, his Expedition with the Worthy Scots Regiment* (London, 1637)

Napier, Archibald, 1st Baron Napier (1576–1645), 'Letter about the Soveraigne and Supreme Power', in *Memorials of Montrose*, Napier, Mark (ed), 2 vols, Maitland Club (Edinburgh, 1868), vol II

Row, James (*c*.1600–*c*.1680), *The Red Shanks Sermon* (London, 1642)

Rutherford, Samuel, *Christ Dying and Drawing Sinners to Himself* (London, 1647)

—— *Letters of Samuel Rutherford* [*Joshua Redivivus*, 1664], Bonar, Andrew A (ed), 2 vols (Edinburgh, 1891)

—— *Lex Rex* (London, 1644)

Spottiswoode, John, *The History of the Church of Scotland* [1655], Russell, M (ed), Spottiswoode Society (Edinburgh, 1851)

Urquhart, Sir Thomas (trans), *Gargantua and Pantagruel* [Books 1 and 2, 1653; Book 3, 1693], 2 vols (London, 1929)

—— *The Jewel* [*Ekskybalauron*, 1652], Jack, R D S, and Lyall, R J (eds) (Edinburgh, 1983)

—— *Logopandecteision* (1653), *Pantochronocanon* (1652), *The Trissotetras* (1645), in *The Works of Sir Thomas Urquhart of Cromartie*, Stirling, S D (ed), Bannatyne Club (Edinburgh, 1834)

SECONDARY TEXTS (including anthologies with critical introductions. Ed)

Buckle, H T, 'An Examination of the Scotch Intellect', in *An Introduction to the History of Civilisation in England*, Robertson, J M (ed) (London, 1904), pp 741–91

Henderson, G D, *Religious Life in Seventeenth Century Scotland* (Cambridge, 1937)

Jack, R D S (ed), *Scottish Prose, 1550–1700* (London, 1971)

Millar, John Hepburn, *Scottish Prose of the Seventeenth and Eighteenth Centuries* (Glasgow, 1912)

Reid, David (ed), *The Party-Coloured Mind: Selected Prose Relating to the Conflict between Church and State in Seventeenth Century Scotland* (Edinburgh, 1982)

Chapter 12

Early Scottish Drama

SARAH CARPENTER

The early history of drama in Scotland is inseparable from the history of the country itself. Theatre is essentially a public rather than a private medium, which demands places for performance and money for staging. Probably more than any other kind of literature, therefore, drama is deeply, if elusively, affected by its social, political and economic circumstances since they determine the provision of these resources. In Scotland the early drama is particularly influenced by two of the major forces in the country's history: the problems of the monarchy, and developments in the Church.

In its early history Scotland suffered from long uncertainties over the throne, particularly in the sixteenth century which experienced a series of infant monarchs and long regencies. Although the monarchy was never positively antagonistic to drama, this prevented a stable context in which either popular or courtly theatre could flourish. The church in Scotland, as in Europe generally, seems to have encouraged drama in the Middle Ages; but the forces involved in the Reformation gradually turned against the theatre. Initially only the religious drama was attacked, for its content rather than its dramatic nature; but eventually most theatre was suppressed altogether, preventing the development of new forms, while most of the evidence for the older kinds of drama—texts, properties and church records—was destroyed. So between them the monarchy and the Church not only affected the course of the early Scottish theatre, and its subject matter; they have also led to an extreme scarcity of texts and records through which we can try to know it. All we have are a few surviving Mediæval records from churches, burgh councils and guilds involved in producing, managing or suppressing various kinds of plays, some accounts relating to performances at court, and a very few texts from the end of this period, the sixteenth century, which seem mostly to have been preserved for their literary rather than their theatrical interest. Nonetheless, the picture we can piece together from this evidence suggests that through the Middle Ages and the Renaissance most of the varied forms of the lively European dramatic tradition existed in Scotland, if sometimes, perhaps, only embryonically.

Although we have next to no texts surviving from the Middle Ages it looks as if some kind of popular drama, or quasi-drama, was flourishing from the thirteenth century onwards. This can loosely be divided into secular and religious forms, though most of the evidence comes in one way or another through the Church. Our earliest evidence is in various thirteenth century prohibitions by the Church of *ludi* (games/plays), sometimes *turpes et inhonesti ludi* (shameful and indecent plays), in sacred places and church-yards.[1] We do not know what these *ludi* were, but it is likely that they involved semi-dramatic dancing and singing, and churches throughout Europe seemed intent on banning them.

During the following centuries Scotland seems likewise to have shared the traditions of European folk drama: seasonal activities, which might involve combat, wooing or crowning ceremonies, sometimes dance. In Scotland we hear of morris and sword dances; there also exists the only Mediæval text for a British folk drama, a 'plough play' dating from about 1500.[2] Plough plays were performed in January to celebrate the start of the new agricultural year by honouring the plough. The text for this one was set to music in a three part courtly song which has preserved the folk ceremony in a sophisticated setting. The action of the 'play' is obscure: the leader addresses the lord of the land, explaining that the old plough ox is so weak he can go no longer. Before he dies a new ox should be found. The workers or 'hyndis' are all called before the lord by name, and then there appears to be an action in which the leader and/or eight men are yoked to the plough as the new oxen. The text is confusing, but it does seem to record a symbolic, energetic, dramatic performance acting out a ceremony of renewal.[3]

The most frequent allusions to Scottish folk drama are, however, to May games. These usually focus on one of two figures. The Abbot of Unreason (or Bonaccord, or Narent) who was appointed in many towns and cities seems to have been a Lord of Misrule figure, who may be related to the church's Feast of Fools. The other very common leader of the May game was Robin Hood. Although he is now generally thought of as an English folk hero, he is recorded in drama almost as soon, and at least as widely, in Scotland. 'Robert Hode' and his fellows are first mentioned as the subjects of popular drama in the mid fifteenth century, and by the beginning of the sixteenth century he is appearing throughout the country, often taking over from the Abbots of Unreason. The evidence suggests that Robin Hood became the centre of a semi-dramatic game celebrating the return of summer. Alexander Scott in the sixteenth century talks of the old May game in which:

> men yeid everich one,   [went]
> With Robene Hoid and Littill Johne
> To bring in bowis and birkin bobbynis.   [boughs] [birch branches]
> ('Of May', 16–18)

Towns and cities from Aberdeen to Ayr financed Robin Hoods, as did the king. By the sixteenth century his role apparently included general authority for organising dramatic festivity. Such was the responsibility, in fact, that people might refuse the position, and even be fined by the burgh council for doing so.

Anthropologists tend to relate drama of this kind to pre-Christian rituals of fertility and luck-bringing, but it is extremely unlikely that, if these were the origins, the participants recognised them. The plays were at least tacitly sanctioned by the church, and organised and financed by the burgh councils. Folk drama of this kind, performed by the people themselves, usually with official support, seems to have served a social and festive function, celebrating community and holiday release.

Reaction against the folk drama began in the mid sixteenth century. In 1555 Parliament ordained that 'na maner of persoun be chosin Robert Hude nor Lytill Johne Abbot of Unressoun Quenis of Maij nor utherwyse'. This seems initially a civil response to fears that the plays caused disturbances and nursed sedition, but as the Reformation proceeded religious opposition increased. The fact that church and government are still forbidding the plays in the 1580s suggests that they died hard, but by the seventeenth century they mostly seem to have disappeared, except for such fragments as the Queensferry Burry Man which exist to this day.

Scotland also shared the other form of popular drama which flourished throughout Mediæval Europe, religious plays based on the Bible. These were also performed by the people themselves, rather than by professional actors; they were outdoor plays, usually associated with one of the summer festivals of the Church, and tended to dramatise and interpret series of episodes from the old and new testaments. These 'cycle', 'mystery' or *corpus christi* plays were performed to glorify God, and to strengthen faith by giving people a vivid and emotional insight into the truths of their religion.

The plays probably began as a series of wordless pageants which processed through a city to its cathedral, either on foot or mounted on pageant wagons. It is not wholly clear from the evidence whether in Scotland these ever developed into full spoken and acted plays, but most Scottish cities had elaborate and spectacular pageants of some sort.[4] The first recorded allusion is to the *ludo de ly haliblude ludendo apud ly Wyndmylhill* (play of the holy blood played at the Windmillhill) in Aberdeen in 1440. Records also survive from Lanark, Perth, Dundee and Edinburgh which suggest that, as in England, each pageant in a series would be the responsibility of one of the trade guilds of the city. The shows were vivid and heterogeneous, a later list from Aberdeen including among its pageants St Laurence, the Coronation of Our Lady, St George, and the Resurrection. A character list from the Perth Hammermen's Guild refers, among others, to Adam, Eve, the 'marmadin' (mermaid), the devil, St Erasmus, and the cord-drawer (to draw out the martyred saint's entrails). Although the records are so fragmentary, they give us glimpses of the visual style of the plays: the payments in Lanark for 'futyn off the cros' (footing of the cross) in 1503, or the Dundee record of 'a credil & thre barnis (babies) maid of clath' (1520), suggest the emotive realism with which episodes like the crucifixion, or the slaughter of the innocents might be presented; while the 'gold fulye (foil) to Cristis pascione' (Lanark), or 'cristis cott (coat) of lethyr with the hoss (hose) and glufis' (Dundee) shows the ritual splendour with which such naturalism was combined.

These religious plays formed a serious and important part of festival celebrations until the middle of the sixteenth century. Performed on Church holy days, on spiritual subjects, managed by the burgh councils, and presented by the guilds, they show the intimate and fruitful interrelationship of Church, government and working life during the Middle Ages. Like the folk drama, they began to disappear during the Reformation, as the 'superstitious kepyng of festvall dayis' which they celebrated was banned. In 1574 the General Assembly of the Church forbade all plays on the 'Canonicall Scripture, alsweill new as old' and local church authorities tried more forceful measures. In Perth in 1577 the church refused to baptise the children of men who performed in a banned *corpus christi* play. By the end of the century this drama seems to have died out altogether. The impetus for this in Scotland clearly came directly from the Reformed Church, but cycle plays were beginning to decline throughout Europe at this time, suggesting a general, but more elusive, cultural shift.

Apart from the popular drama, the other major source of early theatrical activity in Scotland was the court. As the centre of political affairs and ceremonies, as well as of patronage and resources, the court from the earliest times celebrated almost all its major events, as well as its leisure, with dramatic entertainments. Events which combined political, dynastic and personal significance, such as marriages and births, were particular focuses for performances. These were often more than just decorative, as we see from very early on in the hauntingly disturbing glimpse of a *ludus* at the wedding feast of Alexander III in 1285: a ring dance was interrupted by 'ane ymage of ane dede man, nakitt of flesche & lyre [skin], with bair banys'. Mortality is seen to interrupt even the new life of marriage.

By the fifteenth and sixteenth centuries court celebrations were becoming increasingly spectacular, with elaborate theatrical machinery, music, dance and speeches delivered by symbolically appropriate characters. For the baptism of Prince Henry in 1594 there were even plans to draw in one of the pageant cars, bearing a banqueting table and six symbolic ladies, with a real lion. In the end, however, caution prevailed 'because his presence might have brought some feare, to the neerest, or that the sight of the lights and torches might have commoved his tamenes'.[5] Although the emphasis was on spectacle, the courtly context made these entertainments always at least potentially political: political meaning was certainly read into one of the shows devised for the birth of James VI in 1566, when the English envoys to the court were upset by the supposedly insulting gestures of a group of satyrs who 'pat ther handis behind them to ther tailis, quhilkis they waggit with ther handis, in sic sort as the Englishmen supponit it had been devysed and done in derysion of them'.[6]

Elaborate court entertainments could be more deliberately used in the service of political public relations. In 1507 the court of James IV organised the Tournament of the Black Lady, a hugely spectacular affair featuring the Garden of Patience, the Tree of Esperance, and the Black Lady herself, apparently a real negro. Invitations were sent out to foreign nobility, as was the custom with such large scale tournaments, designed to enhance the prestige of the host country. This one was so internationally successful that it was repeated in the following year with even more splendour, the Black Lady being finally elevated to the roof of the hall in a cloud machine in which she disappeared. This dramatic spectacle, in which the king himself jousted, 'with counterfutting of the round tabill of King Arthour',[7] made a significant contribution to Scotland's international image at the beginning of the sixteenth century.

Apart from spectacles for particular purposes, the court also promoted drama for its own entertainment. Mary Queen of Scots in particular encouraged and delighted in courtly dance and masque entertainments, often taking part in them herself and helping to crystallise the opposition of the reformers to her monarchy. 'Thair began', said John Knox of her return to Scotland, 'the masking, which from year to year hath continewed since'. Court poets sometimes contributed to these semi-dramatic entertainments. Some of the poems of Alexander Scott, written in the mid sixteenth century, are composed to dance tunes, as is Alexander Montgomerie's complex allegorical poem of the 1580s, largely in dialogue, *The Cherrie and the Slae*. Both poets may refer obliquely to issues topical at court, and it has been suggested that poems like these were written for dance-and-song performances there.[8]

Montgomerie also composed speeches in Scots for court 'disguisings': 'The Navigatioun' and 'A Cartell of the Thre Ventrous Knichts'. They follow a traditional form in which exotically disguised 'strangers' (usually members of the court) enter, supposedly from distant and mysterious countries, to salute the spectators. 'The Navigatioun', which honours King James while offering political advice, serves to introduce a show of extravagantly dressed foreigners. In 'A Cartell' the three strangers challenge members of the court to ride at the ring, a variety of the common courtly 'mumming' in which the dramatic charcters actually engage with their audience. There also exists a fragment of a masque which James VI himself composed for the wedding of one of his current favourites in 1588. Although a slight piece, giving speeches to traditional gods and nymphs, it touches on the particular relationship between the king and the bride and groom, and the presenter's speech seems designed to be spoken by James himself.[9] All this fits well with the overall mode of courtly entertainment at the time: spectacular semi-theatrical events in which members of the court often participated themselves. It is an interesting borderline use of drama by a restricted but influential circle to enact and confirm its own concerns.

These seem to have been the chief kinds of drama that flourished in Mediæval Scotland, continuing on into the fifteenth and sixteenth centuries. The sixteenth century itself was a time of political and cultural transition, not only in Scotland but throughout Britain. In the troubles of the monarchy and the Church during and after the Reformation new forms of drama were used as potent political and propaganda weapons. These plays, vividly in touch with serious topical issues, give us some insight into the feelings generated by the political events.

Interestingly, the surviving evidence is all of drama used in the interests of reform. Reformation is a natural topic for the dynamic mode of drama, but it also shows that, although the Reformed Church is often blamed for the death of Scottish theatre, the early reformers were not opposed to drama as such. At first they even seem to have used the traditional dramatic forms of the Roman Catholic church to make their points, turning the Church's own weapons against itself. John Knox refers to a Friar Kyllour who presented a reforming 'Historye of Christis Passioun' in Stirling in 1535 that likened the Roman Catholic bishops to the Pharisees who opposed Christ, and so enraged them that according to Knox, 'thei ceassed nott, till that the said Frear Kyllour . . . war cruelly murthered in one fyre' [10] in 1538.

Mostly, however, new ideas were dramatised in new forms. In Dundee in the 1540s anti-papist plays by James Wedderburn were publicly played at the West Port and the town playing field. These were said to be a tragedy on the beheading of John the Baptist, and a comedy of Dionysius the Tyrant, suggesting that Wedderburn used biblical and historical allegories to dramatise the plight of reformers oppressed by tyrannical authorities. Such indirect approaches seem to have been less necessary after the Reformation itself: in 1571 John Knox watched a play apparently directly dramatising the current siege of Edinburgh Castle 'according to Mr Knox doctrin'.

The most interesting of all these plays today, because a full text and some account of the performances survive, is Sir David Lindsay's *Ane Satyre of the Thrie Estaits*. A powerful play in its own right, it is also an illuminating example of the potentialities of sixteenth century political drama. David Lindsay (1486–1555) was not only a probing and accomplished poet, but a high-ranking member of the court, a diplomat, and Lyon King of Arms. He was therefore at the centre of both the literary and the political concerns of his time, with a wide knowledge of European as well as Scottish culture. He seems to have had some involvement with the theatre from the beginning of his long career at court: he was provided with a play coat of blue and yellow taffeta in 1511; as tutor to the infant James V he claims to have played 'fairsis [farces: plays/shows] on the flure'[11] to amuse the prince; and in 1538 he contributed to the celebrations to welcome James V's wife Mary of Guise a 'trieumphant frais' [show] in which a cloud-borne angel exhorted the Queen to obedience and fidelity while delivering to her the keys of Scotland.[12] Lindsay was therefore experienced in drama used both for entertainment and political ends.

Ane Satyre is a political morality play, an allegorical drama which shows Lindsay's familiarity with both English and French dramatic traditions. It seems to have existed in two forms, an earlier version for indoor performance at court, and a longer, much larger-scale production designed for public outdoor performance. Although our texts relate to the later version, we have very revealing evidence about the early production of the play, in a spectator's description of it sent to England by the English ambassador.[13] It appears that it was originally performed at Linlithgow in 1540 with the support of the King, before 'the King and Queene . . . and the hoole counsaile spirituall and temporall'. The play is described as attacking 'the noughtines in Religion, the presumpcion of Busshops . . . and mysusing of preists', a very volatile subject matter before such an audience.

The account gives vivid glimpses of its style—intimate, non-naturalistic, and directly involving the audience. Its characters were a mixture of personifications ('Flattery', 'Experience'), and type figures representing contemporary classes ('Bishop', 'Burgess'). The Poor Man spoke vehemently for the people, 'making a hevie complaynte' against the oppressive Church, and asked for the King. 'And whene he was showed to the man that was king in the playe he . . . saide he was not the king of scotlande for ther was an other king in scotlande that hanged John Armestrang with his fellowes . . . but he had lefte one thing undon'. The Poor Man, rejecting the play king, turns out of the play to James V himself. He alludes to James's suppression of notorious outlaws and suggests that there is another reform for him to undertake in the corrupt Church. This breaking out of the play to implicate the king himself, present in the audience, must have been both comic and disturbing, forcing the spectators into a more personal complicity with the political issues.

Political drama always carries a certain edge of danger, as the fate of Friar Kyllour demonstrates, and this must contribute to its particular theatrical effect. Certainly this performance spilled over the safe boundaries of fictional drama into the real world of its audience: at the end James V is said to have summoned his bishops and told them that if they did not take heed of the play's lessons he would send them down 'unto his uncle of england', Henry VIII whose Reformation was already uncompromisingly in effect.

The texts we have of *Ane Satyre* relate to the large-scale public performances of 1552 at Cupar, and 1554 at the public playfield in Edinburgh. While it has clearly been much adapted and expanded, the new version seems to include much of the old, and it apparently had a lively public impact. The play we have is a large one in every sense (the Edinburgh performance was said to have lasted from nine in the morning till seven in the evening, though if so it must have included substantial breaks). It falls into two halves, separated by an extended meal break. The first traces the spiritual education of the young and innocent King Humanity, who is seduced by Lady Sensuality, abused by various vices, and allows corruption to overtake his country. This is reversed by the dramatic arrival of Divine Correction; but instead of righting things himself, he instructs the king to call a parliament of the three estates (the church, the nobility and the merchants) to reform the abuses of his country. The second half moves from the personal to the public, and the action becomes less linear and more topical. John the Commonweal, emerging from the audience, brings the plight of the country vividly before the parliament. The church is vigorously attacked for its ignorance, self-satisfaction, and harsh oppression of the poor. Resisting reformation, the church leaders are finally unfrocked, revealing fools' clothes beneath their ecclesiastical vestments. Then the Parliament passes edicts of reform, the vices are hanged, and the play concludes with a topsy-turvy mock-sermon on folly by a fool.

The play therefore explores the tensions and troubles within the individual and within the state. Like all Mediæval writers, Lindsay does not see the spiritual as separate from the political, and his solutions for both the king and the government look to God; but nevertheless his play puts the onus for change and control firmly in human hands.

If the subject matter of the play lent it special topical force in its day, it is its dramatic style that has guaranteed its powerful theatrical effect, then and now. It is a play of ideas, and rather than simply following a naturalistic story presents its themes in a lively and provocative mixture of allegory and realism that compels the spectators to think as well as feel. At its simplest this is seen in the easy coexistence and interaction of allegorical and realistic characters on the same stage: the king can talk to Flattery or Deceit, John the Commonweal can argue his case before Divine Correction and Spirituality (the church). Sometimes this interaction is exploited for largely comic effect: a lively scene in which the Shoemaker and the Tailor, having a quiet drink with the beautiful Lady Chastity, are set upon by their jealous wives, depends on the ironic implications of the allegory for the knockabout humour to have its full effect. The wives' conventionally expressed sexual jealousy is undercut when their rival is not an embodiment of sexuality, but of chastity itself. But often a realistic human action conveys more serious allegorical implications. The fact that the seductive Lady Sensuality is eagerly received into King Humanity's bedchamber, while the equally attractive Chastity is sent to the stocks, not only offers an insight into the king's temperament, but forces the spectators to consider the questions of sexuality and control in a wider and more dispassionate context.

Partly because of the interaction of allegory and realism, the tone of the play ranges from high seriousness to farcical humour. Episodes of slapstick comedy not only counterbalance, but are sometimes actually integrated with formal allegory and weighty doctrinal and political issues. As in most morality drama the vices, though always morally dangerous, are given sharply funny personae and many of the theatrical skills and mannerisms of the stand-up comic. Yet their humour often has serious significance in the allegory. A good example is the farcical scene in which Flattery, Falset, and Deceit disguise themselves as clerics in order to wangle their way into the king's favour. After dressing up, they go through a ludicrous and sacrilegious ceremony of mock-baptism, giving each other new and virtuous names to conceal their dangerous natures. But the horseplay of the scene serves to heighten the frightening vulnerability and self-deception of rulers exposed to such concealed and corrupting influences. The unselfconscious movement between serious and comic, allegory and realism, is matched by Lindsay's language. The play is written in an easy vernacular Scots that seems equally expressive in high rhetoric or coarse colloquialism.

Since Lindsay is not bound by the limitations of naturalism he can use vividly theatrical means to convey his points: song, movement, and in particular compellingly emblematic action. The backwards procession of the three estates to the parliament, expressing their complacent wrong-headedness, or the despoiling of the clergy revealing the humiliating clothes of their true natures beneath, have always been strikingly expressive. The stage directions reveal particularly well Lindsay's eye for theatrical effect: 'Heir Spritualitie fames [foams] and rages' (2789) or 'Heir sal thay cleith [clothe] Johne the Common-weil gorgeouslie and set him down amang them in the Parliament' (3802).

Lindsay is clearly not a writer committed to the Reformation: he advocates change from within rather than a rejection of the system itself. But his angry compassion for the poor and oppressed, his vehement satirical attack, his humorous and expressive use of the vernacular, and the variety of theatrical techniques by which he engages the audience, have all made him a model for later Scots drama. Both the subject matter and the style of Lindsay's play seem to be peculiarly characteristic of the best achievements of the Scottish theatre. It is revealing that *Ane Satyre* has been so often revived in the twentieth century, and that both its methods and its concerns seem to be echoed in recent political theatre—*The Great Northern Welly Boot Show*, and the plays of Wildcat and 7:84.[14]

The drama considered so far formed the living theatrical tradition in Scotland. There are also various plays which were probably not performed in the country, but which nonetheless contribute to the overall picture of its early drama. These are often more literary than theatrical in their focus, and show Scottish awareness of contemporary issues and movements in literature.

This is impressively apparent in the Latin tragedies of George Buchanan. Buchanan (1506–82) in fact spent nearly thirty years of his life abroad, studying and teaching largely in France. He was, however, brought up in Scotland, retained his ties with it, and for the last thirty-five years of his life was an influential scholar and educationalist in Scotland—at court, where he contributed both to political events and to court entertainments, in the universities, and as tutor to the young James VI. Buchanan belonged to the important sixteenth century movement of humanism, which was especially concerned to make available to a still largely Mediæval culture the literature and ideas of classical Greece. His writing and scholarship were highly respected internationally.

Among the mid-sixteenth-century humanists, especially in France, there developed a particular interest in translating and imitating classical drama. While teaching at Bordeaux in the early 1540s Buchanan composed four tragedies for his pupils to perform. Written in the living international language of Latin, they were intended to encourage the boys in the skills of performance, and introduce them to the exciting new ideas and forms of Greek literature. Two are direct translations, of Euripedes' *Medea* and *Alcestis*; but there are also two original tragedies, in Greek form but on biblical subjects, *Baptistes* (on John the Baptist) and *Jephthes*. These plays are probably the most successful of all the French humanist drama, and acquired an international reputation. In his original works Buchanan used Greek structures to express Christian ideas. Like Euripedes' drama, both tragedies are concerned with serious moral questions, which are explored and debated, but not wholly resolved. Each focuses on a human situation which crystallises the moral problem involved.

Baptistes presents the religious reformer, John, in opposition to the established church of the Pharisees. The secular ruler, Herod, faced with a genuine problem of civil order, thinks only of his own position and destroys John to buttress his personal authority. Although the play is not wholly coherently developed it presents the issues in vigorous confrontations, raising the problems of tyranny, reform, oppression and violence. It clearly had particular relevance to its own time as religious reform provoked problems for monarchs throughout Europe. It is possible that Buchanan, like his contemporary

James Wedderburn, may have intended the Baptist story to comment on a particular political situation: many years later he suggested a link with the struggle between Thomas More and Henry VIII, and various other historical parallels have been pointed out. But Buchanan's play seems more concerned with the general moral and political issues than with any particular case.

This is certainly true of *Jephthes*, an impressive and moving tragedy which presents the Old Testament story of Jephtha, who rashly vowed to sacrifice to God, in exchange for military victory, the first thing he met on his return home. When his daughter comes to meet him he is faced with the problem of renouncing his sacred vow, or the equally sacrilegious and agonising murder of his own child. The different aspects of the moral problem are explored in taut and anxious discussions with a common sense soldier, a priest, and Jephtha's own wife and daughter, and he finally goes ahead with the sacrifice, urged on by the child herself, and his own conviction that *Non tam quid agitur interest quam cur agas* (918) (It is not so much what is done that is important, as why you do it). The tragedy is a challenging one, expressing both the moral and the emotional aspects of the dilemma poignantly. The characters' positions are not simple, and the moral problem is not resolved by the play. Like Greek drama it expresses the tragedy of an irresoluble human predicament, and seems to deserve the judgement of a contemporary in England that it alone 'amongst all moderne Tragedies is able to abide the touch of Aristotle's precepts and Euripedes' example'.[15]

A completely different play, but also related to the interest in classical literature, is the anonymous *Philotus*, a late-sixteenth-century comedy published in 1603. It reflects the Italian fashion for comedies based on the styles of Plautus and Terence, that focus on love intrigues, disguises and confusions. These lively Italianate comedies became popular throughout Europe. They tend to use sharply defined stock characters and situations, pitting age against youth, love against avarice, and culminating in the triumph of young love. *Philotus* is a play of this kind, although it is not wholly clear whether it was ever intended for the stage. It is in dialogue form, but the first edition actually calls it a 'Treatise ... quhairin we may persave the greit inconveniences that fallis out in the Mariage betwene age and youth'. Several of the characters do, however, refer to spectators; and the comic servant Plesant, who mediates with outspoke colloquial frankness between the audience and the action, is undeniably, at least in origin, a stage figure. The scenes are oddly episodic and unlocalised, leaving gaps in sense which might only be explicable in performance.

The plot of *Philotus*, related to an Italianate novella, is typically complicated. The young Emily, threatened with marriage to the aged Philotus, disguises herself as a boy to escape to her lover. When her long-lost brother turns up he is mistaken for her, shut in with Philotus' daughter whom he seduces after a miraculous 'sex-change', and married to Philotus. After escalating confusions Philotus is confounded and the young couples are eventually married. The interest of the play is in the ingeniously compounded disguises and mistakes, and the briskly vernacular exploitation of the traditional comic predicaments. Emily's disgust at the aged Philotus, her brother's flirtatious playing with sexual roles, and Philotus's comic humiliation are all quite energetically handled. The cynically observing Plesant, and the traditional figure of the Macrell or bawd whom Philotus sends to seduce Emily, both have strong stage presences. They also offer interestingly morally ambivalent characters; but the author of *Philotus*, while he is clearly responsive to stage effect, has done little to develop these, or the play's other themes, in any great depth. Like many plays in this genre, it remains pleasant but slight.

If *Philotus* is only uncertainly intended for performance, the tragedies of James VI's courtier Sir William Alexander were certainly not conceived for the stage at all, and consequently are only nominally related to the drama of Scotland. William Alexander was a noted poet in his day and a companion of the king, whom he eventually followed to London, dedicating to him the four *Monarchicke Tragedies: Darius, Croesus, The Alexandrian Tragedy* and *Julius Caesar.*

Elizabethan and Jacobean tragedy was much influenced by the late-classical plays of Seneca, from whom playwrights took a flamboyant rhetoric, morally epigrammatic style, and vivid sensationalism. Seneca's plays were, however, originally intended for reading rather than the stage, and some academic writers, especially in France, tried to re-create his rather static, non-theatrical style, heavily dependent on moral and reflective monologues. They in turn were imitated by a group of English playwrights with whom Alexander and his tragedies are associated. Alexander himself tended to refer to his works as 'Tragicall Poemes', emphasising their literary quality; by implication he endorsed the view of a similar playwright, Fulke Greville, who asserted openly 'I have made theis Tragedies no plaies for the stage'. Alexander's plays, all loosely related to the topic of monarchy, are, effectively, meditative moral poems. With almost no action, and very little dialogue, they present extended reflective monologues on the issues of mortality and decay, betrayal and trust, and 'the great uncertainty of worldly things' (*Croesus* 2710).

Another reason for the almost negligible impact of Alexander's tragedies on Scottish drama as a whole is perhaps symptomatic of a wider problem. Throughout his career, and especially after the removal of the court to London, Alexander progressively anglicised his drama. Even in the first edition, of *Darius* in 1603, he told his Scottish readers that 'they may not justly finde fault with me, if for the more parte I use the English phrase, as worthie to be preferred before our owne for the elegance and perfection thereof'. Alexander is part of the increasingly English focus of Scottish literature. This, intensified by the king's move to London, had a particularly disastrous effect on the drama. Since there was no commercial theatre in Scotland, the only real source of support for the drama, especially after the Reformation, was the court. Dependent as theatre is on patronage and resources it could not continue to flourish once the court had gone. The drama no longer had a distinctive role in Scotland, and could only look to London.

James VI was a monarch with a committed and active interest in literature, some of which extended to drama. Unlike his mother he seems to have had little interest in performance himself: although he took part in some court masques (possibly even giving himself a speaking part in his own composition) it was said by an observer in 1584 that 'he hates the dance and music in general'.[16] However he certainly took some interest in court entertainments in Scotland, wrote at least one of his own, and devised part of the shows for his oldest son's baptism.

However his move to London seems to have brought little Scottish influence to the English stage. His accession is occasionally reflected in the London theatre, either in complimentary ways, as in Shakespeare's *Macbeth*, or more satirically, as in the play at the Blackfriars theatre in 1608 which is said to have shown him drunken, violent and blaspheming. Similarly the Scots themselves are sometimes satirised, sometimes romantically glorified, in London's early Jacobean drama. James did attend performances of Shakespeare's plays, and his court fostered the Stuart masque, which reached new heights of visual and verbal expressiveness during the early years of his reign. But Scottish drama did not find any real new opportunity or outlet in London.

It is impossible to predict what would have been the course of Scottish drama if the court had remained in Edinburgh. The church, by this time, was a strong influence against the theatre, and there is little evidence that James's interest would have wholly counteracted it. However, in 1599 the king had arranged, and forced the church to accept, public performances by a troupe of English actors in Edinburgh. This could be seen as the first, and only, gesture towards the establishment of a commercial, public theatre in Scotland. Had the king remained in Edinburgh it is at least possible that Scottish drama might have continued to develop in the new forms of the Renaissance. But once the court had gone, the theatre lost its chief patron and Scotland lost its political and cultural impetus. The drama was one of the casualties of the move, and was not to recover its vitality for well over two hundred years.

NOTES

1   Unless otherwise stated all quotations from records can be found in A J Mill, *Medieval Plays in Scotland* (Edinburgh and London, 1927).
2   Text in *Music of Scotland 1500–1700*, K Elliott and H Shire (eds), *Musica Britannica* XV (London, 1957), no. 30.
3   Helena M Shire and Kenneth Elliott, 'Pleugh Song and Plough Play', *Saltire Review*, II:6 (1955), 39–44.
4   Roderick J Lyall points out an unpublished record of a payment in Aberdeen in 1470–71 for making a 'Scafold to the candilmes play', which seems to suggest a performance.
5   *The Works of William Fowler*, Henry W Meikle, James Craigie and John Purves (eds), 3 vols, STS (Edinburgh and London, 1914–40), II, 190.
6   Sir James Melville, *Memoirs*, T Thomson (ed), Bannatyne Club (Edinburgh, 1827), p 171.
7   John Lesley, *The History of Scotland from the Death of King James I in the year 1436, to the year 1561*, Bannatyne Club (Edinburgh, 1830), p 78.

8   Helena M Shire, *Song, Dance and Poetry of the Court of Scotland under King James VI* (Cambridge, 1969), 58ff, 171ff.

9   'An Epithalamion upon the Marques of Huntlies mariage' in *Poems of King James VI of Scotland*, James Craigie (ed), 2 vols, STS (Edinburgh and London, 1948–52), II, 134–45.

10   *The Works of John Knox*, David Laing (ed), 4 vols (Edinburgh, 1846–55), I, 62.

11   'The Dreme of Schir David Lyndesay', *Works. See* General Bibliography.

12   Ibid. II, x.

13   Ibid. II, 2ff.

14   See *History of Scottish Literature*, Volume 4, 'Scottish Theatre 1950–80'.

15   Frances Meres, *Palladis Tamia* (1598), f. 285^v.

16   R Ashton, *James I by his Contemporaries* (London, 1969), p 2.

FURTHER READING

PRIMARY TEXTS

Alexander, William, 'The Monarchicke Tragedies', in *The Poetical Works of Sir William Alexander, Earl of Stirling*, Kastner, L E, and Charlton, H B (eds), STS, 2 vols (Edinburgh and London, 1921–29), vol I
Buchanan, George, *Tragedies*, Sharratt, P, and Walsh, P G (eds) (Edinburgh, 1983)
Cranstoun, James (ed), *The Works of Alexander Montgomerie*, STS (Edinburgh and London, 1887)
Lindsay, Sir David, *Ane Satire of the Thrie Estaitis*, in *Four Morality Plays*, Happé, P (ed) (Harmondsworth, 1979)
Mill, A J (ed), *Philotus*, in *Miscellany Volume*, STS (Edinburgh and London, 1933)

SECONDARY TEXTS

Kantrowitz, J S, *Dramatic Allegory: Lindsay's 'Ane Satyre of the Thrie Estaitis'* (Lincoln, Nebraska, 1975)
McFarlane, I D, *Buchanan* (London, 1981)
The Revels History of Drama in English, Vol 1: *Medieval Drama*, Cawley, A C (ed) (London & New York, 1983); Vol 2: *1500–1575*, Saunders, N (ed) (London & New York, 1980)
Wiles, David, The Early Plays of Robin Hood (Cambridge and Totowa N.J., 1981)

Chapter 13

Scottish Latin Poetry

JAMES MACQUEEN

It has often been pointed out that the literature of Scotland is written in four languages, Scots, English, Gaelic and Latin. Of these four it is the last which has the longest literary history, for works written in Latin have been preserved from as early as the sixth century; the Latin hymns of St Columba, written in the second half of that century, may be regarded as the earliest documented poetry composed on Scottish soil. From then on there was a continuous tradition of Latin verse composition, linked to the Church but concerned not only with religious topics but also with secular events and personalities. Only a little of this now survives, preserved, often only in fragments, in the Lives of saints and in the chronicles compiled in the monastic houses. But what we do have—prayers, hymns, prophecies, king-lists, accounts of battles, and 'histories' going back to the legendary Egyptian origin of the Scots—suggests that an extensive and important part of Dark Age and Mediæval Scottish literature has been irretrievably lost.

The spread of the Renaissance to Scotland brought with it a new interest in the literature of ancient Rome and a new incentive to write in the language of Virgil and the other great poets of the Classical period. So from about 1500 there was a great increase in the production of Latin verse, and for a century and a half numerous Scotsmen found an effective means of expression in the Classical tongue. But it must be stressed that what they produced was in many cases not merely Latin verse composed by Scotsmen. It was in a real sense *Scottish* poetry, and it holds an important place in any assessment of Scottish literature as a whole.

The choice of Latin by poets of the sixteenth and early seventeenth centuries need occasion no surprise. Latin was the international language, and by its use a poet could reach a reading public far more widespread than that which took an interest in works written in the vernacular. Of course there were dangers. It was only too easy to produce a pastiche of lines and phrases culled from poets of the Classical period (or, even worse, from other Renaissance poets), or to compose frigid eclogues or amatory poems laboriously based on Classical forms. But a good Latin poet (and Scotland produced a number of those) was the master, rather than the servant, of his medium, and could use Latin to express himself effectively and memorably over a wide intellectual and emotional range. He could too be a writer genuinely involved in the contemporary world, both national and international, rather than a mere study-bound *imitator veterum*.

This can be clearly seen in the work of the first Scot known to have published Latin verses, James Foullis of Colinton (*c*.1485–1549), a collection of whose poems appeared in Paris, probably in 1512. Foullis writes in a variety of Classical metres, and his poems are heavily loaded with Classical allusions and parallels; but his subjects are principally Scottish. There are for instance almost five hundred lines in elegiac couplets on a recent plague which had struck Edinburgh after a fire in St Giles, and a Sapphic ode in honour of St Margaret. These are works of only modest merit, and the quality of their Latinity is sometimes doubtful. More attractive than either is a short poem which begins as an encomium of Edinburgh's magnificent architecture, but which within a few lines changes to become a satirical illustration of the way in which the merchants of the city endure danger and misery at sea only in order that their wives may dress themselves up to attract other men. This satirical approach certainly has its parallels in Classical poetry, but it is also characteristic of a good deal of contemporary literature written in Scots.

Poems of this sort lead us easily to the early works of the greatest of the Scottish Latinists, George Buchanan (1506–1582). He was educated partly at St Andrews and partly in Paris, where he then taught for several years and developed an enviable facility in Latin verse composition. It was probably at this time that he composed *Quam misera sit condicio docentium literas humaniores Lutetiae* (On the Sad Lot of Latin-teachers in Paris), a work which in the form of a farewell to the Muses gives a lively satirical picture of the life—that of a poet and teacher of poetry—which he was proposing to abandon. The bulk of the poem is made up of a series of vivid scenes from scholarly life—late-night research followed by rude awakening at 4 a.m., the day-long struggle, marked by constant beatings, with lazy or ignorant pupils, the poverty that is the constant lot of teachers and poets alike. Buchanan's descriptive powers are already of a high order, and he can convey a feeling of realism and strong personal involvement in situations which must have been typical not only of Paris but of any university in western Europe.

Buchanan returned to Scotland about 1535 and soon gained employment at court. Here he found himself in a literary milieu where satirical writing flourished. Sir David Lindsay had already produced the *Dreme* and *The Papyngo*, and it was only a few years before the appearance of the first version of *Ane Satyre of the Thrie Estaits*. Looseness of morals in general, and the hypocrisy and corruption of the religious orders in particular, were popular targets, and Buchanan joined in the game with gusto. He had of course besides personal inclination good Classical precedents for satirical composition, and satire in both verse and prose was one of the most effective weapons of the northern Humanists in general. The *Somnium* (The Dream) however, which was Buchanan's first Scottish essay in the genre, does not directly follow the tradition of the Classical satirists. Rather it turns to another tradition, found for instance in Catullus and in Horace's lyrics, in which an author makes a more or less accurate translation of the first few lines of an older poem (for Roman authors a Greek poem), and then develops the work in a different and original way. But Buchanan's starting-point was not a Greek, or even a Latin work. Instead he turned to a *Scottish* poem, composed a generation before, Dunbar's 'How Dunbar was Desyred to be a Frier'. The opening lines of Buchanan's poem, like those of Dunbar's, describe how St Francis appeared to the poet in a dream, offering him the robes of a Franciscan and inviting him to become a member of the Order. Dunbar turns down the invitation by saying that it has come too late, since he has already had personal experience of the Order and its tricks and malpractices. In any case, he concludes, the dream-figure was not St Francis at all, but a fiend in disguise. This ending helps to soften the satirical force of the poem, which in any case is not very strong. Buchanan develops the opening lines in a far more trenchant way. He devotes much of his poem to a strong rejection of the lack of conscience and sheer bestiality which he sees as the hall-mark of the Order. To round it off he ignores the fiend and takes up an idea which occurs in the middle of Dunbar's poem—'Precious few Franciscans have become saints. If you really want to do something for my soul, give me a mitre and a bishop's purple robe.' Thus the poem dissolves in laughter without in any way losing its condemnatory force.

The *Somnium* is an effective poem, and was quickly succeeded by others in the same vein. First Buchanan composed a *Palinodia* (Recantation), which again follows good Classical precedent in taking the form of a withdrawal of the slanders contained in the earlier poem. But of course the form is used with Ovidian wit to add yet more satirical weight to the attack. Finally he turned more strongly for his model to Juvenal, the acknowledged Classical master of aggressive satire, and produced the *Franciscanus* (The Franciscan). This poem in the form in which we have it (like much of Buchanan's early poetry, it was not published until later in his life, and then in a considerably modified form) extends to nearly a thousand lines. Like much of Juvenal's work, it is loosely constructed, and draws its strength mainly from its vigorous attacking force, and from the vivid brilliance with which scenes and characters are portrayed. Like Juvenal too, Buchanan is almost entirely negative, and concentrates his talents on the vices and misdemeanors of those with whom he deals. There is little or no attempt to put forward a positive code of behaviour, or to portray the good alongside the bad. In this he differs from, and suffers by comparison with, his contemporary Lindsay. There is no Jhone the Comoun Weill in Buchanan.

The *Franciscanus* retains some Scottish connection. The climactic incident described in the poem, an exorcism fabricated by a Franciscan called Laing, took place at Dysart at about the time when Buchanan was writing. But many of the charges against the Order are commonplaces of the period which do not apply specifically to Scotland, and it is probable that Buchanan was now aiming more at the wider audience of the European Humanists. In any case he left Scotland soon afterwards, and it is in a European context that his poems of the next twenty years or so have to be judged. Many of these poems are occasional pieces addressed to friends, and there are also several which show that the vituperative and satirical turn of mind had not yet been abandoned. But Buchanan had now begun to explore other avenues. The *Pro lena apologia* (Defence of a Bawd) is a rollicking tongue-in-cheek justification of the activities of the procuress. It shows the same qualities of verbal brilliance and vivid description as had been characteristic of the *Franciscanus*; it is an extended joke, and the poet carries it off magnificently. In other cases he writes in a more serious vein. *Desiderium Ptolemaei Luxii Testaei* (On his Absence from Ptolemaeus Luxius Testaeus) and *Desiderium Lutetiae* (On his Absence from Paris), for instance, are poems of longing and regret, the first for his separation from a friend, the second for his enforced absence from the city which was for him a second home. In form they are pastorals; but Buchanan infuses this over-worked conventional form with his own personality and personal emotions of warm affection and wistful longing. The poems are reminiscent of Virgil's *Eclogues* or Milton's *Lycidas*. They are magnificent illustrations of Buchanan's mature ability to achieve originality within a conventional framework.

Different from this, but equally effective, is *Calendae Maiae* (The First of May), a poem which in the space of a few lines glides effortlessly from the warm breezes of May-day to the Golden Age of earth's first spring, and thence to the never-failing warmth of the Isles of the Blessed, to the soft breezes which gently stir the cypresses by the streams of Lethe, and finally, and triumphantly, to the warmth which will rouse and vitalise the souls of the dead at the Resurrection. 'Welcome, glory of the fleeting years; welcome, red-letter day; welcome, for you remind us of the spring-time of the world, and give us a glimpse of the life that is to come'. The move from particular to universal has seldom been so effectively, or so succinctly, achieved.

Many of Buchanan's poems during this period were written for ceremonial occasions, from the visit of the Emperor Charles V to Bordeaux in 1539 to the capture of Calais by the French from the English in 1558. Encomiastic verse is seldom of very high literary quality, and Buchanan's poems on such themes are on the whole competent and conventional rather than original and inspired. But sometimes he rises to his subject with genuine enthusiasm, and it is surely no accident that his finest effort is an *Epithalamium* celebrating the marriage in 1558 of the Dauphin of France to the young Mary Queen of Scots. This subject allows him to include his famous panegyric on Scotland and its people's eminence both in war and in letters. The passage is skilfully constructed, and bears all the marks of strong personal conviction. In all his long absence from Scotland Buchanan never expressed his feelings for his homeland in a *Desiderium Caledoniae*. But when the opportunity came to integrate those feelings into a more formal composition he seized it with both hands. The Scots themselves, whom Mary brings as a dowry to her French bridegroom, form the heart of the poem, and give it an individuality and a fervour which raise it high above the level of conventional eulogy.

Buchanan wrote many poems addressed to women, but it would be foolish to expect anything that could reasonably be called 'love-lyric'. His Humanistic inclinations drew him rather towards the traditions of Classical epigram, and he expends much skill in giving witty treatment to the emotions of both love and hate. The conflicting and torturing emotions roused in him by 'Neaera'; the loathing he feels for the vile 'Leonora'; these are subjects which he treats over and over again. But the pleasure one gains from them palls with constant repetition. One poem, addressed to an unknown Alisa, who is sick, does promise something rather different. It is an appeal to the deities of death to spare the young and beautiful, and concludes with the pleasing conceit that if Persephone allows Alisa to descend to the realms of the dead she will have cause to regret it, for Pluto will lose his heart to the charms of the new arrival. The poet shows a sympathy and a delicacy of touch which are not often visible in his other poems. Yet all in all it has to be admitted that in his treatment of love Buchanan falls far short of that of his Scots-writing contemporary, Alexander Scott.

The supreme achievement of Buchanan's poetic career was in the eyes of many in subsequent generations his version of the Psalms. This work certainly shows astonishing skill in paraphrasing the originals and moulding them into a wide variety of Latin metrical forms. Today such surface attractions do not generally impress, and they have recently been described as 'rather absurd hybrids'. It must be said however that if we compare their literary quality with that of the metrical version produced in the vernacular a generation or two later and still widely used and loved, we may be able to reach a truer appreciation of Buchanan's skill.

Buchanan returned to Scotland in the early 1560s, and for several years was able to resume his career as a court poet. Verses were composed for masques, to compliment the Queen, her husband and other members of the court, to accompany the gift of a ring to Elizabeth of England, and, on a larger scale, to celebrate the birth of James VI. These works, the competent if rather run-of-the-mill products of an acknowledged laureate, exhibit an increasing tendency first of all towards excessive flattery, and then (especially in the poem on James VI) towards preaching on the duties and responsibilities of a ruler. This second tendency was doubtless the natural product of increasing years, greater security of position, and the changed political and religious situation of the 1560s. But even at this late stage Buchanan still seems more at home when he is dealing with the negative side of things rather than the positive. The poem to the infant James ends not with a triumphant prophecy of future bliss under a ruler who obeys divine law, but with a list of tyrants and enemies of the state, and a warning of the stern punishment exacted by God upon those who break His law. A similar turn of thought can be seen in the elegy which he composed on the death of Calvin in 1564. The first half of the poem shows us the theologian freed from earthly cares and welcomed into heaven and eternal life; the second is an extended description of the tortures of Hell to be endured by Calvin's opponents the Popes of Rome. It is vigorous stuff; over the years the author of the *Franciscanus* had not lost his touch. But polemic like this seems rather out of place in the context of the elegy, and the poem, though a fine piece of rhetoric, in the end suffers from a lack of balance.

The four verse tragedies which Buchanan wrote are dealt with in another chapter, and it remains only to consider his longest poem, *De Sphaera* (The Celestial Sphere). This didactic work in five books was in process of composition over many years, and was never finished. Its subject is a sufficiently comprehensive one, the structure and workings of the universe, and in the eyes of his contemporaries it would have set the seal on his greatness as a poet. Epic verse was regarded as the highest form of poetic composition, and no loftier subject could have been found. Precedents for such an undertaking were plentiful, and current research (this was the era of Copernicus and Tycho Brahe) offered plentiful opportunities to treat the subject in a contemporary context. Buchanan's skill in versification was more than sufficient to enable him to overcome the problems of technical exposition in verse, and always before him he had the great example of Lucretius, with his supreme ability to sugar the didactic pill and add passion and eloquence to the driest intellectual material. To a great extent Buchanan succeeded in his undertaking. His poem is no mere catalogue of astronomical movements and celestial measurements. He often moves beyond such matters to a more general consideration of the human condition, of divine providence, and of the powers of the human mind. And sometimes—though not often enough for many readers—he introduces dramatic or mythological episodes which allow him to exercise his narrative and dramatic skills. The unfinished Book V is especially rich in such material. Its subject is eclipses, but skilfully woven into this are the stories of Endymion, who was loved and visited on earth by the moon when she was in eclipse, and finally taken up into the sky to learn the secrets of the heavens and transmit them to men, and of Gallus, a Roman soldier who predicted an eclipse and thus prevented the panic which would have ensued had it unexpectedly happened during the following day's battle. This latter episode is developed at length by the dramatic device of putting the main expository matter on eclipses into the mouth of Gallus addressing the Roman army. How much more widely this approach might have been used we cannot tell, for Buchanan, despite constant pressure from friends, did not complete the poem. This was probably due rather to the demands of other work, or to failing health, than to loss of interest in the subject. It may even be that as he worked on it he began to realise that by choosing the Ptolemaic rather than the Copernican explanation of the universe he had backed the wrong cosmological horse. But whatever the reason may have been, what we do have is a poem in which scientific exposition combines with narrative skill and ethical idealism to produce a work not only of genuine literary merit but also of lasting interest as a document of sixteenth century attitudes and thought.

Buchanan's work must hold an important position in any consideration of the literature of his times. He was unique among Scotsmen in being a poet of international stature, a man whose works were read and admired throughout Europe. If they now seem remote from the mainstream of Scottish creativity, the reason is to be found not in their failure as works of literature but rather in our failure to provide access to them in a changing cultural and educational system. It is to be hoped that a new edition of his poems will soon rectify this defect, and that the merits of Buchanan's work will once again be easily available to his fellow-countrymen.

Buchanan was a generous patron of younger poets, but his stature was such that they necessarily operated under his shadow. Events of public importance such as the marriage of Queen Mary or the birth of James VI inspired a number of verse tributes, but these are of mediocre quality. Religion too continued to be a driving force. No-one attempted to emulate Buchanan's achievement in putting the Psalms into Latin verse, but the young Andrew Melville (1545–1622) produced in 1573 a metrical version of the Song of Moses (Deuteronomy 32), and this was followed by Chapter 3 of Job, and the lament of David over the deaths of Saul and Jonathan (II Samuel 1, 19–27). At the same time Patrick Adamson (1537–92) wrote a paraphrase of Job. More important than this was his contribution to current religious controversy, *De Papistarum superstitiosis ineptiis* (On the Superstitious Absurdities of the Papists), published in Edinburgh in 1564. Yet even before Buchanan's death new tendencies were beginning to appear. Key figures here seem to be Thomas and John Maitland, the sons of Maitland of Lethington. Thomas Maitland (1550–72) was an acknowledged disciple of Buchanan, and his pastoral poems on the inauguration of James VI, and on the Regent Moray, show clear echoes of the older poet. But in some of his epigrams and elegies there is something that is new, for in them we can observe the emergence of love-poems modelled on those of Catullus and Ovid. This is something not to be found in Buchanan, and it has been seen as the result of the younger poet's contacts with the Continent. It is thus just one of the many signs of European influence on Scottish literature about this time. The Latin poems of John Maitland (*c.*1545–95), later Lord Thirlstane, show no such influence, but he made another important departure by composing verse in both Latin and the vernacular. This bilingual capability can soon be seen in the writings of Mark Alexander Boyd (1563–1601) and even the young James VI himself. The king's contribution to Scottish Latin poetry is not particularly significant, but in Boyd's Latin works, lacking though they often are in literary quality, the new Ovidian influences are much more apparent. His *Hymni*, which are despite their title not hymns but poems on flowers and plants, concentrate largely on stories connected with each, either drawn from Classical mythology or invented by the poet himself. The results are strongly reminiscent of the *Metamorphoses*. Boyd's other main work, the *Epistolae heroidum* (Letters of Heroines) is, as the title shows, openly dependent on an Ovidian original. The poems are but a poor imitation of Ovid's work, since they lack both the skill in versification and the psychological insight of their Classical predecessors. But like the *Hymni* they show a change in attitude towards the writing of Latin poetry. Buchanan had to some extent allowed himself to write fun-poetry—the *Lena* and the attacks on Leonora are good examples of this. But now poetry for pleasure, Latin verse as a pastime for the cultured amateur, was coming much more to the fore. The professionalism, the view that Latin was *the* language of literature, the high seriousness and the ethical idealism which had marked Buchanan's finest works were now rapidly disappearing.

But they had not entirely vanished. After Buchanan's death Andrew Melville emerged from under his shadow to become a sort of unofficial laureate (though contemporaries awarded that title to Montgomerie). His heart can scarcely have been in the job, and he must have turned out poems on events such as the coronation of Anne of Denmark in 1590 and the birth of Prince Henry in 1594 largely because he felt that such events *ought* to be commemorated in Latin. The verse is Virgilian, competent but uninspired. Virgil may also have been the model for Melville's projected epic *Gathelus* on the origin and history of the Scots. This northerly *Aeneid* never really got off the ground. Only 158 lines were published, and 29 more have survived in manuscript. A Scottish national epic in Latin was, it seems, beyond Melville's poetic powers. These are to be seen to a greater extent in verses of a more personal nature such as his poems on the deaths of two acquaintances, John Wallace and David Blake, or in the series of vigorous satirical poems which he directed against the Episcopalian system of Church government. His attack on the English universities also achieved prominence in its day, but is now remembered more for its magnificent title—*Antitamicamicategoria*—than for its satirical content or poetic skill.

Another approach to the composition of a poetical history of Scotland was employed by John Johnston (*c*.1570–1611). His inspiration stemmed not from Virgil but rather from Ausonius, and the result was *Inscriptiones historicae regum Scotorum*, a series of historical epigrams on the kings of Scotland from the fourth century BC to the end of the sixteenth century AD. This was followed by *Heroes ex omni historia Scotica lectissimi*, which dealt in the same way with heroes of Scottish history, and by a number of similar poems, some lauding the virtues of Reformation heroes and others in praise of Scottish towns. Johnston later turned his talent to epigrams on Old Testament figures, and to works concerned with other Biblical subjects. He was a competent versifier, but the epigrammatic technique does not make for ease of continuous reading, and only occasionally does one feel that genuine inspiration or originality is breaking through.

A greater interest in the world about him was displayed by Hercules Rollock (*c*.1550–1599). He was one of the many poets to compose a long *Epithalamium* on the marriage of James VI to Anne of Denmark in 1589. Much more interesting are his occasional poems, in which are included, for instance, verses on a plague which struck Edinburgh in 1585, and on the sad condition to which (he says) Scotland has been brought by the machinations of the Papists. The first of these begins with a laudatory depiction of the capital. Then follows a vivid description of the effects of the plague—the empty streets, the silent law-courts, the corpses dragged by hooks through the darkness to be deposited in open pits. It is the poor who suffer most, while many of the rich make their escape to what they see as safer places. Yet flight is useless, for the plague is a punishment from God, and only true repentance will restore the city and its inhabitants to health. The iambic lines give vigorous movement to the poem, and the conclusion is effectively contrived. Its theme is more extensively developed in the second poem mentioned. Scotland, unconquered over thousands of years, is now being destroyed by civil war. John Knox, the guardian of safety and messenger of eternal peace, has departed to heaven, and Roman rites and dogmas are once more in the ascendant. So the bulk of the poem becomes a long and violent attack on the Catholic Church, rounded off by an appeal to God to drive His wandering sheep back into the pastures of life and cause the enemy's madness to bring about his own destruction. The poem offers a vivid view of contemporary feelings; but it also gives a foretaste of the theological extremism which was, it can be felt, at least in part responsible for the overall mediocrity of Scottish literature in the following decades.

Meanwhile a very different type of poem was being produced by David Kinloch (1559–1617), who chose to follow the tradition of didactic verse, though not on the same lofty plane as that of Buchanan a few years earlier. Kinloch's subject was *De hominis procreatione, anatome ac morbis internis* (On Human Reproduction, Anatomy and Internal Illnesses), admittedly unpromising material for poetic success. Many didactic poets from Lucretius onwards had dressed up their subject-matter by the addition of poetic colouring and diversionary embellishments. Kinloch deliberately eschews such fripperies, but his skill in smooth expository versification is such that if his poem never rises to great heights, it also avoids any descent into bathos or simple dullness. The result is an unpretentious but interesting and readable piece of work.

The removal of the king to London in 1603 had an important effect on Scottish literature. Poets who did not make the journey south found themselves cut off both from the court and from the new influences which were soon to make themselves felt in English poetry. The result was an increasing sense of 'apartness', coupled with a determination to adhere to more old-fashioned poetic values, values which to the more progressive 'smelled too much of the schooles, and were not after the Fancy of the tyme'. The true nature of poetry, as described by Drummond of Hawthornden, the leading Scottish literary figure of the time, had been defined and established by the great poets of the Classical world, and models of poetic quality were to be found in the works of these poets, and of later writers inspired and motivated by them. Clearly this was a background into which poetry in Latin fitted with ease, and it is in no way surprising to find that Scots who composed in the ancient language were prominent in the literary field. Other circumstances however were less favourable. The prevalent Calvinistic attitude, for instance, was inimical to poetic exuberance, and to the idea that poetry could be a source of pleasure. As a consequence, poetic composition in Latin, as in the vernacular, was limited largely to writers who were of the Episcopalian persuasion. Many of these were graduates of Aberdeen, but the real centre of Scottish poetic production, in both English and Latin, was Drummond's seat at Hawthornden. Drummond thus had a considerable influence on Scottish Latin poetry. Although he himself was not a Latin poet, he offered support and friendship to those who were, and also amassed a very considerable library of neo-latin authors. The result was a mini-Renaissance in Scottish Latinity.

The more vivacious and light-hearted side of this can perhaps be best seen in a work which has often (though probably erroneously) been attributed to Drummond himself. The macaronic *Polemo-middinia* (Midden-heid War) is written in what can only be described as joke-Latin. It is first of all hugely enjoyable, and demonstrates clearly that poetic composition, despite the Calvinists, need not be divorced from a sense of humour and boisterous fun. More important than that, it shows that down-to-earth incidents of everyday life can be used as subjects for Latin verse. This is a far cry from the crystalline remoteness of Drummond's English poems. Critics have remarked on the gap that existed between such poetry and the 'folk'. It is genuinely surprising to find that poets who wrote in Latin, though scarcely members of the 'folk', were often much closer to the realities of life and day-to-day human contacts than were their contemporaries who wrote in English.

This can best be seen in the poems of Arthur Johnston. Born in 1577 near Inverurie, Johnston was educated at Marischal College, and spent his life on the Continent (mainly at Sedan) until his return to Scotland in 1622. Soon afterwards he was appointed *Medicus Regius* by James VI and I, and continued to hold that office under Charles I. He died in 1641. His early efforts in Latin verse were in the form of allegorical Ovidian epistles, and were inspired by the dangers facing the Elector Palatine and his wife, James's daughter, at the beginning of the Thirty Years' War. But after his return to Scotland he turned to more local topics. The earlier poems had shown his easy mastery of the Ovidian elegiac couplet, and this became for him the vehicle of an entirely original style. The allegorical approach was largely laid aside, and the polished urbanity of Ovid was adapted to more strongly personal themes. Johnston's *persona* in his work is that of the educated gentleman, relaxed and at his ease in addressing his circle of intimate friends. The form is often that of the epistle, but an epistle which in feeling is Horatian rather than Ovidian, and which in many ways anticipates the epistles of Robert Burns. A good example is the poem *Ad Robertum Baronium* (Epistle to Robert Baron), addressed to the eminent Aberdeen divine of that name. Johnston writes to his friend professing to describe his wretched life in the hard country at the back of Benachie. Here, he says, he toils from dawn to dusk, here he dresses in shaggy hides and exists on a diet of turnips and stream-water. His body is worn and filthy, and his mind is dull and numbed. He has even forgotten how to write Latin poetry! This final twist, so obviously contradicted by the easy flow of the verse, makes it clear that the poem is not intended to be taken seriously. It emerges as a very attractive piece of light verse, and the picture of Farmer Johnston, dishevelled, dirty and horny-handed, is vividly and effectively presented.

Ad Davidem Wedderburnum, Ludimagistrum Aberdonensem, amicum veterem (Epistle to his Old Friend David Wedderburn, Rector of Aberdeen Grammar School) strikes a more serious note. This is a poem full of the sadness and emptiness of old age, relieved only by the memory of early days spent in Wedderburn's company in the hills near their homes, and of their youthful ambitions to scale the heights of poetic success. The poem is full of Classical references, but Johnston unfailingly preserves the delicate balance between the background of mythological landscape and the foreground of Aberdeenshire reality, and there is something extremely attractive in his picture of two Classics-mad schoolboys composing their early hexameters on the banks of the Gadie, and bestowing names such as Delphi and Parnassus on the heather-clad rocks and hollows of Benachie. The poem must rank among his finest.

The lighter side of Johnston's talent emerges again in *De naso Nasonis cuiusdam nasutissimi* (On the Nose of a Certain Nosey, Furnished with a Very Large Nose). This is a fifty-line *jeu d'esprit* in which wildly exaggerated comparisons pile on each other at breath-taking pace to produce a poem as overwhelming as the nose it purports to describe. But the finest of the extended jokes is undoubtedly the *Apologia piscatoris* (a Fisherman's Defence). The poem is cast in the form of a letter to some Presbyterian clergyman who has tried to put a stop to Sunday fishing. In it Johnston produces a host of reasons for being allowed to follow his beloved pursuit on the day of rest, and enlivens his lines with colourful illustrations of all the activities involved in catching salmon. The poem is alive with good-humoured enthusiasm. It effectively combines vivid description with amusing tongue-in-cheek arguments which must have horrified more sober-minded Scots.

Other poems show a similar lightness of touch. There is for instance the *Apologia pro Thaumatia obstetrice ad senatum Abredonensem* (A Defence of the Midwife Iris (?) Addressed to the Town Council of Aberdeen), protesting at the jailing of the local howdie for insolence (presumably directed towards members of the Council), and proclaiming with high humour the disasters that will fall on the community if she is not released. The poem is reminiscent of Buchanan's *Pro lena apologia*, but the local setting gives it an attractiveness which is absent in the earlier poem.

Even when he is writing 'official' verse Johnston can display the same deftness of touch. *Musae querulae de regis in Scotiam profectione* (The Complaints of the Muses about the King's Departure to Scotland) was written to celebrate Charles I's visit to Scotland for his coronation in 1633. In this little group of seven short poems the poet lightly touches on the queen's regret at the absence of her husband, and plays with the fact that it is raining in England but sunny in Scotland. He makes his points with gaiety and charm, and manages to be delicate even on the indelicate subject of the queen's pregnancy, on which, as *Medicus Regius*, he presumably had inside knowledge.

Johnston's range of subjects and of moods is very wide. It would be difficult in the space available to do justice to his many epigrams, some witty, some deeply moving, to his heart-felt appeals for the discovery and punishment of the murderers of two prominent members of the Gordon family in 1630, to his metrical versions, designed to compete with those of Buchanan, of the entire Book of Psalms, or to his *Encomia Urbium* (Praises of Scottish Towns), a series of short poems ranging from Inverness in the north to Dumfries in the south. In all his work Johnston shows his ability to paint vivid verbal pictures and to express straightforward uncomplicated emotions, and these qualities, together with his easy mastery of graceful expression, combine to make him the most enjoyable, as he is the most accessible, of the Scottish Latin poets.

That verbal facility in itself is not sufficient to make a poet can be easily seen from the verses of John Leech, whose works were published between 1617 and 1626. Leech was happy to try his hand at a wide variety of Latin forms, and we have amatory poems, eclogues (bucolic, piscatory, marine and vinitory!), and epigrams, as well as an address to the king and several poems dealing with his unsuccessful attempts to find patronage. The best of these are his verses in anacreontic metres, in which the rhythmic rapidity of the short lines unites with deft and imaginative treatment of the subjects of love and wine to produce poems which are reminiscent more of the Mediæval than of the Classical period. Other poems contain interesting references to such subjects as the recent opening up of the Far East to western Europe, the birth of barnacle-geese from seed fallen from trees into the sea, and the moving islands in Loch Lomond. But on the whole Leech's work is that of a rather minor talent.

One genre threatened but not attempted by Leech was that of epic, and yet there was in literary circles a feeling that a Latin poet *ought* to do for Scotland what Virgil had done for Rome. Melville, it will be remembered, had begun an epic on Gathelus, the mythical founder of Scotland. The next attempt came from the pen of Patrick Panter (*c*.1470–1519) whose chosen hero was Sir William Wallace. The poem was to have been, like the *Aeneid*, in twelve books, but Panter was encouraged by the visit of Charles I to Scotland in 1633 to rush into print when only two and a half books had been completed. After that his enthusiasm apparently waned, and nothing more of his *Valliad* was ever published. In the same year as the appearance of his fragment however there was published an epic work in complete form and of considerably higher quality than anything Panter would have been likely to produce. This was the *Creationis rerum descriptio poetica* (Poetic Description of the Creation) by Andrew Ramsay (1574–1659). In composing this work Ramsay made two important decisions. The first was that he would avoid the manifest difficulties involved in writing on a massive Virgilian scale, and would aim rather at an epic in small compass. The result is a poem in four books with a total of some 1,550 lines, short indeed for an epic, but long enough, when skilfully handled, to allow the poet to make use of epic dialogue and machinery, to draw character convincingly, and to linger over episodes of heroic proportions. The second decision was to avoid a nationalistic theme, and to choose a subject of more universal relevance, the creation, fall, and redemption of man. A combination of brevity with such an extensive theme could have been a matter of considerable difficulty (Milton chose an altogether larger canvas when he dealt with the same subjects a few years later), but Ramsay successfully achieves his object by concentrating attention on the fall in Book III as the centre-piece of his narrative, with the first book given over to the creation and the second to a description of the bliss of paradise, while the redemption is introduced into the fourth book by the good epic device of a debate on possible punishments followed by a prophecy of Christ's redeeming death, just before the final expulsion of Adam and Eve. Book III is certainly the most striking part of the poem, containing as it does the wily temptation of Eve, the tumult into which all nature is thrown by the eating of the forbidden fruit, and the fear and remorse of Adam, all forcefully and convincingly portrayed. Much has in the past been made of Ramsay's little epic as a source for Milton's grander efforts, but if one can forget Milton and approach Ramsay's work as a poem in its own right, it emerges as one of the finest products of Scottish neo-Latinity.

The culminating point in the history of Latin poetry in Scotland came with the publication in 1637 of the *Delitiae poetarum Scotorum huius aevi illustrium* (Gems of the Distinguished Scottish Poets of the Present Time). The prime mover of this anthology was Sir John Scot of Scotstarvet, Drummond of Hawthornden's brother-in-law and himself a composer of Latin verses. The collection, built up over many years, contains specimens of the work of thirty-seven poets, including most of those mentioned in this chapter, but excluding Buchanan, and was designed to stand on an equal footing with similar collections from other countries such as Italy, Germany and France. In the 1,272 closely-printed pages of its two volumes it inevitably contains a certain amount of fairly unexciting material—panegyrics for miscellaneous royal and historical occasions, both British and foreign, complimentary addresses to fellow-poets, routine elegies, epithalamia and pastorals, a three-book history of the Israelites, an ode to Christ in 100 Sapphic stanzas. But there is at the same time much that is of value, not only the works dealt with above, but others such as Thomas Dempster's *Musca* (The Fly), David Echlin's *Ova Paschalia* (Easter Eggs), Thomas Murray's translation of King James's poem on the Battle of Lepanto, and a host of epigrams of all kinds. To open the *Delitiae* is to enter on a voyage of exploration into a little-known and now little-regarded area of Scottish literature, yet an area of which Scotland can rightly be proud. In ending I can do no better than repeat the remark of Dr Samuel Johnson, contained in his account of his journey to the Western Islands: 'Literature soon after its revival found its way to Scotland, and from the middle of the sixteenth century, almost to the middle of the seventeenth, the politer studies were very diligently pursued'. The literature to which he was referring was written in Latin, and he could justly add: 'The Latin poetry of *Deliciae Poetarum Scotorum* would have done honour to any nation'. Elsewhere he makes equally complimentary reference to Buchanan, and what-ever one thinks of Johnson's critical views it is difficult not to agree that the Latin poetry of authors born in Scotland is an important and impressive contribution to Scottish literature as a whole.

FURTHER READING

PRIMARY TEXTS

(For Buchanan, *Opera Omnia* and Scot (ed) *Delitiae*, see General Bibliography)

Foullis, J, *Calamitose pestis elega deploratio . . . et alia quaedam carmina* (Paris, 1512?)
Geddes, Sir W D, and Leask, W K (eds), *Musa Latina Aberdonensis*, 3 vols (Aberdeen, 1892–1910)

SECONDARY TEXTS

Adams, J W L. 'The Renaissance Poets: Latin', in *Scottish Poetry: A Critical Survey*, Kinsley, J (ed) (London, 1955), pp 68–98
Bradner, L, *Musae Anglicanae: A History of Anglo-Latin Poetry* (New York and London, 1940)
Ford, P J, *George Buchanan, Prince of Poets* (Aberdeen, 1982)
Ijsewijn, J, and Thomson, D F S, 'The Latin poems of Jacobus Follisius or James Foullis of Edinburgh', in *Humanistica Lovaniensia*, XXIV (1975), 102–52
McFarlane, I D, *Buchanan* (London, 1981)

Chapter 14

Latin Prose Literature

JOHN and WINIFRED MACQUEEN

The natural affinity of the Celts for the Latin language and for abstract thought ensured that individual Scots played some part in European culture of the Latin Middle Ages, a part best illustrated by the *Benjamin Major* and *Minor* of the mystical theologian Richard of St Victor (d. 1173) and by the enormously influential treatises of the Subtle Doctor, John Duns Scotus (*c.*1264–1308). These belong primarily to the history of European thought, as does the work of Michael Scot (*c.*1175–*c.*1223), who translated much of Aristotle from Arabic into Latin, and whose original works deal almost exclusively with astrology, alchemy and the occult sciences. Scot is connected to Scotland more closely than the others by the legends which came to centre on him, and which at a much later date received memorable literary expression in Walter Scott's *Lay of the Last Minstrel* (1805) and James Hogg's *The Three Perils of Man* (1822), but as the connection between these and Michael Scot's Latin writings is small, we propose to do no more than mention his name. Nor shall we discuss the many writings, some of great historical importance, about logic, medicine, scriptural exegesis, law, mathematics and physics.

That is not to say that the works discussed below necessarily lack European significance—many were first published on the continent or are preserved in MSS now in European libraries. For the educated European Scotland was, and still is, the object of an intellectual curiosity which sometimes degenerated into mere credulity.

The first author to use Latin prose to deal in a literary way with distinctively Scottish issues is a figure earlier than anyone yet mentioned, Adomnan (*c.*624–704), ninth abbot of Iona, author of *De locis sanctis* and the more important *Life of St Columba*. Despite the profusion of miracles attributed to Columba, this latter is a highly intellectual work. Chronological sequence is deliberately treated as of secondary importance; instead the biography is divided thematically into three books, the first of which deals with prophetic revelations granted by and to the saint, the second with miracles of power, 'often accompanied by prophetic foreknowledge', the third with angelic apparitions 'that were revealed to others in relation to the blessed man, or to him in relation to others, and concerning those that were made visible to both, though in unequal measure (that is, to him directly and more fully, and to others indirectly and only in part, that is to say, from without and by stealth), but in the same visions, either of angels, or of heavenly light'. Columba, in other words, is treated primarily as a seer, whose abilities reached across time and space, and were capable of perceiving spiritual as well as physical realities. Adomnan attempts to analyse the function and nature of his gifts.

The modern reader tends to be less interested in this than in some of the stories which he tells to illustrate his theme, and in the unconscious assumptions which underlie these stories. In Book 1, chapter 41, for instance, Columba calls two of the brethren to him and says: 'Now cross the strait to the island of Mull, and look for the thief Erc, in the little plains beside the sea. He came last night, secretly, alone, from the isle of Coll, and he is trying to conceal himself during the day among sand-hills, under his boat which he has covered with grass; so that by night he may sail across to the small island where the sea-calves that pertain to us breed and are bred; in order that the greedy robber may fill his boat with those that he thievishly kills, and make his way back to his dwelling.'

The rather stilted language of the passage cannot disguise the detailed physical reality of the saint's vision—the machair with its sand-hills, the inverted boat covered with grass, the thief himself crouched below, the little breeding island for the seals, which are regarded as a kind of monastic cattle. No element of prophecy is involved; Columba is a clairoyant who sees the man's intentions as well as his position, and frustrates them by having him arrested and sent home with a gift of mutton instead of seal-flesh. An element of saintly compassion for poverty and hunger comes into the story and its immediate sequel, the account of the gift of food sent by the saint, which arrived too late, and was used instead at Erc's funeral.

This element of compassion recurs in chapter 48, which involves a certain measure of prophecy, although the importance in human terms of the event prophesied is negligible. The saint tells one of the brothers: 'On the third day from this that dawns, you must watch in the western part of this island, sitting above the sea-shore; for after the ninth hour of the day a guest will arrive from the northern region of Ireland, very tired and weary, a crane that has been tossed by winds through long circuits of the air. And with its strength almost exhausted it will fall near you and lie upon the shore. You will take heed to lift it tenderly, and carry it to the house near by; and having taken it in as a guest there for the space of three days and nights, you will wait upon it and feed it with anxious care. And afterwards, at the end of the three days, revived and not wishing to be longer in pilgrimage with us, it will return with fully recovered strength to the sweet district of Ireland from which at first it came. I commend it to you thus earnestly, for this reason, that it comes from the districts of our fathers'.

The physical clarity of the vision is again noticeable, as it is in the conclusion of the story. 'This, precisely as the saint foretold, the event also proved to be true. After being a guest for three days, it (the crane) first rose from the ground in the presence of its host that had cared for it, and flew to a height; and then, after studying the way for a while in the air, crossed the expanse of ocean, and in calm weather took its way back to Ireland, in a straight line of flight.'

The close connection of Iona with Ireland is evident in this passage. The

Life of Columba is a product of the Irish colony in Scotland, Gaelic-speaking Dalriada, and represents an early stage in the development of a tradition which was substantially, though by no means exclusively, oral. The *Lives* of saints from other regions of early Scotland—Pictavia and Cumbria (Strathclyde)—encapsulate similar traditions at a later stage of the oral process. From the area of Pictavia, the oldest specimen is the *Life of Servanus* (*Serf*), preserved with the *Life of Kentigern* (*Mungo*) by Jocelin of Furness in a Dublin ms, Marsh's Library V.3.4.16, which may be the same as the *vita sancti Kentigerni et sancti Servani in parvo volumine* ('Life of St Kentigern and St Servanus in a small volume') which in 1432 was catalogued as one of the possessions of the library of Glasgow cathedral. A reference in chapter 8 of Jocelin's *Kentigern* establishes the *terminus ante quem* for its composition as the episcopate in Glasgow of another Jocelin, bishop from 1174 to 1199; it may well be considerably older. The Culdee house of Loch Leven, founded, it is said, by St Servanus, is perhaps the likeliest place of composition, but Culross, Fife, emphasised as the saint's principal church and the place of his resurrection, remains an alternative possibility, although there is no documentary evidence (apart from the *Lives* of Servanus and Kentigern) for an ecclesiastical site there before the establishment of a Cistercian house in 1217.

The style of the *Life* is close to folktale. 'Once upon a time', it begins, 'there was a noble king in the land of Canaan called Obeth son of Eliud, and his wife was called Alpia daughter of the king of Arabia'. Servanus is the elder of twin sons born to this pair by a miraculous conception, but he gives up the succession to follow a remarkable ecclesiastical career in the eastern and central Mediterranean region, which culminates at Rome in his election as Pope. All this he abandons to come to Britain where, despite the opposition of Brude son of Derile, king of the Picts (696–706), he is established by Adomnan, 'abbot of Scotland', as bishop and abbot of the region immediately north of the Firth of Forth—western Fife, that is to say, Clackmannan, Kinross and Strathearn. His earlier wanderings have been guided by an angel, originally responsible for his miraculous conception; this angel has previously armed him with four staves cut from a tree from which Christ's cross had been made; with one of these (which puts down roots and itself becomes a sacred tree) he establishes the site of his church and cemetery at Culross in Fife; with another he kills the dreadful dragon of Dunning in Perthshire. He argues successfully with the Devil in a cave at Dysart, Fife. His death is at Dunning, from which his body is transferred to Culross for burial in his cemetery.

Much of this may seem far from the business and bosoms of Fife people in the earlier Middle Ages, but it is in such societies that tales of wonder tend to have the greatest hold. The reverse side of the coin is the employment by the saint of his miraculous powers to relieve the miseries of ordinary people in such places as Alva and Tullibody. His exotic achievements make him a source of local pride and self-confidence; his more prosaic miracles give comfort to the poor and distressed. The text also lists the sites over which the community at Culross claims to exercise authority, and serves as a guidebook for the devout pilgrim. The *Life* is thus a paradigm of the function of such narratives in early communities.

The later *Legend of St Andrew*, which exists in two forms, is similarly functional, though on the larger scale which befits a greater community. The ultimate founder of the church at St Andrews is the apostle himself, whose relics, it is said, were brought to Pictavia by the Greek monk Regulus or Rule during the reign of the Pictish king Onuist son of Urguist, probably to be identified with the first of that name, who reigned from 727 to 761. He had a later namesake who reigned from 820 to 834. Andrew appears in a dream to Onuist, enabling him to conquer in a battle fought on the following day. As a consequence, the king receives Regulus favourably, and enables him to build a church on a site which becomes known as St Andrews, the metropolitan see, first of Pictavia, afterwards of Scotland.

The see thus acquires the double prestige of a link, first with an apostle, albeit only through relics; secondly, by way of Patras and Constantinople, with Imperial Roman authority. Because the favour of St Andrew had ensured victory against external foes in one time of need, it might be relied on to do the same in others. In addition, by way of Onuist's dream the Scottish saltire banner acquired supernatural associations comparable to those of the *labarum* which had ensured victory for Constantine the Great, the first Christian Roman Emperor, against the pagan Maxentius at the Milvian Bridge (312). *In hoc signo vinces.* The Pictish church thus compensated for the fact that its domain had never been part of the Roman world—a compensation paralleled by the story of the papacy abandoned by Servanus to come to Culross.

The *Legend* has survived in a shorter and a longer version; the first, which does not name the enemy defeated by Onuist, is in the Poppleton MS (Paris, Bibliothèque Nationale MS. Latin 4126), written in England during the fourteenth century. From the point of view of the present chapter, the most important section is ff.26v–32r which includes the legend of St Andrew, and seems to 'represent a collection of materials made by someone in the reign of William' (the Lion, king of Scotland 1165–1214) 'who contemplated writing a history of ancient Scotland'[1] There are two copies of the second version in a fourteenth-century document written in St Andrews, which has now become Wolfenbüttel MS. Cod. Guelf. 1108 Helmst.; these are to be found in ff.28v–30v and 32v–35r. Two further copies derived from the lost St Andrews *Registrum* are to be found in Thomas Innes's *Critical Essay* (1729), ii.797ff., and in British Library Harleian MS. 4628, ff.213–242, copied in or after 1708. This second version identifies the enemy defeated by Onuist as the Saxons under their king Athelstan, unhistorically identified by Fordun (IV:13) as the son of Athelwulf and brother of king Alfred whose death is supposedly commemorated in the name of the village of Athelstaneford, East Lothian. St Andrew thus came to be identified with the struggle against the English which in one form or another was the dominant feature of Scottish life during a period of many centuries.

The Cumbric contribution to this stratum of Scottish Latin prose is best represented by the fragmentary *Life of Kentigern*, composed from earlier native material by a foreign-born ecclesiastic, perhaps a Tironensian monk of Kelso, during the episcopate of Herbert (1147–64), who had been abbot of Kelso before becoming bishop of Glasgow. This *Life* is preserved in a British Library MS., Cotton Titus A xix, ff.76–80, where it is immediately preceded by the *Vita Merlini Silvestris* ('Life of Merlin of the forest'), which occupies ff.74–75. The fragmentary *Life* contains only the miraculous conception and birth of the saint, and it is at least possible that the *Life of Merlin*, in which Kentigern plays a prominent role, and which has a similar basis in folk-material, originally formed part of the same work. The birth-story is a variant of the international tale, the best-known version of which is the Greek legend of the birth of Perseus; secular versions are to be found elsewhere in the British Isles; it is also distantly related to Arthurian tradition by way of *Yvain*, the slightly later (c.1180) French verse-romance of Chrétien de Troyes, and the Welsh prose tale, *The Countess of the Fountain*, which is included in the collection generally known as the *Mabinogion*. The tale is precise in its geographical particulars, emphasising Traprain Law and Aberlady in East Lothian, the Isle of May, and Culross in Fife, and thus serving as charter-myth for a number of features in these localities. The three-fold death prophesied for himself in the *Life of Merlin* by the wild man of the woods (in the text called Lailoken), a prophecy which despite the disbelief of the hearers subsequently becomes a reality at Drumelzier on the Tweed, and is explained as the revenge taken by the wife of Meldred, sub-king of Cadzow (Hamilton) for Merlin's supernatural perception of her adultery, is vaguely paralleled in Geoffrey of Monmouth's *Life of Merlin* (c.1150), and has strong links with early Welsh verse. Whether or not the *Life of Merlin of the forest* originally formed part of a *Life of Kentigern*, it is one of many proofs that the figure of Merlin originally had nothing to do with Arthur. The literary success of Geoffrey's *History of the Kings of Britain*, in which the earlier figure of the boy Ambrosius was mistakenly identified with Merlin, and incidentally with Carmarthen, falsely etymologised as 'city of Merlin', ensured that the association, together with a more southerly location for Merlin, would form an essential part of later Arthurian romance.

The joint traditions of Kentigern and Merlin (as also that represented by the *Life of Servanus*) are related to the developed variety of folk-tale, discussed by many scholars, which has come to be known as heroic biography. From an early date the form was substantially fixed, and usually included such episodes as birth-story, boyhood deeds, acquisition of arms, courtship and marriage, mature exploits, exile and return, notable death and burial. In such biographies the local geography tends to be precise, and to include a substantial measure of charter-myth. The subject usually is a king or secular hero, but in early societies the saint was often regarded as possessing the qualities of both, and as conferring on his community benefits more or less identical with theirs. A miraculous birth-story, for instance, was as necessary to justify his subsequent career as it was for that of Arthur or Perseus. In effect, it was as a direct consequence of his miraculous birth that Perseus was afterwards able to kill Medusa, or Servanus the dragon of Dunning. Equally, it was esential that the hero should be brought into contact, involving some kind of personal triumph, with the notable figures of his supposed day. Thus, the triumph of Kentigern in his encounter with Merlin is the insight which allowed him to recognise that, despite the apparent self-contradiction in his prophecies, Merlin was in fact on the point of death and so in need of the last sacraments, which the saint administers to the horror of his fellow clerics.

As a class, ecclesiastical and secular heroic biographies differ in two distinct ways. The saint obviously cannot himself marry or beget children. Courtship and marriage are thus necessarily excluded from his biography. His position in relation to younger ecclesiastics may resemble that of a father, but a wide range of possible exploits is excluded from his legend. On the other hand, his ecclesiastical status increased the chance that his biography would reach the dignity of a church record composed in Latin and so be preserved. One may reasonably infer that many secular heroic biographies existed in Gaelic, Cumbric or Pictish versions which remained oral and have not survived. Something of their quality may be judged from the Latin *Lives* of saints which were committed to writing and which as a consequence are available to us today.

The *Lives* stand at the point where history, myth and imaginative literature meet. In the Poppleton MS. hagiographical material is combined with secular genealogies, chronicle material, and a speculative attempt at historical reconstruction, the *De Situ Albanie*, composed with the help of Andrew, bishop of Caithness, who died in 1184. The entire contents are presented as at least the raw material of history; this is a consequence of the coexistence within the fairly limited Scottish boundaries of several languages, cultures, and religious traditions, all affected by the proximity of powerful, often hostile, neighbours. Unity and independence came almost to depend on the existence of a Scottish myth with its basis in history and pseudo-history. By way of Geoffrey of Monmouth, Norman England had come to accept the ultimately Welsh story of the foundation of Britain by the Trojan Brutus, whose eldest son, Locrine, the eponym of Lloegria or England, was paramount heir to his father's power. In opposition, the Scots developed the accounts given by the synthetic Irish historians of Scota daughter of Pharaoh and the Greek Gathelus, ultimate ancestors of the Gaelic-speaking Scottish race, to include a settlement of Scots in Scotland which long preceded the Christian era, and which became permanent when Fergus II returned to his country some fifty years before the arrival of the first English settlers in England. The descendants of Brutus were represented by the Britons of Cumbria whose power had never extended much north of the Clyde-Forth line.

The story became particularly important during the Wars of Independence, particularly as in 1301 Edward I of England mounted a legalistic propaganda campaign against the Scots at the Roman *curia*, parts of which depended on the version of history provided by Geoffrey. Here for once he was out-manoeuvred, chiefly by Master Baldred Bisset, a Scots jurist and ecclesiastic, Official of St Andrews and parson of Kinghorn, who has spent some time as a teacher of law at the University of Bologna. Bisset's *processus* ('proceedings'), delivered before Pope Boniface VIII (1294–1303), is a notable piece of Latin forensic eloquence, a 'lucid discourse', as Fordun describes it, which in its use of Scottish historical and pseudo-historical material looks forward to Fordun and Bower and beyond them to George Buchanan's *De Iure Regni apud Scottos*.

Even more impressive is the *Declaration of Arbroath* (1320), sent in the name of the community of Scotland to Pope John XXII (1316–34), who in 1320 had excommunicated four of the leading Scottish bishops together with the king. The Declaration was probably composed by Bernard of Linton, abbot of Arbroath and chancellor of Scotland, and shows with what power a Scottish ecclesiastic, writing in a good cause, could handle the medium of Latin prose. To quote Professor Barrow, 'The Latin in which it is written, terse yet rhythmic, is the work of an accomplished stylist. It wastes scarcely a word, yet it succeeds in summarizing, in much less space, almost everything of importance in the long *processus* of Master Baldred Bisset of 1301'.[2] The most famous passage, with its concluding echo of Sallust (*Cat. Con.*, 33.4), will bear quotation in the original:

A quibus malis innumeris, ipso juuante, qui post uulnera medetur et sanat, liberati sumus per strenuissimum Principem Regem et Dominum nostrum, Dominum Robertum, qui, pro populo et hereditate suis de manibus inimicorum liberandis, quasi alter Machabeus aut Josue, labores et tedia, inedias et pericula, leto sustinuit animo, quem eciam diuina disposicio, et juxta leges et consuetudines nostras, quas usque ad mortem sustinere volumus, juris successio, et debitus nostrorum omnium consensus et assensus, nostrum fecerunt Principem atque Regem. Cui, tamquam illi, per quem salus in populo facta est, pro nostra libertate tuenda, tam jure quam meritis, tenemur, et volumus in omnibus adherere. Quem si ab inceptis desisteret, Regi Anglorum aut Anglicis nos aut Regnum nostrum volens subicere, tamquam inimicum nostrum et sui nostrique juris subversorem, statim expellere niteremur, et alium Regem nostrum, qui ad defensionem nostram sufficeret, faceremus. Quia, quamdiu centum viui remanserint, nuncquam Anglorum dominio aliquatenus volumus subjugari. Non enim propter gloriam, diuicias aut honores pugnamus, sed propter libertatem solummodo, quam nemo bonus, nisi simul cum vita, amittit.

(At length it pleased God, who alone can heal after wounds, to restore us to liberty from these innumerable calamities, by our most vigorous prince, king and lord, Robert, who, for the delivering of his people and his own rightful inheritance from the enemies' hand, did, like another Joshua or Maccabeus, most cheerfully undergo all manner of toil, fatigue, hardship and hazard. The divine providence, the right of succession by the laws and customs of the kingdom (which we will defend till death), and the due and lawful consent and assent of all the people, made him our king and prince. To him we are obliged and resolved to adhere in all things, both upon account of his right and his own merit, as being the person who has restored the people's safety in defence of their liberties. But, after all, if this prince shall leave these principles he has so nobly pursued, and consent that we or our kingdom be subjected to the king or people of England, we will immediately endeavour to expel him as our enemy, and as the subverter both of his own and our rights, and will make another king who will defend our liberties. For so long as there shall but one hundred of us remain alive, we will never consent to subject ourselves to the dominion of the English. For it is not glory, it is not riches, neither is it honour, but it is liberty alone that we fight and contend for, which no honest man will lose but with his life.)

There is a continuity in the political philosophy, as well as the use of historical example, between the *Declaration* and the much later *De Iure Regni*. An implied parallel between Scotland and the Roman republic emerges in the adaptation of Sallust as well as in the general tenor of the passage. This was exploited by later authors, in particular Boece and Buchanan.

One result of Edward I's removal or destruction of the Scottish records was to send John of Fordun (*c*.1320–*c*.1384) on an expedition 'in the meadow of Britain and among the oracles of Ireland, through cities and towns, through universities and colleges, through churches and monasteries, talking with historians and visiting chronographers'. The result of his travels was the *Chronica Gentis Scotorum*, 'Chronicles of the Scottish People', in five books extending from the Flood to the end of the reign of David I (1153), where it was interrupted by his own death. A continuation in note form, the *Gesta Annalia* ('Annals'), brings events up to 1383. Book I extends from the Flood to the establishment during the first centuries BC of the Picts and Scots (the latter under Fergus I) on the northern mainland of Britain. Book II gives a somewhat distorted picture of the Roman period, including the foundation by Regulus of St Andrews and the temporary expulsion of the Scots by an alliance of Britons and Picts. Book III deals with the triumphant return of Fergus II, and the coexistence of Scots and Picts until the ninth century. Book IV extends from the conquest of the Picts by Kenneth son of Alpin to the reign of Macbeth, who killed Duncan in 1040; Book V from the return of Duncan's son Malcolm III (Canmore) to the death of David I. Fordun indicates that he wished the *Gesta Annalia* to be divided into a sixth and seventh book, the sixth concluding with the initial stages of the competition for the throne which followed the death in 1290 of the Maid of Norway. These seven books he probably intended to correspond to the biblical seven days of creation and the seven ages of the world; in this he followed the example of Ranulph Higden, monk of Chester from 1299 to 1364, whose *Polychronicon*, the revision of which was completed in 1340, adopts the same structure and was one of Fordun's main sources.

He used many others—Isidore, Bede, Geoffrey of Monmouth, William of Malmesbury, Sigibert of Gembloux, to name only the most conspicuous. In Ireland he may have consulted such scholars as Gilla-Iosa Mac Fir Bisigh (Mac Firbis) who in 1380 made a copy of an important MS. in the possession of his family, the *Yellow Book of Lecan* (Trinity College, Dublin MS. H.2.16), Seán *mor* úa Dubhagáin, John O'Dugan (d. 1372) and Adam O'Cianan (d. 1373), and he appears to have consulted the Great Register of the Priory of St Andrews, now lost, to which reference has already been made.

The substantial fragment left by Fordun was amplified, indeed transformed by Walter Bower (1385–1449), to become the huge *Scotichronicon*. Bower seems to have been an early graduate of the University of St Andrews, founded in 1410; in 1417 he became abbot of the Augustinian house of Inchcolm, situated on an island in the Firth of Forth, a position which he retained until his death. He was a figure of importance in ecclesiastical administration and government service. He began work on *Scotichronicon* *c.*1441 under the patronage of his neighbour Sir David Stewart of Rosyth, and unlike Fordun survived to bring it to a successful conclusion in sixteen books.

Initially perhaps he intended no more than a revision and updating of Fordun's *Chronica*. Especially in his first five books, Fordun's text is indicated by the word *auctor* in the margin, while his own additions he labelled *scriptor*. The *Gesta Annalia*, however, he expanded in a much more radical way, and of course for the period after 1383 he is himself the sole author. Here indeed, as the recent edition of Books XV and XVI by Professor D E R Watt shows, he at last reveals himself as a genuinely original chronicler; the earlier books are less discriminating, and reveal that Bower's gifts as abbreviator and chronologist were strictly limited. His main aim might almost be described in Professor Watt's words as to introduce 'something for everyone... there are to be lessons for princes on the folly of war and the need for cautious government, for monks on how to follow their rules properly, for laymen by way of accurate information on what has happened in the past, and for everybody by way of edifying stories and reflections which are calculated to improve behaviour and increase devotion'.[3]

Scotichronicon has survived in six full MSS. and in several abbreviated versions, one of which Bower himself produced following criticisms of his 'odious prolixity', *prolixitas odiosa*. Although widely read, *Scotichronicon* reached the dignity of print only in the eighteenth century, and the date of composition ensured that it missed any influence from the early Renaissance. New standards of historical criticism and the rediscovery by scholars of such classical authorities as Tacitus began then to raise problems which the traditional account of early Scottish history failed to satisfy. Some at least of these were tackled in different ways by the two leading historians of the earlier years of the next century. One was John Major (1467–1550), whose great reputation among his contemporaries depended more on his achievement as theologian, logician and biblical commentator ('the last of the Schoolmen'). The other was Hector Boece (*c.*1465–*c.*1536).

By the standards of his time, Major was a pioneer in that he concerned himself not solely with Scotland, but with the island as a whole; his history is of Greater Britain, *Historia Majoris Britanniae tam Angliae quam Scotiae* ('History of Greater Britain, both England and Scotland'), and was printed in 1521 in Paris for a French and European audience. He continued the tradition of the *Declaration of Arbroath*, and anticipated Buchanan, by the emphasis which he laid on the will of the community as the justification for kingly power. He also advocated the political union of Scotland and England; 'It would be of the utmost advantage to both these kingdoms that they should be under the rule of one monarch, who should be called king of Britain, provided only that he were possessed of a just and honest title thereto; and to gain this end I see no other means than by way of marriage; for the kings of each country ought to give their sons and daughters in marriage one to another, even though these were within forbidden degrees of kinship, for which the pontiff could grant a dispensation. And any man, be he Englishman or Scot, who will here say the contrary, he, I say, has no eye to the welfare of his country and the common good'. Major certainly had in mind the fact that James V, to whom he dedicated his work, was the son of James IV and Margaret, daughter of Henry VII of England. Their union had been the 'Marriage of the Thistle and the Rose' (1503) which in a hundred years was to lead to the Union of the Crowns. Even then however the unpopularity of the Union in Scotland is presupposed by the lawyer, Sir Thomas Craig, when in his *De Unione Regnorum Britanniae Tractatus* ('Treatise on the Union of the British Realms'), written in 1605, but not printed until 1909, he repeated and amplified Major's arguments.

By the application of scholastic logic to the written and oral tradition Major was able to demonstrate the improbability of the stories of Brutus, Gathelus and Scota, and so to reject them. He makes no reference to Tacitus. Interestingly, the early stages of his Scottish history come close to what we find in the later *History* of his pupil George Buchanan, who professed to despise his methods; thus he accepts a Spanish origin for the Scots, and a settlement from Ireland under Fergus I in 330 BC; this however he regards as 'a feeble foundation of the kingdom', in no way invalidating the account given by Bede of a major settlement under Reuda, great-great-grandson of Fergus I. In general Major is healthily sceptical of genealogies which directly or indirectly provided Boece and Buchanan with their lists of kings from Roman and pre-Roman times.

Major concludes his survey of English history with the early reign of Henry VIII, but despite the dedication to James V, he concludes his account of Scotland with the reign of James III: 'lest my work should contain any suspicion of flattery, I have left untouched, to be dealt with by other hands, matters of most recent date'.

Major was born in East Lothian, educated in Cambridge and Paris, and taught in Glasgow, St Andrews and Paris; his point of view as a Scot is decidedly southern. Boece belongs more to the north; he was born and brought up in Angus, and although he studied and taught in Paris at the College of Montaigu, where Major and Erasmus also worked, he was summoned home (1497) to teach the liberal arts and later, probably in 1505, to become first Principal of the University of Aberdeen, for which Pope Alexander VI had issued the Bull of Foundation in 1495. To his position at Aberdeen, where he remained for the rest of his life, Boece brought the humanist interests and enthusiasms which he shared with Erasmus, combined, it must be said, with no more than a small measure of the latter's critical tact. He modelled his style primarily on Livy and Cicero; he was interested in reconciling Tacitus with the traditions recorded by Bower and others, but his primary aim, it seems fair to say, was not the pursuit of historical truth, but the production of elegant prose which would use rhetorical rather than historical methods to persuade the reader of the value of Scots antiquities. He avoided the history of his own time; his book, *Scottorum Historiae a prima gentis origine cum aliarum et rerum et gentium illustratione non vulgari* ('History of the Scots from the first beginning of the nation, together with little-known material about affairs and peoples in the outside world'), published in Paris in 1527, ends, like *Scotichronicon*, with the death of James I in 1437. Bower is probably the main source, but the claim that the work contains little-known material is based on the existence of a supposed second authority, Veremundus, perhaps to be identified with Richard Vairement, culdee of St Andrews in the middle thirteenth century, and possible author of the *Historia* which formed the eighteenth item in the lost Great Register of the Priory of St Andrews, already twice mentioned. Boece however was unscrupulous with all his sources; in his earlier books, for example, to what on the evidence of all the surviving material was at most an expanded version of the Scottish royal genealogy, he added incidents and speeches modelled on events in Livy's account of the Roman kingship and early republic. He forced an identification of the Tacitean Caratacus with the Irish 'peace-king' Conaire Mor, best known for his part in the saga, *The Destruction of Da Derga's Hostel*, but also figuring in the earlier stages of the royal genealogy; the exploits of Caratacus he then inflated somewhat and linked to Scottish history by making Caratacus king of Carrick. It troubled him not at all that the account given by Tacitus wholly denies the possibility of any such interpretation.

Boece's work, however, was popular in Scotland and abroad. It was translated into French by Nicolas d'Arfeville, and 'undoubtedly coloured French ideas of Scottish history for a long period'. In England Holinshed made extensive borrowings, and so eventually provided Shakespeare with the plot of *Macbeth*. In 1531 the *Historiae* was translated into Scots by John Bellenden.

Later writers in different ways attempted to compensate, not so much for Boece's inaccuracies, as for his failure to deal with events after 1437. A supplement was added by the Italian Joannes Ferrerius, who spent some time at the abbey of Kinloss in Moray, when he brought out a second edition of the *Historiae* in 1574. Lindsay of Pitscottie wrote a vernacular continuation to Bellenden's translation.

The greatest figures among Boece's successors, George Buchanan and John Leslie, bishop of Ross (1526–96), were more radical; each wrote a new history, Leslie's published at Rome in 1578, Buchanan's in Edinburgh in 1582. Leslie first wrote a continuation of Boece in Scots, of which he later made a Latin translation and expansion which included a detailed epitome of the earlier work. Buchanan made some attempt to correct Boece's errors by means of his own philological investigations, and as has already been noted, by accepting and elaborating ideas first put forward by John Major. In doing so, he failed to mention Major and demonstrated a quite uncharacteristic tenderness for Boece's scholarly reputation. He does not seem to have examined any genealogical material of the kind used by Boece; thus although he refuses to accept that Caratacus in Boece is the same as Caratacus in Tacitus, he still, like Bishop Leslie, includes the name in the sequence of early kings. Buchanan has rightly been criticised for accepting the historical existence of the forty kings alleged to have preceded Fergus II; nevertheless allowance should be made for his scholarly conservatism when faced with long-standing beliefs (even Major accepted the existence of Fergus I and some of his successors) which apparently had some documentary support. He at least approached the problem critically; his failure was that he did not carry his criticisms sufficiently far. It is also undoubtedly important that he had used incidents in this pseudo-history to illustrate the theory of government set out in his *De Iure Regni*.

Buchanan became a Protestant; Leslie remained a Catholic, eventually dying in the monastery of Augustinian canons at Guirtenburg near Brussels where he had spent the last nine years of his life. They stood thus at opposite doctrinal and political extremes, and naturally their interest as historians centred on the Reformation period, in particular on Mary I, the ill-fated Catholic queen of a predominantly Protestant Scotland. Leslie devotes Book X, the longest in his *History*, to events in the early part of her life and short personal reign, in the middle of which he breaks off, claiming that he does not wish to appear over-affected by passion or prejudice. Books XVII–XIX of Buchanan give a diametrically opposed view, the way to which had been prepared by his *Detectio Mariae Reginae Scotorum*, 'Detection of Mary Queen of Scots' (1568), addressed to the English Queen Elizabeth, and by the philosophical dialogue, *De Iure Regni apud Scottos*, 'Legitimacy of Royal Succession among the Scots' (1579), in which he had maintained the views on government which he shared with the Scottish reformers, aspects at least of which were already, as has been indicated, well established in Scotland. He particularly insisted that political sovereignty 'rests and has always rested in the people'[4] and although his primary reference is to Scotland, the philosophic form of the dialogue suggests that he is voicing a universal truth. The Scots, he therefore claims had been right to expel Mary, whose personal life was a scandal and who had acted as a tyrant by holding power against the will of the people. Leslie, it need scarcely be said, saw her as a saint and martyr, victim of a malignant and misguided coterie. His own appointed task was to bring the Scots back to traditional allegiances and the Catholic faith.

In Scotland and elsewhere Buchanan's *History* long retained intellectual and emotional impact, and as late as the nineteenth century Charles Kingsley, an Englishman, could call *De Iure Regni* 'the very primer . . . of constitutional liberty'.[5] *History* and *De Iure Regni* were both fiercely criticised, but this chapter, I hope, has demonstrated their centrality to Scottish political theory and practice. The European reputation of Buchanan ensured that during the next two centuries their influence would extend far beyond Scotland.

For the Renaissance Latinist, prose was virtually indistinguishable from oratory, whether forensic or panegyric. This helps to explain the more outrageous features of Boece's *History*; it is not history as a modern historian would understand the term; rather it is an extended panegyric on the Scottish nation, taking full advantage of the traditional rhetorical liberties. Because he was writing a panegyric, he was in effect not on oath. Leslie and Buchanan are more forensic; very obviously each has a case to urge. During the fifteenth century both kinds of oratory became important for the conduct of public affairs; negotiations between sovereign states were usually accompanied by letters and formal panegyric speeches employing the choicest Ciceronian eloquence which the king's secretariat was able to muster. Training in the classics became essential for the future diplomat or administrator. This may be illustrated by two speeches which survive, that given before the French king, Louis XI, in 1479 by William Elphinstone (1431–1514), later Bishop of Aberdeen and founder of the University in that city; the second given before the English Richard III at Nottingham in 1484 by Archibald Whitelaw (c.1425–98), Archdeacon of Lothian and Subdean of Glasgow, who held the office of royal Secretary for the greater part of the reign of James III.

On a less international scale, panegyric biographies of individual Scottish bishops and abbots figure largely in the surviving literature; Elphinstone's speech, for instance, is preserved in the *Murthlacensium et Aberdonensium Episcoporum Vitae* ('Lives of the Bishops of Mortlach and Aberdeen'), written by Hector Boece and published in Paris in 1522. This collection was put together primarily to provide a setting for the longest item, the panegyric on Boece's patron, Bishop Elphinstone, which incidentally includes an interesting account of the foundation-members of staff in Aberdeen University.

With less rhetorical skill but more attention to humble detail, Alexander Myln (c.1474–c.1549) in his *Vitae Episcoporum Dunkeldensium* ('Lives of the Bishops of Dunkeld') attempted a similar task for his late superior, George Brown, bishop from 1484 to 1514. He also gives vivid details of the troubled installation of Brown's successor, the poet and translator Gavin Douglas. The *Vitae*, completed in 1515, remained in manuscript (NLS, Advocates 34.5.4.) until 1823. The book was completed when Myln had himself left Dunkeld to become abbot of Cambuskenneth; in 1532 he was appointed first Lord President of the College of Justice.

Joannes Ferrerius wrote *Historia Abbatum de Kynlos* ('History of the Abbots of Kinloss'), completed in 1537, and chiefly devoted to the career of abbot Thomas Crystall (1499–1535). This is preserved in NLS, Advocates' MS. 35.5.58, and reached print in 1839.

Much later than any of those, more general in its scope and wilder in its panegyric is a work by the wandering scholar and professor Thomas Dempster (1579–1625), the *Historia Ecclesiastica Gentis Scotorum* (Bologna, 1627), despite its title not an ecclesiastical history of the Scottish nation but in effect a national collection of biographies, extending into Dempster's own time. 'The book', comments DNB, 'is chiefly remarkable for its extraordinary dishonesty', but Dempster's account of his own life, which is included, possesses human interest like that (say) in one of Browning's Renaissance monologues.

Philosophic dialogue modelled on Plato or Cicero was another favourite vehicle of Renaissance humanism. One example has already been cited, Buchanan's *De Iure Regni*, probably modelled on Plato's *Laws*. The imaginary conversation is between Buchanan and his friend Thomas Maitland; most of the talking is done by Buchanan. John Major excludes himself from his *Dialogus de Materia Theologo Tractanda* ('Dialogue on Matters Appropriate for Theological Discussion'), prefixed to *In primum Sententiarum* (Paris, 1510). The speakers here are Gavin Douglas, who gives vigorous expression to the views of the humanists, and David Cranston, a promising theologian, Major's favourite pupil, who died young, and who defends the traditional scholastic terminology. This is a vital document on an important literary and philosophical issue of the time.

The dialogue in its most extended form is represented by *De Animi Tranquillitate* ('Tranquillity of Soul'), published at Lyons in 1543 and written by Florentius Volusenus (*c*.1504–*c*.1547), another wandering Scottish scholar, whose name is often rendered as Florence Wilson. The philosophic discussion takes place in the neighbourhood of Lyons; the participants are Volusenus and his friends and students, Franciscus Michael, who is French, and Demetrius Caravalla, who is Italian. Volusenus begins with an expression of grief on hearing that an English army is threatening to invade Scotland; this leads naturally to the governing topic of the discussion. At one point Volusenus gives a long account of a dream which some years before he had experienced after a day spent on the banks of the river Lossie near Elgin, discussing the problem of contentment with his friend John Ogilvie, afterwards rector of Cruden. His dream was set in the same Moray landscape, now dominated, however, not by Elgin cathedral, but by the marble temple of Tranquillity with its eight pillars, each adorned with a gnomic inscription in Greek. The exegesis of these inscriptions occupies a substantial part of the dialogue, within which the vision serves as the 'myth', more or less as the concluding Vision of Er functions in Plato's *Republic*. From a slightly different point of view, there is a resemblance between the dialogue and such vernacular poems as the *Kingis Quair* of James I or Gavin Douglas's *Palice of Honour*; all are dream-allegories, the visionary and symbolic part of which enriches the content of the remainder. Volusenus is more consciously a Platonist than the vernacular poets; for him, as for Augustine, Plato (with whom he couples the Neoplatonist Plotinus) is the philosopher who comes closest to Christianity.

The conversation in the dialogue is courteous and civilised, and the language appropriately elegant and polished. Volusenus shows his deep knowledge and love of classical authors by frequent quotation and by the perfection of his style. He uses Greek frequently, but always with an accompanying Latin translation. His classicism however is subordinate to his belief in the efficacy and power of the Christian ethic; it is by dependence on Christ alone that tranquillity of soul can be achieved. His humanism, in other words, is the Christian humanism of the early Northern Renaissance, and is related to the Christian philosophy of late antiquity, best represented by the *Consolations* of Boethius.

Scottish Latin prose does not come to an end with the works mentioned here; indeed it remained of some importance even after 1750. But in function it became more limited. The later tendency was for history and philosophy to appear in vernacular dress, with English rather than Scots forming the garment. Latin became more and more restricted to science, mathematics, medicine and law. Paradoxical though it may now appear, when C P Snow's two cultures first moved apart in the course of the seventeenth century, Latin remained firmly on the scientific side of the fence.

NOTES

1 M O Anderson, *Kings and Kingship in Early Scotland* (Edinburgh, 1980), p 236.
2 G Barrow, *Robert Bruce and the community of the realm of Scotland* (Edinburgh, 1976), p 426.
3 'Editing Walter Bower's Scotichronicon' in *Proceedings of the Third International Conference on Scottish Language and Literature (Medieval and Renaissance),* Roderick J Lyall and Felicity Riddy (eds) (Stirling/Glasgow, 1981), pp 70–84.
4 W A Gatherer, *The Tyrannous Reign of Mary Stewart* (Edinburgh, 1958), p 12.
5 Ibid., p 5.

FURTHER READING

PRIMARY TEXTS

(For Buchanan, *Opera Omnia*, see General Bibliography)

Anderson, A O and M O (eds), *Adomnan's Life of Columba* (London and Edinburgh, 1961)

Bower, Walter, *Joannis de Fordun Scotichronicon cum supplementis et Continuatione Walteri Bower, Insulae Sancti Columbae Abbatis*, Goodall, W (ed), 2 vols (Edinburgh, 1759)

—— *Scotichronicon*, Volume 8, Watt, D E R (ed) (Aberdeen, 1987)

Buchanan, George, *The History of Scotland Translated from the Latin of George Buchanan*, Aikman, J (trans), 2 vols (Glasgow, 1827)

—— *The Art and Science of Government among the Scots*, MacNeill, D H (trans) (Glasgow, 1964)

Chambers, R W, Batho, E C, and Husbands, H Winifred (eds), *The Chronicles of Scotland, Compiled by Hector Boece, Translated into Scots by John Bellenden, 1531*, STS, 2 vols (Edinburgh and London, 1938–41)

Craig, Sir Thomas, *De Unione Regnorum Britanniae Tractatus*, Terry, C Sanford (ed), SHS (Edinburgh, 1909)

Dempster, Thomas, *Historia Ecclesiastica Gentis Scotorum*, Irving, D (ed), Bannatyne Club (Edinburgh, 1829)

Ferrerius, Joannes, *Historia Abbatum de Kynlos una cum Vita Thomas Chrystalli Abbatis*, Wilson, W D (ed), Bannatyne Club (Edinburgh, 1839)

Forbes, A P (ed), *Lives of Saint Ninian and Saint Kentigern*, The Historians of Scotland V (Edinburgh, 1874)

Fordun, John of, *John of Fordun's Chronicle of the Scottish Nation*, Skene, W F, (ed), 2 vols, The Historians of Scotland I and IV (Edinburgh, 1871–72)

Innes, Thomas, *A Critical Essay on the Ancient Inhabitants of the Northern Parts of Britain, or Scotland... with an Appendix of ancient MS pieces*, 2 vols (London, 1729)

—— (Repr), The Historians of Scotland VIII (Edinburgh, 1879)

Leslie, John, *The Historie of Scotland... translated in Scottish by Father James Dalrymple... 1596*, Cody, E G and Murison, W (eds), STS (Edinburgh and London, 1888–95)

Major, John, *A History of Greater Britain as well as England and Scotland*, Constable, A (ed), SHS (Edinburgh, 1892)

Moir, J (ed), *Hectoris Boetii Murthlacensium et Aberdonensium Episcoporum Vitae*, New Spalding Club (Aberdeen, 1894)

Myln, Alexander, *Vitae Dunkeldensis Ecclesiae Episcoporum*, Innes, C (ed), 2nd edn, Bannatyne Club (Edinburgh, 1831)

—— *Rentale Dunkeldense*, Hannay, R K (ed), SHS (Edinburgh, 1915)

Skene, W F (ed), *Chronicles of the Picts, Chronicles of the Scots and other Early Memorials of Scottish History* (Edinburgh, 1867)

Volusenus, Florentius, *De Animi Tranquillitate*, Wishart, W (ed) (Edinburgh, 1751)
Ward, H L (ed), 'Lailoken (or Merlin Silvester)', *Romania* XXII (1893), 504–26

SECONDARY TEXTS

McFarlane, I D, *Buchanan* (London, 1981)
MacQueen, J, 'Some Aspects of the Early Renaissance in Scotland', *FMLS* III (1967), 201–22
—— 'Epic Elements in Early Welsh and Scottish Hagiography', in Almquist, B, Ó Catháin, S and Ó Héalai, P (eds), *The Heroic Process* (Dublin, 1987), 453–70.

Chapter 15

Gaelic: the Classical Tradition

W GILLIES

The 'Classical' or 'Classical Early Modern' period of Gaelic literature—both Scottish and Irish—ran from the twelfth century to the seventeenth. In Scottish terms its foundation may be associated with the emergence of the Lordship of the Isles, and its decline with the waning of its basis of patronage—a Gaelic-speaking aristocracy—in the Covenanting and Jacobite periods. On the Irish side convenient historical landmarks would be the coming of the Normans in 1167–69, and, for its demise, the Cromwellian campaigns of 1649–52, in which the bardic schools, as manifestations of organised Gaelic culture, were systematically destroyed.

'Classical' is also used more specifically as a linguistic term, to denote the refined and static version of educated Early Modern speech employed by the court poets. By extension 'Classical literature' was the court literature composed in the Classical language or dialect. This was by no means the only sort of literature being practised in the Gaelic world in Early Modern times; but it was the only sort to be committed regularly to manuscript at the time, and the present chapter will be concerned with it alone.

While the Scottish and Irish Gaelic vernaculars became fully distinct and took on much of their present day character during the Early Modern period, these developments had much less impact at the educated level, and none at the strictest literary level, whose language was designedly supra-dialectal. In many ways one must regard the Classical tradition in Scotland and Ireland as representing a unity; in fact our picture of the whole depends upon the judicious combination of Irish and Scottish evidence at a number of points. In the following account Scottish evidence will naturally be used so far as possible; but Irish testimony will be adduced where Scottish material is unclear or lacking.

Highland society in our period was structured around a series of aristocratic kin-groups—the ruling families of the so-called 'clans'. Some of these ruling families were of old Gaelic stock and had become important earlier on, while others emerged during the period, for instance as Norse influence declined in the Isles, or on account of changing fortunes in the Bruce-Balliol struggles, or in the context of normanisation. Whether Gaelic, British, Norse or Norman in origin, Highland families required a special sort of validation for the aristocratic system to work. As one Irish poet put it: 'If the historical lore (of the Gaelic aristocracy) were extinguished, then the children of your dog-keepers and of your noble kindreds would be equally noble or base. If the men of Ireland really wish to expel Poesy, every (true) Gael's good name will receive scant coverage and every nobleman will be a churl.' This poet's claim, that the aristocracy need their poets to survive, was intended to justify the presence of the families of professional poet-historians which we find attached to Gaelic ruling families in the late Middle Ages.

It is well known, of course, that Celtic chiefs had enjoyed hearing themselves praised by bards since Greek and Roman times. For our period, however, scholars recognise a more explicitly structured and regulated relationship between poets and patrons. Some time in the later twelfth century—or so it appears—a shadowy but undoubted development in poetic industrial relations took place, which had implications for Gaelic literature from Kerry to the Butt of Lewis.

Whereas previously the learned core of Gaelic literary tradition had flourished in a milieu closely associated with the monasteries of the Celtic Church, the latter were now in a decline accelerated by the spread of the Continental Orders, and were no longer in a position to provide the solid base which literature claimed in a Celtic society. The 'new deal', however it was effected, regularised the conditions of patronage whereby a trained poet could receive a free living and various perquisites in return for performing bardic duties for his patron and fulfilling certain obligations to his profession. The literary language itself was regulated: what has been termed 'a mediæval exercise in language planning' gave rise to an essentially artificial language in which conservative or even archaic forms joined forces with some which must have been pretty progressive in twelfth-century terms, while others were excluded: all of this being effected by recourse to principles which are not extant and are frequently not transparent, but which gave rise to rules which were observed unanimously until Classical Irish ceased to be cultivated. Metrical and other requirements were similarly refined or standardised; and the whole edifice was harnessed to the new notion that courtly praise poetry, duly composed on set occasions or under approved circumstances, should now be regarded as the highest expression of the professional poet's art.

We can talk about Scottish involvement in these developments from the early thirteenth century, on account of the well-attested Muireadhach Ó Dálaigh (eponymous ancestor of the MacMhuirich poetic family), whose poetry shows evidence for professional liaisons of the new sort with the family of the Earls of Lennox; and in the case of the more shadowy Giolla Brighde Albanach (Mac Con Midhe?), who may have been a personal friend of Muireadhach's. The fact that one of the earliest surviving pieces of classical praise poetry was composed for Raghnall, King of Man (*c.* 1200 AD), shows that the new system had the prestige to commend itself throughout the Gaelic-speaking world. The initial impetus, however, would doubtless have come from Ireland. The family of Muireadhach Ó Dálaigh, for instance, appears to have been associated with learning for at least three generations in Westmeath, and gave rise to a number of illustrious poetic families in different parts of Ireland. (Muireadhach himself had ended up in Scotland after being forced to leave Ireland in consequence of an act of homicide.)

If details of the foundation of the Classical literary tradition remain mysterious, a good deal can be said about its functioning thereafter. One may think of the *literati* in general as forming a social order—a learned caste, almost—where '*literati*' comprehends also the physicians and lawyers who, like the poets, operated exclusive, hereditary, monopolistic professions, and claimed the support of the aristocracy to enable them to do so. Justification for this view may be sought both externally, as in the way Elizabethan commentators and legislators consistently singled out the Irish learned order as an identifiable focus of resistance; and internally, in the evidence we find for individuals whose families practised one learned profession moving into another field.

Given the unanimity of doctrine implied by five centuries of uncannily consistent poetic usage, it is permissible to attempt a synthetic picture of the typical *file* or professional poet, based on various accounts and on scattered references in the poetry itself. He would be a time-served man who had established himself as an accomplished practitioner and had sued successfully for a vacant position as official poet (*ollamh*) to the head of a noble family (his *flaith* or 'lord'). In some cases his father would have held this position before him, though there is also plenty of evidence that 'poaching' (both of patrons and of poets), and rivalries, quarrels, political realignments, and so on, took place and could affect the bond of patronage.

Our *file*, then, would have spent a number of years learning his craft at one or more of the bardic schools or seminaries which were run by at least the more eminent poetic families in each locality. His courses would have included linguistic and metrical instruction—grammatical, syntactical, and metrical tracts as used in the schools have survived—together with the mass of historical, mythological and genealogical data which he would need to deploy in his verse. His training would have involved much practical verse composition, and he would have had opportunities to make his public début with informal and 'understudy' compositions, or perhaps by reciting his seniors' compositions for them; later he would have found his own level, matching his poetic eminence with the political eminence of a patron.

He was now an honoured member of Gaelic society—as may be seen, for instance, by the appearance of poets as signatories to charters. He had a free living on lands set aside for the local chief's poet. (In this respect our poets were the successors—perhaps literally so in some cases—of the laicised families of erenaghs of the Celtic Church.) He would have enjoyed certain regular gifts, and could command a set fee (*duais*) for an official ode. He was also the close confidant to his chief, to whom he acted as political agent, counsellor or diplomat as the need arose. His principal function was to uphold and protect his chief's good name and fame by his odes, which were due on such occasions as inaugurations, coming of age, marriage, death and so on.

In addition to his role as 'chief's poet' the *ollamh* functioned as a member of the literary 'Estate'—indeed, as the apex of that microcosm of Gaelic society. It fell to him to ensure that young poets were trained up, which could entail running a formal seminary for that purpose. He had to keep up with political developments in the country at large, insofar as they affected the standing and inter-relationships of the ruling kindreds. In this he was aided by the fact that he had the power to travel, to an extent denied to most other sections of the population. The business of visiting was in fact a recognised part of the poet's office: at certain times of the year he left his own territory to go on a circuit (*cuairt*) of other chiefs' halls, attended by a retinue of juniors, pupils and attendants, together with various less exalted men of arts, such as vernacular poets, singers, musicians and entertainers, who collectively formed a poet-band or *cliar*. The *ollamh* was manifestly their 'president'. When it came to the recitation of his formal ode to his host, a central formality in the proceedings, he would be firmly ensconced at the chief's table, while a junior member of the entourage performed the office of reciter (*reacaire*). Again, the poet could be sent officially as his chief's ambassador to another chief (in which case his ode formed part of the diplomatic niceties of the occasion). Additionally, there is widespread evidence for poets keeping in touch with other poets, both by visits and by correspondence.

The most spectacular example of a poetic family's attachment to a noble family is that of the MacMhuirich descendants of Muireadhach Albanach Ó Dálaigh. They provided a succession of official poets to the Lords of the Isles and thereafter to the Clanranald branch of the Clan Donald to the point when, in 1800, Lachlann MacMhuirich could claim 'that he himself was the eighteenth generation from Muireach who had followed the family of Clanranald as bards'. Although there are some difficulties about this testimony we can catch glimpses of the descendants of Muireadhach (but see below) down through the centuries. We may mention Cathal 'archipoeta' who signed a charter of Angus, Lord of the Isles, in 1485; Eóin the contributor of poems to the Book of the Dean of Lismore (early sixteenth century); and several others besides the group of seventeenth-eighteenth century figures who composed the bulk of the surviving corpus of MacMhuirich writings. Of the other poetic families attested the two most important were the Uí Mhuirgheasáin (one of the sources of the Highland name 'Morrison') who were associated with the Macleans of Duart and the MacLeods of Dunvegan, and the MacEwen poets *cum* historians to the House of Argyll and the MacDougalls of Dunollie. In the case of the Uí Mhuirgheasáin we may cite a religious poem by Maghnas son of Maol-Domhnaigh in the Dean's Book; the Gaelic contract of fosterage written up for Ruairidh Mór MacLeod by Toirdhealbhach Ó Muirgheasáin in 1614; the Maol-Domhnaigh who made a considerable impact in Irish poetic circles in the 1640s; and the Donnchadh who was still interested in keeping up with Campbell genealogical lore and who composed an elegy for Sir Norman MacLeod of Bernera as late as 1706, at the very end of our period. As to the MacEwens, we seem to have an elegy composed by a member of the family for Eóin Ciar, chief of the MacDougalls of Dunollie in the late fifteenth century; charter evidence in the sixteenth for their official status as Campbell poets and the hereditary grant of land that went with it; poems to Campbell chiefs in the seventeenth; and at the same time evidence for the involvement of at least one of them in the Synod of Argyll's plan to provide Calvin's Catechism in Gaelic. (The possibility of passing between one of the traditional professions and the Church recurs, both before and after the Reformation.)

The examples cited from these three families should help to define the limits of the poets' profession in at least a general way. We assume that at times and places where there was a Gaelic-speaking chief there would also have been a court poet, even where no literature has survived. Sometimes this assumption may be strengthened indirectly—e.g. by the existence of a learned genealogy for the chief, albeit preserved elsewhere; or by the survival of 'poet's land' place-names or traditions; or should the chief himself or a member of his family be remembered as a composer of Gaelic verse. Unfortunately we lack a Scottish parallel to the poem which Pierce Ferriter composed for Maol-Domhnaigh Ó Muirgheasáin, in which he listed the various bardic seminaries where Maol-Domhnaigh had paused ('like a bee stealing nectar from flower after flower') during his protracted visit to Ireland. On the other hand, an interesting catalogue of some of the chiefs' courts which would have claimed to be 'the destination of the poet bands' (*ceann-uidhe nan cliar*) may be extracted from the story and verses associated with 'Angus of the Satires' (Aonghus nan Aoir), who appears in Scottish tradition as a sort of late Mediæval Egon Ronay, with a pithy comment on the hospitality and fare he received in each chief's house. Extant verses include, besides heads of prominent clans and septs like MacNeill of Barra, MacDonald of Keppoch and Campbell of Glenorchy, a fair number of humbler names (MacDougall of Gallanach, Campbell of Glen Feochan), some from near the edge of the Highland-Lowland divide (Stewart of Garth, Stewart of Ballechin), and, to rub salt in the wounds, a final good word for an originally Norman family— the Chisholms of Strathglass!

Not all the classical poetry we have was composed by members of Scottish poetic families. Some was contributed by Irish visitors. 'It is customary that an *ollamh* should travel with a (diplomatic) message', proclaims one poet of O'Donnell's sent on a mission to the Earl of Argyll; though an earlier poem, by an Irishman who reveals that in his homeland a ship is a curiosity, contains the following honest admission: 'I say, for dread of the storm, alas that it is not a continuous promontory(?) of land across the strait to Angus of Islay.' There is also evidence for the composition of syllabic verse by members of the learned order other than poets—e.g. by medical men or ecclesiastics. This is only natural, given that literacy in Gaelic and familiarity with the literary dialect were the common denominators of the professions; and that the mainsprings of Gaelic linguistic instruction were the poets and the poetic schools. In the same way, a certain number of poems from our period are ascribed to members of the aristocracy or gentry. This ties in with increasing evidence for Gaelic literacy on the part of Highland chiefs—a necessary enough attribute given the diplomatic function of bardic verse—though it is not clear whether this should be attributed primarily to poets acting as tutors to chief's sons, or to chief's sons attending bardic schools. At all events, however, it should be noted that the composition of a formal ode for a chief was strictly reserved for the fully trained professional poet.

The earliest Classical Gaelic compositions relevant to Scotland date from the early thirteenth century; but the manuscripts containing them are mostly much later—sixteenth to eighteenth century. They are on the whole written in the standard Irish scribal hand (the *corr-litir*), and the scribal contractions and other traits conform to Irish practices of the time. (The Book of the Dean of Lismore (1512–42), which was written in Scots notary hand with a homespun quasi-phonetic spelling system based on Scots, is the most important exception.) They may be crudely divided into two classes—patrons' and poets' manuscripts. The former sort includes anthologies written to order, and may contain one or more of the following categories: court, informal or religious verse, heroic ballads, prose romances and tales, history or devotional texts. A specialised but widespread class is the *duanaire*—a book into which the official odes addressed to an individual family were added over the years, so as to form a sort of verbal portrait gallery of its principal members. Amongst the 'poets' manuscripts' we find source-books for the patrons' anthologies (including aphorisms and other space-fillers), and professional and technical literature of various sorts—linguistic and metrical, historical, genealogical and mythological.

Much has been lost: there are gaps where we know Gaelic literature flourished, and some horror stories about the destruction of manuscripts. The space of time which elapsed between the cultivation of the manuscript literature and the awakening of antiquarian interest in it—which occurred, ironically, in the cry for manuscripts to validate MacPherson's *Ossian*—was all too often a fatal one.

Returning to the court poet, one can visualise him adding an illustrious visiting poet's ode to his patron's *duanaire*, or his own most important compositions. For the latter he would doubtless have kept a copy to show visiting or visited colleagues, some of whom would make their own copies of it, as he would of theirs. If it were an exemplary piece it might come to be studied by apprentice poets in the schools, and citations from it might appear in their technical manuals. Or it might become anthologised and appear in numerous later copies. But the primary purpose of composing it was for immediate, public performance, as part of a celebration: the epinician odes of Pindar are in many ways comparable.

It seems that the declamation of the Gaelic panegyric was accompanied by the music of the harp; but what form this accompaniment may have taken is hard to say. We shall see that the verse in question is arhythmical, and also embellished with a pervasive and integral word-music. These two factors narrow the field of likely instrumental accompaniment and suggest that whatever form it took it cannot have been intrusive during the recital of the verses. (Something more prominent or elaborate could, of course, have been inserted *between* verses.) It has also been suggested that the recitation of the ode took the form of a plainsong-like chant; but again the positive evidence is not strong.

At any rate there is no doubt but that the primary medium for experiencing bardic verse was the aural one. This ties in with the rather fuller testimony regarding composition: quite a number of references, both in poems and in accounts of the poets, lay stress on a ritual of seclusion and concentration by the composing poet, with the poem itself only attaining written status after the act of composition was complete. This is striking when one considers that these odes can contain scores of quatrains, and, if literally true, it says a lot for the mental training of the poetic schools. Celtic scholars have also been reminded of the ancient mantic and visionary connotations of various words for 'poet' and 'poetry'. This emphasis is no doubt much as the poets would have wished it, being very much in keeping with the image they cultivated for the outside world. It could be argued that the fact that they were written down at any stage in the process casts doubt on their 'pure' orality. But in fact features which can definitely be termed 'visual' are rare and peripheral; and when we find that poets who habitually compose with rigorously correct forms can be quite slapdash and erratic when they write down even their own compositions on paper we may conclude that since ignorance is out of the question and obfuscation not apparent, simple unconcern about the written medium is the likeliest explanation. It is in the courtly love poetry, with its more intimate, boudoir ethos, that we find the acrostics and 'crossword clues' to ladies' names, and such-like indulgences *ad oculos*.

Formally speaking, Classical poetry is distinguished by its use of the set of syllabic metres known collectively as *dán*. These metres are syllabic in the sense that each of the four lines in adverse contains a fixed number of syllables—typically seven—and each line's completeness is determined by its syllable count. Unlike other classes of versification found in Gaelic, the number and position of stresses is of no concern in this syllabic poetry, except at line ends, where fixed cadences are obligatory. In the following verse stressed syllables are italicised; the cadences are ´— — in first and third lines and —´ in second and fourth lines throughout.

Le*at* sl*a*bhraidh c*ao*la c*o*n t'*a*thar,
   gach *a*rg c*u*mhdaigh ar do ch*ui*d,
a th*oi*ghe 's a ch*á*in gan chomhroinn,
   t*á*in is gr*oi*ghe Dhomhnuill d*ui*d.

Given that in historic times Gaelic has always been a stress-timed language, a metrical system based on regular stresses would appear more in keeping with the genius of the language; and many scholars have sought an exotic source for *dán*, seeing its origins in Mediæval Latin hymn-metres.

The syllabic principle is complemented by rhyme, which occurs both structurally and ornamentally: structurally to mark off the ends of lines or couplets and to link them with one another; and ornamentally to achieve a series of echo-effects between succeeding lines. Thus in the quatrain just quoted *chuid* and *duid* achieve the obligatory end-rhyme between *b* and *d*; while in *cd* rhymes between *thoighe*, *cháin* and *chomhroinn* on the one hand and *groighe*, *táin* and *Dhomhnuill* on the other fulfil an obligation to provide a rich aural resonance. (The order of the 'echoes' in *d* is to some extent variable: here we have 1,2,3 : 2,1,3.) It should be noted that rhyme does not necessarily involve literal identity of consonants after the stressed vowel; rather it is based on a series of phonetically based consonant classes. A third category of metrical device is provided by alliteration: sequences of stress-bearing words within the same line may be bound together by having the same initial sound. Examples in the quatrain above include *caola con* in *a*, *cháin ... chomhroinn* in *c* (where the unstressed preposition *gan* does not impede alliteration), and likewise *cumhdaigh ... chuid* in *b*.

Now verse of this sort, observing the categories of metrical constraint just described, had been composed for almost half a millennium before the Classical period. Some Mediæval examples show the same degree of elaboration as the Classical poets observed. But the Classical *dán díreach* ('strict *dán*') codified and made obligatory the requirements for the accepted metres, and added a whole series of more detailed rulings on such matters as avoidance of jingle, the position of alliteration in the line, initial mutations in complex phrases, and rhymes involving consonant clusters. A less strict form of *dán*, known as *óghláchas*, was in order (perhaps even prescribed) throughout our period for compositions other than the formal odes of master-poets; but where the latter conditions were fulfilled there was no room for choice. In the following quatrain by Muireadhach Albanach *no* stressed word lacks a rhyming or assonating 'partner' save the initial *éistidh*, and every line contains alliteration:

> Éistidh riomsa, a Mhuire mhór,
> do ghuidhe is liomsa badh lúdh;
> do dhruim red bhráthair ná bíodh,
> a Mháthair Ríogh duinn na ndúl.

And the prescription involved language too: acceptable and non-acceptable declensional and conjugational forms for thousands of nouns and hundreds of verbs had to be known and observed. The grammatical tracts which deal with such matters often authorise several permitted variants: e.g. the dependent form of *do-gheibhim* may take the form *faghaim*, *foghaim*, *faghbhaim* or *foghbhaim* (and one source authorises a set of forms without the initial *f-* besides). Given the metrical constraints described above we may be sure the poets had need of their variants.

Classical Gaelic poetry as a whole drew on an extensive and rich field of literary reference for the purposes of allusion, simile, apologue, and so forth. It was based almost entirely on native literary, historical and mythological sources, the most important of which were as follows.

(1) Mediæval Irish scholars, the predecessors of the classical *filidh*, had constructed a unified account of the pre-history of Ireland and of the Gaels. Inspired by their discovery of Grecoi-Roman and Biblical antiquity they had set out to fill the gap that became apparent in the West, from Creation to the coming of St Patrick. They portrayed a series of civilisations or eras prior to the coming of the Gaels, whose journeyings they also chronicled—from Babel to Scythia (compare the name 'Scotti'), and thence via Egypt and Spain to Ireland. Thereafter the preoccupation became increasingly genealogical, as the ancestry of existing noble families was taken back to the descendants of the sons of Míl of Spain (the 'Milesians'). The main focus throughout was

on the sovereignty of Ireland. This elaborate origin myth took account of non-Gaelic neighbours like Britons, Picts and Angles, but only in a peripheral way. It is termed the 'synthetic history' of Ireland, and it drew to some extent on pre-existing mythological and literary material, origin legends and genealogical traditions; but it owed an enormous amount to rampant speculation and plain fabrication.

(2) Correlated with this scheme of the past, but also known in their own right, were the literary cycles of Early Ireland—the tales and lore of the Ulster, Fenian, Mythological and King-cycles.

(3) Complementary to these sources was the 'historical geography' of Ireland, or *dindshenchus* (a body of lore which explained the stories behind place-names of legendary significance) and similar reference works.

(4) The *filidh* also had access to certain non-native literature, including a selection of Classical and Mediæval Latin texts; but this was never an important part of their field of reference.

Of the classes of composition practised by the *filidh* the most fundamental was the formal panegyric to a chief, the importance of which is reflected in the amount of comment the *genre* has attracted over the years. This comment has not all been favourable, it should be said. Thus bardic eulogy has been criticised for its effects on the recipient: English commentators on Ireland in the reign of Queen Elizabeth, and those concerned to enforce the King's rule in his Scottish realm, alike saw eulogy as a stimulus to uncivil acts; while at least one Irish poet stressed the spiritual dangers, chiding his fellow-poets for consigning men to Hell by plying their trade of 'fashioning soft words' where salvation depended on truthful self-examination.

An additional twist has been added by modern literary critics who focus more on the poems themselves, and have trouble with their supposed mendacity and the 'impure' (i.e. mercenary) motive that prompts them: eulogy is, as it were, an affront to the good name of Poetry. To be sure, few have failed to praise its technical artistry; and some have valued its intellectual challenges, its linguistic *élan*, or its heroic values; but on the whole it nowadays receives a fairly bad press as literature. That common estimate may be correct at the end of the day; but it is sometimes based on certain misconceptions about praise poetry, which may appropriately be dealt with here. First, there are undoubtedly departures from factual truth in Gaelic bardic eulogy—the 'exaggerations' and 'insincerities'. But they are there as part of an idealised chiefly portrait which is part of the *given* in this eulogistic tradition. Hence one cannot automatically condemn a bardic poem for calling a weakling a mighty man or a petty warlord the prince of the Gaels. It is the genre that calls the tune. And here we should also recall that, working within their conventions, the *filidh* themselves had developed a sense of measure, recognising the possibility and undesirability of excessive praise in a specific case, just as they held that unmerited satire would rebound on its composer. Secondly, one should not think of official eulogy and elegy as a mere 'bread and butter' exercise: it had an important role and function in the life of the community, whether in celebration or in mourning; and there was no lack of seriousness or sincerity in the poets' commitment to traditional Gaelic society.

And thirdly, at least where the more considerable poets are concerned, it is wrong to think of the bardic poet as merely a grovelling toady; backed up by the solidarity of his profession he can cajole, hector or remonstrate, suggest political action or criticise present policy—and frequently does so.

The value system against which the individual chief is measured does not change. In many respects it can be traced back to the earliest court poetry we in Old Irish, and parallels in other literatures suggest that certain features may be of Celtic or even Indo-European provenance. Praise-worthiness derives from certain cardinal attributes, such as nobility, wisdom, strength, generosity, and physical perfection. Praise is expressed by means of largely conventional symbols of these attributes or by subtler allusion. There is, in effect, a quasi-ethical system in which the praiseworthy is the absolute, and the subject of each praise poem ('hymn' might be a better term) is shown to be praiseworthy by associating him with the praiseworthy traits. Thus he can be a 'key to knowledge' or a 'pillar of strength' or a 'treasure house for poets'. Many of the symbols are multi-functional: 'salmon' or 'nut', for instance, have primary connotations of knowledge and wisdom (through their literary-mythological associations), but may also connote strength and rule in the case of the 'king of fishes', and fecundity and solidarity in the case of the nut in its cluster. Or again, depending on context, a tree can be a genealogical symbol, both of ancestry and of posterity; or it can represent pre-eminent height, or overshadowing protection, or stout resistance to the flood, or shapeliness and beauty, or a source of nourishment and provision. The commonly used symbols included selected animals, birds and fishes; note also that certain parts of the human body are capable of becoming praiseworthy—e.g. luxuriant hair, radiant face, ruddy cheek, clear eye and shapely calf. There is need of more work on the origins and articulation of these systems.

Praise-poetry also promotes the idea of 'the Gaels'—the native aristocracy, united in their descent from the sons of Míl. This is done by calling the subject of a praise-poem 'descendant' or 'scion' of some famous character from prehistory, and associating him with one of the many poetic names for Ireland or one of the 'high-places' of Ireland from literature or *dindshenchus*. It made a specific patron King of all Gaeldom for a moment to call him 'heir of Neil from Cobhthach's plain'. In a given poem these generalised references alternate with much more specific ones referring to the patron's actual forefathers and domains. (In a Scottish poem, of course, these names are Scottish ones.)

One key ideological element remains to be mentioned: the role of the poet himself, the provider of fame. The set of symbols associated with illustriousness, the images of brightness such as 'star', 'sun', 'flame', etc., are accompanied by the susurrus, 'no poet, no king'. The good ruler is praised for his generosity to poets, thereby assuring himself of a good name. A striking recurrent image is that of the patron as husband, the poet as wife, which can lead the poet to claim the right to sit and to sleep next to the patron, or to claim to be the latter's bride, with a right to unique intimacy and faithfulness from his 'spouse'. The poem *Feuch féin an obair-se, a Aodh* was long held to be a superb love-song by a girl torn between husband and lover, until it was pointed out that it is in fact a poet's apology to his patron on being wooed away to another master. Various other reflexes of this special relationship recur, and it is an important and distinctive element in the court poetry as a whole.

A bardic eulogy normally has a theme, arising out of the circumstances of the recipient, the occasion, and so on. This theme is usually encapsulated in the first line of the poem, which acts as a sort of key signature for the whole. (It is also, incidentally, required that the last line echo the first line.) Examples might include 'Archibald [Earl of Argyll] is prince of the Gaels', 'Pay attention to me, o king of the Maguires', 'Decay is near for Poesy'; the first lines quoted indicate that the first is celebratory, the second minatory, the third elegaic in tone.

The poem may contain more than one 'movement', or 'moment'—e.g. an elegy may keep distinct '*le roi est mort*' and '*vive le roi*'. A particularly prevalent device is the *apologue* (i.e. parable or exemplum), preceded by a general rehearsal of the theme or résumé of the facts the poet wishes to comment on, and followed by an application of the apologue to the previously mentioned circumstances. In some cases it appears that apologues have been preserved minus the rest of their poems: they can be masterpieces of economical tale-telling.

On the whole, however, large-scale structural organisation is of small importance, given the nuclear stanza form and the basically linear progression natural to the oral-aural milieu. There can be verbal or conceptual linkage from the end of one verse to the beginning of the next, sequences of verses with minimal differentiation (and hence maximum emphasis on the slowly unfolding 'story'), and priamel (i.e. 'not A, nor B, nor C ..., but X'). The fact that these poems were composed for public recitation added its own constraints and licences. There is much apostrophe, a large canvas, primary colours; there is frequent switching between second and third person (i.e. between addressing the chief and addressing the assembled court); and full use is made of key-words or key-concepts to which the poet brings us back at intervals, often to 'fix' the conclusion of one section in our minds before moving on to another.

It is sometimes suggested that bardic verse was understood only by the *filidh* themselves. This seems unlikely. There would certainly have been a spectrum of levels of understanding; but the whole purpose of these compositions was to get a message, which could be a delicate and complex one, across to the people who mattered in the clan. The complex word order, with chevilles and apostrophes worked in, can certainly cause problems for the modern reader on occasion; but we do not know how much help the hearers of *dán díreach* received from the tempo and punctuation of the *reacaire*. Given that a significant proportion of the Highland aristocracy can be shown to have been literate in the Classical language, it seems preferable to take occasional references to the difficulty of understanding bardic verse as being tendentious or malicious.

Some of the most sustained examples of the high art of the *filidh* are to be found in bardic religious verse. Some poets were particularly associated with religious verse—e.g. Muireadhach Albanach's brother Donnchadh Mór Ó Dálaigh, and later Aonghus Fionn Ó Dálaigh and Tadhg Óg Ó hUiginn. In its central form bardic religious verse presents a slightly odd reflex of ordinary court poetry, with God as patron and the poet as a would-be Christian penitent, courting His favours. 'Bend my knee for me, o Lord,' the poets expostulate. Also prominent are the themes of the Passion and of Judgement, the relationships between mankind and Christ being conceived in a framework of brehon law.

The principal editor of these poems, Fr. Lambert McKenna, was moved to suggest that they were composed to be read out like secular poems, 'for the displaying of professional skill', or to be created for 'their author's own pious pleasure, or by way of practice in technique.' That this may not have been the whole story is suggested by a poem of Donnchadh Mór's which concludes:

> Rob sgiath dídin an duan-sa
> do mharbhaibh na mór-shluagh-sa;
> dom aos aithnidh don fheadhain
> dar n-aithribh dar n-oideadhaibh.

> Guidhim fós an bhFáidh bhéaras
> neamh da gach neach mheibhréabhas,
> go rod-beara ar neamh a-nonn
> gach fear dá ngeabha a ngabham.

(May this poem (*duan*) be a protecting shield to the dead of these great hosts; to my acquaintances amongst the group, to our fathers and our fosterfathers.

I pray too to the Prophet who will give Heaven to each one who will memorise (this): may He convoy over into Heaven every man who recites my words.)

The theatrical tone of bardic verse is well suited to ecstatic exclamation, and its method of envisioning a conventional scene by means of rapid 'close-ups'—e.g. the lattice of coagulating rivulets of blood caused by the crown of thorns—gives it a claim to be considered seriously as meditational poetry. A doubt remains as to how and why this genre actually became associated with the Classical *filidh*. Conceivably there is a clue in their regular use of the term *deachmhadh* ('tithe') to describe it.

A very different speciality of the *filidh*, at least by repute, was satire. From the earliest references in their own learned literature and professional mythology down to modern folklore about poets we find consistent mention of their power to wound with words. Both as individuals and as a group they were acknowledged to have supernatural powers, including thaumaturgy: Highland tradition credited 'Mac Mhuirich Mór' with the power of stirring the elements just like some saint of old. They saw themselves as validators of their patrons' rule (by means of their praise) who were capable of withdrawing their sanction if a ruler's justice faltered. In their traditional world-view, if the rule was blemished the ruler must be blemished and it fell to the poets to expose his shame. It was also acknowledged that that power should not be exercised unreasonably: poets themselves could be discredited; and the individual chief's poet in our period was bound to defend his patron against unjust satire from other poets.

There are several references in Irish historical sources to satires being delivered—most famously in the case of Sir John Stanley, whose obit in the Annals of the Four Masters records that he died (in 1414) after being satirised in revenge for his harrying of the Ó hUiginn bardic family in Meath. And the possibility of hiring Irish poets to satirise the Irish aristocracy was not lost on the English authorities in that period. While acknowledging that the poets themselves had a vested interest in playing up their supernatural aura, we must nevertheless recognise that their claims to represent a source of authority within traditional Gaelic society were made in all seriousness, and carried weight because of the weight attached to good name in an aristocratic, honour-based society. That said, it must be admitted that we do not possess many actual satires—partly, no doubt, because such compositions would not commend themselves for inclusion in the *duanaire* class of manuscript. On the other hand, a number of poems survive in which the poet talks about satire in a menacing way when addressing a patron who is not treating the poet as he should. (The main difference between Gaelic satire and the Horatian tradition of an indignant individual poet inveighing against the excesses of his contemporaries is that here, at least in theory, an individual chief is singled out for 'blacklisting' or 'excommunication' by the poets as a class.) To judge from some examples in the Book of the Dean of Lismore it would appear that in the Classical period a full-blooded satire consisted of a character assassination by means of 'anti-praise'—imputation of an absence of the praiseworthy qualities and an abundance of satire-worthy defects and vices. Where the good chief attracted epithets of radiance, nobility, generosity and purity, the victim of satire was portrayed in terms of darkness, meanness and degradation, with their own repertoire of symbols to suit.

Implicit in the duty of defending one's patron against satire is the idea of poetic combat, which also manifests itself in early references to competitions for pre-eminence in poetry and, in practical Early Modern terms, in evidence for rivalry to secure patronage. This did not become institutionalised as a literary genre in the way that flyting did in the Scots tradition; at least, it does not make a great impact in surviving sources. Nevertheless, we have a couple of elegies for Allan MacDonald of Clanranald (ob. 1509), one conventional one from a 'friendly' source in the Red Book of Clanranald and one decidedly unfriendly one which has reached the Dean's Book from a less official source; these could well be taken as a pair in the present sense. As for man to man flyting between *filidh* the evidence is largely indirect; but it seems likely enough that it could take place. One should mention here *Iomarbhágh na bhFileadh* ('The Contention of the Poets'), a many-handed poetic controversy in strict metre dating from the last years of the Classical period, in which the claims of the Northern and Southern Half of Ireland to pre-eminence in the vanishing Gaelic continuum were debated with conspicuous learning, advocacy and sometimes artistry.

Better attested, though still meagre in bulk beside the more prestigious poetry of eulogy, is the involvement of the *filidh* in a species of love poetry which combines native themes and techniques with the modes and concepts of *amour courtois*. The circumstances of its emergence in *dán* remain obscure in several ways. The majority of dateable examples are from later sixteenth and early seventeenth century Ireland, when we know that some members of the nobility were taking an interest in English literature; but a group of Scottish examples, the work of both professionally trained and amateur poets, is found in the Book of the Dean; and the same source also preserves some poems attributed to the late fourteenth century Gerald, Earl of Desmond, who has been cited as possibly the first practitioner of this sort of poetry (though in fact these poems do not represent the central categories of later *dánta grádha*) and as evidence for a Norman-French channel of transmission for the exotic elements. The question is further complicated by evidence for continental love-themes of a more popular sort, and in some ways nearer to the proposed continental models, in Irish and to a lesser extent Scottish Gaelic popular songs.

Love may be expressed in praise-terms, and a grammar of attributes and analogues for the ideal lady is in evidence. To some extent the materials for it already existed, in the descriptions of lovely ladies in the early prose tales, in religious poetry addressed to Mary, and in honorific verses to the wives of chiefs in bardic eulogy. Sometimes the lady appears as a supernatural visitant who disturbs the poet's sleep; again there are echoes of the early tales. Once bitten by love, the poet is in a state of illness, delirium or madness, and a well-developed symptomatology of love exists to be drawn on. The minds that delighted in metaphysical paradoxes in bardic religious verse revelled in the possibilities of love as a living death, being not oneself, and having one's heart given or stolen away. An antiquarian or legalistic streak is to be seen in the poets' readiness to cite literary precedents for their predicament. Other features worth noting include the 'farewell to last night', the 'love versus sex' debate, and the gossips and jealous husbands who frustrate the lovers' designs. A number of poems provide 'crossword' clues to the girl's name (couched in terms of the old ogham alphabet) and there are a couple of acrostics—one elaborate Irish one containing both the man's and the girl's name. Finally there are the departures from the 'first position' of *amour courtois*—poems where the poet renounces Love, or curses women, or pours scorn on 'pale and wan' lovers and sends up the symptomatology.

The *filidh* composed on a wide variety of informal subjects, sometimes in *dán díreach* and sometimes in the looser *óghláchas* metres. Some of the most famous poems of all fall into this category. Examples include Muireadhach Albanach's lament for his dead wife, the poems connected with his trip to the Holy Land, and the informal 'deathbed' poems in his name; Ó Maoil-Chiaráin's poem for his son Fearchar who died while on a poetic visit to Ireland; and Gofraidh Fionn's elegy for his son. Again, at certain junctures winds of political change ruffle the poets' mantles and they provide us with poems on the passing of old orders which can be more accessible than many of the odes to individuals. The Dean's Book contains a fine example on the passing of the Lordship of the Isles, and there are several from the time of the Plantation of Ulster. Humour is not unrepresented: there are mock eulogies and elegies to unheroic subjects and tours de force on awful pipers or those who snore like them. Moralising is also common—on the vanity of human aspirations, the fickleness of friendship, the fleetingness of youth, and so on. A discreetly muted note of aggression creeps into Cathal Mac Mhuirich's parody of a colleague's imperfect command of *dán díreach*, with its cruelly accurate imitations of the other's solecisms. Often the pattern of survival in manuscripts, together with the actual tone of the poems, suggests the clubbish atmosphere of somewhere like the bardic schools, a men's world of badinage and wordplay.

In a well-known section of the introduction to his Gaelic translation of John Knox's *Book of Common Order* (published in 1567) John Carswell apologised for his imperfect command of Classical Gaelic—it was actually very good—saying that only a few scholars of poetry and history were fully competent to write in it. That he should have felt it necessary to do this is indicative of the touchy exclusiveness that characterised the Classical tradition. An *ollamh* could compose an informal piece on a flippant topic as an 'exercise for the left hand,' or a super-charged version of the verse and prose medley known as *crosántacht* and properly associated with *crosáin* ('buffoons'); but neither a junior poet nor a musician nor even an aristocratic amateur could offer a formal ode in strict metre. One of the extant inaugural odes (to Feidhlimidh Ó Conchobhair) was composed by Torna Ó Maol-chonaire, a member of a family of historians rather than poets. It is interesting not only because of its testimony on inauguration practices, but also because it is composed in a loose form of a rather distinctive metre usually associated with informal compositions. It has been plausibly suggested that there could be a connection—a delicate gesture of deference from one branch of the *literati* to another.

The other main areas of Early Modern Gaelic literature which can be associated with the court tradition were the heroic ballads—the genuine lays which formed the starting-point for MacPherson's Ossianic creations—and the heroic-romantic tales. In each case there is some evidence to associate the literary poets with them. For the ballads there is their syllabic metre and the use of the terms *duan* and *laoidh* (which are equally applied to court eulogies), together with the antiquarian element which is prominent in some of them. Similar considerations, including continuity from the Mediæval period, and their status as written texts, apply to the prose romances, though many details remain obscure. What the *filidh* did not concern themselves with was the vernacular stressed-metre poetry—at least until the very end of our period, when we find Niall MacMhuirich composing two elegies for Allan Mac-Donald of Clanranald (who died from wounds received at Sheriffmuir in 1715), one Classical and one vernacular. Prior to that the normal situation would presumably have been more like that which we find with the seventeenth century MacLeods of Dunvegan, whose court found room for Ó Muirgheasáin the trained poet and also for the vernacular compositions of Roderick Morison ('The Blind Harper'), not to mention the songs of Mary MacLeod.

When the end came, as the heads of Gaelic noble families turned away from traditional Gaelic culture, the literary links with Ireland withered away, and even within the Highlands the channels of literary intercourse became attenuated, the representatives of the literary families found themselves constrained to find new callings—as clerks or ministers or tenant farmers. In some cases they or their descendants became associated with the vernacular literature, with important consequences for the latter.

Estimates as to the achievement of the Classical period vary. The older generation of Gaelic scholars, in the later nineteenth century and the earlier part of the twentieth century, tended almost to venerate the Classical poets as proud symbols of a period in which Gaelic had an indigenous and stable high culture, beyond the contagion of the Ossianic controversy and the trauma of the Highland Clearances. Accordingly, these scholars emphasised the 'classical' virtues of polish, elegance, power of expression, nobility of sentiment, sense of order and loyalty to discipline. In more recent times Olympian virtues such as these have become less popular in general, and the reputation of bardic verse has suffered accordingly, more emphasis now being placed on the shortcomings of excessive formalism, lack of passion and directness, and so forth. Nevertheless, it has continued to be defended, albeit in a more discriminating way, by the critics who are most closely acquainted with its ways. As one ought really to expect, there is better and worse bardic technique in it, and good and bad poetry. Less predictably, considering the volume and time-span and the number of practitioners represented, there is virtually no incompetent versification: whether or not this was a good thing in other respects, the training of the bardic schools created a safety-net to ensure certain minimum standards for the profession, which the more creative and adventurous would use as a starting point. Again, the relationship between the Classical and vernacular traditions is now more clearly understood; and we recognise that the learned, literate tradition has influenced, in one way or another, the creation of such diverse vernacular works as Duncan Bàn Macintyre's *Moladh Beinn Dobhrain*, *Òran na Comhachaig*, and William Ross's *Òran Eile*, while Iain Lom's independence of spirit and readiness to shame the MacDonald chiefs into taking action on the Keppoch murders can similarly be traced back to the way in which the Classical *filidh* regarded their role in society. There was an irony in this continuity of tradition, however: in their heyday the learned poets would have drawn a firm line between their own activities and those of vernacular composers; indeed some references suggest that they would not have dissented strongly from the Lowland estimate of the Highland bard.

FURTHER READING

PRIMARY TEXTS

Bergin, O, *Irish Bardic Poetry* (Dublin, 1970)
Knott, E, *The bardic poems of Tadhg Dall O hUiginn*, 2 vols (Dublin, 1922–26)
Watson, W J, *Scottish Verse from the Book of the Dean of Lismore* (Edinburgh, 1937)

SECONDARY TEXTS

Black, R I, 'The genius of Cathal Mac Mhuirich', *TGSI*, 50 (1976–78), 327–66
Gillies, W, 'Courtly and satiric poems in the Book of the Dean of Lismore', *SS*, 18 (1977), 35–53
—— 'Gaelic and Scots Literature down to the Reformation', *Actes due 2ᵉ colloque de langue et de litterature ecossaises*, Blanchot, J-J and Graf, C (eds) (Strasbourg, 1979), pp 63–79
—— 'The Classical Irish poetic tradition', *Proceedings of the 7th International Congress of Celtic Studies* (Oxford, 1983), pp 108–20
Knott, E, *Irish Classical Poetry* (Dublin, 1957)
Thomson, D S, 'The Mac Mhuirich bardic family', *TGSI*, 43 (1960–63), 276–304
—— 'Gaelic Learned Orders and Literati in Medieval Scotland', *SS*, 12 (1968), 57–78
—— 'Three seventeenth-century bardic poets: Niall Mór, Cathal and Niall MacMhuirich', in *Bards and Makars*, Aitken, A J, McDiarmid, M P and Thomson, D S (eds) (Glasgow, 1977)
—— (ed) *The Companion to Gaelic Scotland* (Oxford, 1983)
Watson, W J, 'Classic Gaelic poetry of panegyric in Scotland', *TGSI*, 29 (1914–19), 194–234

Chapter 16

The Ballad and Popular Tradition to 1660

HAMISH HENDERSON

Scotland, like Switzerland, is—and seems always to have been—a 'multi-ethnic' country, and the various strands of its popular tradition necessarily reflect this chequered linguistic past. Never throughout its entire history has the country had one single unitary language, covering its whole area. It is only in the present decade, with the death of the last Gaelic-speaking monoglots in the Western Isles, and the gradual loss of ground of Scots to English in the former's once impregnable seeming redoubt in the North-East, that the great metropolitan world-language seems set to move in for the kill.

To throw these centennial cultural confrontations into sharp relief, we may recall that when in the mid fourteenth century John Barbour, archdeacon of Aberdeen, was writing his *Bruce*—a poem whose rough-hewn couplets sometimes evoke the rhythm and even the idiom of the Scots ballad stanza—Gaelic was still being spoken, sung and composed in less than 30 miles from the 'ryall bruch', on the middle reaches of Deeside. And St Machar's, the cathedral he officiated in, itself recalls by its very name the ubiquitous band of Celtic saints who christianised—or re-christianised—half western Europe in the Dark Ages.

That Highlanders and the men of the 'plain land' fought together against the English host at Bannockburn is attested by Barbour himself:

> The ferd bataile the noble king   [fourth]
> Tuk till his awne go*ver*nyng.
> And had in-till his cumpany
> The men of Carrik halely
> And off Arghile & of Kentyr
> And off the ilis quharof wes syr
> Angus of Ile, and but all tha
> (XI, 337–43)

Much of the material used by Barbour in his *Bruce* must have been assembled from orally transmitted accounts in the immediate aftermath of the War of Independence. But that some of these were perpetuated in song is expressly stated by the archdeacon:

> I will no*cht* reher*s* the maner
> For quha-sa lik*is* thai may her
> Young wemen quhen thai will play
> Syng it amang thaim ilk day.
>
> (XVI, 527–30)

Indeed, reading the many passages which vividly describe early fourteenth century warfare, one cannot help surmising that echoes of actual balladry have occasionally found their way into the narrative:

> Then *with* a will till him thai yede   [went]
> And ane him by the bridill hynt,   [seized]
> Bot he raucht till him sic a dynt   [fetched] [blow]
> That arme and schuldyr flaw hi*m* fra.
>
> (III,112–15)

If so, echoes of this sort constitute—together with one verse of a song of triumph over the English defeat at Bannockburn, which is preserved in Fabyan's *Chronicle*, and quoted by Marlowe in *Edward II*[1]—the earliest (and tantalisingly fragmentary) indications of the existence of 'ancestor' ballads which anticipate the 'riding ballads' of the sixteenth century by over 200 years.

There is, moreover, a curious ballad-like link with Barbour's *Bruce* at the beginning of a 246-line poem entitled *ane taill of Sir colling ye knyt*. This poem, under which the date 1583 is scribbled, is an earlier version of the classic ballad *Sir Cawline* (No. 61 in Professor F J Child's *English and Scottish Popular Ballads*), which appears in the mid-seventeenth-century English MS. used by Bishop Thomas Percy as the basis for his famous collection *Reliques of Ancient English Poetry*. The first lines of the Scottish poem (which is written in consecutive lines unbroken into stanzas, but which often betrays an underlying stanzaic pattern) are as follows:

> Jesus Chryst and tryniti
> That deitt wes on the ruid   [cross]
> to send him grace in all digne
> That luiffis the Scottis bluid
> This be ane knyt corporall
> hardie was and guid
> Sir Coling was the knyt's name
> ane kingis sone was hie
> ut Edvaird the bruce he fuir to fecht   [went]
> In Irland biyond the sie[2]

In the Percy version, the opening lines are:

> Jesus, lord mickle of might,
>   Thay dyed ffor us on the roode,
> To maintaine us in all our right
>   That loves true English blood.

> Ffor by a knight I say my song,
>   Was bold and ffull hardye;
> Sir Robert Briuse wold fforth to ffight,
>   In-to Ireland over the sea.
>
>   (1–8)

Child dismissed these stanzas as 'manifestly belonging to a historical ballad', and the version he printed begins at verse 3 of the Percy MS. ballad, but this recently recovered Scottish poem effectively restores them to their rightful place. The story-line of *Sir Colling* retails the heroic combat of the hero with 'ane alreche [eldritch] knyt', a three-headed giant and a lion—all widely diffused folklore motifs—but the opening lines firmly attach the action to time and place, in the way beloved of traditional singers the world over.

On the evidence of the text, therefore, it looks as if the attitude of the 'Sir Colling' poet to his 'folk' source material bears some resemblance to that of the English 'Gawain-poet', who—at the beginning of that astonishing masterpiece *Sir Gawain and the Green Knight*—frankly acknowledged the oral sources of his tale:

> I schal telle hit as-tit, as I in toun herde,
>   with tonge.

In Barbour's *Bruce*[3] 'Schyr Colyne Cambell' appears among the Scots fighting in Ireland with Edward Bruce, and it seems a reasonable inference (in view of the localisation at the beginning of the poem) that the unknown makar of *Sir Colling* borrowed the name of his hero from this passage. The Scots who fought with the Bruces in their Irish campaign were (according to M P McDiarmid) mainly from the Gaelic-speaking west, and the 'Sir Colling' of the poem accomplishes his feats of valour in order to win the hand of the daughter of the lord of Argyll.

When Barbour was writing his heroic documentary, by far the greater part of Scotland was still Gaelic-speaking, and there are quite a number of passages in late Mediæval and Renaissance Scots poetry which testify to the currency of tales about Gaelic legendary characters among the Lowlanders. The most frequently mentioned heroes are Fyn Makowll (Fionn MacCumhail) and Gow Macmorn (Goll MacMorna). When the Pardoner, in Sir David Lindsay of the Mount's *Ane Satyre of the Thrie Estaits*, is laying out his wares to tempt the gullible (and not so gullible) public he describes two of his wonder-working relics as follows:

> Heir is ane relict lang and braid
> Of fine Macoull the richt chaft blaid,
>   With teith and al togidder:
> Of Collings cow heir is ane horne;
> For eating of Makconnals corne,
>   Was slaine into Baquhidder.[4]

Here we have an incongruous mixture of fabulous legend and local news item, for—*pace* Campbell of Islay, who suggested that the horn of Colling's cow must surely belong to some beast with mythological significance—it seems more likely that the poet, in characteristic Scots 'doon-takin' style, was contrasting the exalted memory of the legendary hero with the sort of small-clachan gossip which would find ready entry to a country newspaper in this or any other century.[5]

The religious reformers of the sixteenth century were also well aware of the strength of Gaelic popular tradition, and they naturally sought to combat it in the interests of the Protestant faith. This is explicitly acknowledged in the dedicatory epistle to that remarkable work, the translation into Gaelic of the *Book of Common Order* executed by John Carswell, Bishop of the Isles, and printed in Edinburgh in April 1567. Carswell, writing in the literary Gaelic common to both Ireland and Scotland in his day, has this to say about the secular tales circulating in the bounds of Argyll:

> And great is the blindness and darkness of sin and ignorance and of understanding among the composers and writers and supporters of the Gaelic, in that they prefer and practise the framing of vain, hurtful, lying, earthly stories about the Tuath de Dhanond, and about the sons of Milesius, and about the heroes and Fionn Mac Cumhail with his giants, and about many others whom I shall not number or tell of here in detail, . . .'[6]

Some of the 'Ossianic' tales here denounced by Bishop Carswell can be collected in the North Highlands to this day, so we can be sure that in the sixteenth century they must have been in common currency from Caithness to the Mull of Kintyre. And it is probably not being too sanguine to assume that already many versions of the international tales to be found (in some cases) throughout Europe and into Asia had already penetrated the Gaelic world, and assumed their localised identity. When, in 1859 and 1860 the great Highland collector John Francis Campbell of Islay (Iain Og Ile) assembled the texts of stories gathered for him by various helpers, he found that many of them closely resembled wonder-tales already being put on record in various parts of Europe. The pioneering work of the Brothers Grimm had sparked off similar collecting efforts in a number of countries, and in the massive index *The Types of the Folktale*, begun by the Finnish scholar Antii Aarne and later vastly enlarged by the American Stith Thompson, the Scottish Gaelic versions which will be found listed beside (for example) versions in Czech, Lithuanian, Turkish, Italian or Greek, are mostly those printed in Campbell's *Popular Tales of the West Highlands.*[7] Since then the number of such stories collected in Scots Gaelic versions has increased twenty-fold following the setting up of the School of Scottish Studies in 1951. For this, the dedicated and self-sacrificing collecting work of the late Calum Maclean is largely responsible.

The international folktales which have surmounted the barriers of language, geography and culture can usefully be referred to by their numbers in the Aarne-Thompson index: e.g. Campbell's 'Cath nan Eun' (the Battle of the Birds) is AT 313. In many cases the versions of international tale types which have found their way into the Gaelic world must have crossed the broad culture-zone inhabited by speakers of English and Lowland Scots. Until comparatively recently, the number of folktale versions in English and Scots which had been put on record was surprisingly small, but the fieldwork of the School of Scottish Studies among the Scots-speaking 'travellers' (or tinkers) has disclosed an enormous folktale treasury until now hidden away in their own secret world. Examination of this vast corpus of narrative artistry, and comparative study of the same or similar tales on record as being in the repertoires of storytellers as far away as Turkey, Iran and India, make it clear that we are dealing with an international *Märchengut* going at least as far back as the Middle Ages—and, in the case of maybe a hundred tale types, probably a good deal further.

An example of one of these—which must stand for many—is the type already mentioned, AT 313 ('The Girl as Helper in the Hero's Flight', alias 'The Magic Flight'), of which the Jason and Medea legend provides one early example. 'Every schoolboy knows' how Jason arrived in Colchis in search of the Golden Fleece, how Medea helped him to accomplish the tasks set him by her father Aeetes, and how they made good their escape together. This is certainly one of the basic folktales of the human race; indeed, it is easy to see why, for the storyline can be summarised briefly as the boy winning his girl and carrying her away in defiance of her father's wrath and pursuit. That the story penetrated the Gaelic world very early is indicated by the vast number of versions—'several hundred', according to Bealoideas XII (1941)—in the archives of the Irish Folklore Commission; it is referred to as 'one of the most popular of all Irish folktales'. Scottish Gaelic versions have been put on record by J F Campbell, and by collectors working for Edinburgh University. However, the version which is in many ways the most illuminating, as far as the more obscure corners of the tradition are concerned, is one couched in the most delectable, racy Aberdeenshire Scots, which was collected from Geordie Stewart, a 'traveller' then aged 24, in Jeannie Robertson's wee house in Causewayend, Aberdeen. This is *The Green Man of Knowledge*, a tale which provided the title for Alan Bruford's excellent short collection of stories from oral tradition.[8] Although the characters in Geordie's story speak in mid-twentieth-century 'Aiberdeen-awa', internal evidence links his version with the already mentioned anonymous romance *Sir Gawain and the Green Knight*, which is written in the North-West Midland dialect of English, and is believed to have been composed in Lancashire in the last third of the fourteenth century. There is evidence to suggest that an unrecovered English folk version is one at least of the sources of this remarkable poem; if that is the case, Geordie Stewart's *Green Man*[9] could well be a far out relative of that hypothetical folk artefact, which I have always hoped might turn up among the 'Pikies' and 'Diddiecoyes' (English travellers). The complex relationships involved prompt two reflections:

1) We are unlikely to do justice to the ramifications of folktale diffusion if we do not allow for extensive interpenetration between contiguous folk cultures, and

2) an ancient Celtic substratum likely underlies much of the folklore of England, as well as that of Lowland Scotland.

(The text of Geordie's story, together with a survey of the historic-geographic distribution of this tale type will be found in *Scottish Studies*, vol. 2, part 1, 1958.)

A much lighter piece of work, the *Schwank* (comic folktale) 'Silly Jack and the Factor' (= AT 1600, 'The Fool as Murderer'), which was one of Jeannie Robertson's favourites, is in her 'wey o't' as firmly and elegantly domiciled in the Scottish North-East as 'The Green Man of Knowledge'; consequently, the listener (or reader) could be forgiven for imagining it to be a local short story belonging to the eighteenth century at the earliest, but a glance at its widespread distribution throughout northern Europe (and particularly along the Baltic coast) leads to the irresistible conclusion that here, too, we are dealing with a piece of popular tradition which must have been imported to Scotland—if not, like the Pardoner's relics,

> 'fra the Cam of Tartarie,
> weill seald with oster-schellis',[10]

quite possibly on a vessel bringing merchandise from one of the Hanseatic ports, after 'the Illuster and Vailyeand Campioun, Schir William Wallace' wrote to re-open the trading connection.

Just as many of these prose narratives were undoubtedly imports, so many of the narrative songs which were to find their way into Child's *English and Scottish Popular Ballads* were just as certainly incomers from across the North Sea, or 'land-loupers' which came up from the South, after crossing the English Channel—in some cases starting their fabulous migration in the Mediterranean world.

A revealing example of this latter peregrination is provided by 'Lord Randal My Son'—as Salinger calls it in *The Catcher in the Rye*—which is No. 12 in Child. The version printed by Sir Walter Scott in his *Minstrelsy of the Scottish Border* in 1802 can claim to be one of the two most famous ballad texts in the world (the other is 'Edward'), and generations of Scots poetry lovers have undoubtedly accepted without question the wholly Scottish national identity of this haunting piece. However, the truth is that it is only one version of a very widely diffused international ballad, and that the earliest indication of its presence in a particular culture comes from Italy, where it seems to have been popular 350 years ago. A Veronese broadside of 1629 gives the first three lines of 'L'Avvelenato' (The Poisoned Man), an unmistakable first cousin of Lord Randal:

> *'Dov' andastu iersera*
> *Figliuol mio ricco, savio e gentile?*
> *Dov' andastu iersera'?*

Since then, dozens of versions have been recorded up and down Italy. In

Germany 'die Schlangenköchin' (literally, the woman who cooked snakes) is manifestly the same ballad. Although the texts we have are all from the nineteenth century, or later, it is plain that they represent a centuries-old tradition, as do (for example) the Dutch, Swedish, Danish and Hungarian variants.

'Lord Randal' is an 'all-dialogue ballad': that is, the entire action is unfolded through conversation between the protagonists—here a mother, and her son who has been out hunting or courting (or maybe both). The ballad commonly called 'Edward' (whatever the hero's name) is No. 13 in Child; it, too, is an all-dialogue ballad involving a son and a mother. The version sent by Sir David Dalrymple (later Lord Hailes) to Thomas Percy for inclusion in his *Reliques of Ancient English Poetry* is generally now accepted to be a re-write by a gifted poet (probably Hailes himself) of a traditional ballad which had probably reached him by oral transmission. Professor Archer Taylor, who made a detailed study of Child 13, regarded it as 'a revision of a folksong, a re-writing which may justly compare with Goethe's "Heidenröslein" '.[11] Although the name he gave the ballad was 'Edward', Child did not make the Hailes' version his A or principal text; the pride of place in this section of his great thesaurus goes to 'Son Davie', which was collected by William Motherwell from a Mrs King of Kilbarchan, and printed by him in his *Minstrelsy, Ancient and Modern* in 1827. This is, quite unmistakably, an unamended version collected from a folksinger.

It may well be asked, at this point, how legitimately we may enrol ballads like the Scott 'Lord Randal' and the Hailes 'Edward'—or indeed the Motherwell 'Son Davie'—which were all put on record in the eighteenth century or later, among the products of popular tradition 'before 1660'. The answer has to be sought in studies like the one, already mentioned, by Archer Taylor; if a ballad story appears in the tradition of a number of countries— in the case of 'Edward' there are numerous Swedish, Danish and Finnish versions—we can confidently assume a much longer history than the evidence of collection might indicate. Taylor's own conclusion about 'Edward' was that it probably originated in Scotland or England during the Middle Ages, and subsequently travelled to Scandinavia.

Supporting evidence is provided by the 'props' in the older versions; the murderer has a hawk, a hound, a steed, and a bloodied sword; he has landed property ('towirs and ha'), and the whole atmosphere is aristocratic; as Taylor expresses it, 'this courtly background ... implies customs and manners quite foreign to the world in which the modern traditional forms move'.[12] Here he is evidently thinking of the versions collected in this century in the United States.

As the indefatigable Aberdeenshire collectors Gavin Greig and the Rev James Duncan of Lynturk did not recover a version of 'Edward' in the early years of this century—although theirs is one of the largest folksong collections in the world—Taylor was forced to conclude that Child 13 had died out in the country of its presumptive origin. This conclusion suffered a spectacular disproof in 1953, when the great Aberdeen ballad singer Jeannie Robertson (1907–75) sang a version for collectors which she had learnt from her aunt

Maggie Stewart. Jeannie was a settled urbanised 'traveller' (or tinker), but her version undoubtedly makes the most 'aristocratic' impression of the lot. Here are the first two verses, as quoted in the present writer's article 'At the Foot o' yon Excellin' Brae':

> 'Oh, what's the blood 'its on your sword,
> My son, David, ho son David?
> What's that blood 'its on your sword?
> Come, promise, tell me true'
> 'Oh, that's the blood of my grey meir,
> Hey, lady Mother, ho, lady Mother,
> That's the blood of my grey meir,
> Because it wadnae rule by me.'
>
> 'Oh, that blood it is owre clear,
> My son David, ho, son David,
> That blood it is owre clear.
> Come, promise, tell me true.'
> 'Oh, that's the blood of my greyhound,
> Hey, lady Mother, ho, lady Mother,
> That's the blood of my greyhound.
> Because it wadnae rule by me.'
>
> $(1–16)^{13}$

Another of the ballads in the repertoire of Jeannie's aunt Maggie was 'Little Sir Hugh and the Jew's Daughter' (Child 155). Here again, we encounter what is manifestly a Mediæval ballad, although the earliest recorded text belongs to the eighteenth century (sent to Percy from an unidentified Scottish source, and printed by him in 1765). Another justly celebrated version is that provided by Mrs Brown of Falkland, the Aberdeenshire lady who was the repository of many of the finest orally-transmitted ballads ever recorded. Mrs Brown's version mentions 'merry Lincoln', thus providing proof positive that the story of the ballad derives from the legend of Hugh of Lincoln, which is told in the Annals of Waverley, under the year 1255, by a contemporary writer. This Hugh was a boy supposed to have been crucified by the Jews; outbreaks of irrational panic occasioned by such rumours led to brutal persecutions of the Jews in a number of countries throughout the Middle Ages.

Yet another ballad undoubtedly originating in Mediæval England is 'Young Beichan' (Child 53), which clearly has some connection with the legend of Gilbert Beket, father of Saint Thomas, the martyred Archbishop. However, the essential features of the storyline—the hero being rescued from prison 'in furrin parts' by his jailor's daughter, and the latter eventually coming by sea to claim him, and prevent his marrying another woman—are widely diffused motifs found in several separate national traditions. Mrs Brown knew two quite distinct versions of this ballad, and gave them both to Robert Jamieson in 1783; one is Child's A text ('Young Bicham') and the other his C text ('Young Bekie'). For this latter Mrs Brown provided a tune.

In his *The Ballad and the Folk*—one of the most important books about the ballads published in this century—Professor David Buchan endeavours to show that Mrs Brown was able, although an exceedingly literate woman who wrote verses and read Ossian, to recreate her ballads at every singing, using the techniques employed by non-literate singers:

> The traditional singer does not learn individual songs as fixed texts, but learns instead both a method of composition and a number of stories. By this method he re-composes each individual story every time he performs. While, however, he re-creates the story's narrative essence, he actually creates the individual lines and shapes the individual structure at the moment of performance: he composes the text as he re-composes the story. Each rendering of the story is, then, an 'original text'.[14]

Buchan's central contention is that Mrs Brown was able to perform this feat. The springboard from which he took off will be found in an article by Bertrand H Bronson; reprinted in *The Ballad as Song* (University of California Press, 1969); referring to two versions of 'The Lass of Roch Royal' (Child 76) recorded in 1783 and 1800 respectively he opined:

> What Mrs Brown was trying for in the version of 1800 was, not to recover her own text of 1783, but to recover, or re-create, the ballad itself, the essential, ideal 'lass of Roch Royal', as it exists in solution in the sum of all its traditional variations...What was it she had carried in her memory? Not a *text*, but a *ballad*: a fluid entity soluble in the mind, to be concretely realized at will in words and music.[15]

And yet, in the same article, Bronson raises the very objections that are bound to occur to anyone who examines Mrs Brown's texts with any care:

> Her versions seldom show the gaps and chasms, the rugged and abrupt leaps of narrative which are such characteristic and vivid features of traditional balladry. They show, on the contrary, an expository skill, a faculty of neat transition and summary, which is doubtfully welcome at this stage of art. It is symptomatic too, that there are almost no real obscurities of phrase or idea, such as often appear in pure oral transmission. There are occasional moral observations and pious reflections, especially at the ends of her ballads, which are little above the broadside level and which jar our sense of fitness. It can hardly be an accident that where the erotic note is bluntly struck in other versions, in Mrs Brown's it is side-stepped or soft-pedalled.[16]

Buchan's promotion of Mrs Brown of Falkland as a 'singer of tales' able to recreate her ballads at each singing has been strongly challenged by Holger Olof Nygard, by Flemming Andersen and Thomas Pettitt and by the present writer.[17] What is and will remain undisputed is that—however they came into being—the ballad texts put on record by Mrs Brown in 1783 and 1800 are among the very finest ever collected.

Her obvious favourites nearly all belong to the 'magical and marvellous' category, and include such treasures as 'Gil Brenton', 'Willie's Lady', 'The

Twa Sisters', 'Allison Gross', and 'Thomas Rhymer'. These can all be assigned to a period long anteceding the mid seventeenth century, irrespective of the dates when they were first put on record. These ballad texts are unexampled for aesthetic power and grace, and would alone entitle their preserver to the gratitude and love of subsequent generations.

It is when we approach the broad acreage of the Scottish historical ballads that we can feel less defensive about dates and centuries. 'Gud Wallace' (Child 157) is evidently based on a story in the fifth book of Blind Harry's *Wallace*— although, as in the case of Barbour's *Bruce*, it is by no means unlikely that an earlier ballad or ballads on the same subject may have entered the epic poem, and then (so to speak) found an oral outlet from its confines.

A fragment of a Border ballad probably composed not long after the event it describes is preserved by Hume of Godscroft in his *History of the Houses of Douglas and Angus* (1644): this is 'The Knight of Liddesdale':

> The Countesse of Douglas out of her boure
>   she came,
> And loudly there that she did call:
> 'It is for the Lord of Liddesdale
>   That I let all these teares downe fall'.
>
> (Child 160)

Sir William Douglas, the knight of Liddesdale, was assassinated in 1353, while hunting in Ettrick Forest, by the retainers of his godson William Lord Douglas—the motive being, according to Godscroft, a well founded suspicion that the dead man had been having an affair with his murderer's wife. The sole piece of evidence for this—but not one to be disregarded—is the above mentioned lost ballad.

A far more resounding event which became famous in Border song and story was the Battle of Otterburn, fought on 19 August 1388; this affray had the honour of being described in vivid French prose by Froissart, and in heroic songs by English and Scottish ballad makers; the best known of these— by name at least—is 'Chevy Chase' (Child 162). There were in fact two distinct ballads about the battle, and the other 'The Battle of Otterburn' (Child 161)— is generally regarded as the older. It is certainly the one which spawned the variants collected in the eighteenth and early nineteenth centuries which put the Scots—as opposed to the English—point of view. It is also the one which modern Revival singers have put back into 'folk' currency in recent years:

> 'But I have dreamd a dreary dream,
>   Beyond the isle of Sky;
> I saw a dead man win a fight,
>   And I think that man was I'.

This is strong poetry, and there is nothing in the other rather laboured ballad to match it.

In the *Complaynt of Scotland* there is a reference to the 'Hunttis of Chevat' as being among 'the sangis of natural music of the antiquite' sung by shepherds. Another song mentioned there is 'The Battel of the Hayrlau'; this undoubtedly refers to the famous set-to between MacDonald of the Isles and a Royal Army under the Earl of Mar which took place in 1411 in the Garioch district of Aberdeenshire. The earliest known text of the 'folk' ballad of Harlaw—'folk' as opposed to the ornate literary ballad about the battle which Ramsay printed in his *Ever Green* (1724)—appeared in Alexander Laing's *The Thistle of Scotland* (Aberdeen 1823); it is a three verse fragment, and it includes an incongruous reference to 'the red-coat lads'. Since then several lengthy versions of the ballad have turned up, including a splendid one sung by Jeannie Robertson; this is in the archives of the School of Scottish Studies. Like all 'modern' versions it seemingly flies in the face of history by giving the Forbeses a leading part in the battle, and killing off 'the great MacDonald' (who in fact did not die at Harlaw). These anomalies have led several critics—including Child himself—to dismiss the 'folk' ballad as a comparatively modern production, but David Buchan has subjected the historical facts behind the ballad to fresh scrutiny, and powerfully reinforced the idea that the nineteenth and twentieth century versions are in fact descendants of a very old traditional song, inevitably altered and occasionally 'distorted' in the course of time.[18]

Although the Robin Hood ballads are distinctively English, and their setting is invariably Nottingham and environs, there is plentiful evidence that they were as popular in Scotland as they were south of Border. In April 1577 the General Assembly of the Kirk of Scotland requested the King to 'discharge [prohibit] playes of Robin Hood, King of May, and sic others, on the Sabbath day'. A fragment of 'Robin Hood and Little John' (Child 125) was recorded from John Strachan, an Aberdeenshire farmer, by Alan Lomax and the present writer in 1951, and a version of 'The Bold Pedlar and Robin Hood' (Child 132) turned up in Aberdeen in 1954; it was sung by Geordie Robertson, a veteran North-East traveller.

A possible contact in the Middle Ages with the Celtic world of Welsh-speakers is suggested by the nomenclature of one ballad: this is 'Glasgerion' (Child 67), which was preserved in the Percy MS. A Scottish variant, 'Glenkindie', was collected from an old woman in Aberdeenshire at the end of the eighteenth century. Kittredge's head-note to this ballad in the one-volume reduction of *English and Scottish Popular Ballads* (1904) draws attention to the appearance of 'The Bret [Briton] Glascurion' in Chaucer's *House of Fame*, where he is joined with the harpers Orpheus, Orion (Arion) and Chiron. Glascurion is also mentioned by Gavin Douglas (copying Chaucer) in his *Palice of Honour*. There is a strong possibility that this character can be identified with Y Bardd Glas Keraint (Keraint the Blue Bard), who is said to have been 'an eminent poet of distinguished birth, son of Owain, Prince of Glamorgan'. The version in the Percy MS. opens:

> Glasgerion was a King's own sonne,
> And a harper he was good.
>
> (Child 67)

The Glenkindie version likewise sets the hero in a courtly setting:

> Glenkindie was ance a harper gude,
> He harped to the King.
>
> (Child 67)

In *The Ballad and the Folk*, Professor Buchan (amplifying a definition of J E Housman) describes the most promising area for the creation of the 'muckle sangs':

> Traditional balladry flourished in a nonliterate, homogeneous, agricultural society, dominated by semi-independent chieftains, that is situated in a remote, hilly, or border region where cultures meet and feuds and wars abound; this kind of society provided both subjects for ballad-story and occasions for ballad performance, and lasted till the advent of widespread literacy.[19]

In view of the abundant evidence of ballad composing up and down Scotland and England, this definition may seem uncomfortably narrow; however, there can be no doubt that it fits the two areas in Scotland which *have* manifestly created a great mass of balladry: the Borders, and the North-East. In the latter, several songs reflecting the 'clannit society' which lingered on in some parts as late as the eighteenth century have been put on record. 'Captain Car', alias 'Edom O' Gordon' (Child 178) bears gory witness to the ferocity of the blood feud which raged between the Gordons (Catholic partisans of Mary Queen of Scots) and their bitter rivals the Forbeses (supporters of Protestantism, and the 'King's Party'). In 1571 Adam Gordon sent Captain Thomas Ker to take the house of Towie in Strathdon and, because the mistress of the house refused to surrender it, it was burnt together with the whole household. The infamy of this deed was grist to the ballad composer's mill, and frequent reshaping engendered stark poignant poetry:

> O bonny, bonny was her mouth,
> And chirry were her cheiks,
> And clear, clear was hir yellow hair,
> Whereon the reid bluid dreips!
>
> Then wi his spier he turnd hir owr;
> O gin hir face was wan!
> He said, You are the first that eer
> I wist alive again.
>
> He turned hir owr and owr again;
> O gin her skin was whyte!
> He said, I might ha spard thy life
> To been some mans delyte.
>
> 'Busk and boon, my merry men all,   [prepare] [pray]

> For ill dooms I do guess;   [fates]
> I cannae luik in that bonny face,
> As it lyes on the grass.'
>   (Child 178)

'The Baron of Bracklay' (Child 203) conflates two episodes in the feud between the Gordons and the Farquharsons of Inverey; the first of these took place in 1592 and the second in 1666. A verse from Child's A text (Laing's *Scarce Ancient Ballads* 1823) expresses in two lines the ineluctable obligation of 'deidly feid':

> Up spake the son on the nourice's knee,
> 'Gin I live to be a man, revenged I'll be.'
>   (Child 203)

Writing about the terrain in which the so-called Border Ballads flourished, A L Lloyd stated:

> The bare rolling stretch of country from the North Tyne and Cheviots to the Scottish southern uplands was for a long time the territory of men who spoke English but had the outlook of Afghan tribesmen; they prized a poem almost as much as plunder, and produced such an impressive assembly of local narrative songs that some people used to label all our greater folk poems as 'Border ballads'.[20]

Well, whether the Borderers spoke 'English' is a moot point, but an inspection of the 'riding ballads' of the Border Marches amply demonstrates that the comparison with the folkways of Pathan tribesmen might not be resented by the one side only. G M Trevelyan found another parallel which transfigures the wild Border reivers who figure in these ballads into epic heroes of classical antiquity:

> Like the Homeric Greeks, they were cruel, coarse savages, slaying each other as the beasts of the forest; and yet they were also poets . . .[21]

Personally, thinking of the manifold grotesqueries and bizarre incidents which give occasional ludicrous colour to the 'riding ballads', I have sometimes wondered whether an apter parallel might not be with Harry the Horse, Spanish John and their Brooklyn gangster mates in the Prohibition-era short stories of Damon Runyan. Just as much blood soaked the sordid reality of that particular period, in any case.

In this connection, it is curious that T F Henderson in his *Scottish Vernacular Literature* referred to the ballads as 'solemnly serious, and devoid of wit and humour'.[22] Even a cursory reading will show that many are impregnated through and through with what can properly be called sardonic gallows-humour; Christian Morgenstern (of *Galgenlieder* fame) is of the same *galère* as the makers of 'Hughie Graham', 'Dick o' the Cow' and 'Jock o' the Side'.

Nearly all of the best known of the Border ballads belong to the sixteenth century: that is, to the century immediately prior to the Union of the Crowns in 1603, and a majority of them belong to the second half of it. It is almost as if the Borderers were determined to make gainful use of the threatened Border while the going was good. An excellent description of the *mores* then prevailing has been provided by George MacDonald Fraser in his book *The Steel Bonnets*,[23] and a rare imaginative poetic assessment of the songs themselves by James Reed in his *The Border Ballads*.[24]

In many ways the most impressive of these blood-drenched story-songs is 'Johnny Armstrong' (Child 169), which chronicles the arrest and execution of a redoubtable magnate of the 'Debatable Land' by James V. In the *Complaynt of Scotland* this ballad is styled 'Jhonne Ermistrangis Daunce', and indeed the feelings it evokes are very similar to those Carlyle describes when recollecting his first hearing of 'McPherson's Rant'—also a song about the execution of a freebooter:

> Sae rantinly, sae wantonly,
> Sae dauntinly gaed he.
> He played a tune and danced it roon
> Below the gallows tree.

The dance of the tragic hero is a recurring theme in literature, and nowhere is it executed with more death-defying smeddum than in these two splendid songs. The ballads, still danced in the Faroes, may no longer have called Scots on to the dancing floor in the sixteenth century, but if any ballad in the whole Child canon could reasonably have entered the lists as a candidate for this sort of treatment, it is certainly 'Johnny Armstrong'. In all versions of the ballad King James V is quite explicitly charged with perfidy in the apprehension of Johnny. In this case, as in most others, the sympathies of the ballad maker are strictly with the local hero: he seldom operates on a 'national' scale.

It is a curious fact that in spite of the highly spectacular career of Mary Queen of Scots—ballad material of the most enticing, one would have thought—there are only two ballads which refer to her, and she is not the central figure in either. One is 'Earl Bothwell' (Child 174); this is about the murder of Riccio, and the subsequent assassination of Darnley at Kirk o' Field. It is however a highly partisan English production which must have been composed very soon after Mary's flight to England (May 1568); it ends 'now in England shee dothe remain'.

The other is 'Mary Hamilton' (Child 173), which at one point spawned the well known 'singer's digest' usually called 'The Queen's Maries'. Although at first sight this ballad seems firmly localised at the court of Mary and Darnley, and to have some connection with an incident of 1563 which involved the Queen's apothecary and 'a Frenchwoman that served in the Queen's chamber', there are several puzzling features which have never been adequately explained. First, the name of the protagonist. The Queen's four Maries (who had been with her in France, and returned to Scotland with her in 1561) were surnamed Fleming, Livingstone, Seton and Beaton: yet Hamilton is the name found in most versions of the ballad hitherto recorded.

Furthermore (as Child points out, following Charles Kirkpatrick Sharpe) 'there is a quite extraordinary coincidence between the ballad and the fate of a Mary Hamilton who, in the reign of Peter the Great, was one of the maids of honour to the Russian Empress'. There are also the strange references to the 'jolly sailors, that sail upon the main'; these are charged not to

> 'Let on to my father and mother
> But what I'm coming hame—'
> (Child 173)

which suggests in fact that Mary Hamilton is to die in a foreign land.

Whatever the truth of this still unresolved problem—and it really does seem as if we have here a unique confluence of two distinct ballad traditions—the fact remains that the queen herself is a marginal figure; in Child's A version (Sharpe's Ballad Book, 1824, p 18) she is even referred to as the 'auld queen', a truly incongruous epithet if Mary is accepted as the queen concerned.

Her son King James VI fares no better. His appearance in one of the most celebrated of all ballads is hardly to his advantage; he is tacitly accused of conniving at the murder of the bonny Earl of Moray (hero of Child 181), who was 'unmercifully slain' by the Earl of Huntly at Donibristle in Fife in February 1592. Huntly held a commission to apprehend and bring Moray to trial, on suspicion of his being in league with Bothwell against the king. Edward J Cowan argues that the ballad was 'kirk inspired':

> Moray was widely regarded as the champion of the kirk, as were all who had borne his title. What is less familiar is that three days before Moray's death, Sir John Campbell of Cawdor was assassinated in Argyll. It later transpired that Cawdor's slaying was part of a widespread conspiracy, in wich Huntly was involved, to assassinate the young Earl of Argyll. The murders of Moray and Cawdor were thus connected in a conspiracy which aimed to destroy the two great champions of Scottish protestantism.[25]

The ballad cannot have helped but lower still further James's already base public image: it must be regarded as a trenchant piece of propaganda in favour of the Presbyterian party. It is one of the mysteries of this type of orally powered artistry that such a made-to-order polemical song should, with the passing of the years, have engendered the powerful elegiac poetry of what emerged as a magnificent terse clear-cut narrative song.

We may take leave of the theme of historical and Border ballads with a mention of one of the finest, and also one of the least known. This is 'Lord Maxwell's Last Goodnight' (Child 195). There existed for many years a feud between the Maxwells and their rival clan the Johnstones. John, 9th Lord Maxwell and Sir James Johnstone came to an arranged tryst on 6 April 1608, each bringing one follower. After the parley began, there was an affray between the two followers, and in the confusion which followed Lord Maxwell shot Sir James Johnstone in the back. He fled the country, and the ballad maker composed for him a suitable 'Goodnight' or 'Farewell'.

> Adiew, fair Eskdale, up and down,
>   Where my poor friends do dwell!
> The bangisters will ding them down,   [bullies]
>   And will them sore compel.
>
> But I'll revenge that feed mysell   [feud]
>   When I come ou'r the sea;
> Adiew, my lady and only joy!
>   For I maunna stay with thee.
>   (Child 195)

Four years later Lord Maxwell returned to Scotland, was betrayed into the hands of the Government by the Earl of Caithness (who was a kinsman of his), and beheaded at Edinburgh on 21 May 1613.

'Thus was finally ended', noted Sir Walter Scott, 'by a salutary example of severity, the "foul debate" betwixt the Maxwells and the Johnstones, in the course of which each family lost two chieftains: one dying of a broken heart, one in the field of battle, one by assassination and one by the sword of the executioner'.[26]

Lord Byron, in the preface to *Childe Harold's Pilgrimage*, says: 'The good-night in the beginning of the first canto was suggested by Lord Maxwell's goodnight in the Border Minstrelsy'. This is by no means the only debt Byron owed to balladry: 'So, We'll Go no More A-roving' is without doubt a reminiscence of the chorus of one version of 'The Beggar Man' (Child 279) in Jeannie Robertson 'wey o't':

> Nae mair I'll gang a-rovin'
>   Sae late into the nicht;
> Nae mair I'll gang a-rovin'
>   Though the meen shines ne'er sae bricht.   [moon]

This is of course the ballad which in popular tradition is credited to King James V, in his guise of the 'Gaberlunzie Man'.

There seems to be a general consensus, among folklorists as well as sin-gers—and, indeed the general public—that of all the ballads of the British Isles it is Scottish produce which 'bears the gree'. A glance through Child's great collection affords ready confirmation for this widely shared opinion. But why should this be? It really does seem that our ballad makers had what has been called a 'fierier imagination' than their English counterparts; furthermore, the presence in the cultural hinterland of an exceedingly strong oral tradition in the Celtic world proper has been adduced as a partial explanation. Writing about the song 'Mo Nighean Donn a Cornaig' in a paper 'Realism in Gaelic Poetry' Samuel MacLean MA (i.e. the poet Sorley MacLean) has this to say:

> The subject is tragedy of crime and circumstances, the murder of a young girl by her brothers to prevent a marriage of which they disapproved. The poem is characteristic in its simple intensity, its sheer economy of word, the lack of any romantic appurtenances, the horror that makes little comment, letting the story

speak for itself. It crystallises an attitude to tragedy strangely common in Lowland Scots poetry as well as in Gaelic poetry. It is life contemplated with intense emotion, an emotion that is all the greater because of its reticence; there is no haze or mysticism of any kind. Hence it is essentially a realistic poem if the realism is on the level of the realism of tragic poetry.[27]

The theme of 'Mo Nighean Donn a Cornaig' is in fact related to that of 'The Cruel Brother' (Child 11), but Sorley's words touch on deeper resemblances. Sir James Fergusson is clearly referring to the same general poetic sensibility when he writes:

> ... In those generations of the sixteenth and early seventeenth centuries that produced the best of the ballads there must have existed remarkably widely the instinct for those strokes which distinguish the ballads and make them one of Scotland's principle contributions to European literature. These characteristics I would distinguish as direct movement of the story to its catastrophe, economical statement, a telling choice of episode and memorably succinct dialogue. The story does not move laboriously on from point to point, as in the medieval romances, but—in the best of the ballads—by a swift succession of scenes, almost in the manner of a film, between which much is left to the imagination of an audience obviously accustomed to exercise that faculty.[28]

These particular characteristics are, of course, shared by all European ballad communities, and can be attributed to the techniques and workings of oral creation and recreation themselves—the reader is referred to Chapters 8–11 in David Buchan's *The Ballad and the Folk*—but the Scots seem to have taken particularly kindly to this type of 'folk art'. Maybe it has something to do with the terse epigrammatic speech of the people, documented in dozens of historical anecdotes. Fergusson himself says that 'reported speech from authentic history is full of phrases which might have come straight out of the ballads—or gone straight into them', and he gives several examples of this. Here is one which he does not. In *The Historie and Cronicles of Scotland*, completed in the 1570s, Lindsay of Pitscottie described the meeting of James V and Johnny Armstrong (June 1530) as follows:

> ... When the King saw him and his men so gorgeous in their apparel, and so many braw men under a tyrant's commandment, throwardly he turned about his face, and bade 'take that tyrant out of his sight, saying, What wants yon knave that a King should have?'

In the version of the ballad in Allan Ramsay's *The Ever Green* 'copied from a gentleman's mouth of the name of Armstrong, who is the 6th generation from this John', verse 26 reads:

> Ther hang nine targats at Johnys hat,
>   And ilk ane worth three hundred pound:
> 'What wants that knave that a king suld haif,
>   But the sword of honour and the crown!
>   (Child 169)

Later in Pitscottie's account comes the following passage:

> He, seeing no hope of the King's favour towards him, said very proudly, I am
> but a fool to seek grace at a graceless face.

Verse 22 of the same version of the ballad runs as follows:

> To seik het water beneth cauld yce,
>   Surely it is a great folie:
> I haif asked grace at a graceless face,
>   But there is nane for my men and me.

Variants of this last-quoted verse appear in versions of the ballad published
in seventeenth century English broadsides and miscellanies—see Child's head-
note to No. 169, Vol. 3, pp 362–363—but verse 26 of the *Ever Green* copy is
unique.

Pitscottie, therefore, in the sixteenth century is quoting practically verbatim
a ballad version not printed until the eighteenth, but presumably circulating
in his own day—or does Ramsay's ballad owe something to Pitscottie? Or
do both the historian's account and the ballad version echo actual speech
borne to each on the wing of oral transmission? It would be a bold man who
would support only one of these possibilities, to the absolute exclusion of the
others.

This merciless tight-lipped sardonic utterance is echoed in scores of folk-
rhymes which have come down to us from earlier centuries. Here are a few
examples:

> Says Tweed to Till
>   Whit gars ye rin sae still?
> Says Till tae Tweed
> Though ye rin wi speed
>   And I rin slaw
> Yet for ae man ye droon
>   I droon twa.

And this—again from the Borders:

> Happy the craw
> That biggs on the Lammerlaw   [builds]
> And drinks o' the Water o' Dye
> For nae mair may I.

And this, from Aberdeenshire:

> Twa men sat doon on Ythan Brae
> And the teen tae the tither did say,
> And fit-like men may the Gordons o' Gight hae been?

The supreme example in our whole ballad-literature of this devastating, epigrammatic terseness is surely the final stanza of 'The Twa Corbies' (the Scottish analogue of the English 'The Three Ravens'):

> Mony's the ane for him maks mane,
> But nane sall ken whaur he is gane.
> Ower his white banes, when they are bare,
> The wind sall blaw for evermair.
>
> (Child, 26)

If, as has been argued, this version was 'worked over' by Scott or Charles Kirkpatrick Sharpe, that only underlines how fortunate we have been to have ballad-collectors and editors whose speech-habits and mental attitudes so closely corresponded to the authentic tradition of ballad-Scots.

There seems little doubt that many of the ballads found in Scotland now, and probably current in the sixteenth century—for example, 'The Death of Queen Jane' (Child 170), which is about Jane Seymour's demise shortly after giving birth to the future Edward VI—came to us from England. Ballad-Scots merges into ballad-English, for the simple reason that England and Scots-speaking Scotland—and indeed English-speaking Ireland—really form one single great ballad zone. The narrative songs moved around with astonishing ease, and breached dialect and language boundaries like an underground army.

The multi-ethnic origins of Scottish folk culture must surely be regarded as constituting in the main a strength and not a weakness. The hybrid is often more resourceful and resilient than the pure-bred. Scots folksong has been able to welcome and assimilate material of the most diverse origins. As Gavin Greig wrote in the first article he contributed to the *Buchan Observer* in December 1907:

> As we pursue the subject we are carried beyond the bounds of Scotland and quite away from the present time; for the field of folksong admits of no delimitation either in a geographical or a secular way, reaching forth ultimately to the ends of the earth through countless affinities, and back to primeval times through an unbroken chain of derivation.[29]

The ballads, therefore, illustrate and shed further light on a phenomenon already documented in the work of the great makars Dunbar and Henryson—that much Scottish literature is both 'Inglis' and 'Scottis'. There was a two-way process: many ballads migrated 'on the hoof', so to speak. 'Geordie' went South and 'The Bold Pedlar' came North. There was fusion at several levels—but no one listening to a recording of Frank Jordan of Shropshire singing 'The Outlandish Knight', and then (for example) to one of John Strachan of Fyvie singing 'Glenlogie' could doubt that he was listening (in every sense) to two different voices.

The Border, marauders' highway and frail political barrier, was—and remains to this day—a cultural and linguistic watershed. Anonymous Scottish ballad-composers and ballad-singers have given these great songs 'a local habitation and a name'.

NOTES

1 'Maydens of Englonde, sore may ye morne/For your lemmans ye have loste at Bannockisbourne!/With heve a lowe./What wenyth the Kynge of Englonde/So sonne to have wonne Scotlande?/With rumbylowe.' According to Fabyan, 'This songe was after many dayes sungyn in daunces, in carolles of the maydens and mynstrellys of Scotlande, to the reproofe and dysdane of Englishmen, *wt dyverse other which I over passe.*' See *Edward II*, Act 2 Sc. ii, 190–95.
2 Marion Stewart, 'A Recently Discovered Manuscript', *Scottish Studies*, 16 (1972), p 23.
3 *Barbour's Bruce*, M P McDiarmid and J A C Stevenson (eds), 3 vols, STS (Edinburgh and London, 1980–81), III, 126.
4 Sir David Lindsay, *Works* D Hamer (ed), 4 vols, STS (Edinburgh, 1931), II, 205.
5 It is this ludicrous contrast, in my view, that makes the passage funny. However, others have drawn attention to the practical usefulness of the horn in pastoral society; to the lasting popularity of the song *Crodh Chailein* (Colin's Cattle); and even to the sacred aura surrounding the bull of Cooley in the Irish heroic saga Táin Bó Cuailnge.
6 John Carswell, *Book of Common Order*, edited and translated by Thomas M'Lauchlan (Edinburgh, 1873), p 19.
7 (Edinburgh, 1860–62).
8 Alan Bruford (ed), *The Green Man of Knowledge and other Scots traditional tales* (Aberdeen, 1982).
9 The text of Geordie's story together with a survey of the historic-geographic distribution of this tale type will be found in *Scottish Studies*, vol. 2, part 1, 1958.
10 School of Scottish Studies Sound Archive, SA 1954/90/B9.
11 Archer Taylor, *'Edward' and 'Sven i Rosengård' A Study in the Dissemination of Ballads* (Chicago, 1931), p 26.
12 Archer Taylor, p 55.
13 *Scotland and the Lowland Tongue*, J D McClure (ed) (Aberdeen, 1983), pp 109–10.
14 David Buchan, *The Ballad and the Folk* (London and Boston, 1973), p 52.
15 Bertrand H Bronson, *The Ballad as Song* (Berkeley, 1969), p 71.
16 *The Ballad as Song*, p 72.
17 Holger Olof Nygard, 'Mrs Brown's Recollected Ballads', *Ballad and Ballad Research* (Seattle, 1978); Flemming Andersen and Thomas Pettitt, 'Mrs Brown: A Singer of Tales?', Journal of American Folklore, 92, 1979; Hamish Henderson, 'The Ballad, the Folk and the Oral Tradition', *The People's Past*, E J Cowan (ed) (Edinburgh, 1980).
18 David Buchan, 'History and Harlaw', *Ballad Studies*, E B Lyle (ed) (Cambridge, 1976), pp 29–40.
19 Buchan, *The Ballad and the Folk*, p 47.
20 A L Lloyd, *Folksong in England* (London, 1967), p 159.
21 G M Trevelyan, *The Middle Marches* (Newcastle, 1935), p 25.
22 T F Henderson, *Scottish Vernacular Literature* (London, 1898), p 370.

23   (London, 1971).
24   (London, 1973).
25   Edward J Cowan, 'Calvinism and the Survival of Folk' in *The People's Past*, pp 32–57.
26   Sir Walter Scott, *Minstrelsy of the Scottish Border*, T F Henderson (ed), 4 vols (Edinburgh and London, 1902), II, 175.
27   'Realism in Gaelic Poetry', *TGSL*, XXXVII, 89.
28   In *Scottish Poetry: A Critical Survey*, James Kinsley (ed) (London, 1955), pp 99–118 (p 110).
29   Gavin Greig, *Folksong of the North-East* (Hatboro, Pennsylvania, 1963).

FURTHER READING

PRIMARY TEXTS

Bronson, Bertrand H, *The Traditional Tunes of the Child Ballads*, 4 vols (Princeton, N.J., 1959–72)

Buchan, David (ed), *A Scottish Ballad Book* (London and Boston, 1973)

Child, F J, *The English and Scottish Popular Ballads*, 5 vols (Boston, 1882–98; repr New York, 1965)

Keith, Alexander, *Last Leaves* (Aberdeen, 1925)

Shaw, Patrick S, and Lyle, Emily B (eds), The Greig-Duncan Folk Song Collection (Aberdeen, 1981-   )

SECONDARY TEXTS

Andersen, F, and Pettitt, T (eds), *The Ballad as Narrative* (Carbondale, 1961)

Bold, Alan, *The Ballad* (London, 1979)

Bronson, Bertrand H, *The Ballad as Song* (Berkely and Los Angeles), 1969

Buchan, David (ed), *Scottish Tradition* (London, 1984)

Entwhistle, William, *European Balladry* (Oxford, 1939)

Fowler, David C, *A Literary History of the Popular Ballad* (Durham, N.C., 1968)

Gerould, Gordon H, *The Ballad of Tradition* (Oxford, 1932)

Gunmere, F B, *The Popular Ballad* (Boston, 1907)

Hodgart, M J C, *The Ballads* (London, 1950)

Howes, Frank, *Folk Music of Britain and Beyond* (London, 1969)

Leach, MacEdward, and Coffin, Tristram R (eds), *The Critics and the Ballad* (Carbondale, 1961)

Muir, Willa, *Living with Ballads* (London, 1965)

Reed, James, *The Border Ballads* (London, 1973)

Wells, Evelyn Kendrick, *The Ballad Tree* (London, 1950)

INDEX

The index is arranged word-by-word.
Authors are indexed under their own name; their works appear twice, under title, and listed with the author.